ENCOUNTERS WITH AUTISTIC STATES

A Memorial Tribute to Frances Tustin

ENCOUNTERS WITH AUTISTIC STATES

A Memorial Tribute to Frances Tustin

Edited by
Theodore and Judith L. Mitrani

JASON ARONSON INC.
Northvale, New Jersey
London

Front cover photo credits, counterclockwise from top right:
-Frances Daisy with parents George and Minnie Vickers, 1915.
-Frances during her Tavistock training in 1947. Photo by Graham Tustin (Arnold's nephew).
-Frances and husband Arnold in 1984. Photo by Theodore Mitrani.
-Frances in 1994. Photo by Judith Mitrani.

The editors gratefully acknowledge permission to reprint excerpts from *Charlotte's Web*, copyright © 1952 by J. White, reprinted with permission of Penguin Books Ltd. and HarperCollins Publishers.

This book was set in 11 pt. Granjon by Alabama Book Composition of Deatsville, Alabama.

Library of Congress Cataloging-in-Publication Data

Encounters with autistic states: a memorial tribute to Frances Tustin
    / edited by Theodore and Judith L. Mitrani.
        p. cm.
    Includes bibliographical references and index.
    ISBN 0-7657-0066-2 (alk. paper)
    1. Autism.   2. Autism—Treatment.   3. Tustin, Frances.
  I. Tustin, Frances.   II. Mitrani, Theodore.   III. Mitrani, Judith L.
  RC553.A88E53   1997
  616.89'82—dc21   97-3469

Printed in the United States of America on acid-free paper. For information and catalog write to Jason Aronson Inc., 230 Livingston Street, Northvale, New Jersey 07647-1731. Or visit our website: http://www.aronson.com.

About the Contributors

Anne Alvarez, M.A. is Principal Consulting Psychotherapist and Co-Convenor of the Autism Workshop at the Tavistock Clinic, London, and a visiting Professor in the Department of Child Neuropsychiatry at the University of Turin, Italy. She is the author of *Live Company: Psychoanalytic Psychotherapy with Autistic, Borderline, Deprived and Abused Children* and numerous published papers. A member of the Association of Child Psychotherapists, Mrs. Alvarez conducts her private practice with children and adults in London.

Francis M. J. Dale trained at the Tavistock Clinic in London, where he is a Consultant Child and Adult Psychoanalytic Psychotherapist. He is a member of the British Association of Psychotherapists and has worked in various child guidance settings as well as the Marlborough Family Service (London) and as a consultant for staff in residential settings. He has been involved in organizing and running training courses at various branches of the London Center for Psychotherapy, including the branch in Devon, where he is currently the Director of a 3-year training course in psychoanalytic psychotherapy accredited by Exeter University.

Susanna Isaacs Elmhirst, M.D. was, for many years, a training and supervising analyst at the Institute for Psycho-Analysis, London, and is a Member of the British Psycho-Analytical Society. Her work in the treatment of psychotic states in children and adults is widely known and published.

Renata De Benedetti Gaddini, M.D. is a pediatrician, child psychiatrist and psychoanalyst. She is a full member of the Italian Psychoanalytic Association, Professor of Child Psychopathology at the University of Rome, Member of the National Committee on Bioethics, the "Osservatorio per lo studio della Famiglia" (Italian Ministry of Social Affairs), the Association for Child Psycho-Analysis, the American Academy for Child and Adolescent Psychiatry, the International College of Psychosomatic Medicine (of which she has been vice-president) and the International Psycho-Analytical Association's Standing Committee on Psychoses. She was the founding president of the Italian Association for the Study and Prevention of Child Abuse and Neglect. Her studies on the early development of mental life, on the potential space of growth, on pre-object relatedness, and on regression are included in over 200 publications and in a number of books to which she was invited to contribute.

James S. Grotstein, M.D. is a training and supervising analyst at the Psychoanalytic Center of California and the Los Angeles Psychoanalytic Society and Institute, Clinical Professor of Psychiatry at UCLA, author of the book *Projective Identification*, and the editor of several others—most notably, *Do I Dare Disturb the Universe*—as well as over 160 psychoanalytic articles published in both American and international journals and books. Dr. Grotstein is currently working on a new book on psychoanalytic technique.

Genevieve Haag, M.D. is the author of many published clinical and metapsychological papers. She has worked extensively with autistic and psychotic children. She is a member of the Paris Psychoanalytic Association and practices privately in Paris, France.

Victoria Hamilton, Ph.D. studied philosophy and psychoanalysis at University College, London, under the professorships of Richard Wolheim and Joseph Sandler and trained in adult and child psychotherapy at the Tavistock Clinic. She is a training and supervising analyst at the Institute of Contemporary Psychoanalysis, a member of the Los Angeles Institute and Society for Psychoanalytic Studies, and a member of the Association for Child Psychoanalysis. She has authored many published papers and reviews and the second edition of her first book, *Oedipus and Narcissus*, has been recently published by Karnac, Ltd. Her second book, *The Analyst's Preconscious,* was published in 1996 by Analytic Press.

Didier Houzel, M.D. is a professor of Child and Adolescent Psychiatry at the University of Caen (France) and is a full member of the French Psychoanalytic Association. His interests are especially focused on the exploration and analytic treatment of autism and childhood psychosis. He has benefited from many years of supervision with Frances Tustin and with Donald Meltzer.

JoAnn Culbert-Koehn, M.S.W. is a Jungian analyst in private practice with adults and children in Santa Monica, California. She is a former Director of Training at the C. G. Jung Institute of Los Angeles and a former Co-Director of the Hilde Kirsch Children's Center. She has lectured in the United States and in Europe on issues of separation and birth trauma, and she teaches in an innovative program in Santa Fe, New Mexico, integrating the work of Jung, Klein, and Bion.

Bianca Lechevalier, M.D. is a former resident of the Hospital of Paris, former Chief of the Child Neuropsychiatric Clinic of the Paris School of Medicine, and a member of the Paris Psychoanalytic Society. The author of numerous published papers and chapters in books, she maintains a private practice in psychoanalysis with children and adults in Caen, France.

Suzanne Maiello earned her *Laurea* in psychology from the University of Rome. She is a member of the Association of Child Psychotherapists (Great Britain, Tavistock Section) and a founding member and former President of the Associazione Italiana di Psicoterapia Psicoanalitica Infantile. Ms. Maiello is the author of publications in European and English journals, teaches and supervises in Tavistock-model training courses in Italy and abroad, and is in private practice with children and adults in Rome.

Judith L. Mitrani, Ph.D. is a senior faculty member of the Psychoanalytic Center of California and guest faculty at the Los Angeles Institute and Society for Psychoanalytic Studies and at the Southern California Psychoanalytic Institute. Dr. Mitrani is the author of *A Framework for the Imaginary: Clinical Explorations in Primitive States of Being*, and she has published numerous papers in the area of primitive mental states in both international and American journals. She has been an Associate Editor on the North American Board of the *International Journal of Psycho-Analysis*, and currently serves on the editorial board of the *Journal of Primitive Mental States* and as the founding Chair of the International Frances Tustin Memorial Trust. She is in private practice in psychoanalysis in Beverly Hills, California.

Theodore Mitrani, Ph.D. is a psychoanalyst in private practice with children and adults. He is a senior faculty member of the Psychoanalytic Center of California where he also serves on the Education Committee as Curriculum Chair and as a Director of the Board of the Society. He is a supervising analyst at the Graduate Center for Child Development and Psychotherapy and is guest faculty at the Los Angeles Institute and Society for Psychoanalytic Studies. He is a member of the board of trustees of the Frances Tustin Memorial Trust and an Editorial Board Member of the *Journal of Primitive Mental States*.

Thomas H. Ogden, M.D. is Co-Director of the Center for Advanced Study of the Psychoses, faculty member of the San Francisco Psychoanalytic Institute, and a training and supervising analyst at the Psychoanalytic Institute of Northern California. He is a graduate of the Yale School of Medicine and the San Francisco Psychoanalytic Institute and has served as an associate psychiatrist at the Tavistock Clinic, London. He is a member of the North American Editorial Board of the *International Journal of Psychoanalysis* and is the author of many published papers as well as several books, among them *The Matrix of the Mind, The Primitive Edge of Experience, Subjects of Analysis,* and *Projective Identification and Psychoanalytic Technique*. He maintains a private practice in San Francisco.

Maria E. Pozzi is a child psychotherapist and an associate member of the British Association of Psychotherapists. She works in Stevenage Child and Family Consultation Clinic and in private practice with both adults and children. She is a visiting tutor at the Tavistock Clinic and at the London Center for Psychotherapy and lectures internationally on separation issues.

Maria Rhode works in private practice and as a consultant child psychotherapist at the Tavistock Clinic in London, where she is a member of the autism workshop. She has written a "Tribute to Frances Tustin" in the *Journal of Child Psychotherapy* as well as numerous papers on autism and infant observation.

Charlotte Riley, Psy.D. is a supervising and training analyst at the Los Angeles Institute and Society for Psychoanalytic Studies and the Institute for Contemporary Psychoanalysis. She did her child psychoanalytic training at the Tavistock Clinic in London. Dr. Riley has also supervised and taught interns at the Los Angeles Child Development Center, the Wright Institute, and the Reiss-Davis Child Study Center. Previous publications have appeared in the *Journal of Child Psychotherapy* and *Winnicott Studies*.

David Rosenfeld, M.D. is a training and supervising analyst at the Psychoanalytic Association of Buenos Aires (APdeBA), a professor of mental health of the Faculty of Medicine at Buenos Aires University, and author of three books, a dramatic play, and numerous papers published in analytic journals and texts. His latest book, *The Psychotic Aspects of the Personality*, culminates decades of clinical work with psychotic, borderline, autistic, drug addicted, and psychosomatic adult and child patients in analysis.

Sheila Spensley, Ph.D. is a consultant clinical psychologist and psychoanalytic psychotherapist at the Willesden Center for Psychological Treatment in London and is a training supervisor in both adult and child psychotherapy. She is the author of numerous clinical papers and of the biographical book *Frances Tustin*.

Jane Van Buren, Ph.D. is a training and supervising analyst at the Psychoanalytic Center of California, a faculty member of the Wright Institute, and adjunct faculty member at both the Southern California Psychoanalytic Institute and at the Los Angeles Institute and Society for Psychoanalytic Studies. She is the author of *The Modernist Madonna: Semiotics of the Maternal Metaphor* as well as numerous published journal articles. Dr. Van Buren lectures internationally.

Isca Wittenberg, M.D. is a consultant child and adult psychotherapist and psychoanalyst for those training in analytic child psychotherapy at the Tavistock Clinic in London, where she was formerly Vice-Chair. She works in private practice in England and teaches there as well as in Europe and overseas. Among her many publications are two books that have been translated into several languages: *Psychoanalytic Insights and Relationships* and *The Emotional Experience of Learning and Teaching*. She also authored, with Donald Meltzer, the now classic volume *Explorations in Autism*.

There is a saying that it is better to light one small candle than to go on cursing the darkness. It has been my privilege to light one small candle to shed its light on the dark scene of psychogenic autism. With my advantages and opportunities, it would have been a professional dereliction not to attempt to do so.

Frances Tustin (1986, p. 310)

Contents

Preface

by Judith L. Mitrani

Axioms in philosophy are not axioms until they are proved upon our pulses: We read fine things but never feel them to the full until we have gone the same steps as the author.

John Keats

It seems fitting that these remarkable papers should be gathered here to pay tribute to Frances Tustin. Each of the authors featured here knew Frances and her work, and they have been left to carry that work forward into the future. It is an honor for each of us to share with the reader some memories and insights of this most extraordinary human being, a gallant pioneer in the treatment of primitive mental states of most elemental dimensions. The authors represented on these pages have read the "fine things" written by Frances Tustin. Many have "gone the same steps" as she did, and thus her axioms "have been proved upon their pulses." Others present alternative vertices that would have pleased Frances, as this was much in line with her own spirit of ongoing inquiry and reevaluation.

Indeed, Frances Tustin stepped lively and maintained strong life signs for us to feel. Just one month before her death, we sat together, side by side, talking and laughing and weeping one last time. I can recall so many instances when the telephone would ring in her room at Rayner's—the retirement home where she spent those last months of her life—and she would answer, as always, "Frances Tustin here!" Almost invariably it was someone—a friend or an admirer—who wished to visit her (she kept a little book of all the visits to come, looking forward, always forward) and I could tell by her response that the caller on the other end of the line was asking what they could bring her. Could she have flowers in her room? Could she have sweets? Was there anything she needed? Anything she wanted? Time and again Frances would reply in earnest, "Oh no, I don't want things! *I just want people! Bring me words!*"

And so, here we are, gathered together—as many have been in memorial tributes held in her honor in numerous parts of the world—bringing words: words for her, about her, and about her work and our experiences with her, as well as the work she inspired and enabled us to do. After all, Frances left *each* one of us a legacy of words: words we remember, words to share with one another, words we have used and will use to comfort one another and others, words that she found so comforting.

Frances Tustin died on November 11th, 1994—Remembrance Day in England—only a short time after her 81st birthday. This book is our "remembrance day" for Frances. It is indeed hard to believe that she is gone. I understand that just as Frances' words nourished us and helped us to grow as therapists and analysts, now her ashes add to the nourishing medium in which flowers grow and bloom in Amersham, England, not far from her home: That little bungalow into which she welcomed so many. Frances always had a place in her home and in her heart and mind for a new student.

Few would dispute Tustin's place alongside Melanie Klein and Anna Freud as one of the foremost child analysts in the world. She was an honored member of the Association of Child Psychotherapists, a Trustee of the Winnicott Foundation, an Honorary Affiliate of both the Psychoanalytic Center of California in Los Angeles and the British Psychoanalytic Society in London, and a dear friend and faithful supporter of all those who knew her.

Right after the start of my training, even before I knew her personally, Tustin's work had an enormous impact on my own. I feel especially fortunate to have had Frances in my life, as my friend and mentor for over a decade. As she did with so many others, she encouraged me when I first began to write seriously about my clinical experiences, she vetted my papers one by one, always concerned that I be protected from undue criticism. She supported my ideas when they seemed sensible if heretic at times, while gently letting me know when I was off course in my thinking. She helped me to better grasp her ideas and cheered enthusiastically when I voiced my own. She delighted in my successes, and she felt with me—holding me firmly in both her heart and mind—during those times when I experienced failure.

I remember when my first paper was rejected. She cheered me up with a favorite story of hers. It was all about *her own* first paper, one she had written on the treatment of an anorexic girl. Frances was so proud of this paper that she sent it to Melanie Klein to read. Mrs. Klein wrote her a "Dear Frances Letter" saying something like, "This is a very nice paper, but it is simply *not my work*!" As one can imagine, Frances was *so* disappointed to read this, that she carried on about it for days. After a time, out of deep concern, her husband, Arnold, finally asked her *what on earth* was making her so heartsick. When she replied that Mrs. Klein had read her paper and had said that it wasn't *her* work, Arnold—sage that he was—simply said, "Well of course, you silly twit, it isn't *her* work, it's *your* work!" In so many ways, Frances helped me to appreciate that we *each* must do our own work, that we each have something to offer. Without a doubt Tustin's work offers us some of the most original and important extensions of Kleinian theory to date. I believe she would be proud of all those authors included in this volume who have each done their own work while helping to communicate her ideas.

For me, although her death has left a terrible void, it is *not* a "black hole." It has indeed been difficult to bear—no longer to be able to ring her up and hear the lilting inflection of her almost-always cheerful and ever-youthful voice answering "Frances Tustin here!"—but her invaluable body of work, her written words, remain. Frances authored five books and dozens of articles, published and translated into several languages. There are, as well, all the memories of her that endure in letters, photos, tapes, videos and—of course—in the hearts and minds of those who knew her. It is these memories that filter in to fill the gap and to make the loss of her physical presence bearable.

I remember when my husband, Ted, and I first met Frances in the summer of 1984. It was in London where Frances spoke at a conference, along with Herbert Rosenfeld, John Bowlby, and Susanna Isaacs Elmhirst. I thought I'd never seen anyone who looked so much like Mrs. Santa Claus. She was small and round, with cotton candy for hair, and huge blue eyes that twinkled, even beyond the tenth row in which we sat. Five minutes into her paper, a big, burly, and bearded colleague of mine leaned over to me, grasped my forearm, and whispered, "Oh, God, I just want to climb into her lap!" This exclamation did not surprise me one bit, as my colleague's desire merely echoed my own as-yet-unspoken sentiments.

Added to that first vision of Frances, her words and her spirit touched me in a spot where none had gone before. She seemed to me to be so open and *so accessible* that I dared to call her at her home, near the end of our month-long stay in London, before returning to the States. That was the first time I would hear the telephone greeting that was to become such a big part of my life: "Frances Tustin here!" I was positively smitten—enchanted! I didn't know what to say. I wanted to ask her to adopt me, but instead I asked if Ted and I could take her to tea. She welcomed my overtures with a warm invitation, directions to Amersham by Tube, and a very generous offer to pick us up at the train station the next day.

We spent that summer's day with Frances, first for mid-morning coffee and cakes at home with Arnold, who charmed us with limericks about what he called Klein's "theory of the flying breast" and "Bion-be-gone." Afterwards, Frances took us for lunch at Amber's of Amersham, a fashionable boutique and tea room that had taken up residence in a seventeenth-century Tudor mansion built upon the remains of an eleventh-century silk mill, still running and powered by a stream that wound decoratively through the center of the house.

The millinery of the shop resided in the old pony barn, attached to the house where even the Queen's own ladies-in-waiting (who often frequent this chi-chi salon) sit in what used to be the stalls, trying on hats and veils. Frances pointed out this section of Amber's with great joy, as she told us of a similar set-up—also a pony barn—which Arnold had himself converted into a play therapy room for her and the children she treated in their old place on the hill in Amersham. Indeed, this was heaven! We munched on sandwiches and cakes, washed down by cream tea, and chatted on for hours about psychoanalysis.

At one point, a young adolescent boy—who had been sitting eavesdropping with his parents at another table—came over and asked us if we were *really* psychoanalysts. He begged just to sit with us in order that he might better be able to hear what we were talking about. Tustin's answer was typical of her humble attitude and her de-idealizing style. She simply said "Yes we are psychoanalysts, and *of course* you may join us, but you know, *we're just balmy people treating balmy people!*"

Of course, for all her genuine modesty, Frances was much more than just a "balmy person treating balmy people." Her work with autistic children has spawned numerous clinics in Europe and South America, where her keen interest in the psycho-biological interplay between body and mind fostered cooperation between experts from different fields. Her sincere empathy concerning the sufferings of both these enigmatic children and their parents, and her poetic yet common-sense understanding of what she called "shell-type" or "encapsulated" children has also informed our treatment of autistic pathology in neurotic, borderline, and psychotic adult patients in analysis, thus broadening her contribution to the treatment of primitive and proto-mental sensation states. Her work has appealed to and has been applied by clinicians of all analytic orientations to problems ranging from drug addiction to eating disorders, from depression to narcissism, and on and on, as will become apparent as the reader turns the pages of this book.

One year before her death, her 80th birthday was celebrated by an international gathering in France of hundreds of workers in the field. The proceedings of this *Homage* have since been published. A similar tribute to her work took place in London that year and was published in the *Journal of Child Psychotherapy*. Additionally, an issue of the *Journal of the Squiggle Society* was published in her honor. In 1994, James Grotstein edited an issue of *Psychoanalytic Inquiry* which was devoted to the problem of autism and included discussions by Tustin as well as some of her exponents around the globe.

Shortly after Professor Arnold Tustin—her husband of over fifty years—died in January of 1994, Frances told me that she felt that they had been like two trees, grown together for so long that their roots were inextricably bound up with one another, and so when one died the other would whither away soon after. I think now that she was trying as gently as she could—months before the diagnosis of her cancer was made—to prepare me for her death.

However, in spite of the debilitating disease she suffered from, she did not whither away. When I was by her side at Rayner's—for those few days during the last month of her life—she was bright, alive, still learning and teaching, surrounded by friends and students from all over the world. One very special day, Maria Pozzi and I took Frances—all dressed up in her favorite purples and pinks—to say farewell to her little bungalow and flower garden on Orchard Lane in Amersham, the day before the new owners were to take possession, and we three enjoyed our last tea together at Amber's, where, there too, she was surrounded by loving friends.

Frances used to say that the most important thing to keep in mind, while working with autistic states, is to "keep moving forward" and not to get discouraged. And this she always did. For example, only a few days before her death, when we spoke on the telephone for the last time, she told me about the article for The British journal *Nature* which she was then dictating to Wendel Caplan in hope of making her work on autism even more accessible to the public. She was always trying to find new ways to go forward, to reach out, and to help more distressed children and their parents. She kept going forward with attempts to help people connect with one another, to help mothers and their children—as well as therapists and their patients—to form lively links.

Frances always deeply regretted that she and Arnold were never able to have children of their own. I recall her telling me about David Munrow, the son of friends from their Birmingham days, who later grew up to pioneer the Early Music movement. When David was a small child, Frances lost a baby in a toxemic pregnancy and he lovingly offered himself as her honorary son. She seemed to consider many of her students as "honorary sons and daughters," taking active interest in each of us and making efforts to link us to one another as a sort of "family." I will always be grateful to her for the supportive links that I have been able to forge with others who knew her—Vickie Hamilton, Charlotte Riley, David Rosenfeld, Cesare Sacerdotti, Tom Ogden, Graeme Taylor, Neville and Joan Symington, Renata Gadinni, and especially Maria Pozzi, who shared some of those last moments with Frances and me. Perhaps it was because Frances lacked children that the love she received from her students meant such a great deal to her.

Frances liked to tell the story of a woman who had suffered a great personal loss and had thus fallen into a deep, dark depression. This woman had locked herself inside her house and would see no one. However, all of her friends came around bearing candles to brighten the night, to warm her, and to let their bereaved friend know that they had not given up hope, and finally the mourner emerged into the light her friends carried for her. This seems to me to be a fitting metaphor for what we as therapists do with those patients who have retreated into an autistic enclave.

[margin note: What friend?]

Frances so enjoyed and was deeply moved by each one of the letters and cards that she received in those months after her husband's death and during her own long illness. She truly felt surrounded by friendly "candles" in her time of darkness. All of us will long treasure her many written contributions—her humanity, her integrity of mind, her generosity of spirit, and her capacity for deep emotional contact—that light our way through the dark passage of our work with troubled patients. As she herself wrote, in the work quoted in the frontispiece of this volume, Frances lit "one small candle" to shed some light on the dark scene of psychogenic autistic states. She truly remains an inspiration for all the contributors to this Memorial, who wish to add twenty more candles to light the readers' way.

Acknowledgments

The editors wish to acknowledge the following persons who made it all possible: Our sincere thanks to Cesare Sacerdotti, for his good sportsmanship, wise counsel, generous encouragement, and for putting the interests of this book above his own; to Grace Kono of "Keystrokes," who transformed IBM discs into Macintosh, transcribed the translations, scanned papers generated on archaic typewriters, and spent numerous all-nighters perfecting the art of transcontinental e-mail; to Michael Moskowitz, who went to bat for us; to Dr. Jason Aronson, for his faith and good judgment; to all the many friends of Frances Tustin—near and far, people and institutions—who conveyed their warm and enthusiastic support and in so doing contributed to this book much more than they might imagine; to our families, friends, and colleagues, who tolerated our "primary editorial preoccupation"; and of course, to each and every contributor, with whom we have come to feel a deep sense of camaraderie.

Introduction

Theodore Mitrani

This volume is a homage to the memory of Frances Tustin the person and to the body of phenomenological descriptions, psychoanalytic insights, diagnostic classifications, technical adaptations, theoretical formulations and metapsychological developments which constitute her teachings. Her work was focused on the nature of those psychogenic, sensation-dominated autistic phenomena encountered in the analytic setting. The value of the analytic wisdom Tustin bequeathed us—as it emerged from nearly half a century of clinical and supervisory experience—has been recognized for its importance by prominent child and adult analytic workers from many geographic and cultural areas of the Western world and Asia, only partially represented in this collection of papers.

Within these twenty chapters, the reader will find adaptations of Tustin's meticulous observations with regard to the analytic treatment of autistic children, extensions and applications of her findings to the treatment of learning disabilities, personality disorders, psychotic phenomena, eating disorders, substance abuse, and an array of primitive states in *statu nascendi,* mainly with adults. Evocative depictions of countertransferential experiences—an indispensible resource to the therapist in his or her work with autistic states of mind—distinguish the many clinical vignettes offered in nearly every contribution to this publication.

Not unlike other formulations shaped by nonconforming minds inquiring into a particular field at the cutting edge, Tustin's legacy has at times been misunderstood—in both aspects of theory and technique—by some analytic and nonanalytic workers. Perhaps the former group could not reconcile her formulations within the schemata of established theoretical notions, and the latter may have found her teachings too far from the mainstream of educative and behavioral models or neurophysiological frames of reference. Echos of some of these misunderstandings and clarifications of the same may be found in some of the present offerings. Differing views and new insights and inferences, rooted in the individual experiences of other contributors, are also featured in this volume. Constructive critiques and reappraisals are an essential part of the very fabric of lively, unfolding scientific progress. Indeed they were actively sought out and encouraged by Tustin, who hoped her own contributions would continue to evolve, to be reevaluated and revised both by colleagues and students in the light of new clinical facts and findings. It is the hope of the editors that, in assembling this enlightening array of essays, we have been able to do justice to Frances Tustin's bold and nondogmatic spirit.

In the first chapter of this compendium, Suzanne Maiello meticulously follows the evolution of Tustin's thinking, which ultimately reaches the conclusion that there is no primary autistic phase in normal development. The question of a possible prenatal pathological development of autistic-born children, along with the possibility of its connection to maternal depression during pregnancy, is considered by the author as she explores the issues of sensuous awareness of the fetus, with particular attention to the area of tactile and auditory experiences, their interplay in normal development, and the possible pathological consequences of the failure of prenatal sensuous integrations. The dream material presented in this chapter depicts an experience of tactile-auditory integration, and clinical material from the analysis of an autistic child illustrates the failure of interaction between these two sensuous modes.

In Chapter 2, Tustin's concept of the unbearable ecstasy of at-onement and her attentiveness to the importance of the containing function of the mother with regard to this elemental experience, Bion's distinction between "reverence and awe" and defensive idealization, and Meltzer's notion of the "aesthetic conflict" are explicated and discussed by Judith Mitrani as each of these themes—separately and in combination—have some essential bearing upon the provocation or mitigation of envy, the process of introjection and the development of both healthy and pathological internal object relations, the resultant nature of the super-ego, and individual self-esteem. Mitrani discussed the ideas contained in this paper during her last face-to-face conversation with Tustin, just one month before her death, and poignantly recalls that conversation. Additionally, she presents clinical case material as a background for and an illustration of the phenomena described, and she offers certain conclusions that may have some impact upon the analyst's attitude and technique.

The use of the voice as a medium for symbolic communication is contrasted by Maria Rhode, in Chapter 3, with its use as a source of sensations in the mouth against the background discussion of the treatment of a young autistic child, who uses an abnormally resonant monosylable as an autistic object to provide a sense of safety in situations that threatened him with such catastrophic dangers as being cut in half and of losing parts of his body and his mouth. Possession of the sound is shown by Rhode to be linked with possession of the umbilical cord and the nipple. Increasing confidence in the therapist's capacity to survive is seen as leading to a softening of the autistic object and to some development in the capacity for symbolic play and language.

In Chapter 4, which is focused on several aspects of a six-year-long therapeutic process with a young autistic girl, Charlotte Riley emphasizes the importance of the therapist's capacity to sustain her experience of periods of lack of contact, meaninglessness, and hopelessness for as long as the patient requires without reacting or withdrawing from such experience. It is this recognition and emotional endurance on the part of Riley that contributes to a rather moving transformation in her patient, from a rigidified world in the depths of a double "black hole"—where the baby's primal depression is intensified by the mother's, in the absence of paternal support—toward a recognition of a new object-relationship, which allows for and facilitates a new world in which increasing communication of targeted feelings, needs, and empathy accompany the dawning of symbol formation.

Through her vivid description of one case of a child with learning disabilities, which was supervised by Tustin years ago at the Tavistock clinic, Victoria Hamilton demonstrates, in Chapter 5, the relevance of disturbances in the elemental sensation-ego to both the emotional and cognitive-intellectual functioning of children with compliant, moulding symptomatology who oftentimes cannot play. This description, with its detailed verbatim of sessions from the treatment, is accompanied by a series of drawings by the child which sharply highlight the polarity between her lulling and numbing trends and her growing awareness of attachment to the therapist and the analytic process. In the course of her discussion, Hamilton articulates fresh considerations about her work with this patient from the vantage point of 25 years of experience.

In Chapter 6, JoAnn Culbert-Keohn introduces a central concept in Jung's description of psychic life: his "theory of the opposites." In one of his last works, Jung wrote, "The opposites are the ineradicable and indispensable preconditions of all psychic life." Similarly, among the salient clinical revelations in Tustin's writing on mismanaged psychological birth is her idea of the importance of integrating the opposites of hard and soft. Tustin wrote about "the third" emerging from the infant's integration of hard and soft as "the birth of a new way of functioning." Jung also believed that a third element is produced when opposites are brought together and contained. Culbert-Koehn—a prominent developmental Jungian analyst who has integrated her years of experience in Kleinian and Bionian analysis into her Jungian foundations—presents three clinical examples of adult patients who suffer very primitive reactions to analytic breaks which provoke them to reexperience their difficult physical/psychological births while undergoing a Jungian analysis in which the integration of the opposites of hard and soft facilitate forward movement in the analytic process.

In Chapter 7, Isca Wittenberg—a contemporary of Tustin's who has previously, along with other's in Donald Meltzer's group, written about her "Explorations in Autism"—brings extracts from the analytic treatment of a child and an adult, as well as from infant observation, to illustrate her hypothesis that there is a group of children who adopt autistic defenses as a barrier to falling into a state of despair and hopelessness that dates from an infantile experience of a mother who is depressed and unable to deal with her own or her baby's fear of death and dying. Wittenberg's contribution, dedicated to this particular aetiological category of autistic states, identifies a pattern in which babies who are born highly sensitive and intelligent, "with a great lust for life and beauty, are overwhelmed with depressive anxiety" when their preconception of a lively, responsive, and caring object (i.e., the mindful breast) fails to materialize. In addition, they seem to hold themselves responsible for this disturbance in the mother and attempt to protect her omnipotently. The necessary failure of such attempts, against the background of the initial disappointment in life and hope in Mother, triggers a shift from trust in the human object to a "hard-object," such as some nonstop activity used as an escape from the terror of hopelessness and death.

A long-time student, associate, and—more recently—biographer of Frances Tustin, Sheila Spensley draws on Tustin's innovative concepts in relation to the latter's understanding of the isolation of children with autism, as well as on those contemporary developments in her thinking. In Chapter 8, Spensley gives an overview of the theoretical growth that followed the discovery of autism and explores the repercussions of Tustin's insights concerning autistic states, with their implications for the psychoanalysis of adult patients. Spensley then relates these advances in understanding to the treatment of an eating disorder in a patient whose psychoanalytic inaccessibility has been especially marked.

In Chapter 9, David Rosenfeld presents a clearly organized account—including case illustrations—of the ways in which Tustin's teachings have influenced his work with patients ranging from autistic children to drug addicts, holocaust survivors, psychosomatizers, hypochondriacal organ transplant recipients, and various other categories of patients with autistic enclaves. Throughout his descriptive journey, Rosenfeld develops classificatory nomenclature and demonstrates, in his clinical vignettes, the centrality of sensation-dominated disturbances in a variety of patients, discussing the occurence of autistic pockets concealed within the larger, more-obvious syndromes of established pathologies. His considerations help to shed new light on the ways we might identify, conceptualize, and treat certain symptoms.

Thomas Ogden's paper on "Personal Isolation" is reprinted in Chapter 10. It is an outgrowth of ideas that originated in the context of a correspondence between Tustin and himself that lasted many years and which, as Ogden states, "stands as one of the great pleasures of [his] professional life." The author further states that Tustin's letters

"were always thought provoking and to the point, never mincing words, and never once betraying a note of possessiveness of an idea or an insistence on the wisdom of her point of view. There were points of disagreement between us to be sure, but it was always clear to both of us that we shared a deep respect for the work involved in attempting to address the most primitive and frightening reaches of human experience. The quality that most characterize her letters was a generosity of spirit. Even in the final years of her life, when she was weakened by illness, she never tired of trying to help me to learn (as opposed to trying to teach me) nor did she ever stop attempting to learn from me."

It might be said that Tustin's theories speak to the origins of semiotic processes and their relationship to the "black hole," which she defines as a gap or hole in the fabric of one's being. Tustin explains that the failure to overcome the dread of nothingness gives way to an atrophy of the normal autosensual pulses and rhythms of bonding and the possibility of communication. Lacan proposes that the notion of lack and of fragile being dawns in infancy, emphasizing the haunting of the human subject by a sense of limitation and the fear of death, because the creation of the chain of signifiers only *substitutes* for the loss of the object of primary identification. For Lacan, the hole (lack) stimulates the formation of the signifier, whereas for Tustin, the dread of the hole or wound prevents the creation of signs and symbols and the development of a sense of inside and outside. Lacan's tragedy is found in the futility of the semiotic, while Tustin's is found at the very root of psychosomatic expression. In Chapter 11, historian and psychoanalyst Jane Van Buren compares Tustin's ideas about schizoid withdrawal and the truncation of symbol formation with Lacan's ideas on the semiotic process, and she illustrates her thesis with clinical vignettes.

Chapter 12 features a touching tribute to Tustin by Susanna Isaacs Elmhirst, a prominent British analyst who, with Bion, helped pioneer the Kleinian movement in Los Angeles. Elmhirst, who met Frances Tustin for the first time when the latter was in training at Tavistock and participated in the observation of the former's infant twins, writes of her appreciation of Tustin's open-minded, scientific approach to theory building—which allowed for the growth of Tustin's understanding of autistic phenomena—and especially her capacity for reevaluation of the concept of a "normal autistic phase" in development.

The function of early defenses, as one meets them in the psychoanalytical process, is explored in Renata Gaddini's paper in Chapter 13. Over many years, Gaddini had discussed many of her ideas on the "fear of change" with Tustin. Gaddini especially recalls a conversation the two of them had on a long journey from Rome to Sienna, in which Gaddini reported to Tustin a "dialogue" with a 7-year-old autistic patient who was, at the time, well on her way toward acquiring speech. This little girl was obsessively asking Gaddini whether a folding chair, which was part of the analytic setting, "would close her button in," and Gaddini had recalled the child's terror of being flushed away with the water in the toilet. Gaddini's paper does not specifically concern the "fear of change" in autistic children; however, like Tustin, she has learned much from these children who—on the basis of the unbearable shock of awareness of bodily separateness—have built a system of protective-if-alienating autosensual abberations. Here, Gaddini attempts to describe the defense of the self as distinct from the ego's defenses (built on their basis) and she suggests that there are two distinct varieties of loss against which patients seek to protect themselves. The first is "self loss," of the type the young child meets when confronted with separation before acquiring a capacity for representation. In this case, the suffering is "agonic" because it is unthinkable and therefore the mind is not yet capable of coming to the rescue. Here, imitation is probably the earliest form of self-defense. Another type of suffering has quite a different nature and is typical of those conditions where loss and mourning have been worked through. The ensuing need for reparation is met with symbolic operations typical of mental processes.

In Chapter 14, Anne Alvarez's contribution focuses mainly on the transforming and potentially multifaceted significance and function of stereotypical behaviors in the autistic child. She regards such rituals as indirectly object-related, contrary to the conclusions of those nonanalytic observers who do not make use of the experience of the countertransference. Indeed, she is clear in her critique of the inadequacy of observations made and inferences reached exclusively from the perspective of a one-person psychology or from an organicist premise, which she suggests is "like listening to music while tone deaf." The author shows how her positions emerged from within her intensive, long-term work, especially with one autistic boy whom she saw well into his manhood. Her longitudinal study, throughout which she continued to evolve professionally in response to the difficulties she encountered with this patient and with the helpful insights of colleagues (e.g., Tustin's notion of the autistic object), allowed Alvarez to witness developments in an autistic person rarely reported in the analytic literature.

James Grotstein has stated that "Frances Tustin was an intrepid pilgrim who made extraordinary progress in rescuing a hitherto obscure clinical entity and placing it in the forefront of psychoanalysis. Her clinical expertise was phenomenal as were her personal portraits of her patients' behavior and the anxieties behind them." In Chapter 15, Grotstein places Tustin's important contributions within the context of a growing body of empirical doings on autism that he suggests "she did not have access to but which, although seemingly at variance with some of her conclusions, reveal all the more how difficult her therapeutic task had been and how miraculously and steadfastly she continued to meet this challenge."

A student and close confidante of Tustin's near the end of her life, Maria Pozzi discusses, in Chapter 16, some aspects of the treatment of a young woman. Pozzi recalls some of the highlights of her weekly consultations with Tustin that took place during the first year of this long treatment, and she writes about how Tustin's ideas and influence have been alive in her work ever since. Although some autistic defenses held back her patient's emotional and social development, and a persistent sense of void and lack of identity had impaired her patient throughout her teens, Pozzi demonstrates how, through painstaking analysis of autistic barriers and later defense mechanisms employed by this patient, her patient's sense of identity and some direction in her life begins to emerge.

In Chapter 17, Francis Dale provides a clear rendition of the powerful and demanding countertransference experience and its aftermath as the therapist attempts to register, with no compulsion to understand, the experience of a 3-year-old autistic boy in his care. In the course of sorting out his own experience, Dale reaches a number of theoretical conclusions. He suggests that the baby does not think but instead *sensates*; that the transference can be said to emerge only with the appearance of a transitional space between therapist and patient; that the concept of the self arises from the owning of one's body along with the recognition of the boundary between me and not-me, contingent upon the maturation of the peripheral nervous system and the frontal lobes; and that the "hard-object" may function not only to block contact with the object (as suggested by Tustin) but also to facilitate contact, as do the nipple and tongue. Technically, Dale insists that the work with autistic states calls for the therapist's capacity to move, with relative ease, between mindlessness and mindfulness and to let go of "shared mental realities, cognitive frameworks, theories and mental safety nets," as a prerequisite for making contact with the autistic child.

In Chapter 18, Bianca Lechevalier hypothesizes "a mode of adhesiveness" occurring at the point of first contact with one or both depressed parents. Transmitted nonverbally, some undigested horror or grief in the parent, deprived of meaning for the baby, creates a nameless dread against which the adhesiveness defends. Lechevalier grounds her hypothesis in a clear and compressed case description of a 10-year-old girl manifesting autistic symptoms and seen since the age of 4 months. The reader is taken on a long and arduous journey, culminating in the attainment of bodily existence and symbol formation as the child becomes aware of her own mortality, thus relinquishing a state of sensation-dominated omnipotent fusion with the mother. Additional examples—of adults in the grip of stultifying pseudo-identifications and concretization—are discussed, and the role of the countertransference as a central tool in analysis is clearly demonstrated.

The origin of thoughts is a question that philosophers have been discussing for a very long time. In Chapter 19, Didier Houzel confronts two categories of hypotheses: Nativism and Empiricism. In the latter category, the Sensualism of Condillac suggests that the whole of psychic functioning depends on sense data. Houzel suggests that the psychoanalytic inquiry into infantile autism, as carried out by Frances Tustin—with whom he had many years of professional and personal contact—leads to the reformulation of the question, especially with regard to the connections between sensations and emotions. He proposes that rather than a genetic continuity between the two, there are instead dialectic connections. On the one hand, sense data constitutes the material that allows for the representation of emotional experiences, while on the other hand only those emotions experienced within human communication are able to give meaning to sensorial experiences. Thus he finds that, in the treatment of autistic children, it is at the very core of the transference and countertransference dynamic that one can give meaning to sensorial experiences and can reach our representation of the emotional experiences.

Genevieve Haag's contribution, in the final chapter, consists of two parts. The first is a theoretical and metapsychological discussion, intertwined with clinical vignettes, in the course of which she broadens and deepens our notions of elemental states of mind in an original way suggesting, for example, that adhesive identification be regarded not only as a pathological symptom but also as a necessary developmental phenomenon. In a thoroughly critical style, Haag reviews many of Tustin's most important contributions, found both in Tustin's published writings and made available to Haag through her long years of consultation and correspondence with Tustin. Here she makes enlightening links between Tustin's teachings, her own findings, and those of other important contributors, such as Anzieu, Bick, Green, Grotstein and Meltzer. The second part of the chapter features a number of exceptionally detailed case examples, examined in the light of the previous discussion and illustrating the laborious task of owning up to one's body and to the links among its various parts. The significance of the crucial developments in this process is highlighted in relation to the concepts of both the sensation−ego and the body−ego.

1

Going Beyond: Notes on the Beginning of Object Relations in the Light of "The Perpetuation of an Error"

Suzanne Maiello

> *When beliefs need some modification,*
> *We make it with much trepidation,*
> *For our world is then new,*
> *And things seem all askew,*
> *Till we're used to the new formulation.*
> Professor Arnold Tustin

Frances Tustin knew that "The perpetuation of an error" would be her last paper when she read it to the Association of Child Psychotherapists in London during the study weekend in 1993. It was published in 1994, only a few months before she died. It was her last published work, the legacy she left us with.

The error that Frances wanted to correct concerned her former acceptance of the idea that there is a normal developmental stage of primary autism. I believe that her new findings not only modify the definition of autistic pathology but have deep implications for the basic issues of the beginning of object relations.

Tustin's thinking had a deeply empathic quality and never left the ground of close observation of both external and internal reality. Her long analysis with Bion had taught her that thinking was an emotional experience, with the

How?

aim of deepening the understanding of oneself and others through the creation of meaningful links both between ideas and people. Her thinking was imaginative and often expressed itself in metaphors, but it was never speculative. She knew how cautious we must be in formulating ideas about the most primitive levels of mental functioning. She used to say that results can only be inferred, and that the only means for their validation is the exchange of similar experiences with other authors. Her intellectual honesty and her clinical sensitivity were the gifts that made her the extraordinary supervisor she was. Frances Tustin had the gift to help others to grow.

how does growth differ from change?

In the late 1970s, she supervised my work with my first autistic child patient. This is what she said at the end of one supervision:

Now I haven't . . . given you specific interpretations, but I've given you, as I feel, the stage of development that this child is struggling with, and you'll find your own way of saying it to him. In some ways, I've repeated myself . . . but it helps you to work it over in all sorts of different ways, so it just becomes part of your scheme of understanding and you don't have to think: Oh dear, now, what did Frances say about this? The important thing is to be flowing and spontaneous and real and natural with these children. . . . If you can get this scheme of understanding, just let it sort of spring up in your mind, grow up in your mind like a plant. This is the soil as it were that I am giving you. And then, your interpretations will come up like plants and you will be able to say things in a natural way that will be meaningful to him. [personal communication, 1978]

Since the little boy was my first autistic case, I had a long way to go and much to learn. Frances gently told me so by extending the metaphor and saying:

The fact that we make mistakes is a good thing, because those, in a way, are the growing points. If we were always so perfect and so marvelous, there would never be any growing points. . . . I don't know if you do gardening. But in transplanting plants, the new roots grow from the wound where you have cut off the leaves, and where you have done a wound at the bottom, the new roots grow from those wounds. [personal communication, 1978]

Outgrowing Theory

It sometimes happened that a child did not "fit" the theory. If Tustin came up against a clinical phenomenon for which there was no corresponding theoretical formulation she knew of, she would search for one. If she found no entirely satisfactory existing term, she would suggest a new one to describe, as precisely as possible, the phenomenon she had observed.

When her little patient, John, had become able to tell her about the "black hole" he felt in his mouth, she was worried, because the Kleinian formulations with which she had been trained did not seem to cover that kind of experience (Tustin, 1994b). She set out to find a concept that made sense of the child's experience so that she could think about the experience and share it with other workers. She would not hesitate, if necessary, to extend or modify her frame of reference.

Frances Tustin had a keen sense for language. Her search for knowledge always included the search for the right words to name what she had observed. She paid tribute to Bion when she said that she had learned from him an attitude of respect for words. But working with autistic children who live in an asymbolic nonverbal world had also made her very conscious of the limits of verbal language and therefore of the difficulties connected with translating these children's modes of functioning into words that could both express their mental state as precisely as possible and be shared with her fellow workers. She said:

> Inevitably, we come to a point beyond which our understanding of these elemental situations cannot go. Ultimately, it is beyond the power of mind to study itself, or to express non-verbal mental experiences in words. When writing about them, we are constantly haunted by the discrepancy between what we can intuitively apprehend, and what we can manage to express. . . . [1986, p. 168]
>
> The original experience, which was preverbal, is distorted by the use of words, but it is the nearest that both patient and therapist can come to it. [1986, p. 194]

Tustin often used evocative imagery and called upon poets to convey the atmosphere of what she felt to be the sensation-dominated world of autistic children. Poetry is rooted in those primordial states, and poetic language— with its rhythmical and melodious flow and its freedom from grammatical and syntactic constraints—appeared to her to reach down to those deep levels.

Tustin's own writing is in plain, clear and rigorously descriptive scientific language. She was a great "translator," capable of using simple words with theoretical precision without depriving them of the richness of their emotional evocative resonance. Her idea of growing was never connected with becoming big or acquiring scientific power, but with the eagerness to learn from her ongoing experience and the capacity for change. This is what her last paper, "The perpetuation of an error," is about. "Growing" to her meant outgrowing a previous setup, if it no longer corresponded to her clinical experience or to new observational findings. She writes:

> One lesson we should learn from this error is that our loyalty should be to *understanding* rather than to personalities. [1994a, p. 6]

She saw the reason for the tendency to take personalities as points of reference, as well as for her own clinging to the concept of normal primary autism, in the fact that psychoanalytic work is highly anxiety-provoking. With the intellectual honesty that distinguished her she wrote:

> I clutched at it (the concept of normal primary autism) as to a raft because I felt baffled, helplessly adrift and "at sea." [1994b, p. 13]

Tustin was all but a cult figure. Her generosity in sharing her knowledge and in linking her younger colleagues among each other was extraordinary. Her books are dedicated to her autistic patients, their parents, and to the people who discussed their clinical work with her. She concluded "The perpetuation of an error" by thanking the colleagues who read the drafts and "helped it to grow" (1994b, p. 21), and she meant what she said.

Rectifying the Error

In *Autism and Childhood Psychosis* (1972), Tustin introduced the term "normal primary autism" and started using it systematically. However, she never seemed to be really satisfied with it. In *Autistic States in Children* (1981a), she began explicating her doubts: "It is tenable that the primary state of autism is not absolute. There are likely to be flickering states of awareness of separateness. . . ." (p. 5).

In "Thoughts on autism with special reference to a paper by Melanie Klein" (1983), Tustin never used the term "normal primary autism" at all and described the normal primary stage of development as a "psycho-physical state of auto-sensuousness" instead. She stated that this "primal sense of 'me-ness' is bound up with feelings merged with the mother" (1983, p. 168) and she stressed the difference between normal and pathological development by saying:

> If this primal autosensuous "me-ness" is disturbed, it goes along a deviant path. This pathological version has features in common with normal primary auto-sensuousness, but it has a precocity and artificiality . . . which are not part of normal development. [1983, p. 168]

A few years later, in the second chapter of *Autistic Barriers in Neurotic Patients* (1986), under the title "The growth of understanding," Tustin transferred her insights to the level of existing theoretical concepts:

> Following Mahler . . . I began to use the term "autistic" for the earliest state of normal infantile development, as well as for pathological states . . . but since then the word "autism" . . . has become so contaminated with pathological associations that it can no longer be usefully used for *normal* states. [p. 36–37]

In the preface to *The Protective Shell in Children and Adults* (1990), Tustin not only criticized the use of the term "autism" for normal development but corrected her former view of the existence of a normal state corresponding to primary autism by saying: "It is no longer tenable to postulate an undifferentiated autistic state of an absolute kind in earliest infancy as normal" (p. XII).

In 1991, the *International Journal of Psycho-Analysis* published "Revised understandings of psychogenic autism." In that paper Tustin wrote:

> I have come to the conclusion that I made a mistake in following the general trend of psychoanalytical writers in using the term autism for an early stage of infantile development, as well as for a specific pathology. I now realize that it is more correct, and leads to clarity in our thinking, if the term *autism* is solely reserved for certain specific pathological conditions in which there is an absence of human relationships and gross impoverishment of mental and emotional life; these impairments being the result of the blocking of awareness by an early aberrant development of autistic procedures. [1991, p. 585]

Finally, Tustin's revised understanding of primary autism became the object of her last paper—"The perpetuation of an error"—published by the *Journal of Child Psychotherapy* in 1994. She stated:

> *There is not a normal infantile stage of primary autism to which the pathology of childhood autism could be a regression* (italics added). [1994b, p. 3]

In that paper, Tustin made another point of fundamental importance. She viewed autism as a pathology that develops in *two* stages. She wrote:

> I began to realize that, in seeing this perpetuated state of unified "at-oneness" with the mother as a *normal* situation in early infancy, we had been extrapolating from a *pathological* situation and mistakenly seeing it as a normal one. This was an error we must be careful not to repeat. I now realize that the infantile state that was being re-evoked in the clinical situation was an *abnormal* one. I have come to see that autism is a protective reaction that develops to deal with the stress associated with a traumatic disruption of an *abnormal* perpetuated state of adhesive unity with the other—*autism being a reaction that is specific to trauma*. It is a two-stage illness. First, there is a perpetuation of dual unity, and then the traumatic disruption of this and the stress that it arouses. [1994b, p. 14]

Tustin was aware that the abandonment of the idea of the existence of a normal primary autistic state would have important consequences, insofar as "it affects our basic assumptions about serious disorder" (1994b, p. 4). She also foresaw that the revised view of the aetiology of autism would "bring about a significant re-orientation in our approach to the treatment of autistic children" (1994b, p. 18).

For my part, I believe that this modification has deep implications not only in theoretical and therapeutic issues concerning childhood autism but more in general in our understanding of primary mental states and their development. The formulation of autism as a pathology that develops in two stages— whereby the actual autistic retreat is preceded by a stage of abnormal adhesive unity—leads to the question of the onset of the first pathological stage in children who are autistic from birth and never take to the breast. At the same time, the conclusion that there is no such stage as normal primary autism represents a challenge to our thinking about "the dawning of human relationships and their development" (1994a, p. 124).

In following the history of psychoanalysis from its origins, we see how, from the very beginning, the observation and analysis of psychopathological stages led—at first—to the formulation of theories about the conditions of their onset and evolution and—at a later stage—to formulations about normal development. In the two brief and concentrated pages in which she traces the history of her error (1994b, pp. 4–6), Frances Tustin refers to her former definition of normal primary autism as corresponding to Freud's concept of auto-erotism, which precedes in his theoretical model the equally non-object related stage of "primary narcissism" (Freud 1914).

Tustin's conclusion that there is no such state as normal primary autism leaves us with the basic issue of the time and mode of the beginning of human interaction and relatedness. It may also leave us with the worry of the confrontation between different psychoanalytic schools, and we might be tempted to get involved in the question of who or what comes first, that is, whether there must be a subject—an I—before it can invest objects and establish relationships, or whether a subject becomes such through the experience of significant primary object relations.

Frances Tustin never fostered theoretical dispute. Without ever losing her clarity and coherence, she tried more and more, as her life came to an end, to bridge gaps rather than to exasperate differences. She believed in the strength of observation and creative thinking, not in the power of persuasion. Her intellectual freedom was essential to her.

In her reminiscences of her analysis with Bion, Frances Tustin quoted the concluding paragraph of his Sao Paulo discussions:

> You do not have to be limited by the limitations of your lecturers, teachers, analysts, parents. If you are there is no room for growth. [Bion 1980, p. 127]

And, in thinking about her own experience, she wrote:

> Dr. Bion aroused in me the courage to see things from a different perspective from the current and accepted ones, and also different from his. He provoked me to think for myself—to have a mind of my own. [1981b, p. 175–176]

Going-On-Thinking

I believe that the best tribute I can pay to Tustin at this point is to go on thinking and to write down the ideas that came to my mind when I first read

"The perpetuation of an error." My first reaction was an almost physical sensation of liberation, as if a door had been opened and new spaces had become accessible and could be explored.

I think that in this last paper, Tustin made two trailblazing statements. The first is that *there is no normal primary autistic stage*. This means that there is a disposition for some form of relatedness from the very beginning. The second statement is that *autism is a two-stage illness*. If it is correct that autistic retreat from trauma corresponds to the second stage of illness, the question of the time of onset of the first stage arises, which is characterized by excessive adhesive at-oneness. In the case of children who show the symptoms of the second stage of autism from birth, the first stage would necessarily begin in prenatal life.

Prenatal Roots of Autism

As long as Tustin maintained the view of the existence of a stage of normal primary autism, there was no reason for searching for possible prenatal situations that could contribute to set in train autistic reactions. This did not prevent her though, already in *Autistic States in Children*, from thinking about prenatal experiences:

> In the early weeks of life, sensations of being in the watery medium of the womb appear to linger on and to be carried over into the child's earliest experience of the outside world. This means that the child's earliest illusions are imbued with womb experiences. [1981a, p. 80]

In the later years, when her doubts concerning normal primary autism had increased, Tustin pointed out that the mothers of her autistic patients had invariably been depressed during pregnancy or after birth. She was convinced that "depression or harassment in the mother will affect the fantasies she has about her child both before and after birth" (1986, p. 95–96). If depression during pregnancy affects the mother's fantasies, these in turn seem to affect the unborn child.

The "water bath" situation commented on by Tustin in the clinical material of an autistic child seemed the realization of the evocative image she had used many years earlier. The child seemed to have been "re-enacting a very early state in which sensations of being in the watery medium of the womb linger on to create a kind of postnatal womb" (1986, pp. 209–210). It is at this point that she quoted Freud's statement that "there is much more continuity between intra-uterine life and earliest infancy than the impressive caesura of the act of birth allows us to believe" (Freud 1926, p. 138).

A few years later, Tustin carried her understanding another step further when she wrote:

> I am convinced that there must be something in the genetic constitution or in the *intra-uterine experience* of the autistic child which predisposes him (or her) to resort to autistic encapsulation as an exclusive mode of protection (italics added). [1990, p. 26]

An even more specific statement follows:

> Since some children seem to be autistic from the day they are born, I suggest that aversion reactions associated with precocious and aberrant ego developments can occur as early as the last trimester of pregnancy. [1990, p. 87]

The Language of Liquidity

Ever since first meeting Frances Tustin, I had heard her using words and expressions that referred to liquid states, to flowing and fluidity. In 1979, she wrote in a letter: "Lectures seem to be flowing from my pen," and later, in another letter: "I swim in clear and limpid water" (1981d).

In describing autistic children, Tustin said that something that had once been "flowing" had become "frozen"; these children's lives would begin to "flow" again when they emerged from their protective encapsulation. This primary flowing state seems an evocation of the watery intra-uterine environment. When she described the anxieties of autistic children, Tustin would use words such as "spilling away, leaking, liquefying, dissolving." In her evocative expressions she often referred to images of liquidity. She would speak of "torrential overflow," "watery bewilderment," "wet universe," "fluid shapes," and "floating weightlessness."

Tustin used this language of liquidity long before she began to think about prenatal life and its possible connection with primary autism. It was part of her and her deep intuitive insight into the earliest stages of human development. Since the early days, she used the expression "flowing-over-at-oneness" to describe the primary sensuous experience of at-oneness. Later, she gave the expression a more precise meaning. Referring to a paper by Hermann (1929), who described "flowing over" as a precursor of projection, Tustin suggested that "'flowing-over-at-oneness' is the process by which the illusion of 'primal unity' is maintained" (1981a, p. 80). At this point, she already hinted at the primitive *protective* function of the state of "flowing-over-at-oneness" against unbearable anxieties of spilling away or dissolving. To my knowledge, she did not follow this idea much further, except in a letter (1982), in which she commented on the material of my little autistic patient who had begun to have a perception of his body existing in space. Tustin wrote, referring to a paper by David Rosenfeld (1981): "In this paper, he suggests that the earliest body-image . . . is based on the notion of liquids flowing through the body. This seems to me to link with my notion of *the predecessor to 'projective identification' being 'flowing-over-at-oneness'"* (italics added).

Projective identification, which is an attempt to counteract an unbearable feeling of separateness, presupposes both the perception of being in a solid state and some awareness of being an individual. "Flowing-over-at-oneness" could be seen as an earlier version of projective identification that could operate at a time or in a state when the sense of being is still more fluid and fleeting, and prevalently connected with an experience of liquidity.

Tactile Perceptions and Adhesive Pathology

During the first stage of autistic illness, Tustin describes the child as being abnormally merged, undifferentiated and "at one" with the mother's body. This appears to be a pathological reaction to the first and unbearable moments of awareness of bodily separateness. She calls this reaction "adhesive-at-oneness" or "adhesive equation" (1994b, p. 15).

In some cases, this first stage of autistic pathology may have its roots in prenatal life. Since adhesive-at-oneness is connected with touch, the question of tactile experiences before birth needs to be thought about. Tustin describes the isolating effect of the addictive use autistic children make of tactile sensations when they produce autistic shapes and when they clutch autistic objects. "In autistic states, the sense of touch over-rides sight and hearing" (Tustin 1990, p. 218). The crucial point is that tactile sensations are misused to shut out any other kind of sensuous experience, because *touch is the only sense that ensures the absence of distance from the object.*

In the prenatal environment, the child does not have to search for a continuity of "no-distance" tactile sensations. These are available at any moment. If some children are born autistic, it is tenable that they have used tactile sensations in an exclusive and shutting-out way already during prenatal life. If we tentatively extend Ogden's concept of the "autistic contiguous position" (1989, p. 47) to the prenatal period, we might say that, while, for a normal child, tactile sensations would contain the possibility of moving towards presymbolic experience, these sensations would be used by the later autistic child in an asymbolic way, that is, as a barrier against the onset of the symbolization process. Here, the term "presymbolic" would indicate an openness to growth and to other less concrete sensuous experiences, while an "asymbolic" use of tactile sensations would be a sign of "unmentalized experience" (Mitrani 1992, p. 550n; 1995) that blocks further development. Tustin attributes the resulting state of autistic-born children to prenatal "aversion reactions" (1990, p. 87). These imply an excessive clinging to tactile continuity and a shutting out of auditory and visual experiences that inevitably entail fleeting perceptions of distance and otherness.

In this connection, the question of why autistic children do not suck their thumbs must be thought about. Sucking is, after all, a tactile experience. Is it because the thumb, coming from outside, can appear as a "not-me" object? Or is the thumb rejected because the child experiences that it cannot remain in the mouth forever?

Sucking can be described as composed of three concurring elements: thumb-in-mouth gives a tactile sensation of surfaces in contact (bi-dimensional skin-to-skin sensation) and a tactile sensation of fullness (three-dimensional sensation of the thumb filling the mouth and the mouth containing the thumb). For sucking to occur, another element must be present, namely the rhythmical inward-bound pull that brings about interaction between mouth and thumb. The inward pull reinforces the possibility of an experience of containment, and therefore of tri-dimensionality; and the alternation between pulling and letting go introduces movement (inward-bound/outward-bound) and a direction in space, as well as a time-structuring rhythmic element. Autistic children need static sameness and exclude from their experience the sensations that sucking would expose them to, namely some rudimentary fleeting awareness of time and space, of containing or being contained, and of interaction with a "not-me" object.

When thinking about such elemental situations, I strongly feel the limits of verbal language. Expressions such as "awareness," "perception" and "experience" describe psychic events that occur in the mind of an "I" that is sufficiently separate from the "other" to be aware, perceiving, and experiencing. I wish we were able to cover our words with veils, or blur them until they *almost* lose their excessively clear-cut shape and meaning every time we try to explore these primordial states. Since we cannot do this when we write, the reader will have to contribute to understanding by "unfocusing" the words whenever they appear to be too neat and solid for conveying the atmosphere of misty dimness that envelops the dawning of consciousness.

We know that children in the womb are able to suck their thumbs actively from the fifth month of prenatal life. Some autistic-born children may never have sucked at all, even during intra-uterine life. Others may have stopped sucking at some point for some reason. For what reason, or for what reasons? Can we make a tentative connection with Tustin's statement that several mothers of her autistic child patients had been depressed during pregnancy? Tustin is assertive about the fact that autism is a reaction to trauma. Since some children are autistic from birth, trauma would necessarily have occurred prior to birth.

Grotstein (1983) suggested that maternal depression during pregnancy can have the effect of a biochemical assault upon the unborn child in the "amniotic bath," and Herbert Rosenfeld (1987) described the impotence of the fetus in the presence of the "osmotic pressure" of the mother's state of mind. Might we conclude that such threats could induce even the unborn child to seek refuge in a life-blocking tactile adhesiveness and become deaf to other stimuli?

Auditory Perceptions (Rhythmic-Musical Shapes), Deafness, and Echolalia

Frances Tustin thought that "'normal primordial' shapes would seem to spring from auto-sensuous rhythms and responses at the root of our 'being.' They would seem to affect the individual's capacity for empathy, and thus for relationships with people" (1986, p. 149). Pointing more specifically to the auditory level, she affirmed that musical shapes ". . . pattern the individual notes that make up the sensation of sound into those percepts and concepts which are particularly related to the dimension of time" (1986, p. 162).

Music is made of both melody and rhythm. Melody can be described as an up and down moving and potentially continuous line. Rhythm brings in a structural element in time. It introduces elements of accentuation and of separation, and thus the principle of discontinuity.

Speech, like music, has a component of both melody and rhythm. The rhythmic element introduces accents, irregularities, and caesuras in the smooth line of the vocal melody. In a wider perspective, the alternation of speech and silence, of vocal presence and absence, is also a rhythmic event. But "speech seems to be a specific kind of musical shape" (Tustin 1986, p. 162). The specificity of speech, as opposed to music, consists in its being the vehicle for thoughts and emotions that human beings use for everyday interpersonal communication. In normal interaction, the rhythmic melody of the speaking voice is the carrier of symbolic messages, that is, it conveys the products of mental activity.

If we try to go deeper into the idea that the first stage of pathology of autistic-born infants would occur during prenatal life, we must briefly recall the evolution of the fetus's hearing capacity in normal development. We know that hearing is fully developed by the age of four months of intra-uterine life (Tomatis 1981, Prechtl 1989).

> By that time, the child perceives the medium and high sound frequency range corresponding to the mother's voice. The low frequency range corresponding to the sounds produced by the maternal organism (the heartbeat, the cadence of breathing and the digestional noises), are perceived at an even earlier stage. Low frequency sounds have a soothing effect on the fetus and slow down its motor activity, whereas sounds of the medium and high frequency range are enlivening and stimulate its motility. The sounds are not only heard by the child, but they seem to leave traces in its memory and constitute a kind of sound-code from which the child's future language will develop. The fetus receives and retains in its memory not only the melodious and rhythmical aspects of the mother tongue, but also the personal inflections and modulations of the maternal voice. [Maiello 1995 p. 26]

The fetus's reactions to the maternal voice, which is *not* continuous and conveys clues about her emotional state, are different from those it has to the low-frequency-sounds produced by her organism, which are continuous and nonmental. Among the bodily sounds that reach the fetus, I believe however that the mother's heartbeat plays a special role.

Rhythm has a time-structuring function through the fact that it introduces discontinuity, but it also conveys—if it is regular—a sense of reliability. Reliability is linked with events being foreseeable. The sensation of "going-on-being" may be connected with the mother's heartbeat in prenatal life. Its structuring and soothing function may correspond to the role of the regular and repetitive bass beating the time in music. The fact that the maternal heartbeat disappears at the moment of birth, together with the other background noises produced by the maternal organism, may well be one of the potentially shocking changes at the end of prenatal life. This loss may become seriously traumatic, if the child has been abnormally merged, undifferentiated, and adhesively "at one" with the maternal environment during its intra-uterine life.

Tustin gives a moving account of one of these "heartbroken" patients:

Their "heartbreak" goes beyond what we usually mean by the term. The feeling of brokenness goes into the very fabric of their being. . . . Since the sucking rhythm had become associated with the beating of the heart, it was the "teat-tongue-heart" that was felt to be broken. Of course, all this was wordless, and to put it into words seems clumsy and even absurd. But it helps us to understand that for these patients bodily awareness of their separateness had been experienced as an interruption to the pulsing rhythm of their "going-on-being." [1990, p. 156]

For these patients, we can imagine that pre- and postnatal tactile and auditory losses have merged and result in a traumatic heartbreak. The last heartbeat means that a life has ended. This is true also for the mother's heartbeat at the end of prenatal life.

Rosetta, an autistic little girl I began seeing from the age of 5, seemed to have become able to deal with this traumatic experience. During the third year of therapy, she began to show some awareness of the passing of time, and therefore of separations.

The first thing Rosetta did when she entered the room for the last session before a brief holiday was to look at my wristwatch and ask me at what time her mother would pick her up again. She then put her ear to my watch and listened. After some time, I asked her what she heard. She got up, looked at me and said: "Toc, toc, toc." She then bent her head and leaned lightly with her ear against my chest. She listened for a while and then said: "The heart."

I think that at this point Rosetta had reenacted previously heartbreaking experiences. The holiday break was about to begin. She checked to hear that I had a beating heart in my body, that I was alive, and maybe that I (and she) would remain alive during our separation. In fact, she seemed able to bear that the sound of my heart was *there,* namely inside me, and that she could hear it *only* if she was at no distance from me. She was aware now, and could tolerate that my heart was not a "me-thing," and could name it.

In distinguishing tactile and auditory sensations, I am aware that I try to separate elements of an experience that is probably more unitary for the newborn infant, and even more so in the fetus's primordial state. In fact, Tustin used to speak of "clusters of sensations." It is necessary to do so, if we want to get a better understanding both of the functional specificity of touch and hearing, and of the basic differences between normal and pathological pre- and postnatal development.

We see how, in Ogden's *autistic contiguous position,* tactile sensations can be used either in a presymbolic or in an asymbolic way (1989). What can we say about hearing? Hearing is a less "concrete" sensuous mode than touch. It is, together with vision, a "long-distance mode of perception" (Tustin 1990, p. 51). Whereas tactile experience is possible *only* if there is no space separating the two surfaces that come into contact with each other, hearing (and, after birth, sight) cannot function properly in a no-space situation.

Therefore, we can state that auditory and later visual experiences contain a higher potential for symbol-formation than touch, because symbolization cannot begin without at least a fleeting awareness of separateness, and therefore of space and distance. Distance is the very thing autistic children cannot bear. It was the premature traumatic experience of separateness that necessitated their radical self-protection against any awareness of space, and hence of "not-me" experiences.

Although autistic children are neither blind nor deaf, they do not look or listen. They eliminate the normal functioning of the senses that are connected with distance by equating every potentially symbol-promoting experience with an asymbolic "no-space" tactile situation. As Tustin writes:

I have come to realize that vision and hearing, as a result of the undue dominance of the sense of touch, become excessively imbued with tactile sensations. [1986, p. 145]

We see that in normal development, the unborn child not only hears but seems to listen actively to the mother's voice and to be enlivened by it. Moreover, traces of the prenatal auditory experience are present in the infant's memory and emerge later in its language development. I call this trace of memory of prenatal auditory experience a "sound-object" (1995). Again, I am aware that the term "object" is too distinct and too "solid" a word to convey the idea of what the "protomental activity" of the fetus brings to its awareness in terms of experience (Mancia 1981). However, I do not call it a "shape," because I wanted to imply its possible function as a precursor of the later internal maternal object.

Is it possible to think that the autistic-born child is able to "plug" its hearing capacity by shutting down the normal auditory receptivity to the mother's voice already in the womb? If the idea of a prenatal "sound-object" and its function as a precursor of the postnatal maternal "breast-object" is tenable, we could say that the autistic-born child may have missed the opportunity for its "sound-object" to develop. Could this have happened with Tustin's cases in which the mothers were depressed during pregnancy? Could the children have withdrawn from the mother's depressed feelings that resonated in her voice already at that stage, clinging to tactile sensations instead? This withdrawal would prevent the child from having such basic experiences as those of the alternation of presence and absence, the emotional oscillations expressed in the tone of voice, as well as its symbolic content. The normal fetus possibly uses the maternal voice as a kind of prenatal auditory nourishment that is necessary for its protomental activity to set in train the formation of the "sound-object" that will allow the child to meet its realization at the breast after birth.

In African cultures, the young pregnant woman, at her first experience of motherhood, is urged by her mother to talk to her child, particularly at the beginning of pregnancy, that is, at a time when the danger of miscarriage is major, and even more so if she feels upset or nauseous. These cultures seem to have an archaic knowledge of the lifegiving and relation-creating power of the voice.

Autistic children often do not speak. If they do, their speech is echolalic, although they understand verbal language. However, they use both what they hear and what they say in an asymbolic way. Echolalic speech repeats "sameness" and is a powerful means against differentiation. Tustin writes: "Echolalia is a manipulation of words and sounds, as if they are tangible physical objects in order to make them into 'me'" (1986, p. 113). That autistic children do not suck implies that they also miss the normal "mouthing" experience at the breast. Ricks (1975) found that autistic children often do not "lall" or "babble."

Rosetta

The following clinical material from Rosetta's therapy exemplifies the relation-killing effect of echolalia, which reproduces sameness and shuts off both difference and similarity. A few weeks before the session in which she had listened to my heartbeat, Rosetta brought a toy parrot from home. The parrot had a battery, a microphone and a loudspeaker inside and repeated, exactly like a real parrot, everything that was said. The articulation of the words was blurred, but the intonation was imitated with irritating perfection.

The little girl interacted with the parrot by pronouncing words and sentences that he immediately repeated. She was totally absorbed in her activity and completely excluded me from communication with her. At some point, I started talking about what I thought was happening and what Rosetta was doing to our relationship. The parrot readily produced an indistinct melodious caricature of my comment. Rosetta continued talking to him without taking any notice of my words. At this point, I had the choice between trying to make another comment, knowing that the parrot was ready to ridicule any attempt to give a meaning to the situation, and withdrawing into silence, allowing the echolalic exchange of "sound-shapes" to go on.

Tustin wrote about the strenuous resistance of these children against unforeseeable "shapes," and about their unflinching efforts to endlessly reproduce "shapes" that are familiar to them (1986). What they pay attention to is the tone of voice and "the sound of words rather than the meaning" (1986, p. 162). In other terms, they treat words as if they are made only of their musical and rhythmical components and are not the result of the symbol-producing process that we call thinking.

Here is another example drawn from Rosetta's material of the same period of therapy. It shows how, on the one hand, she was more in touch with reality and more capable of both listening and talking in a communicative way and also, on the other hand, how quickly she could deprive vocal messages of their emotional meaning, retaining only their musical and rhythmical shape in order to control them and to shut out the experience of relatedness.

During a Monday session, Rosetta showed me her hand and said that it was wounded. I said that she had come to the doctor for me to take care of her wound and heal it. She replied affirmatively. While I talked to her about the past weekend break, I alluded with slight movements of my hand, without touching her, to a doctor's nursing gestures, first of softly rubbing ointment onto her wounded hand and then of wrapping a bandage around it. While I did this, I said first, slowly, in a low and soft tone of voice: "ointment, ointment," and then, accompanying my swifter circular hand movement, "bandage, bandage, bandage." This is not something I would usually have done. It was the first time Rosetta had shown me her perception of pain and her need for help. I had probably imagined that I could better reach her elemental level of emotional functioning if I alternated my verbal interpretation with more rhythmic speech and with the representation of nursing gestures. Rosetta was very satisfied and wanted me to give her the same treatment on other parts of her body. At that point I could already feel that a repetitive mode was taking over and that she was doing away with the previous interactive experience.

In the following session, she wanted to reproduce the same situation. She said, "ointment, ointment . . . bandage-bandage-bandage" with exactly the same intonation and rhythm as I had done the day before, but there was no wound anymore. She had turned the words of healing into a protective shield against pain.

It is probable that the unusual part of my comment, that had been intended to meet her need also at a presymbolic level, had been a mistake and had resulted in inducing her to use my response to her request in an asymbolic way, by retaining the musical-rhythmical and tactile aspects of my words and doing away with the emotion of relatedness. She might have been able to stay with the experience of pain and need longer if I had spoken in the usual plain verbal form.

When I did not reproduce the material and rhythmical pattern she wanted me to repeat, instead talking to her about how difficult it was to accept that things were not exactly as they had been last time, she started smelling her hands and feet and superficially repeated the nursing gestures herself, while saying the rhyme on and on. Both the words and the gestural representation had lost their original symbolic content.

The Dawn of Two-Ness

If it is tenable that, in autistic-born children, the first stage of pathology begins in intra-uterine life, we can conclude inversely that in normal development, sensuous "proto-integrations" that are prevented by its withdrawal would take place.

We shall never bring positive proofs of these hypotheses, for we will never know what the unborn child really experiences. The only thing we can do is to infer with caution and respect from dream or infant observation material. The dream that follows tells us about the interplay between tactile and auditory sensations and helps us to imagine how primary sensuous integrations may develop. The dreamer is a 45-year-old woman:

> I am standing in an undefined inner space. A man whom I don't know comes towards me. He is slim, but there is nothing special about him. We embrace and start dancing. It all happens quite naturally. We have neither

sought nor chosen each other. We dance together in perfect harmony to the sound of music that comes from somewhere, our bodies moulded to each other. But there is nothing sexual about our closeness. There is no tension or excitement, just a deep and total sense of well-being. Our legs and feet are in such perfect agreement that they sometimes step out of the beat of the music, without ever losing their harmonious correspondence. The most wonderful of all sensations is to feel our steps moving in syncopation with the rhythm of the music while effortlessly maintaining their movements in perfect accord. [Maiello 1995, pp. 28–29]

The dreamer associated her dancing steps with the fetus moving in the amniotic fluid, in constant contact with the liquid medium and with the uterine walls, the umbilical cord, and the placenta. At the tactile level, the sense of well-being has to do with the bodies being molded to each other, and with the perfect harmonious correspondence of their movements. The blissful "we-ness" is not so much connected with a relationship but rather with what we could imagine as the first awareness of constancy of the body–ego, which has boundaries, is self-centered, and capable of enjoyable movement. "The ego is first and foremost a body ego . . . ultimately derived from bodily sensations, chiefly from those springing from the surface of the body" (Freud 1923, p. 26). The tactile part of the experience evoked in the dream seems to correspond to Ogden's description of the autistic contiguous position (1989).

The auditory component in the dream-sensation is represented by the music which "comes from somewhere." The source of sound is undefined, and so is the direction from which it comes. But clearly it comes from *outside*. It gets into the dancers' feet, but it is "not-me" music. The dancers' most intense pleasure is derived from their safely connected legs and feet *stepping out* of the measure of the music and finding a rhythm of their own, without loosing the joyfully syncopated communication with the musical "other."

The dream has to do with Tustin's "rhythm of safety" and evokes what Meltzer (1986) called the "song-and-dance level," which he sees as a stage that leads on to the development of actual symbolic communication. The deep feeling of well-being is derived both from the secure tactile union of the bodies and from the auditory experience of "consonance" with *and* differentiation from the music. The tactile component seems to bring about the awareness of being a "me," and the auditory component, the perception of the "other." This corresponds to the mental situation described by Grotstein (1980) as "dual track," that is, the simultaneous sensation of fusion and separateness. The consensual combination of tactile and auditory sensations seems to establish a primary sense of self existing in space and time. In differentiating between "ego" and "self," Tustin writes: ". . . the sense of self and of individual identity is dependent upon relationships with other people" (1986, p. 44) and "to have a 'self,' we need to have awareness of 'others'" (1990, p. 158).

When there is sufficient basic trust in "going-on-being," oscillations between "at-oneness" and separateness become possible. This experience paves the way for psychic growth. Since the child hears and listens to the mother's voice during intra-uterine life and reacts to its presence, but has no control over it, I would suggest that its sound may give the fetus its first fleeting awareness of "otherness." The tactile body–ego is defined at first in terms of surfaces and boundaries, but the maternal voice with its enlivening and meaningful music may introduce a proto-experience of tri-dimensionality (Meltzer et al. 1975) during intra-uterine life.

This would mean that absolute bi-dimensionality would pertain to asymbolic pathological development, while normal presymbolic functioning of the mind would have a tri-dimensional potentiality from the time when hearing is fully developed in intra-uterine life. If this idea is tenable, the experience of the maternal voice and its meaningful music could be seen as the basis for the development of the infant's "self."

Going Beyond

In a comment on my autistic child patient, who during one session had started crawling underneath the carpet from one side to the other side of the room, and pronounced his first non-echolalic word, "tunnel," Tustin wrote:

> It is my experience that psychological birth is expressed by the "black hole" or by going down a dark tunnel. It is at this point that the child emerges from the state in which he is only aware of surfaces to being aware of insides and outsides (i.e., from bi-dimensionality to tri-dimensionality). I think the tunnel is a re-evocation of going down the birth canal in physical birth. . . . It is a preparation for the valley of the shadow of death. It seems to me that some people are only psychologically born on the day of their death (1981c).

In the afterthoughts to "The perpetuation of an error," Tustin wrote about the possibility of transforming pain into suffering by becoming able to look at the trauma, to represent it, and to deal with it. She said: "A psychic catastrophe can become a psychic opportunity" (1994b, p. 17). The metaphor of the growing plant that Frances Tustin had used 15 years earlier to encourage me in my first clinical experience with an autistic child was the poetic version of this same idea. "The mistakes," she had said, "are the growing points. The new roots grow from the wound where you have cut off the leaves." After Bion's death, she wrote in her reminiscences of her analysis with him: "Growing is the goal. But it is not under control. The pilgrimage takes us we know not where. . . ." (1981b, p. 178). Frances did not know where her new insights would take her, but she never hesitated to go forward on her path and, if necessary, to cross borders. She had the courage to go beyond and taught us what growing means.

References

Bion, W. R. (1980). *Bion in New York and Sao Paulo*. Perthshire, Scotland: Clunie Press.

Freud, S. (1914). On narcissism. *Standard Edition* 14:67–102.

———— (1923) The ego and the id. *Standard Edition* 19:3–63.

———— (1926). Inhibitions, symptoms and anxiety. *Standard Edition* 20:75–175.

Grotstein, J. S. (1980). Primitive mental states. *Contemporary Psychoanalysis* 16:479–546.

———— (1983) A proposed revision of the psycho-analytic concept of primitive mental states. II: The borderline syndrome. Section I: Disorders of autistic safety and symbiotic relatedness. *Contemporary Psychoanalysis* 19:580–604.

Hermann, I. (1929). Das Ich und das Denken. *Imago* 15:89–110; 325–348.

Maiello, S. (1995). The Sound-Object. *Journal of Child Psychotherapy* 21, 23–41. [First published (1993) as L'oggetto sonoro. *Richard e Piggle* 1, 31–47.]

Mancia, M. (1981). On the beginning of mental life in the foetus. *International Journal of Psycho-Analysis* 62:351–357.

Meltzer, D., Hoxter, S., Weddell, D., and Wittenberg, I. (1975). *Explorations in Autism. A Psychoanalytical Study*. Perthshire, Scotland: Clunie Press.

Meltzer, D. (1986). *Studies in Extended Metapsychology*. Perthshire, Scotland: Clunie Press.

Mitrani, J. L. (1992). On the survival function of autistic manoeuvres in adult patients. *International Journal of Psycho-Analysis* 73:549–559.

——— (1995). Toward an understanding of unmentalized experience. *Psychoanalytic Quarterly* 64:68–112.

Ogden, T. H. (1989). *The Primitive Edge of Experience*. New Jersey: Jason Aronson.

Prechtl, H. R. (1989). Fetal behavior. In *Fetal Neurology*, eds. A. Hill and J. Volpe. New York: Raven Press.

Ricks, D. (1975). Vocal communications in preverbal, normal and autistic children. In *Language, Cognitive Defects and Autistic Children*, ed. N. O'Connor. London: Butterworth.

Rosenfeld, D. (1981). The notion of a psychotic body image in neurotic and psychotic patients. International Psychoanalytic Congress. Helsinki, Finland, July.

Rosenfeld, H. A. (1987). Afterthought: Changing Theories and Changing Techniques in Psychoanalysis. In *Impasse and Interpretation*. London: Tavistock.

Tomatis, A. (1981). *La Nuit Utérine*. Paris: Editions Stock.

Tustin, F. (1972). *Autism and Childhood Psychosis*. London: Hogarth.

——— (1978). Excerpt from tape recording. Unpublished.

——— (1979). Excerpt from manuscript letter. Unpublished.

——— (1981a). *Autistic States in Children*. London: Routledge and Keagan Paul.

——— (1981b). A modern pilgrim's progress: reminiscences of personal analysis with Dr. Bion. *Journal of Child Psychotherapy* 7:175–179.

——— (1981c). Excerpt from manuscript letter. Unpublished.

——— (1981d). Excerpt from manuscript letter. Unpublished.

——— (1982). Excerpt from manuscript letter. Unpublished.

——— (1983). Thoughts on autism with special reference to a paper by Melanie Klein. *Journal of Child Psychotherapy* 9:119–131.

——— (1986). *Autistic Barriers in Neurotic Patients*. London: Karnac Books.

——— (1990). *The Protective Shell In Children And Adults*. London: Karnac Books.

——— (1991). Revised understandings of psychogenic autism. *International Journal of Psycho-Analysis* 72:585–591.

——— (1994a). Autistic children who are assessed as not brain-damaged. *Journal of Child Psychotherapy* 20:103–131.

——— (1994b). The perpetuation of an error. *Journal of Child Psychotherapy* 20:3–23.

2

Unbearable Ecstasy, Reverence and Awe, and the Perpetuation of an "Aesthetic Conflict"

Judith L. Mitrani

Beauty is truth, truth beauty, —that is all Ye know on earth, and all ye need to know.

John Keats, "Ode on a Grecian Urn"

In this chapter I will attempt to explicate and discuss some aspects of Frances Tustin's concept of the unbearable ecstasy of at-one-ment emphasizing her attentiveness to the importance of the containing function of the mother with regard to this elemental experience; Bion's distinction between "reverence and awe" and defensive idealization; and Meltzer's notion of the "aesthetic conflict" as each of these themes—separately and in combination—have some essential bearing upon the provocation or mitigation of envy, the process of introjection, the development of both healthy and pathological internal object relations, and the resultant nature of the superego and individual self-esteem. I will offer clinical case material both as a background for and an illustration of the phenomena described, as well as certain conclusions that may have some impact upon our attitude and technique in psychoanalysis.

Background

Over one weekend break in the sixth year of her five times per week analysis, Jessica—a woman in her late thirties—attended a concert of classical music.

23

Featured on the program was a female violinist who was to play Jessica's favorite concerto.

Jessica adored music. She had herself been formally schooled in the violin since the tender age of 2. She had, in her youth, played with numerous amateur orchestras, and nearly all the members of her immediate family were musically inclined. This by way of saying that for Jessica, attending concerts was always an intensely emotional experience.

On this particular occasion, Jessica sat quite close to the stage, directly in line with the spot where the soloist would be standing. After the overture, in anticipation of the concerto to come, Jessica found herself glancing about the audience, soon realizing that she was looking for me.

When the soloist walked on stage, Jessica was stunned. The woman who stood before her was incredibly beautiful, an ethereal vision of long black hair flowing over porcelain white shoulders left bare above a deep blue strapless satin gown. As the violinist began to play, Jessica could not decide which was the more lovely: the sound of the music that flooded her ears, or the sight of this Rumanian gypsy dancing and swaying to that music, which bedazzled her eyes. Jessica was enraptured and ecstatic.

After the concert, as the sights and sounds of the evening lingered on in Jessica's mind, she thought once more about my perceived absence and her ecstasy gradually degraded into a profound sadness. She was aware of a deep and almost unbearable feeling of regret over not having been able to share this experience of sensual wonder with me.

In the Monday hour in which these events and feelings were reported, Jessica talked about her mother, a beautiful woman of Rumanian descent. She said that her mother—who was nearly always depressed during the patient's childhood—had little sense that she (the mother) was either beautiful or desirable. The patient thought that this might be partly due to her father's openly expressed intention to obtain a divorce from her mother even before Jessica's birth.

Jessica's violin lessons were initiated, encouraged, and supported by her mother, who also participated actively in her studies by accompanying Jessica, when possible, at the piano. The mother also sang—at one time semi-professionally—but had always longed to play the violin, and was thrilled when her daughter seemed to demonstrate both an interest and talent in this direction.

Jessica said that she had felt good when she left the hour on Friday, and she now thought that this might be one reason why she had hoped to see me that evening at the concert. Since she could not find me, she concluded that I must not be there, and felt disappointed at not being able to share the beautiful concert experience with me. She now was aware that she wanted very much to convey this experience in the session, but she feared—much to her dismay—that I could never really have that experience since I had not been there.

The patient also made reference, both direct and indirect, to my *perceived* physical beauty. As she did so she burst into tears, which seemed to pour out of her in an uncontrollable way, streaming down her cheeks and soaking her hair and the collar of her dress. When she noticed this, Jessica expressed a concern that both her hair and dress had been ruined, and she reported a sense of dread that she would not be able to *pull herself together* when our time was up so that she could face the day that lay ahead of her.

While Jessica spoke, I was reminded of a dream she had reported the week before about a teacher whom she had a crush on in elementary school, a beautiful woman with prematurely graying hair (which I also have). Additionally, I noted that—like the violinist—I am of Rumanian heritage. While wondering *if* and *how* Jessica might sense this, I recalled the uncanny feeling in the Friday hour of the previous week, when it seemed that we were so closely attuned to one another that the sensation of our touching one another was unmistakably palpable.

I also recalled that this hour was one of those rare and memorable ones when our thoughts—her associations and my interpretations—seemed to be burgeoning, one from the other, in such a graceful and organic way that it had felt at the time like we were creating a modern ballet or a poem. Jessica's comments at the end of that hour had spoken to her experience of something "beautiful" about our contact as well.

With this in mind I said to Jessica that I thought that she was communicating something of the ecstasy she had experienced, not only at the concert but also in our Friday hour, when she had perhaps experienced herself, me, and our connection as a thing of beauty. Jessica nodded in agreement with this and added that she had felt foolish when she left at the end of the hour, thinking that while she was sorry to end the analytic week, I probably felt tired and would be looking forward to my weekend off.

To this I replied that it seemed that she had come away from the Friday hour with two contrasting experiences of me: one as a beautiful mother-analyst who loved and supported her, and the other as a tired, depressed, and unsupported mother-analyst who was relieved to be rid of her. Since she was not certain which experience was true, she had searched the concert crowd for my face in hope of finding me there, sharing in the beautiful experience of both herself and of myself making beautiful analytic music together, swaying in tune with one another, rocked safely in the rhythm of the melody of the Friday hour. I also said that perhaps she had taken my absence from the concert—like my absence during the weekend break in our contact—as a confirmation of my depression and fatigue.

Jessica responded to this saying that she had felt awfully overwhelmed after the concert but that she did not know why. Hearing her, I recalled that our Friday hour had been so rich that I had needed to make notes on it afterward, in part to preserve it, in part because this is one way in which I feel I can help myself to contain whatever leftover emotion might otherwise spill into subsequent hours with other patients. I was then moved to say that I thought Jessica might be telling me that she had needed to see her feelings of admiration toward the beautiful mother-me reflected in my presence.

Perhaps Jessica needed to see that I could *also* feel myself to be beautiful, but when she imagined me absent from the concert, her worst fears were realized. Perhaps her experience of the mother-me as tired, depressed, and relieved to be rid of her for the weekend had seemed painfully confirmed. In that moment, her feeling of ecstasy had dissolved, spilling over in an overwhelming encounter with disillusionment, perhaps leaving a very little baby-Jessica feeling incapable of the task of holding herself together over the long weekend.

One might say that beauty and its associated attributes—goodness, hope and truth—are the cornerstones of mental health. However the experience of the beautiful mother must first be had *with* that mother, not merely *of* her (Reid 1990). This notion is analogous to Winnicott's (1956) observation of the baby's need to first experience being alone in the presence of the object in order that it might gradually develop *the capacity to be alone,* rather than being *overcome with loneliness* and despair. He also discussed the baby's need for a mirroring object, which I believe is closely related to the issues under discussion in this paper.

As the hour unfolded, it became clear that Jessica had needed me to partake in the experience of myself as a beautiful mother-analyst, to catch the overflow of the ecstasy she felt in my presence in the Friday hour, and to confirm this experience when its reality was threatened by the pain of separation—by the presence of the absence. It might be said that for Jessica, it was the "absent object" (O'Shaughnessy 1964) that constituted the hell of two-ness—perhaps first felt at birth and reexperienced over the weekend break—which was the antithesis of the paradise she had known as the blissful at-one-ment with the womb-mother, recaptured within our emotional contact in the Friday hour.

The Aesthetic Conflict

I was reminded of Jessica's experience while reading a paper by Donald Meltzer (1988). In that paper on "the aesthetic conflict," Meltzer states:

> It has probably escaped no-one's attention that the percentage of beautiful mothers recorded in the course of psycho-analysis far exceeds the national average and that this appellation clearly refers back to childhood impressions often completely out of keeping with later more objective judgments by the patients of their middle-aged parent. [p. 8–9]

Here Meltzer prompts our consideration of the possibility that the view of the "beautiful mother," often presented by patients in analysis, harkens back to some early "proto-aesthetic" experience; one that is however not without conflict.

> "Rocked in the cradle of the deep" of his mother's graceful walk; lulled by the music of her voice set against the syncopation of his own heart-beat and hers; responding in dance like a little seal, playful as a puppy. But moments of anxiety, short of fetal distress, may also transmit itself through heart-beat, rigidity, trembling, jarring movements; perhaps a coital activity may be disturbing rather than enjoyable, perhaps again dependent on the quality of maternal emotion; maternal fatigue may transmit itself by loss of postural tone and graceless movement. [p. 17]

In this passage Meltzer indicates that the baby knows its mother inside and out—as both the bad and the beautiful—and is impacted on a sensual level by each of her physical, mental, and emotional qualities even before its birth. This notion reverberates with findings from current fetal observation (Mancia 1981, Piontelli 1985, 1987, 1988, 1992a, 1992b), psychoanalytic-clinical inference (Bion 1976/1987, 1977, Freud 1926, Hansen 1994, Maiello 1995, Mitrani 1996, Osterweil 1990, Paul 1981, 1989, 1990, Share 1994), and imaginative conjecture (Bion 1979).

Indeed Meltzer purports that ". . . every baby 'knows' from experience that his mother has an 'inside' world, a world where he has dwelled and from whence he has been expelled or escaped, depending on his point of view" (p. 21), and he goes on to posit that, after birth:

> The ordinary devoted mother presents to her ordinary beautiful baby a complex object of overwhelming interest, both sensual and infra-sensual.

Her outward beauty . . . bombards him with an emotional experience of a passionate quality, the result of his being able to see [her] as "beautiful." But the meaning of his mother's behavior, of the appearance and disappearance of the breast and of the light in her eyes, of a face over which emotions pass like the shadows of clouds over the landscape, are unknown to him. [p. 22]

Meltzer seems to suggest here that mother is an enigma to her baby. The baby may have known her, and yet—perhaps shaken by "the impressive caesura of the act of birth" (Freud 1926)—it has suddenly become uncertain of what it knows. Is she a beauty or the beast?

When Meltzer proposes that

This is the aesthetic conflict, which can be most precisely stated in terms of the aesthetic impact of the outside of the "beautiful" mother available to the senses, and the enigmatic inside which must be constructed by *creative imagination* (italic added). [p. 22]

it seems that he is implying that the baby's sensory experience of the beautiful (good) mother must be confirmed by what the baby finds inside the mother, and that the baby's experience of the mothers inner world—her mood, her emotional and mental life, her attitudes—is colored by *creative imagination*, that is, by its own phantasies via the process of projective identification.

However further along, Meltzer appends the above conclusion, submitting that the baby must wait—like Kafka's "K"—"for decisions from the castle of his mother's inner world" (p. 22). With this addition, it would seem he is suggesting—and, I believe, is correct in doing so—that *it is not just the baby's "creative imagination" that imbues the inside of the mother and the baby's prenatal and postnatal experience of her with meaning,* since, as he so astutely observes, the baby must derive its cues from the mother's conscious and unconscious communications; that is, the baby must wait for its mother to confirm its greatest hopes or its gravest fears.

To put it another way, the baby asks: "How does mother view or experience herself?" and it must anxiously await the answer *from its mother.* I believe that the baby's question—and the mother's answer—constitute one aspect of the type of reality testing that Melanie Klein (1975) referred to as the means by which the baby finds validation for the enduring existence of the good breast, the good internal object, and the good experience it represents.

An example of this type of reality testing, and the consequences of a distorted message being received from the castle of the mother's inner world, may be seen in the following material from the four times per week analysis of another patient, whom I will refer to as Carla.

Carla

When Carla was a very young child, her mother died, only a short time after they were abandoned by Carla's father. Carla came across in our first meetings as a hard, arrogant, street-wise "chick." Her hardened impermeable cynicism seemed to serve as a "second skin" (Bick 1968), which took on concrete form, as if it were woven into the tight, black, leather clothing she often wore. Thus she seemed to have replaced her absent father by taking on a masculine toughness, to shield herself from any awareness of the feminine vulnerability that lay just beneath the surface.

However, in the second year of her analysis, that fragile part of Carla began to emerge, like a baby crying out to be born and to be allowed close contact with what she seemed at times to experience as the caring presence of a mother-analyst. In one session it occurred to me that the depth of Carla's cries might correspond to the strata from which they emanated, as if they were being released from some subterranean pocket that held at bay her most painful experiences of infancy. When I told her as much, she said, "I feel like something terrible wants out of me. I don't want it to come out. I'm so afraid that I'll never stop crying."

Thus, Carla seemed to be attempting to communicate about the terror of spilling out. She became afraid that she would not be unable to collect herself at the end of the hour when she came in contact with the loss of some very basic sense of security: a loss that may have originated even earlier than the memorable events of either Father's abandonment or Mother's death. Months later we came close to understanding some of the most primitive origins of Carla's fears of being spilled and gone, as well as the template for the development of her leathery protection against the threat of such dissipation. Both this anxiety and the defense against it appeared to be connected to a primary experience of the mother as it became enacted in the transference relationship, which I will next attempt to describe.

In the third year of her analysis, I noticed that almost invariably when Carla returned from the weekend breaks, she would greet my arrival at the waiting room door with a warm and enthusiastic smile. Then, she would scan my face quite intensely, passing through the doorway on the way to my consulting room. The intensity of Carla's scrutinizing gaze often left me feeling unusually self-conscious. Carla was very beautiful and always perfectly made-up when she came for her sessions, and I frequently was given over to wondering if my lipstick was on crooked, if I had forgotten to powder my nose, or if perhaps I had applied mascara to just one eye and not the other.

These banal ruminations were discomforting and intractable, and I found myself tempted to dismiss them as irrelevant. However, as these were uncommon if not all together absent preoccupations with others of my patients, I opted to allow them to brew a bit to see what percolated out of them. This lead to the emergence of some fleeting thoughts: might I be envious of this young and beautiful girl? Might Carla be looking for something in my face that might reflect her own? Was I felt to be failing her in some way that was both disconcerting and implacable?

No matter how many times this sequence would occur, by the time my patient had settled on the couch, I noticed that her enthusiasm for me and her analysis would suddenly be transformed into a tough, leathery air of indifference and disgust, as if she resented having to submit to *my* "rigid requirement for yet another hour and another week."

One day I had the opportunity to turn our attention to this shift in her attitude toward me. I said that I wondered if the change might somehow be connected to feelings and fantasies provoked in her by what she seemed to see in my face when I came to the door. She replied with despair, "It could be, but I don't know how. After all, *you always look the same.*"

Carla then went on—as if changing the subject—to tell me that she had been happy that she had managed to arrive in plenty of time to get to the restroom before her session. However when she found that "it was all locked up," she was left feeling as if she might burst open. Then, by way of denying the urgency of her need and the significance of her disappointment, she added resolutely that it was *"really* OK."

At that moment, it seemed to me that the story of the locked restroom contained clues to the meaning of her radical transition from joy in the waiting room to disdain on the couch. I now considered that Carla had been filled to bursting with positive feelings about our connection, which she could barely hold inside when she arrived. However, she had soon been disappointed when she felt me to be emotionally shutting her out—just as she had felt shut out of the restroom—as she searched my face for signs of *my own joy* as evidence that I might have been open to the overflow of her excitement, that I might therefore be able to provide her with some relief from these as well as other (perhaps less positive) overwhelming feelings. Instead, she seemed to find me ". . . always . . . the same" or locked-up.

I told Carla that it seemed to me that she had been hoping that my face would reflect the enthusiasm with which she had come to see me that day—especially when she felt that it was not too late for her to get some relief—but that her hopes had somehow rapidly turned to disillusionment. She nodded in agreement, so I continued, telling her that I thought that she might be bringing to our attention a very little-she, unable to bear that feeling of disillusionment, a thin-skinned little one who had consequently resolved to toughen up for fear of bursting open.

Carla responded by saying quite poignantly that she had only hoped that I would be as happy to see her as she was to see me. I acknowledged her hope and added that she also seemed to need to feel that a flowing-over and joyous baby-she could be seen and held in my facial expression, so that she would not spill away and be lost again. I soon added that I thought that this need to be held together was so intense and urgent that—when it seemed to her that I *could not* reflect and reciprocate her joyous feeling for me—that she had transformed herself to match what must have felt to her to be a locked-up, leathery-tough, mommy-analyst. I felt that perhaps this transformation was intended to enable her to create a sense that she could catch and hold herself by bringing us closer together with no gap in between.

Carla wept softly and finally told me that, as I was speaking, she had flashed back upon the image of her mother's face looking just as it had when, as a very little girl, she would watch her with loving admiration as she sat before the mirror on her dressing table. After a long pause she then told me—for the first time—that when her mother was a child she had been disfigured in a terrible automobile accident and, as a result, her face had always looked strange, disgusted, and remote, with a leathery skin full of scar tissue resulting in a frozen, unchanging expression of disdain. Carla then tearfully expressed the painful realization that she could never tell if her mother really loved her.

It seemed to me that—in some dimension—the baby-Carla may never have felt lovable or held lovingly, safely, and responsively in her mother's gaze, as Mother's unalterable expression might have hindered her ability to reflect her daughter's joyous states of ecstasy, admiration, and love for her. Unfortunately for Carla, the ecstasy of one-ness with the mother (Tustin 1981/1992) may well have been left uncontained, rebounding off the expressionless surface of her mother's face, an ecstasy apparently unreflected in the mother's experience of herself.

I could also imagine that Carla's mother—depressed, abandoned, and betrayed, with little in the way of self-esteem and self-love to reflect back to her daughter—may have failed to confirm the little girl's *experience of her mother's inner goodness*. Thus, Carla's appreciation of her own inner goodness and beauty—lacking resonance with a sense of a good inner object—may have dissipated and faded away over time.

Carla's perception that I "always look[ed] the same" seemed to evoke these very early painful feelings of being unlovable in the transference. At the same time, I became the receptacle for that maternal object with the frozen, disfigured face that manifested itself in the countertransference as extreme self-consciousness and obsessive doubts about my makeup being lopsided or missing and indeed may well have affected my facial expression, contributing to a vicious cycle. As our understanding of Carla's experience deepened over time, the way in which we saw each other and ourselves shifted, she felt better about herself and our connection, and we could begin to touch upon some of the omnipotent phantasies that contributed to the untoward sense of guilt and shame against which she so mightily defended herself.

Fuller (1980) reminds us that the negative of the *aesthetic* is the *anesthetic*, and he suggests that aesthetic emotion is connected to primal experiences of the self submerged in its environment, with the subsequent gradual differentiation of the self out from it. I believe that a premature or abrupt loss of that early fleeting experience of at-one-ment with the beauty of the world often leads to states of anesthesia where little can get in or out. The most extreme consequences of such disruptions might be seen in cases of infantile autism, as described by Tustin (1981), where the natural processes of projective and introjective identification are massively truncated. Indeed it seemed that, at best, all that my patient Carla could gain for herself, in adhesive identification (Bick 1968, 1986, Meltzer 1975, Meltzer, et al., 1975; Mitrani, 1994a, 1994b, 1995, Tustin, 1981/1992, 1986, 1990) with her mother, was a tough, leathery protection against that penetrating disillusionment that threatened to puncture and deflate her own beautiful baby-buoyancy.

Reverence and Awe versus Idealization

In a paper read at a joint scientific meeting of the Southern California Psychoanalytic Society in 1967, Bion (1992) describes an encounter with one patient who came to him after a previous analysis from which he had benefited but with which he was nonetheless dissatisfied. At first Bion expected to find greed at the bottom of this patient's distress, but it soon became clear to him that there was something else going on.

Bion described his patient's outpourings, which were so fragmented "that they would have required an omniscient analyst to sort out and make sense of" (p. 289). Bion's interpretations were either labeled "brilliant" or they were met with extreme disappointment and hostility to the point of depression. He finally concluded that:

> There is a great difference between idealization of a parent because the child is in despair, and idealization because the child is in search of an outlet for feelings of reverence and awe. In the latter instance the problem centers on frustration and the inability to tolerate frustration of a fundamental part of a particular patient's make-up. This is likely to happen if the patient is capable of love and admiration to an outstanding degree; in the former instance the patient may have no particular capacity for affection but a great greed to be its recipient. The answer to the question—which is it?—will not be found in any textbook but only in the process of psychoanalysis itself. [p. 292]

In his customary style, Bion avoids saturating his concepts, leaving them somewhat ambiguous, and thus allowing us the freedom to use our own capacity for "imaginative conjecture" to fill in the blanks, so to speak. I will yield to the temptation to do so with the understanding that the reader may draw his or her own conclusions, which may very well differ from my own.

I think Bion seems to be saying that, in this instance, *he had met with a patient for whom Klein's theory of envy did not apply.* Indeed he seems to be making it clear that he did not see his patient's disappointment and hostility as constituting an attack on the good breast or the analyst's good interpretations. Neither did he seem to see the patient's fragmented presentation as the result of an envious attack on thinking or on the links that might have rendered his communications meaningful and relevant (Bion 1959).

Instead, Bion appears to conclude that his patient was attempting to have an experience of an object who might be able to understand and transform the inchoate experiences of the as-yet-unintegrated-baby-he and was therefore seeking the realization of his preconception of an object who can contain these experiences as well as his innate capacity for love, reverence, and awe.

The containing capacity—initially found and felt to be located in this type of *external* object—when introjected leads to the development of an *internal* object capable of sustaining and bearing feelings of ecstasy and love: an object that might form the basis of the patient's own self-esteem. This aim certainly calls for an analyst who truly thinks well enough of himself and his own goodness that he is not dependent upon the goodness and cooperativeness of the patient in order to continue to function analytically.

Discussion with Frances Tustin

During one of my final conversations with Frances Tustin (1994), with whom I enjoyed a close personal and professional relationship, we had the opportunity to discuss this distinction which Bion makes between the manic defense of idealization and the healthy striving to be in contact with an object deserving of reverence and awe. Prior to this time, Tustin had never read—nor had she even been aware of the existence of—this paper of Bion's, which I chanced to bring to her attention in the following way.

When we were together in England, just one month before her death, I knew that Frances had little time to live and I wanted to express to her—in most explicit terms—how much her work had affected me. I wished to do this partly out of my own need to show my gratitude toward her this one last time. However I also felt the need to reassure her, since she seemed to be plagued by a fear that she had not contributed enough, that what she had contributed would soon be lost or forgotten, or that it would have no effect on anyone after her death.

When I told Frances how profoundly she had helped and inspired me in my thinking and practice, she demurred, as if she felt I was in danger of idealizing her. She said that I gave her "much too much credit for [my] good work and hard-won success," and she heaped upon me many other compliments that, although sincere, left me feeling somewhat rejected. Suddenly I felt a headache coming on and my good spirits faded. When Frances noticed my mood had changed she asked what the trouble was. I was quite candid with her about what I had felt and about what had followed, and I said that I hoped she would be more mindful of the way she handled people's gratitude for and admiration of her.

After recounting my experience and those of the patients discussed in this paper, we talked over how she herself had stressed the idea that the "ecstasy of at-one-ment" (Tustin 1981/1992) could only be borne if it were adequately contained by the mother herself (p. 224–226). In the most primitive states of mind, "beauty is associated with moments of bodily completeness in which there is an experience of ecstatic fusion with the earth-mother" (Tustin

1981/1992). If left uncontained, such ecstasy might be experienced as a dangerous overflow of bodily excitement equated with "a devastating sense of two-ness" (p. 106), too much to be borne in mind, perhaps disintegrating into a painful if not unbearable somatic agony. When the beautiful experience of at-one-ment is unable to be kept in mind, not only does it leak out and dissolve into its antithesis—the ugly tantrum of two-ness—but the baby is now doomed to an eternal despairing search for that "ever-present auto-sensual bit" needed to "flesh out" its experience of being.

Frances considered this for a long moment, after which we went on to talk for hours about the relationship of the experience of "ecstasy" to that of the beautiful mothers refered to both by Meltzer (1988) and by Winnicott (1945), as well as about Bion's ideas about reverence and awe. We both knew that I was having difficulty facing the loss of her friendship and support, and that I was chafing at the prospect of her death. However, in that moment it seemed to both of us that even more salient was my need to secure—in our last contact—her aid in containing all of my love and gratitude for her.

Some Conclusions

In part, as a result of that last conversation with Tustin, I have arrived at the conclusion that *the resolution of what Meltzer called the aesthetic conflict might be predicated, at least in part, upon the capacity of the mother to contain the baby's reverence and awe of her,* along with her capacity for tolerating his hatred, envy, and terror of loss. This may prove clinically crucial when we consider the process of internalization or introjection by the patient—of the analyst and his/her functioning—which is essential to insure a successful treatment.

It might be said that the apprehension of beauty (Meltzer 1988) is linked to the existence—at the core of the inner sphere of the personality—of a container, not just for our painful experiences, but for those joyful ones as well; a containing object with the capacity to endure not just our feelings of hatred toward the object (and therefore toward the self), but one that is enduring of and resonating with those loving feelings felt toward the perceived external object, one in which the capacity for realistic self-love and esteem are rooted. As Kahlil Gibran wisely wrote in *The Prophet*:

> And a poet said, Speak to us of Beauty.
> And he answered:
> Where shall you seek beauty, and how

shall you find her unless she herself be your
way and your guide?
And how shall you speak of her except
she be the weaver of your speech?
(1923/1976, p. 74)

It must not escape our awareness that our capacity to love—and therefore
to forgive ourselves—depends largely upon the way in which our loving
feelings have been accepted and validated by an other. It seems—when all is
said and done—that we are limited, in part, in our capacity for self-esteem by
the limitations of our parents' capacity (and later our analyst's) to contain and
therefore confirm our feelings of reverence and awe. I believe that herein lie
several technical implications of enormous import.

For example, we must consider that if we interpret the patient's genuine
reverence and awe of us (when we are felt as truly "good objects") as a defensive idealization (as if we were instead being experienced as bad objects)—
perhaps out of some rigidly inappropriate adherence to our theories—we will
fail in our function as a container for experiences of true goodness, and
consequently this essential internal function will fail to develop in the patient.
Instead, the "'Super' ego" (Bion 1962, p. 97)[1] will be augmented and its
devastating effects will intensify where forgiveness and the striving for life
might otherwise healthfully prevail. Additionally, the development of an
enduring faith in the existence of goodness and beauty, with increasing hope
for their apprehension, will be stultified.

When hopefulness perishes, nagging doubts about the goodness of the
object—and therefore about the worthiness of the self—perpetuate in spite

---

1. Bion coined the term "Super" ego to denote an internal organization lacking
any of the usual characteristics of the superego we commonly understand in psycho-
analysis. This "Super" ego is "an envious assertion of moral superiority without any
morals . . . the resultant of the envious stripping or denudation of all good and is
itself destined to continue the process of stripping . . ." (Bion 1962, p. 97) concomitant with what Bion calls the "minus K" (or "-K") condition associated with negative
narcissism. He describes this condition as follows: "In -K the breast is felt to remove
the good or valuable element in the fear of dying and force the worthless residue back
into the infant. The infant who started with a fear of dying ends up by containing a
nameless dread. . . . The seriousness [of this situation] is best conveyed by saying
that the will to live, that is necessary before there can be a fear of dying, is a part of the
goodness that the envious breast has removed" (p. 96).

of repeated proofs of such goodness and worthiness. Moreover, increased envy and defensive idealization will proliferate hyperbolically (Mitrani 1993). As analysts, we must be aware of our strengths and limitations and need be willing to consider, to accurately evaluate, and to acknowledge to ourselves the impact of the messages we send to the baby-in-the-analysand from the "castle of our inner world" if we are to provide an emotional experience for the patient that serves to mend old wounds and facilitate new growth.

References

Bick, E. (1968). The experience of the skin in each object relations. *International Journal of Psycho-Analysis*, 49:484–486.
———— (1986). Further considerations on the function of the skin in early object relations. *British Journal of Psychotherapy*. 2(4):292–301.
Bion, W.R. (1959). Attacks on linking. *International Journal of Psycho-Analysis* 40:308–315.
———— (1962). *Learning From Experience*. London: Heinemann. (London: Karnac Maresfield Reprints 1984).
———— (1976/1987). On a quotation from Freud. In *Clinical Seminars and Four Papers*, ed. F. Bion. Abingdon: Fleetwood Press.
———— (1977). *Two Papers: The Grid and Caesura*. Rio de Janeiro: Imago.
———— (1979). *The Dawn of Oblivion*. Perthshire, Scotland: Clunie Press.
———— (1992). *Cogitations*. London: Karnac Books.
Fairbairn, W.D. (1952). *Psychoanalytic Studies of the Personality*. London: Tavistock.
Freud, S. (1926). Inhibitions, symptoms and anxieties. *Standard Edition* 20:77–175.
Fuller, P. (1980). *Art and Psychoanalysis*. London: Writers and Readers.
Gibran, K. (1976). *The Prophet*. New York: Alfred A. Knopf.
Hansen, Y. (1994). The importance of the birth experience in early integrations. Unpublished paper presented at the conference on The Detection and Understanding of Primitive Mental States for the Psychoanalytic Center of California, Santa Monica, CA, June.
Klein, M. (1975). *Envy and Gratitude and Other Works*. New York: Dell Publishing.
Maiello, S. (1995). The sound object. *Journal of Child Psychotherapy* 21(1):23–42.

Mancia, M. (1981). On the beginning of mental life in the fetus. *International Journal of Psycho-Analysis* 62:351–357.

⤳ Meltzer, D., and Williams, M.H. (1988). The aesthetic conflict: its place in the developmental process. In *The Apprehension of Beauty: The Role of Aesthetic Conflict in Development, Art and Violence.* Perthshire, Scotland: Clunie Press.

——— (1975). Adhesive identification. *Contemporary Psycho-Analysis,* 11(3):289–310.

Meltzer, D., Bremmer, J., Hoxters, S., et al. (1975). *Explorations in Autism.* Perthshire, Scotland: Clunie.

Mitrani, J. L. (1993). Deficiency and envy: some factors impacting the analytic mind from listening to interpretation. *International Journal of Psycho-Analysis* 74(4):689–704.

——— (1994a). On adhesive-pseudo-object relations: part I- theory. *Contemporary Psychoanalysis* 30(2):348–366.

——— (1994b). Unintegration, adhesive identification, and the psychic skin: variations on some themes by Esther Bick. *Melanie Klein and Object Relations* 11(2):65–88.

——— (1995). On adhesive-pseudo-object relation: part II- illustration. *Contemporary Psychoanalysis* 31(1):140–165.

> ——— (1996). Notes on an embryonic state of mind. In *A Framework for the Imaginary: Clinical Explorations in Primitive States of Being.* New Jersey: Jason Aronson.

O'Shaughnessy, E. (1964). The absent object. *Journal of Child Psychotherapy* 1:134–143.

Osterweil, E. (1990). *A Psychoanalytic Exploration of Fetal Mental Development and Its Role in the Origin of Object Relations.* Unpublished doctoral dissertation.

Paul, M.I. (1981). A mental atlas of the process of psychological birth. In *Do I Dare Disturb the Universe,* ed. J. Grotstein, pp. 551–70. London: Karnac.

——— (1989). Notes on the primordial development of a penitential transference. *Melanie Klein and Object Relations* 5(2):43–69.

——— (1990). Studies on the phenomenology of mental pressure. *Melanie Klein and Object Relations* 8(2):7–29.

Piontelli, A. (1985). *Backwards In Time.* Perthshire: Clunie Press.

——— (1987). Infant observation from before birth. *International Journal of Psycho-Analysis* 68:453–463.

——— (1988). Pre-natal life and birth as reflected in the analysis of a two-year-old psychotic girl. *International Review of Psycho-Analysis* 15:73–81.

———— (1992a). On the continuity between pre-natal and post-natal life: a case illustration. Paper presented to the Psychoanalytic Center of California, Los Angeles, CA, April.

———— (1992b). *From Fetus to Child: an Observational and Psychoanalytic Study*. London: Routledge.

Reid, S. (1990). The importance of beauty in the psychoanalytic experience. *Journal of Child Psychotherapy* 16:29–52.

Share, L. (1994). *When I Hear a Voice it Gets Lighter* N.Y.: Analytic Press.

Tustin, F. (1981). *Autistic States in Children*. London/Boston: Routledge and Kegan Paul (Revised edition, published 1992.)

———— (1986). *Autistic Barriers in Neurotic Patients*. London: Karnac Books.

———— (1990). *The Protective Shell in Children and Adults*. London: Karnac Books.

———— (1994). Personal communication. Hyde Heath, England.

Winnicott, D.W. (1945). Primitive emotional development. In *Collected Papers: Through Pediatrics to Psycho-analysis*, pp. 145–156. New York: Basic Books, 1958.

———— (1956). Primary maternal preoccupation. In *Collected Papers: Through Pediatrics to Psycho-analysis*, pp. 300–305. New York: Basic Books, 1958.

3

The Voice as Autistic Object

Maria Rhode

*The need for a containing object would seem, in the infantile uninte-
grated state, to produce a frantic search for an object—a light, a voice, a
smell, or other sensual object—which can hold the attention and thereby be
experienced, momentarily at least, as holding the parts of the personality
together.*

Esther Bick

In her paper on "Autistic Objects" (Tustin 1980), Frances Tustin described
how autistic children use the sensory qualities of hard objects to provide them
with a delusional experience of strength, and in this way to block out the
experience of the black hole and the terror of annihilation. She showed how
autistic children can learn to read and write, which may mislead observers
into believing that they are witnessing evidence of symbolic capacity, where in
fact words may be recognized—and erroneously linked—in a mechanical
way, based on the shape that is felt to "touch" the child's eye.

In her earlier treatment of the subject, Tustin (1972/1995) gave observational examples of children who used autistic objects felt to be part of their
own body, *me*. One of these children was Baby Susan, whose development
was followed weekly as part of an infant observation. Her mother always kept
her on her lap to bathe her, and Susan, who was contented lying on her
tummy, regularly became very agitated lying on her back. At the age of 2
weeks,

41

When she is again put on her back so that her front can be powdered she starts to cry but stops as she mouths to the breast. When she doesn't get the breast, she starts to cry again. Finally, she stops as her fingers and the string of her bib accidentally get into her mouth during the threshing around she does whilst crying. [p. 60]

At 8 weeks, the observer noticed Susan making an "m-m-m" sound while sucking at the breast. She continued making this sound at the bottle or when sucking her fist. When she was 3 months old, she started crying while on her back on her mother's lap, but managed by putting her fist in her mouth, which she accompanied by a quiet "m-m-m." When her fist was dislodged by a sneeze, she began to cry again.

Then, at 1 year old,

> Susan . . . is tottering around the room on unsteady plump legs. Her mother goes into the kitchen to make tea. Susan's eyes follow her mother to the door and she sits down with a bump. She looks at the door through which her mother has disappeared. However, she soon gets up again and turning her back on the door, picks up a large rubber ball. She cradles this in her arms and hugs it to her chest. She then puts her lips to the ball and totters round the room making m-m-m sounds. When her mother returns Susan takes the ball away from her mouth. [p. 62]

Tustin made the point that Susan was using the ball as though it were part of her body, in the service of "the illusion of having an ever-ready completion to her mouth." This nonautistic little girl was employing an autistic means of coping in the service of development, of being able to wait for her mother: She took the ball away from her mouth as soon as her mother came back, and indeed Tustin commented that in the observations at three months and one year, "we have reached the point where the autistic object merges into becoming the *transitional object*" (p. 62).

I have reproduced this sequence of observations in detail because it beautifully illustrates the use of vocalization as an autistic object, one trembling on the edge between sensation and meaning. Susan's "m-m-m" sounds contain a reference to an absent object (her mother) in whose presence she used to make them, as well as being a self-generated sensation in her mouth that could be used to wipe out the importance of the object. It is this interface between sensation and symbol that I shall attempt to explore in this chapter with regard to the use of the voice, an interface corresponding to the one between symbolic meaning and the autistic recognition of shapes that Tustin delineated about the capacity to read.

Thomas

Thomas B was brought for a consultation at the age of 3 years and 10 months. He was his parents' only child; his mother had a teenage daughter by her first marriage. Both parents had grown up abroad, and Mrs. B still felt exiled in England.

Although Thomas was a much-wanted child, the pregnancy and delivery were sufficiently difficult to make his parents decide not to have any more children. He was born with a harelip, which was surgically corrected when he was 3 months old. Mrs. B's father, to whom she was devoted, died suddenly at this time, and she felt emotionally isolated as her husband's work took him away for long periods of time.

Mrs. B's job was important to her, and she soon went back to work. Thomas's first *au pair*, who came from his mother's native country, stayed until he was 1 year old. He was very fond of her, as he was of her successor, who left when he was just under 2 and a half. His parents said that he managed the necessary adjustments without obvious difficulty, but the arrival of the third nanny coincided with a visit from his maternal grandmother, who was very critical of her.

Mrs. B felt extremely undermined. Thomas had babbled richly, and clearly understood the meaning of many words. However, by the age of 2 he had not developed speech, and his parents began to be concerned. By the age of 2 and a half, he was patently disturbed, turning his back on people and avoiding eye contact and cuddles. He was diagnosed as autistic at a London teaching hospital and this diagnosis was confirmed by neuropsychologists at a psychoanalytic center. No organic damage could be detected. His mother gave up work to look after him full time, which she was determined and eager to do, but which increased her sense of isolation.

Video of Thomas's Early Development

Mr. and Mrs. B had made a video of their child, spanning the whole of his life from the time he was 3 weeks old, which they allowed me to see when he had been in treatment for some 18 months. This presented me with a dilemma. I was aware that my experience of the transference might be influenced by this information. On the other hand, the video provided invaluable evidence on questions about which the parents had not felt able to trust their memory. They found it helpful to discuss it as part of making sense of the past; it also helped me to deal with difficult feelings which Thomas aroused in me during treatment.

The video showed clearly that Thomas was not one of those children, later diagnosed autistic, who have difficulties in relating from the moment of birth. The first sequences showed him completely absorbed in intense eye-contact with his father at the age of 3 weeks. His parents were obviously ecstatic, and a very moving atmosphere was conveyed of the baby bathed in their loving voices. At 3 months, after his operation and his grandfather's death, he appeared less focused than before, with a greater tendency to tremble and shake, particularly when there was a loud noise in the background. He soon recovered, but the tendency to startle at loud noises persisted for years.

Many sequences showed him upset after a plane flew over the house, with Mother explaining to him, "That was a plane." She was clearly sensitive to his feelings when something distressed him, like the sound of airplanes or the overly boisterous games in which his sister fell down with him onto a bed. Mother always intervened to put a stop to incidents of this kind, but she was at times unable to respond when he looked sad.

Much of her interaction with Thomas, as shown on the video, consisted of getting him to smile for the camera, and later on to point to different parts of his face and body when she named them. He did this very obligingly, and at first with pleasure, although a mechanical quality crept in with increasing repetition, and his smile, which had been spontaneous at first, increasingly took on a calculating, smirklike tinge.

The video included scenes of Thomas with his first *au pair*, who left just after his first birthday. They were clearly very attached to each other, and played peekaboo games with great shared enjoyment, and with none of the manic quality with which he often performed for the camera. She used to play with his lower lip when he was vocalizing so that he produced a "b-b-b" sound, and after she left, he could be seen doing this himself, with an inward-looking expression in his eyes, as though he were remembering her. However, in another sequence just after she left, he threw toys downstairs, panicked, and thrust his fingers into his mouth. His attempt to work through his feelings about her disappearance was unsuccessful and, in order to manage his distress, he turned to sensations in his mouth that he could provide for himself.

He appeared to make a reasonable attachment to his second *au pair*, and his babbling and capacity for interest in toys seemed normal, as were his motor milestones. His verbal comprehension during his second year appeared normal too, although the calculating quality in his expression increased in those episodes in which he obliged his mother by pointing to the parts of his body that she named.

When Thomas was 2 years and 4 months old, the situation seemed to alter dramatically. He looked as though a terrible traumatic event had taken place, although the parents could not think what it might have been, other than the departure of the second *au pair* and the difficult three months with the new nanny and the maternal grandmother. His eyes looked haunted and terrified, his expression was mostly withdrawn, and a new tinge of cruelty could be seen in his smile. This cruelty was particularly in evidence in a sequence in which he impaled a ladybug on the point of his finger.

His vocalization patterns changed as well at this point. Previously, he had produced a rich variety of babbling sounds, and had squealed "ee-ee-ee" to accompany his own movements when he ran around. Now, instead, "ee-ee-ee" became associated with the movements of a toy train, which he drove very close past his face. For long stretches of time he ran up and down emitting a highly resonant, vibrating "deeee" noise, and maintaining a state in which he was completely cut off from everyone. His parents found this extremely distressing, and this went on until he had been in therapy for some months. When he was in this state, as his father said, "We can't get through to him at all."

First Sessions

By the time I first saw him, when he was two months short of his fourth birthday, Thomas was emerging slightly from the worst of his withdrawal. He was a well-built, sturdy little boy whose eyes no longer had the vacant look typical of autism, though he still avoided eye contact.

When I saw him, together with his mother, he ran all over the room looking for things to open and places to get into. Although his mother said that he was fascinated by toy trains, the only toy that held his interest was a plastic teapot with a detachable lid. He was holding the knob of the lid in his right hand, with his left thumb in his mouth, when his mother began to cry while telling me of her father's death when Thomas was 3 months old. He shrieked, dropped the lid, and his thumb shot out of his mouth as though someone had torn it away. He shook as though he were falling apart. It was a dramatic enactment of how he experienced his mother's grief: as the traumatic tearing away of a sense of completeness in his mouth, just as Tustin has described. He was quite inaccessible to any words of comfort and, although he calmed down gradually when his mother took him on her lap, he still looked lost and distraught.

When I saw him on his own, he avoided the teapot but went around the room again like a whirlwind in search of things to open or places to occupy. I had very little sense of emotional contact. He climbed onto the windowsill with no regard for the danger. However, he did seem to be listening when I stopped him and spoke about his need to behave as though nothing could hurt him. He was interested in the join where a label was sewn onto the bedspread, and he tugged at the label as though trying to make sure that it would not come off. At the end of the session, he lifted up his T-shirt and felt his tummy button, as though reassuring himself that it was in place; then he carefully touched each of his nipples.

Geneviève Haag (1985) has written about autistic children who experience separateness from their object as the loss of one half of their body. She has suggested that this may be expressed in a preoccupation with joins such as hinges or skirting-boards. In Thomas's case, this preoccupation was with the join between label and bedspread. Unlike Tustin's "Peter" (Tustin 1981), who derived from his tummy button the safe feeling of being "all buttoned up," I think that Thomas was experiencing his tummy button as the place from which something had been lost, leaving him with the need to hold together the two sides of his body (the nipples).

In the course of therapy, he habitually clenched his teeth and fists and stiffened his arms or bent his body over rigidly, after moving a heavy wooden shutter towards himself so that it seemed to be cutting him in half down the midline. His anxiety about the join between label and bedspread may well have expressed the conflation of his worries about his bodily integrity with those about Mother's vulnerability. She confirmed that at home he was meticulously careful never to break anything. Over the summer following this first contact, Thomas became clean and dry, as well as being slightly less cut off, and his parents decided to bring him to therapy.

Early Themes in Therapy: Bodily Disintegration and the Battle for the "Hard Extra Bit"

From the first, Thomas was very much involved in the therapy. He was eager to come and reacted to holidays instead of ignoring them. At first he reacted by becoming ill. Later he showed his mother that he did not wish to come back. After a year, he cried broken-heartedly during the approach to Christmas. He soon established a ritual sequence during the sessions. He would gaze after his mother when she left, as if holding onto her with his eyes. Then he would march into the room stamping, as if asserting his right to be there. He attempted to take possession of the room, shaking off my hand and behaving as though I did not exist.

In the early months, he regularly slammed his box shut and pushed it out of the way on the table to make room for his head; he would then make the box come towards him and push his head off the table. This was varied by his lying on the table and letting his head or one leg fall over the edge, and then repeating this over and over again. Sometimes, he would try to rest his foot against the table leg, but it always slid off onto the floor.

I understood this as meaning that he felt displaced by a hard, dangerous rival object (the box with its hasp, which he repeatedly fingered). The hard table leg was experienced as something slippery that he could not get a grip on rather than as something strong that could support him. Thomas needed to maintain constant contact with the table so that all of his body could feel "there" by virtue of the sensations engendered by such contact. These prevented experiences of fragmentation like the baby Susan's, or those described by Cornwell (1983) in an infant observation where the young baby reacted with terror to losing the contact between tummy and mattress. Similarly, Winnicott (1988) reported that an adult psychotic patient felt her head was coming off her shoulders when he moved his hand away from under it, and he linked this with the Moro reflex.

For Thomas, feeling displaced meant losing his head or his leg. He practiced arching his head and shoulders upwards away from the floor when his head was hanging over the edge of the table, as though to prove that he could retain control of them. With his head over the edge, he would produce hollow-sounding "eeee" noises in the direction of the floor, as though measuring the distance by echography. The atmosphere he conjured up was desolate: It sounded as though he were plumbing an abyss, rather than a distance of some two feet, in a world with no answering human voices in it.

On the other hand, at this stage he did not welcome any approach from me. When I spoke about his terror of falling and then held my hand under him, he pushed it aside forcefully. At the time this felt hurtful; with hindsight, I think that he was afraid of being engulfed. It became clear that he and I were engaged in a battle for the thing that Tustin (1972) called "the strong extra bit," and that the alternative to possessing this "extra bit" was falling into the abyss and bodily disintegration.

When Thomas felt blocked or displaced by a hard object—a locked cupboard door, its protruding doorknob, the slippery table leg—he typically reacted with a manic annexation of the hard object's qualities. While I was clearing up at the end of a session, he would bang against a locked cupboard door then arrange his bottom over the knob and shoot off galloping across the room, shouting "deeee" with a triumphant smirk on his face. I thought that he felt excluded and pushed over the edge by a hard, protruding Daddy-nipple that caused my mind to be shut to him. He dealt with this by anally incorporating the Daddy-bit, which imparted to him the power to run across the room instead of falling down. This power seemed to be concretely embodied in the "deeee" sound: the strong Daddy-sensations were present in his mouth— as self-generated sound vibrations—and simultaneously in his anus. By filling up my room with sound, just as he filled up his mouth, he could equate room and mouth with each other and could circumvent the problem of the locked door and the knob.

The lost, unanswered "eeee," with which he had plumbed the depths of the abyss, had been transformed into a strong, hard, nipple-sound in his mouth by the addition of the initial "d." This consonant—besides belonging to the word "Daddy"—requires the tongue to touch the roof of the mouth and then to move away from it. In this way the integrity of the mouth is verified. This integrity must be taken for granted if the sounding of the letter is to be completed in a natural way, with a normally pitched voice. Thomas, who could not take the integrity of his mouth for granted, reassured himself of it by means of the sensations generated by the abnormally resonant pitch of his "deeee" noise.

Sometimes Thomas demonstrated even more clearly the transference implications of sounds. Instead of anally incorporating the knob on the cupboard, he would touch his lips to my leg with a seductive expression and then look up at me triumphantly before galloping off saying "deeee." He behaved towards my leg—a protruding part of my body—as though it were a masculine part-object that he seduced away from me and for which his mouth and I were in competition.

The Countertransference
and Identification with the Aggressor

For many months, the aspect of Thomas's character that was most in evidence was embodied in his triumphant narcissistic smirk. He swaggered into the room, rearranged its contents with a lordly and contemptuous air, and very effectively made the point that he was the boss, acting according to a plan of his own in which I was irrelevant. He took this to delusional lengths, "pouring" out of an empty jug when I temporarily restricted his supply of water, with which he had deliberately drenched the furniture. I felt impotent and full of hatred much of the time.

Meanwhile, Thomas's material was in stark contrast to his manner. Besides enacting the terror of falling off the table, he spent much of the session manipulating the Victorian wooden shutters, which consisted of two panels of wood joined by a hinge. He bent the hinge so the shutter formed a triangle, the apex of which he brought up to his mouth and nose as though it were about to cut his face in half; he would then verify that he still had both sides of his face by pressing each cheek in turn against the flat surface of the shutter.

Sometimes Thomas varied this sequence by moving the edge of the shutter quickly towards his head as though to cut it off. There was a metal crossbar hanging down from the shutter. This made a loud clanging sound such that the threats to his head and face were accompanied by deafening noise. He clearly equated this noise with a strong voice. On one occasion, when he was hitting himself very hard on the head with his hand and I intervened with a firm voice to stop him, he flung the shutter against the window so that the metal bar made a thundering noise, and he faced me defiantly as though insisting that he was the one with the louder voice.

I believe that Thomas was communicating to me the despair and hatred that he might have felt when, as a baby and toddler, he suffered repeated experiences of pain and loss that could not be sufficiently understood. On the basis of the above-mentioned material, I believe he experienced the hard Daddy-bit both as something that blocked his way into his mother's mind and also as the sharp, terrifyingly loud executive agent of the threat to his mouth and to the rest of his body. This would seem to link up with the lasting fear of airplane noises, revealed in the video. His means of coping then was to claim this terrifying object as part of his own mouth—to equate himself with the aggressive nipple. Later in treatment, this extended to the way he flaunted his pointing fingers: He gestured with them in a way that made them look like magic wands with which he was arranging the room and indeed the whole of reality.

The vulnerability behind this could be seen in the way in which he sometimes brought his fingers close up to his face, as though constructing a protective filter between his eyes and space. There seemed to be no middle ground between a contemptuous omnipotence and total vulnerability and terror. Indeed, when he brought threatening hard objects close up to his mouth, pulling it into a wounded grimace, this grimace would shade imperceptibly into his narcissistic smirk.

During the time that I was experiencing impotence and hatred in the sessions, I heard from his parents that Thomas's impervious galloping had markedly decreased at home and he was cooperating much better at school. Gradually, the smirking diminished during sessions, mostly confined to beginnings and endings, except around holiday times. Genuine emotional contact became possible, particularly when I spoke about how sad he often felt. Instead of galloping, he would sit across the room from me, gazing intently into my eyes. In Geneviève Haag's terms, he was at these moments able to use eye contact and emotional communication to free himself from the need for the adhesive sticking, which otherwise served to avert the fear of falling through space (Haag 1991).

He also began to show evidence of introjection. I sometimes said "mm-hmm," and he reproduced this in an ordinary 4-year-old's voice. It was during one of these times, after some fifteen months of treatment, that he shaped his mouth into a circle and vocalized "O" while looking at my mouth. I believe that the emotional contact, and the visual evidence that I had a mouth like his, allowed him to voice an "o" instead of experiencing the shape of his mouth as a hole. Reid (1990) has described a similar coming together of eye contact and vocalization in a recovering autistic boy.

Voice, Umbilical Cord, and Autistic Object

From the beginning of his therapy, it was clear that Thomas used the sensation generated in his mouth by his "deeee" noise to reassure him that the nipple was a part of his mouth—this in order to circumvent the terrifying experience that a separate nipple would inflict upon him. He would "deeee" when the shutter threatened his face; when he needed to gallop across the room in order not to fall down; when he examined the spout on the teapot, which was clearly not part of his mouth; when he used his "magic" fingers to suck water, instead of sucking from the hard, unreceptive base of the jug.

At the end of his first year in therapy, Thomas focused increasingly on drawstring cords that were part of his clothing: the cords that fastened the waist and hood of his anorak, and the ties of his shorts or track-suit bottoms. Shortly before the first summer holiday, he came into the room, stamping and making his "deeee" noise, and I said to him how important it was to show me that he was going to be there, that he had the strong voice that made this possible. He responded by looking straight at me and clutching the drawstring cord on his shorts. This made me think that he was equating the possession of a strong voice with the retention of an umbilical cord as well as with the sensation of the nipple in his mouth. It reminded me of his attention to his tummy button during his assessment session.

Subsequently, he twice came to his session clutching a stick. He very purposefully touched the end of the stick to his tummy button. I said to him that holding the hard stick made him feel joined up to me by the tummy button, and this made him feel safe. He was then able to put aside this autistic object during the session, though he clutched it again when I warned him that it was nearly time to go.[1]

Umbilical Links to the Object

Thomas always ended his sessions lying face-to-face on a child-sized Teddy bear. I understood this as another means of protecting himself from experiences of fragmentation and spilling out at the end of the time. His exact vertical alignment with the bear seemed to be a development of the theme of his head and leg being pushed off the edge of the table. When I talked about his need to feel that all the parts of his body were there, he began to move off the bear; first at right angles with only his head remaining on it, eventually parallel and completely separate. Occasionally, he managed this separateness by maintaining eye contact with me, but mostly he coped by sucking his thumb while clutching his anorak cord with the fingers of the same hand and resting his other hand on the bear. This is of course the same linking configuration that was in play before he dropped the teapot lid in the assessment session.

When he lay on the bear, it provided him with a sense of bodily cohesion by serving as a sort of tactile mirror image. One way of managing without lying on it was to link up with it in such a fashion that it became, in Tustin's words, "an ever-ready completion of his mouth." Such sequences illustrate the umbilical cord qualities of this kind of thumb-sucking.[2]

---

1. Hughes (1996) has described a similar relationship to the tummy-button of a series of autistic objects used by her four-year-old patient.

2. Compare Winnicott (1960) on the use of string as a denial of separateness.

Sometimes, instead of sucking his thumb, Thomas would attempt to bridge the gap by reaching out towards the bear with the waist cord of his anorak. On one occasion, when the distance was too great for this, he instead grabbed at the bear's protruding ear and made his "deeee" noise. This was another instance of using his voice to claim the nipple/cord as part of his own body.

Tustin (1990) once speculated that those autistic children who were born with difficulties in relating might have had an abnormal relationship to the umbilical cord before birth. This speculation was later given credibility by the ultrasound studies of Piontelli (1992). Tustin did not explicitly develop this theme, but I assume that the abnormality she referred to would have consisted of treating the cord as though it were a part of the baby's body rather than a vital link to the mother. Thomas was not one of these children: The video sequences showed an excellent capacity for relating at the age of 3 weeks. However, he suffered repeated traumatic separations with little support in digesting them. He may well have experienced these as a catastrophic loss of the feelings and parts of himself that he had lodged in the lost person, and he coped with this loss by overemphasizing the sensual element of an emotional link. An instance of this would be the way he provided himself with the same sensations on his lips that his *au pair* had provided for him, after she had left and his attempt at a *fort-da* game went wrong. It is along these lines that I would understand his attempts to force me into a role similar to that of the bear: the role of a placental mirror image.

Maiello (1995) has proposed that the development of hearing in the fourth month of gestation permits the differentiation of the intra-uterine environment—in terms of ongoing or episodic sounds from the mother's different internal organs—as well as recognizable external voices that come and go. Thomas once inserted the end of his waist cord into his ears: He was claiming possession of the structure that mediated sounds and all that they implied. Thus, he would often establish eye contact while making his "deeee" noise and holding his hands over his ears. In this way he could try to engage with me as a separate person while safeguarding himself by simultaneously making his head resonate with his own sounds and keeping other frightening ones out.

The structure of his babbling reflected his relationship to the bear in that he produced di-syllables when lying on it and monosyllables while lying on the floor. Haag (1995) has suggested that the stage of children's babbling that is characterized by di-syllables indicates the sense of possessing both halves of the body, and I have given instances elsewhere of structural parallels between autistic children's idiosyncratic use of words and their object relations (Rhode 1995).

Towards a Separate Object: Depressive Anxieties

For several sessions after Thomas had brought the stick which he used as an autistic object and which was linked to the umbilical cord and to his "deeee" noise, he brought along instead a particular kind of drinking cup. This was a closed plastic cup with a lid attached by a hinge, which opened to permit the insertion, through a hole in the top of the cup, of a straw made of the same plastic. Occasionally, Thomas sucked the straw, but he was more concerned with biting the lid. He seemed to be testing out whether it was strong enough to survive.

This suggested to me that the need for a constant source of sensation in his mouth—for a nipple that he could use as an umbilical cord rather than as a truly separate object—derived from his fear that a separate object could not withstand his aggression. This would fit with the many early losses he suffered. The temporal coincidence of his mother's grief for her father with Thomas's operation for harelip would also have contributed to his experiencing vulnerability in his object as an attack on his mouth. This links with his dramatic reaction to his mother's tears in the first consultation. In contrast to this, when his mother could not comfort him—during his spells of heartbroken crying, leading up to his second Christmas holiday—and began to cry herself, he was able to distinguish between himself and her sufficiently so that instead of collapsing, he very movingly tried to comfort her. It should be emphasized that from the beginning of therapy, he was strikingly better in sessions to which he was brought by both parents.

The mouth sensations generated by the "deeee" noise could thus be thought of as a constantly available straw that Thomas could use as an umbilical link at moments when fears about the survival of the nipple as part of the breast threatened to overwhelm him.

The Hard "In-Between" Object

During the middle part of every session, Thomas lay on the floor close to me and experimented with different relationships to the plastic rubbish bin, which he manipulated in relation to his face. If he ever let go, he would look at it with a highly persecuted expression as though expecting it to attack him.

In the last session before the Christmas holiday of his second year, he poured water out of the jug then jiggled the bin on its side with quick, short movements while his thumb was in his mouth and his fingers gripped his anorak cord. I spoke about how important it was to feel he could make me come back. He responded with very good eye contact and tensed up his body, and I said that he made himself strong so that things did not spill out of him like the water and get lost while I was away. He then began to roll the bin towards me: When it left his hand, he pulled his mouth into a grimace and tensed up. I said he felt that part of his mouth was lost when he let go of the bin and of me, and he responded with a loud "deeee," as though to counteract this fear. The bin had become the embodiment of the "hard extra bit" that was essential to his bodily integrity, and for which we were still felt to be competing.

The "In-Between Thing" as a Link: Body Parts, Grasp, and Babbling

When we had worked over such themes, Thomas sometimes felt safe enough to sustain—for a few moments—a game in which we rolled the bin back and forth between us. The bin could then be a shared link instead of a vital bit that we competed for. On one such occasion, he accompanied the to-and-fro movement of the bin by babbling repeatedly, "A-g-a, a-g-a." The harmonious structure of subject-link-object allowed the emergence of harmonious, normal babbling with a parallel structure of vowel-consonant-vowel. At the same time, he was using the back-and-forth game with me to link up the two sides of his body. At first he used one hand to roll the bin to me and receive it back, then the other hand; finally he rolled the bin back and forth between his own two hands.

Haag (1991) has described the way in which the link between mother and baby, comprising "the dual interpenetration of eyes and nipple-in-mouth," is incarnated in the subjective experience of bodily linkages. Thomas's material illustrates this and shows the importance of this link for the development of undistorted babbling.

In another sequence in which he babbled while rolling the bin between us, he took the important step of gripping the edge of the bin between fingers and thumb, whereas previously he had manipulated it with flat fingers. This material shows how the ability to grasp, so often lost or impaired in autistic children (Alvarez 1992), is derived from experiencing the in-between-thing— the nipple—as a link, rather than as a threatening hard intrusion that might slice his face in half. When I once misjudged rolling the bin back and it returned a bit too fast for him, he was unable to continue with the game or with babbling. Instead he resumed his flat hold on the bin, clutching his anorak cord with his thumb in his mouth, and joined himself to the bin with a loud "deeee" from very close up.

Proto-words: Communication or Magic

Thomas sometimes produced word-like sounds. However these were used to establish a particular kind of object relationship by magical means, rather than for symbolic communication. For instance, at school he would join in on the last word of "Ready-steady-*go*" in such a way as to feel virtually "part of" the group. He sometimes said "da-dee," which could have evolved into 'daddy,' but which I think was a magical way of constituting himself as the complete primitive combined object.

On one occasion he said "da-da-dee" while pressing his cheek flat against the side of his box and holding the lid open at right angles. This vocalization might be seen as reflecting the structure cheek-box-lid. Similarly, he once took into his mouth the hard edge of a bowl into which he had poured water. I said that the hard safe thing that stopped things spilling out was supposed to be part of his mouth, and he responded, "Da-dee." ("Da" is said with a wide-open mouth, whereas saying "dee" replicates the position of teeth and lips grasping the edge of the bowl.) However, when I made the mistake of echoing "daddy" with evident pleasure, he reverted to his "deeee" noise.

An important part of mother-infant interaction, at the time that speech is beginning, consists of the mother's amplification of the child's proto-words. This amplification is based on the assumption that proto-words are intended as approximations to ordinary language. Normally, this process is mutually enjoyable and leads to the growth of verbal interchange (Papousek 1992). Thomas, however, experienced my amplification of his "da-dee" as a threat. He may have misunderstood my pleasure as robbing him of his achievement (Barrows 1996), like the video sequences in which he pointed to parts of his body to please his mother. This would have meant my laying claim to the hard edge of the bowl instead of his being allowed to retain it to complement his mouth, and may have forced him back onto the use of "deeee" as an autistic object.

The converse took place when he tore a thread out of his sleeve with his teeth: He held it taut and plucked it, listening to the sound and vocalizing "ee." I said that I was supposed to be his sleeve, part of his mouth: that he was holding on by biting and could not be sure that having the sound in his mouth need not mean biting it off me. This led to good eye contact, and he began to babble, saying "da-dee" and other proto-words.

The "Softening" of the Autistic Object

After a holiday, some eighteen months into therapy, I wished to replace the bin, as Thomas was visibly worried by some cracks in its base that he had not made. He often reassured himself by tapping against the sides as though testing their integrity, while doing the same for his mouth by producing a series of hard consonants, "t, k, t, k." I decided to overlap the old and new bins for a session so that the cracks should not appear to have vanished as if by magic. This had unforeseen consequences.

Thomas insisted that I should hold the new bin on my lap. He then launched into a to-and-fro game with the old bin, babbling as he did so, and without the lengthy preliminary work that was otherwise necessary before he could do this. In the next session, he brought along a soft toy instead of a hard object, placed the new bin on my lap, and held the soft toy against his cheek while sucking his thumb and touching the old bin. When I spoke about the holiday, and how difficult it was to believe that I would come back unless I were part of his mouth, he was able to let go of his toy, and he rolled the bin over to me.

The reassurance of there being a hard bin to complete each of us allowed him to let go of his, without fearing that I would snatch it from him, or that he would merge with me and lose his identity. (He first waved "good-bye" to me after a session in which I had acknowledged that he needed to feel strong and hard so as not to sink into me as he sank into the soft pillow.) Instead of insisting that the bin was an extension of his own anorak cord, he could loosen his hold on both the hard bin and the soft toy and begin to allow the integration of the hard and soft aspects of his object in the way that Tustin (1981) has described. This went together with a softening of his whole attitude.

Discussion

Thomas's history illustrates a constellation which Tustin thought typical of many autistic children. Innate predispositions in the child coincide with a temporary vulnerability in the mother, who needs the child as a source of reassurance and therefore has difficulty in seeing him as separate and helping him to digest his experience (Tustin 1981, 1994). I have already suggested how this may have interacted with other traumatic events—such as his operation and repeated losses—to cause him to confuse his own sadness with his mother's and to experience them as a catastrophe in his mouth.

Thomas's material illustrates the correspondence between the two tripartite structures of "baby-umbilical cord-placenta" (Paul 1981) and "mouth-nipple-breast." In each case, the hard autistic object is seen to correspond to a distortion of the middle element—a distortion of the link. Thomas turned to the autistic object to protect himself on the one hand from the terrors of being cut in half, of losing parts of his body, of falling and spilling out; and, on the other hand, from losing his identity through merging with a yielding maternal object.

Britton (1995) has written about similar anxieties in borderline adults who experience them as a consequence of the full emergence of the Oedipus complex—"the closure of the Oedipal triangle." He has suggested that the paternal element may be blamed for the mother's inability to receive emotional communications and has distinguished two different types of defense according to whether the patient fears the paternal element or idealizes and identifies with it. This is reminiscent of the way in which Thomas dealt with his fear of a hard, dangerous nipple by identification.

The triad of mouth-nipple-breast may be thought of as the Oedipal triad on the autistic level, on which two, soft, receptive organs (breast and mouth) are either linked by the hard nipple or compete for it. Examples of this are Thomas's annexation of the knob on the cupboard door and of my leg as well as the different kinds of play with the bin. A third possibility involves the narcissistic obliteration of the nipple—the element that defines difference—so that mouth and breast are felt to be stuck together like mirror images rather than linked. In *The Hands of the Living God,* Milner (1969) reproduces a drawing by her patient, which can be seen either as a face receiving the nipple of a breast into its mouth or as two faces kissing with mouths pressed together. This may be related to the way in which Thomas's painful grimace—when his mouth was threatened by a sharp object—often shaded into his narcissistic smirk.

Thomas used his voice as an autistic object—that is, for the generation of hard sensations that made him feel strong and safe rather than as a medium for symbolic communication. This use of his voice was linked both with his umbilical cord and with his thumb when it took over the functions of the nipple. Other vocalizations reproduced the structure of Thomas's relation to his objects. I view this in accordance with Meltzer's notion of a "theater of the mouth" as a site for the generation of meaning (Meltzer 1986). An example of this in Tustin's work is Peter's use of the word "boiler," which she interpreted as a "boy with an extra bit" (Tustin 1981).

As Boubli (1993) has pointed out, it will be difficult to use the mouth for the production of communicative vocalization if each associated sensation is "too massively present" in the mouth and too immediately associated with major anxieties. Indeed, Abraham (1916) described a 17-year-old who suffered from a crippling inhibition in speaking because his mouth was completely occupied with what would now be regarded as the autistic practices of sucking at his tongue, cheeks, and teeth.[3]

Meltzer (1974) suggested that, among the necessary conditions for developing speech, the child should have internal objects who communicate with each other. An autistic child may experience this with extreme concreteness as being intolerable. For instance, an autistic girl seen by Mrs. Christine Porter learned to write her name but remained mute: This seemed to be connected with her inability to tolerate her therapist's voice, which she repeatedly attempted to squeeze out of its voicebox. One possible reaction is to emphasize the sensory aspects of the voice.

Sidney Klein (1980) has described the extreme importance which adult patients with autistic traits attach to the qualities of the analyst's voice, as opposed to the meaning of his words. Rodrigué's (1955) 3-year-old patient's blissful hallucinations seemed to occur in response to the analyst's voice. This may be one element in the well-documented sensitivity to music shown by many autistic patients.[4] For instance, Barrows (1996) has suggested that her patient's highly musical voice served as a container for good aspects of the personality.

---

3. I am grateful to Daphne Briggs for drawing my attention to the paper by Abraham.

4. For a discussion of this, see Sobey (1996).

Haag (personal communication) has noted that autistic children who become interested in "Daddy-sounds" in the central heating pipes, rather than being persecuted by them usually begin to speak soon afterwards. This stands in contrast to Thomas's defiant claim to the loud "voice" of the metal bar in the shutters. Such ideas may be relevant to elective mutes, whose difficulties lie not in symbolic incapacity but in the impossibility of using their voice to communicate in certain situations.[5]

At the time of writing, the appearance of soft toys and Thomas's occasional ability to let go of the bin suggest the beginnings of the ability to tolerate separateness. This is essential if the voice is to be freed from serving as an autistic object, instead to become the medium for symbolic communication between separate people.

References

Abraham, K. (1916). The first pre-genital stage of the libido. In *Selected Papers on Psycho-Analysis*. London: Hogarth, 1927; Fourth Impression, 1949.

Alvarez, A. (1992). *Live Company*. London: Tavistock/Routledge.

Barrows, K. (1996). The rabbit in the brown paper bag: the starvation of the self. Unpublished paper.

Boubli, M. (1993). Les mots dans la bouche. Des objets au premier langage parlé. In *Les Contenants de Pensée*, ed. Kaës, R. and Anzieu, D. Paris: Dunod.

Britton, R. (1995). Second thoughts on the third position. Paper read at a Clinic Scientific Meeting, Tavistock Clinic, London, England, Oct.

Cornwell, J. (1983). Crisis and survival in infancy. *Journal of Child Psychotherapy* 9:25–31.

Haag, G. (1985). La mère et le bébé dans les deux moitiés du corps. (Paper read at 2nd World Congress of Infant Psychiatry, Cannes, 1983). In *Neuropsychiatrie de l'enfance* 33:107–114.

——— (1991). Contribution à la compréhension des identifications en jeu dans le moi corporel. Paper read at Congress of the International Psycho-Analytical Association, Buenos Aires, Argentina, July.

——— (1993). Personal Communication, October.

---

5. An elective mute treated by Mrs. Margaret Goodchild brought much material about falling and losing half of his body of the kind described here.

———— (1995). Presentation of a diagnostic grid on the progressive stages of infantile autism as observed in treatment. English translation by Daphne Briggs. In press.

Hughes, M. (1996). Unpublished paper.

Klein, S. (1980). Autistic phenomena in neurotic patients. *International Journal of Psycho-Analysis* 61:395–402.

Maiello, S. (1995). The sound-object: a hypothesis about prenatal auditory experience and memory. *Journal of Child Psychotherapy* 21:23–41.

Meltzer, D. (1974). Mutism in infantile autism, schizophrenia, and manic-depressive states: the correlation of clinical psycho-pathology and linguistics. *International Journal of Psycho-Analysis* 55:397–404.

———— (1986). Concerning the perception of one's own attributes and its relation to language development. In *Studies in Extended Metapsychology*. Perthshire, Scotland: Clunie Press.

Milner, M. (1969). *The Hands of the Living God*. London: Hogarth.

Papousek, M., (1992). Parent-infant vocal communication. In *Nonverbal Vocal Communication*, ed. H. Papousek and U. Jurgens. London: Cambridge University Press.

Paul, M. (1981). A mental atlas of the process of psychological birth. In *Do I Dare Disturb the Universe?*, ed. J. S. Grotstein. Beverly Hills: Caesura.

Piontelli, A. (1992). *From Fetus to Child*. The New Library of Psychoanalysis. London and New York: Tavistock/Routledge.

Reid, S. (1990). The importance of beauty in the psychoanalytic experience. *Journal of Child Psychotherapy* 16:29–52.

Rhode, M. (1995). Links between Henri Rey's thinking and psychoanalytic work with autistic children. *Psychoanalytic Psychotherapy* 9:149–155.

Rodrigué, E. (1955). The analysis of a three-year-old mute schizophrenic. In *New Directions in Psycho-Analysis*, ed. M. Klein, P. Heimann, and R. Money-Kyrle. London: Tavistock.

Sobey, K. (1996). Striking the right note: the role of music in facilitating the move from sound play to symbolism and verbalisation in children with autism. Unpublished Masters Thesis. London: Tavistock.

Tustin, F. (1972). *Autism and Childhood Psychosis*. London: Hogarth Press. Reprinted, London: Karnac Books, 1995.

———— (1980). Autistic objects. *International Review of Psycho-Analysis* 7:27–39. Reprinted in Tustin (1981).

———— (1981). *Autistic States in Children*. London: Routledge. Revised Edition, 1992.

———— (1990). *The Protective Shell in Children and Adults*. London: Karnac Books.

———— (1994). The perpetuation of an error. *Journal of Child Psychotherapy* 20:3–23.

Winnicott, D.W. (1960). String: A technique of communication. *Journal of Child Psychology and Psychiatry* 1:49–52.

———— (1988). *Babies and their Mothers*. London: Free Association Books.

4

Between Two Worlds: Hope and Despair in the Analysis of an Autistic Child

Charlotte Riley

> *Between two worlds life hovers like a star*
> *Twixt night and morn, upon the horizon's verge*
> *How little do we know that which we are*
> *How less what we may be!*
>
> Lord Byron, "Don Juan" XV, st. 99

This chapter evolved in the course of my struggle to disengage myself from a quicksand of hopelessness, lifelessness, and meaninglessness, which I was experiencing in my analytic work with one autistic child, whom I will call "Joanna." The struggle led me to think about our experiences with hope and despair in the countertransference.

Joanna

Joanna is an 11-year-old girl with a psychiatric diagnosis of autism, who came into analysis when she was age 6. For approximately three years—although the work was very difficult, and I endured intense feelings of lack of contact and nothingness at times—the predominant experience was of hopefulness. The child progressed more than expected, both within the analysis and in her functioning and relationships outside. Above all, she continued to turn to me in the analysis to cooperate in making sense of her world, both inner and outer, despite periods of autistic unrelatedness.

Around Joanna's 9th birthday, a fairly dramatic turn for the worse occurred. She turned away from me both physically and psychically, turned away from relating to external attachment figures, and expressed a marked preference for a hidden world of psychotic fantasy, replete with delusional omnipotence and possible hallucinations. She became much more inaccessible and negativistic outside treatment, and she was assaultive to others. Thus began the two year period in which I found myself feeling increasingly hopeless about the patient, about myself as her analyst, and about our work together.

In the sessions, I experienced virtually intolerable feelings of utter lack of contact with another human being, utter meaninglessness, and overwhelming helplessness. I frequently felt totally passive, as if I were present only in body, and as if I were "killing time" until the end of the session. This alternated with my more forceful attempts to break through the patient's autistic isolation and make contact. As I have become able to achieve sufficient distance—or more accurately, transitional analytic space (Ogden 1986, Winnicott 1967) in which to begin thinking about the transference-countertransference experience with this patient rather than being submerged in its concreteness—I realize how much evidence of progressive change occurred during this period. At the time, I was either blind to such progress or was unable to hold onto it internally in the face of the patient's recurrent turning away from psychic growth and relatedness.

The start of the period of increased hopelessness in this analysis coincided with the advent of pubertal changes in Joanna. I will discuss some of the ways puberty and adolescence have been experienced. However, first I will give a brief background sketch of Joanna and the earlier period of her analysis.

In the Beginning

When she first came to me, Joanna had been diagnosed as atypical; her subsequent psychiatric diagnosis was "high-functioning autistic." She showed features of both autism and childhood schizophrenia as Mahler (1968) and Tustin (1992) have described them and of both the encapsulated and confusional children delineated by Tustin (1992). The question of organicity had been evaluated and no evidence was found. Obviously this does not preclude the likelihood that most such children have a biological predisposition to autism.

Joanna's parents had believed that they had the perfect baby because she was so "easy," sleeping a great deal, presenting no difficulties, and feeding well. However, all developmental milestones were significantly delayed. The first sign of emotional turmoil, with inconsolable crying, occurred at 20 months when Joanna began to walk. When moved to a new room, before the birth of her sister, Joanna again became extremely agitated at bedtime. Indeed her sister's birth, when she was 2 years old, emerged in her analysis as a very traumatic time for her.

During the mother's pregnancy with her sister, Joanna was evaluated for the first time and found to be seriously delayed with very little speech. She was unconnected to other people, making little eye contact. She made no effort to communicate her needs, had limited and blunted affect, and frequently carried around hard objects. After significant intervention with Joanna and her parents at a treatment center, she still spent more than half her time in school lying on the floor, staring into space. Her flaccid, uncoordinated body tone was very noticeable. She had long, rather wild blond hair.

The progress that sustained my hopefulness during the first three years of Joanna's analysis was marked by steps in establishing some rudimentary sense of identity. In an earlier paper (Riley 1989b), I have shown how she worked through certain psychotic anxieties, as described by Winnicott (1962, 1974) and Tustin (1992). She concretely demonstrated her primary experience of being unheld and dropped. At the first analytic break, she felt physically broken apart from me in the transference, and she dramatically enacted her terrors of leaking away and dissolving with an intense bout of diarrhea in the session. Anxieties about fragmentation were apparent when she spilled cake mix all over my office and then ate it off the floor. As she felt these anxieties contained by me, she wrote the first letter of her name—"J"—in the spilled cake mix. Soon after, she brought a doll and had her say, "I don't have a name yet. I'm not ready. I have to do some thinking first."

Joanna next became able to express her rage in explosive tantrums at separations from me, culminating in the vengeful statement that she would, "throw [me] in the dark basement where there's boys and girls and monsters." There followed the appearance of a firmly bounded, containing "no-mommy," who could say no to her omnipotent demands. This culminated in the achievement of sufficient psychic structure to permit her to describe her first dream.

Outside her analysis during this period, Joanna became a much more active participant at school. She learned to read to herself and her body became less flaccid, more upright, thinner and more attractive. Her parents reported a transformation in her relations with them, in which she could seek them out, express affection, and converse with them. These were some of the reasons for my considerable optimism during these three years of the analysis.

The Dawn of Puberty

As she was turning 9, Joanna began to develop secondary sexual characteristics, with the accompanying hormonal changes. At this time, she began coming into her sessions, lying on the couch with her back to me, and "spacing out" (as we called it) to her psychotic fantasy world. Occasionally, she smiled to herself and was perhaps hallucinating. When I spoke, or when anything drew her attention to me, she yelled, "I don't want to talk to you. I never want to talk to you again. I want to space out forever." If I persisted in an attempt to get through to her, or to interrupt her spacing out, she kicked, hit or bit me, and she had to be physically restrained.

This behavior was persistent and evoked feelings of alarm and despair in me. It was painful to become her enemy. Intense feelings of rejection—of being hated and permanently thrown away—mirrored experiences from her internal world, elaborated especially around her unconscious memories of her sister's birth. I gradually came to feel that, in the transference, I was felt as the absolute representative of a despised and overwhelmingly frustrating external reality from which she was decisively turning away.

She had shown me that in her spaced-out world, she felt in perfect omnipotent control, able to *make* reality become whatever she wanted by the mere act of wishing it. For example, she felt she could "grab" and steal anything I wore that was orange—her favorite color—merely by looking at it. Thus, she stole my magic powers or switched identities and became me. She told me in fragmentary communications that she listened to a "gang" in her mind who told her not to talk to me or others, to follow them to absolute safety in the "spaced-out world." At home and at school, Joanna became more negativistic and assaultive.

In what way was Joanna's dawning puberty influencing these changes? Frances Tustin has described the following normal situation in earliest infancy:

Differentiated states [of consciousness] fluctuate with states when the sense of bodily separateness is diminished. . . . In such states the outside world, and the objects in it, are experienced as a continuation of the subject's body. . . . However, some mothers and babies become unduly equated with and undifferentiated from each other. If bodily separateness is experienced too forcibly in this state of equation . . . for this particular baby (usually a hypersensitive and extremely sensuous infant), the infant suffers . . . "an agony of consciousness." The sensation is experienced as a mutilating loss of part of the body [usually the mouth]. . . . Patients have used the phrase "a black hole" to describe this experience. It is an engulfing "nothingness." It is the source of a traumatic type of depression. Unconceptualized, reactive, manipulative protections develop which form a protective static cocoon for the vulnerable infant. . . . The stage is set for the clinical manifestation we call "autism." [1990, pp. 217–218]

Mrs. Tustin also states that,

Autistic barriers can break down in situations of unbearable stress or biological change. . . . Biological situations that can threaten the autistic barriers are such events as puberty, having a baby, and aging. As the autistic barriers break down, the individual becomes flooded with psychotic "black hole" depression, which had previously been kept at bay by autistic reactions. [1990, p. 80]

I believe that such a threat was experienced by Joanna amidst the changes of puberty. Indeed, change itself is always threatening, and pubertal changes are profound and dramatic. Joanna tried at first to ignore the development of her breasts and the growth of pubic hair. When she began to notice them, she was terrified. She tried to pull out her pubic hairs, saying that they "itched" her. "Itching" was her expression for any unexpected bodily sensation, including sexual feelings, which were not within her delusional control, and was felt as a threatening impingement. In addition, "itching" expressed her feelings of skin discomfort when she felt her body surface was not entirely "smooth," as she wished it to be. For Joanna "smooth" meant continuous with, and not separate from, the body of her primary object.

When Joanna looked down at her breasts and then looked at mine, she appeared terrified and confused. We were able to understand this as her terror that her delusional fantasies of being able to pluck or bite off parts of her mother's or my body (especially the breasts) and to stick them onto her own were felt to have been realized in external reality. She would then be left with a terrifyingly damaged object and thus be vulnerable to similar sudden losses of pieces of her own body. Later, when menstruation began, Joanna would yell, "I'm not having a period." This was not expressed as a wish or protest but was a delusional, omnipotent command to reality, by which Joanna believed she concretely prevented her periods. The terrors that she could dissolve and leak away, expressed in the earlier diarrhea episode, were of course revived and magnified with the onset of menstruation.

In the countertransference, I found myself feeling unfairly betrayed by fate that Joanna should undergo such an early puberty. I have since come to realize that I had been sharing Joanna's delusion of living in a world of timelessness. I had felt as if we were sequestered inside a bubble, as if reality and change could not affect us in the privacy of my consulting room. It came as a blow that indeed it could! In retrospect, I believe that my predominant feeling throughout these two years that no progress had occurred illustrates the degree to which I was taken over by Joanna's massive fantasy of reversing the forward movement of time and change.

Nevertheless, progress was occurring. For example, Joanna was still confused between units of time: a day, a week, a year were all interchangeable. However, after she moved to a new class for older children, she brought pictures of the late 1960s rock group, "The Monkees" (her then current obsession) when they were *older* and *younger*. She went over in great detail what was the same and what was different about them. She liked them (and of course, herself) much better when they were younger, but she saw that they had changed.

Joanna's sense of "I-ness," as Tustin (1986) called it, was enormously fragile. Puberty and adolescence reopened primitive identity fears and contributed to Joanna's drive to turn away into psychosis and my corresponding despair. As one's body and body experience begin to change, one is called upon to tolerate not knowing who one *is* or who one will *become*, in the most basic physical sense. Added to this are social pressures for role changes. In her spaced-out world, Joanna could instantly become anyone she wished, for example a member of "The Monkees." Thus, she could solve the intolerable problem of being *herself*, and could achieve an instant identity, requiring no growth or struggle. However, more recently, she wonders what job she will have, indicating that she has begun to think about her identity and the future.

With the enormous threat to omnipotence that the changes of puberty have brought comes an awareness of the terrors of bodily separateness which Tustin has elaborated on. Adolescents often feel isolated. For Joanna, the feeling of utter and complete isolation was ushered in by an awareness of separateness, and for her, this feeling goes back painfully to her state of mind in infancy. One way in which adolescents ordinarily deal with their sense of isolation is through an intense relationship with a group. Joanna's solution to these and other problems of early adolescence has been to turn away from the terrors and frustrations of making friends to an obsession with "The Monkees."

In bits and pieces of communication, she has shown me how she is never alone, because "The Monkees" are always with her as soon as she thinks of them. Thus, she reverses her experience of feeling alone and simultaneously solves the problem of her new sexuality, and the necessity to relinquish her parents, and to make a new heterosexual object choice. She imagines she is married to one of "The Monkees"; being married, she believes, means owning someone exclusively so they are never apart from you and never frustrate you.

Thus, the many issues of early adolescence are dealt with by turning away from relationships with real people and the working over of the inevitable frustrations such relationships engender. Normal adolescents use fantasies about rock stars as trial action, preparing themselves for true heterosexual relationships and linking themselves to their peer group through shared preoccupations. In contrast, Joanna's fantasies are idiosyncratic and felt as concretely happening. They turn her away from the external world. As Tustin (1992) points out, these psychotic defenses make the patient inaccessible to the nurturing and growth-enhancing comforts and pleasures which are available from caretaking figures in her environment. The intensity and pervasiveness of these psychotic defenses contributed greatly to my sense of hopelessness.

Hopelessness in the Countertransference

Three elements of my countertransference experience of hopelessness were especially striking to me. First, I would point to the experience of total *isolation* that I was immersed in for much of the time. It is hard to find words to adequately describe the feelings engendered in me by being physically present with another person who is so utterly absent, unreachable, and entirely preoccupied in a world of her own. The sense of nonexistence and of nullification was often overwhelming. For long periods, absolutely nothing I could think to say or do seemed to reach Joanna.

This sense of total unrelatedness is of course one of the most difficult things for humans to bear: Spitz's (1945) babies died from it. At times, I was concretely inside the experience of not existing for the other. I felt dazed, overwhelmingly somnambulistic, and inchoate.

At other times, I understood that this was a very close approximation of the state in which Joanna has spent much of her life. This was the infant who seemed perfect because she made almost no demands and slept so much. I think this extreme isolation was the product of a vicious circle: a baby who had innate incapacities to do her part in object-seeking and initiating a relationship, and parents who, for complex reasons and no fault of their own, accepted this nonrelationship and did not react with alarm or vigor to pull their baby into the world of human relatedness. Joanna consequently developed more and more confusional and autistic methods of sealing herself off in her own world so that when her parents became able to reach out for her more actively, they were met with no response and failure. For these reasons, my ability to metabolize and emerge from my sense of isolation and nonexistence, to persist in my efforts to reach Joanna despite repeated failures, was of critical importance in the analysis. At times, Joanna found words for her sense of isolation, for example when she said, "I called for help, but nobody heard my call."

A related experience that contributed to my feeling of hopelessness was the sense of utter *meaninglessness* that pervaded the analysis. Psychoanalysis and much of human life is about generating meaning in the context of human relatedness (whether in internal or external reality). Joanna's autistic defenses were aimed at denuding experiences of both relatedness and meaning, because these involved a rudimentary recognition of separateness that threatened her with annihilation. Over and over again in the analytic work, something profoundly meaningful would occur: Real communication between us would occur, only to be followed by Joanna's retreat to the spaced-out world because identity and separateness were implied. I was left wondering whether the communication ever happened, or I forgot it entirely for long periods, or thought that it was only a random bit of echolalia floating by.

In one session, Joanna came in seemingly agitated, totally out of contact and lost in the spaced-out world. I tried numerous comments and "clever" interpretations that had no effect. Eventually, I relinquished my attempts to force contact and to "know" what was going on and sat quietly, managing on this occasion not to withdraw into isolation and sleepiness. Eventually, Joanna sighed, and I said, "Feeling bad Joanna?" She made eye contact for the first time in the hour and said she wanted us to read from *Charlotte's Web* (White, 1980). This is the children's story of a pig, Wilbur, who is to be killed at birth because he is a runt. He is spared temporarily, to be a child's pet, only to be fattened up for "bacon and ham." Moved by his despair, the spider Charlotte befriends him and saves his life by weaving *words* into her web, such as "Some Pig," which the humans take as a sign of Wilbur's uniqueness.

Joanna found the page where she wanted me to begin. I read aloud the poignant chapters (White 1980, pp. 25–41) where Wilbur is terrified and alone at night, and Charlotte the spider first speaks to him and makes it clear she will help. For a while, Joanna remained in contact and sat very close to me, but at the point where the spider speaks her name—"Charlotte"—she spaced out again. (Joanna called no one by name because of the separateness names implied). As the end of the session approached, she was unable to speak to me or to answer any questions about her thoughts.

The whole matter of Joanna asking me to read aloud with her is an interesting example of the problem of meaning and meaninglessness. The two books she asked for were *Charlotte's Web* and *The Lion, the Witch and the Wardrobe* (Lewis 1970). Both were endlessly rich in meaning regarding Joanna's psychic world and struggles. At times, as I read to her, it was clear that we were two people sharing the experience of the story and its meanings. At these times, Joanna could tolerate my pausing to comment on the feelings or meanings and even their relation to herself and myself in the transference; sometimes she could elaborate on the idea. At other times, what was *apparently* the same situation—me reading to her, as she had requested—was a totally different experience. The words were not being heard for their meaning but were woven into a kind of boundaryless "autistic shape" (Tustin 1986, pp. 119–140), which was continuous with Joanna's spaced-out world.

At these times, Joanna silently read the words of the book with her eyes while I spoke them with my mouth: In her experience we were one person. At these times she would tolerate no discussion, and ordered me to "Continue!" She seemed to be trying to weave me into her own confusional web of endless "continuing," where there was no interruption, or "stopping" as she called it, no separateness, and therefore no communication. Language had, at such times, become a sensuous shape without meaning. I was felt to be under her absolute control, a part of her. Gradually, I became able to trust my sense of when the stories were *communications,* with meaning about her own experience that could be interpreted, and when the stories became one-dimensional, with Joanna using her "continuing talk," as we called it, to evade the feelings evoked by separateness. My experience—of having communication and meaning repeatedly erode—turned into disconnection and meaninglessness and was debilitating.

Rereading Winnicott's "Dreaming, Fantasying, and Living" helped me to understand my experience of meaninglessness in Joanna's analysis. Her life in her "spaced-out world" was an extreme version of what he calls 'fantasying.' He describes it as follows:

> Dream fits into object-relating in the real world, and living in the real world fits into the dream-world. . . . By contrast, however, fantasying remains an isolated phenomenon, absorbing energy but not contributing either to dreaming or to living. . . . Inaccessibility of fantasying is associated with dissociation rather than with repression, . . . rigidly organized dissociations. . . . In the fantasying, what happens happens immediately, except that it does not happen at all. These similar states are recognized as different in the analysis because if the analyst looks for them he always has indications of the degree of dissociation that is present. [Winnicott 1971, pp. 26–27]

Winnicott adds that what such fantasying does is "to fill the gap" (p. 29). It is this gap—the separateness between two human beings—that Joanna encountered each time she dared meaningful communication with me, and from which she retreated into fantasying.

The third element in the countertransference hopelessness I want to comment on is *helplessness*. A number of writers have pointed out the close link between feelings of hopelessness and helplessness. It is one of the more painful aspects of our work that we are so often called upon to contain states of helplessness for our patients.

The only thing that mitigates experiences of extreme helplessness and allows for their integration is the availability, in internal or external reality, of human contact: good-enough objects to contain or hold us and to see us through. As therapists, we are all subject to our own therapeutic omnipotence, which provokes us to avoid the reexperiencing and reworking of helplessness. Experiences of helplessness that are uncontained, too long-lasting, or exploited in the service of the object's needs lead to hopelessness. Gerald Adler (1972) points out that intense countertransference feelings of hopelessness relate to the patient's very early unsuccessful relationship to the maternal figure and probably reflect the helplessness felt by the mother in the original situation.

All first-time mothers contend with powerful feelings of helplessness stemming from the combined newness of the mothering experience along with their identification with their babies and the reexperiencing of their own infantile helplessness. If we add to this picture a baby who is innately passive and predisposed to autism, without the lively responses that so encourage new mothers, it must be a mother of rare psychic strength who can meet the challenge and not give up, overwhelmed by helplessness.

If the mother is dealing with difficulties regarding separateness or a depression of her own, a situation of mutual helplessness may arise between mother and baby. Tustin (1992) describes the "black hole" experience of psychotic depression in autistic children. I have commented previously that the baby who then comes upon the mother's depression, preoccupation, or disconnection may experience

> Something like the overlapping of two black holes. . . . The combination of the infant's primal depression, the mother's temporary depression, and [in some cases] the lack of paternal support might feel to the infant like an endless series of black holes with no firm "psychic skin" to catch his torrential overflows. Perhaps the baby would have a sensation of falling into or through the mother which would evoke terror and cause a further turning away. I think that this experience of coming upon the mother's hole of depression, her temporary lack of a firm, permeable psychic skin to hold him, may be experienced as a fatal quality of softness where there is nothing to hold onto. [Riley 1989, p. 39]

Such a situation was being repeated in the transference-countertransference interaction with Joanna, who seemed to react initially by falling into a passive flop. This is a situation that generates great despair in the infant and child, and it was Joanna's despair about the mutual helplessness and disconnectedness between herself and her mother that I had to contain in the analysis.

The course of any analysis may be characterized by alternations between times when archaic, disturbed object relationships are reexperienced in the transference and those times when a new object-relation is being experienced based on holding, containment, and understanding. The reexperiencing of the old, pathological relationship in the transference is accompanied by painful feelings and by *hopelessness* when the patient experiences it as concrete and unchangeable. When these experiences are contained and understood adequately, a new object-relation is released in the transference, accompanied by *hope* because change has become possible. Of course, the positive, hopeful relation to the analyst also draws upon past experiences with good objects from the patient's internal and external worlds. However, Winnicott (1963) and others brought to our attention the significance of the new relationship being experienced for the first time in an analysis. It is this new object-relationship, characterized by the possibilities of transformation, that is at the center of the experience of *hope* for patient and analyst.

The Dawning of Hope

Perhaps the clearest images from Joanna's analysis of the old pathological object relations and the new transformative ones are to be found in her images of the pigs. The second time Joanna came to see me for an evaluation, when she was 6, she picked up a toy pig with piglets suckling and said, "The babies are drinking too much milk—for the mommy." When I asked if the mommy was getting empty, she looked directly at me answering, "Yes, she's going to sleep." Here is the old unresolved situation in which she feels she has overwhelmed a helpless mother. The states of sleepiness that she and I both experienced in the analysis suggested the mother going to sleep, that is, the reexperiencing of this relationship of mutual helplessness leading to hopelessness. More recently, however, she has turned to the pig Wilbur who finds a friend in Charlotte—a friend who is in contact with his pain and saves him through her use of words. This is the new object-relation being forged bit by bit in the transference—and characterized by hope.

This brings me back to the fact that once I had regained sufficient observing ego to look at this period of countertransference hopelessness with some perspective, I could see signs of change or progress that I had either been unaware of or kept losing sight of at the time. Joanna's active turning away from me during this period was very different from a passive flop into helplessness or an objectless state. When she attacked me verbally and physically, she felt I was *there* to be fought against; reality was there to be fought against. She would yell that she was going to "stop those stoppers." Inherent here was a sense of the separateness of herself and me, the mobilization of her aggression and protest (also different from the passive flop), and the use of splitting and projective identification: defenses more advanced than those of auto-sensuousness. I gradually realized that not only was I her "stopper" but that Joanna repeatedly projected the sane part of herself into me—the part of *herself* that does know the limits of her powers, and that can *stop* herself from acting-out at times.

The evolution of Joanna's "monsters" illustrates her movement from a relatively primitive autistic state to a more differentiated one. Joanna has always been afraid of monsters. Tustin (1990) has described the atavistic fear of predators from which autistic children seem to feel unsheltered. She says,

> The onset of autism is sometimes associated with the birth of another baby. . . . However, instead of feeling in competition with just one baby, such children feel in competition with a swarm of rivalrous sucklings who threaten to crowd them out or crush them to death. I have come to realize that it is this terrifying delusion that has been the main precipitant of their autism. It is at the root of avoidance of people. [1990, p. 49]

This is the situation Joanna was dealing with early in her development and in analysis. Whenever she became aware of separateness, she felt terrifyingly alone and unprotected from monsters' mouths coming to eat her. This was the situation of "the dark basement where there's boys and girls and monsters" that dominated much of her early play with the pig and suckling piglets, and which led to her total avoidance of other children at school.

More recently, Joanna has been able to describe fantasies about her monsters; they are often discrete, namable "monsters" from Sesame Street who are coming to eat her. Now, in her relatively organized state, and with her increased use of projective mechanisms, she understands and elaborates interpretations of her fears as projections of her own aggressive impulses, fantasies and acted-out attacks. Thus, after she kicks, hits, or bites someone, she can think about her own monster-feelings getting control of her; or when she fears a fantasized attack, she can describe her own corresponding aggressive wish, for example to eat me so that she would have my head inside her and then she could "make the rules." She is no longer the helpless, passive victim in a flop.

A further sign of progress is the intermittent evidence of depressive anxieties regarding loss, mourning, and concern for a damaged object. Joanna began to return from vacation breaks in a more organized, coherent state. Having obviously maintained an image of me, she was glad to see me. Following the first summer break—during the two year period I am discussing—Joanna told me about an experience from her vacation which had obviously had intense meaning for her. She described a program at her school on the Civil War where she saw an American flag. She had been both fascinated and terrified to look at it. I was very moved as she remained in full contact with me and described how "The flag was old and tattered, and it had a hole in the middle from a bomb. I was afraid it would ruin our whole land." She placed her hand over her heart, and my impression was that she had had an experience and had maintained a coherent image, which corresponded to—and perhaps finally had begun to *symbolize*—her internal situation. The flag was the prized but terribly damaged, depressed maternal object. She asked, "And do all the people in our country love our flag?" Her explosive rage and annihilation anxiety at separation had left both her and her loved primary object with a hole at the center. But in the school program, the flag had been safely preserved for people to look at, think about, and admire.

I also felt there was a breakthrough at home when a male daycare worker with whom she was obsessed was leaving. Alongside her delusional shouts—"he *must* be my husband, he *must* be mine"—she began to lie in bed on nights before returning to daycare and weep mournfully about his *not* being there anymore and how much she missed him. She shared these feelings with her mother instead of turning away and spacing out in her usual fashion. In these ways I believe Joanna was dealing at a new level with the terrible sense of loss she experienced at some point in her early life, and certainly at the time of her sister's birth.

Harold Searles (1979) states, in a paper entitled "The Development of Mature Hope in The Patient–Therapist Relationship"

> Any realistic hope—as contrasted to unconscious denial-based, unrealistic hopefulness—must be grounded in the ability to experience loss. One who has survived the griefs over losses, over disappointments in the past has known what it is for hope to triumph over—to survive—despair. In the same regard, hope comes into being when one discovers that such feelings as disappointment and despair can be shared with a fellow human being—when one discovers, that is, that the sharing of such feelings can foster one's feeling of relatedness with one's fellow human beings. . . . [1979, p. 484]

This is the road that Joanna and I are struggling to travel.

I have titled this chapter "Between Two Worlds." By this I mean a number of things. Among these is the sense in which I felt myself suspended, shuttling between Joanna's psychotic, "spaced-out world" and ordinary reality. I also mean the two worlds of hope and despair. However I think the most important meaning lies in the word "between." Through thinking about this case, I have finally returned to the transitional area between reality and fantasy, knowing and not knowing. I no longer feel concretely overwhelmed by

Joanna's psychosis and despair. I can tolerate that there are both reasons for hopefulness and for a very guarded prognosis.

Thomas Ogden (1982) makes these comments on transitional phenomena and hopelessness:

> The therapist must be able to bear the feeling that the therapist and the therapy are worthless for this hopeless patient, and yet at the same time not act on the feelings by terminating the therapy. . . . The "truth" [of the hopelessness] . . . must be treated as a transitional phenomenon wherein the question of whether [this] "truth" is reality or fantasy is never an issue. As with any transitional phenomenon, it is both real and unreal, subjective and objective, at the same time. In this light, the question "if the patient can never get better, why should the therapy continue?" never needs to be acted upon. Instead, the therapist attempts to live with the feeling that he is involved in a hopeless therapy with a hopeless patient and is, himself a hopeless therapist. This, of course, is a partial truth which the patient experiences as a total truth. . . . [1982, p. 30]

The hard fact is that we *do not know* whether, or how much, Joanna can progress. We can only live and work with what we have in the present. I am now again able to locate the transitional area, where it feels possible to tolerate the paradox (Winnicott 1971, p. xii), and to bear not knowing.

It is precisely this transitional space that Joanna has not yet found with any reliability. She feels either merged with her object, in omnipotent control, or utterly cast out, alone and left to die. She can only fleetingly feel that separateness is tolerable because the attentive other is reliably there, that in the space between herself and the other, communication can occur. Communication is the sharing of experience with another. It generates meaning and may make even the deepest pain and terror bearable.

Similar issues may arise in virtually any case, in periods of negative transference, or wherever the transference is focused particularly on the repetition of an old pathological object-tie that the patient cannot yet relinquish and which he cannot believe could change. Our task is to contain the feelings of despair, *without action*, for as long as it may take before the patient can feel them to be adequately communicated and gradually understood. I have suggested that transference-countertransference experiences of isolation, meaninglessness, and helplessness are key elements here.

In addition to the work we each do on our personal countertransference responses, perhaps we all have to struggle against the primitive superego demands that rise up in us at such difficult times. The primitive superego requires that we know the answer immediately, cure the patient quickly, and fix the situation so that neither patient nor analyst will feel that things are so wrong. This superego *blames* us from within for the patient's ills; it feeds on pressures from without, such as a patient's spouse, or a child's parents, complaining about the patient's behavior. These primitive superego demands can temporarily paralyze us.

However, if we can support ourselves and each other in being aware of these experiences, we may remember that we have lost sight of progress that has occurred. We may also remember that we sometimes must become temporarily immersed in the patient's dynamics to fully empathize and contain his experience. Then patient and therapist may have the courage to carry on bearing the painful doubts and hopeless feelings, and important new meanings may emerge over time. This in turn may generate the experience of the new, hopeful object-relation in the transference. Something has happened, between the patient and another person, which the patient had previously given up on or believed impossible. It is this new object relationship, based on holding, containment, understanding, and transformation, that we hope the patient may eventually internalize and take away from the analysis.

Postscript

At the Memorial held for Frances Tustin in Los Angeles (October 1995), I read a version of this chapter and spoke of my contacts with Mrs. Tustin, including invaluable consultations with her on this case. I quoted a letter she wrote to me, typical of her warm communications with colleagues, in response to my review (Riley 1993) of the revised edition of *Psychotic States in Children* (Tustin 1992). She said, "I was so grateful to you for discussing the phrase 'psychogenic autism' so helpfully. It means the work is still growing! . . . I'm blessed with intelligent, helpful friends. It makes growing old more bearable." I commented that it meant a great deal to me that Frances and I had connected in this way through our work and that this was our last direct communication.

At the Los Angeles Memorial, I told a story that had occurred to me while I was in London at the Tavistock Clinic Memorial for Mrs. Tustin (February 1995). There, tributes from all over the world were given and read. Someone remarked on Frances' great satisfaction toward the end of her life, at the international interest and elaboration of her work. This brought to my mind the day in Los Angeles when I heard of Frances' death. I had a session with Joanna that afternoon, and I felt a strange sense of someone missing in the room. No doubt, sensing my sadness, Joanna asked me to read the chapter called "Last Day" from *Charlotte's Web* (White 1980). In this chapter, Wilbur has just won first prize at the fair:

> Charlotte and Wilbur were alone. . . .
> "Charlotte," said Wilbur after a while, "why are you so quiet?"
> "I like to sit still," she said. "I've always been rather quiet."
> "Yes, but you seem specially so today. Do you feel all right?"
> "A little tired, perhaps. But I feel peaceful. Your success in the ring this morning was, to a small degree, my success. Your future is assured. You will live, secure and safe, Wilbur. Nothing can harm you now. These autumn days will shorten and grow cold. The leaves will shake loose from the trees and fall. Christmas will come, then the snows of winter. You will live to enjoy the beauty of the frozen world . . . Winter will pass . . . The frogs will awake, the warm wind will blow again. All these sights and sounds and smells will be yours to enjoy, Wilbur—this lovely world, these precious days . . ."
> Charlotte stopped. A moment later a tear came to Wilbur's eye. . . .
> "Why did you do all this for me?" he asked. "I don't deserve it. I've never done anything for you."
> "You have been my friend," replied Charlotte. "That in itself is a tremendous thing. I wove my webs for you because I liked you. After all, what's a life, anyway? We're born, we live a little while, we die. A spider's life can't help being something of a mess, with all this trapping and eating flies. By helping you, perhaps I was trying to lift up my life a trifle. Heaven knows anyone's life can stand a little of that." [pp. 163–164]

They continue their conversation and Charlotte tells Wilbur that she won't be going home to the barn because she is dying. Wilbur is desperate, but Charlotte tells him that it wouldn't make any sense for him to stay at the fairgrounds with her.

> Wilbur was in a panic. He raced round and round the pen. Suddenly he had an idea—he thought of the egg sac and the five hundred and fourteen little spiders that would hatch in the spring. If Charlotte herself was unable to go home to the barn, at least he must take her children along. [p. 166]

Wilbur finally persuades Templeton, the rat, to climb up and get the egg sac from Charlotte's web.

Wilbur had already decided how he would carry the egg sac—there was only one way possible. He carefully took the little bundle in his mouth and held it there on top of his tongue. He remembered what Charlotte had told him—that the sac was waterproof and strong. It felt funny on his tongue and made him drool a bit. And of course he couldn't say anything. But as he was being shoved into the crate, he looked up at Charlotte and gave her a wink. She knew he was saying good-bye in the only way he could. And she knew her children were safe.

"Good-bye!" she whispered. Then she summoned all her strength and waved one of her front legs at him. [pp. 170–171]

Back at the barn, Charlotte's babies eventually hatch out and Wilbur is ecstatic at having so many new friends. But one day, the warm wind comes and blows the babies away.

Wilbur was frantic. Charlotte's babies were disappearing at a great rate . . . At last one little spider took time enough to stop and talk to Wilbur before making its balloon.

"We're leaving here on the warm updraft. This is our moment for setting forth. We are aeronauts and we are going out into the world to make webs for ourselves."

"But *where?*" asked Wilbur.

"Wherever the wind takes us . . ."

Cries of "Good-bye, good-bye, good-bye!" came weakly to Wilbur's ear. He couldn't bear to watch any more. In sorrow he sank to the ground and closed his eyes. This seemed like the end of the world, to be deserted by Charlotte's children. Wilbur cried himself to sleep. [p. 179–180]

When he awakes, Wilbur hears a tiny voice and discovers three of the baby spiders making webs in the barn doorway. They pledge their friendship.

As time went on, and the months and years came and went, he was never without friends . . . Charlotte's children and grandchildren and great grandchildren, year after year, lived in the doorway. Each spring there were new little spiders hatching out to take the place of the old. Most of them sailed away, on their balloons. But always two or three stayed and set up housekeeping in the doorway. [p. 183]

We too may hope that Frances Tustin's psychoanalytic offspring will continue to set up housekeeping wherever the wind takes them and continue to develop her legacy of friendship and profound insight.

References

Adler, G. (1972). Hopelessness in the helpers. *British Journal of Psychology* 45:315–326.

Lewis, C.S. (1970). *The Lion, The Witch and the Wardrobe.* New York: Collier Books.

Mahler, M. (1968). On Human *Symbiosis and the Vicissitudes of Individuation.* Vol. I. New York: International Universities Press.

Ogden, T. (1982). *Projective Identification and Psychotherapeutic Technique.* New Jersey: Jason Aronson.

———— (1986). *The Matrix of the Mind.* New Jersey: Jason Aronson.

Riley, C. (1989a). Discussion of Frances Tustin's paper "The dread of dissolution." *Winnicott Studies,* 4:37–42.

———— (1989b). Thinking about psychotic anxieties: moments in the analysis of an atypical child. Paper given at scientific meeting, Los Angeles Institute & Society for Psychoanalytic Studies, Los Angeles, CA, October.

———— (1993). Review of *Autistic States in Children. Winnicott Studies* 8:76–84.

Searles, H. (1979). The development of mature hope in the patient-therapist relationship. In *Countertransference and Related Subjects,* 479–502. New York: International Universities Press.

Spitz, R.A. (1945). Hospitalism: an inquiry in the genesis of psychiatric conditions in early childhood. In *The Psychoanalytic Study of the Child,* 1:53–74. New York: International Universities Press.

Tustin, F. (1986). *Autistic Barriers in Neurotic Patients.* London: Karnac Books.

———— (1990). *The Protective Shell in Children and Adults.* London: Karnac Books.

———— (1992). *Autistic States in Children, Revised Edition.* New York: Routledge.

White, E.B. (1980). *Charlotte's Web.* New York: Harper & Row.

Winnicott, D.W. (1962). Ego integration in child development. In *The Matu-*

rational Processes and the Facilitating Environment. New York: International Universities Press, 1965.

———— (1963). Psychiatric disorder in terms of infantile maturational processes. In *The Maturational Processes and the Facilitating Environment.* New York: International Universities Press, 1965.

———— (1967). The location of cultural experience. In *Playing and Reality.* London: Tavistock, 1971.

———— (1971). *Playing and Reality.* London: Tavistock.

———— (1974). Fear of breakdown. *International Review of Psycho-Analysis* 1:103–107.

5

The Analysis of a 9-Year-Old Girl with Learning Disabilities: Reflections on Supervision with Frances Tustin, 25 Years Later

Victoria Hamilton

To Frances Tustin, who kept watch over those who had fallen to "the low dark verge of life"[1]:

Be near me when my light is low,
When the blood creeps, and the nerves prick
And tingle; and the heart is sick,
And all the wheels of being slow.

Be near me when the sensuous frame
Is rack'd with pangs that conquer trust;
And Time, a maniac scattering dust,
And Life, a Fury slinging flame.

Be near me when my faith is dry,
And men the flies of latter spring,
That lay their eggs, and sting and sting
And weave their petty cells and die.

Be near me when I fade away.
To point the term of human strife,
And on the low dark verge of life
The twilight of eternal day.

Alfred Lord Tennyson, *In Memoriam*

Introduction

I met Frances Tustin in 1969, during my second year of training at the Tavistock Clinic. She supervised the five times weekly analysis of my third training case, a 9-year-old girl I call "Miranda." My first memory of Mrs. Tustin is of looking down onto the car parked from the common room

---

1. The verses at the beginning of this paper are part of a collection of poetry and music I taped for Frances Tustin during her last days when friends were keeping vigil by her bedside.

window in the Department of Children and Parents and seeing this rather small, round lady, dressed in purple, with a peaceful smiling face, who walked with a bit of a limp. She looked approachable and ordinary. This is something Frances always emphasized: autistic children lack a sense of being ordinary (or ordinary being). The Frances who could appreciate the black hole of nothingness and the beauty of a circle was sensible, not sentimental. Despite her growing influence on a large number of students and thinkers throughout the world, Frances was down to earth and skeptical of those who aggrandized her descriptions of autistic processes into what she called "high fallutin" theories.

When the time came for me to start my third case, I set off with some trepidation to Frances Tustin's flat in West Hampstead. The room was cozy and quiet, with soft warm lamps, a velvet embossed sofa with pillows on which Frances would put her feet up, a little purple velvet chair, and tea and biscuits. Frances exuded qualities that psychoanalysts rarely write about: generosity of heart and spirit, and kindness. She was a born teacher, never telling one what to say, or what one should have said, but able to say firmly "No, I wouldn't do that because. . . ."

Usually, she made suggestions that built on a theme that was on the edge of consciousness. She was always looking for that flicker of light in a dark situation. This spiritual quality made her a gifted teacher and supervisor and had much to do with her unique success in the psychodynamic treatment of autistic children. In these children, "the human spirit has been well-nigh extinguished" so that "the feeble flame of psychic life has to be fanned by every means at our disposal" (Tustin 1995, p. 153).

In our last conversation before she died, when Frances could only speak in a whisper, I wrote down the ideas on sensation and spirituality that Frances wanted to publish in *Nature* magazine. That day, Frances talked about her belief that there are several kinds of autism but that the basic autistic state is one of being outside, "averted" from the world of people, of "not belonging." Autistic people share an experience that the world around them—the people-world—suddenly stopped, and, in that minute, the child ceased to belong. Frances emphasized that the state of not belonging was more subtle than the experience she previously described in terms of a "too sudden separation," or rupture from the mother.

In the foreword I wrote for the new edition of Tustin's first book, published by Karnac Books (1995), I concentrated on the links between Tustin's descriptions of autistic processes and the concepts she drew upon and developed in order to theorize about her experiences and findings. What is so fascinating is that her descriptions of autistic states changed very little, although she expanded the concepts she used in order to link her work with contemporary developments in neuropsychology, biology, infancy research, as well as psychoanalysis. The ordinary language we use to describe our experiences with patients carries a richness, flexibility, and uncertainty that theoretical concepts lose. It is not therefore surprising that a thinker like Tustin, with a background in both science and literature, could fit her vivid descriptions into different, even conflicting, theoretical frameworks.

At times, we see a theoretical model restricting her imagination, whilst at others, theories open up new explanations and ways of seeing. For example, Didier Anzieu (1985), Daniel Stern (1985), Colwyn Trevarthen (1979) and many other contemporary researchers opened up her understanding of the *psychobiological* basis of autistic states just as her early formulations of "primal depression"—of the "black hole"—were inspired by the works of Melanie Klein, Wilfred Bion, Margaret Mahler, Edward Bibring, John Bowlby, and Donald Winnicott.

Miranda

Turning now to the case supervised by Frances Tustin, I will present selected sessions with some accompanying paintings. I had not looked at my case notes on Miranda's analysis since 1972, and the sessions came back to me afresh. The 9-year-old girl I shall call Miranda was the youngest of three sisters, the older ones being Maria, age 12, and Miriam, age 15. I saw Miranda for nine months, five days a week. Miranda was referred because of severe learning difficulties—she could not read or write—and her therapy ended dramatically when her mother substituted special tutoring for the therapy hours. Miranda's IQ was 117. Interestingly, she was good at math and this was demonstrated in her counting and scoring of activities she engaged in during the therapy hours.

Miranda's therapy could not be called successful, although her parents told their social worker that they were pleased with her and that her reading and writing had greatly improved since coming to therapy. It was obviously brief, so that the intensity and pervasiveness of Miranda's fears were barely touched. However, in retrospect I wonder whether the limited outcome did not result in part from the lack of understanding at that time—among psychoanalytically minded therapists—concerning the cognitive aspect of learning difficulties, as well as the absence of contact between Miranda's family and myself.

Nowadays, if I were referred a child with these problems, I would expect that he or she would be seen by an educational therapist, and I would myself be aware of the special perceptual problems in sequencing that these children encounter. Dyslexic and dysgraphic children do not see or make gaps. Thus words, letters, or lines on a page are joined, thereby reordering the normal sequence. I would also expect a learning disabled child to be above average intelligence, although that child might present herself as "stubborn," "resistant," "lazy" or "superficial" as a protection against feeling different and deficient. However, 25 years ago, analytically minded therapists tended to believe that therapy alone was the treatment of choice for most disorders.

I note that I have almost no record of Miranda's family history. The father was in the restaurant business, the mother was a housewife. Miranda was breastfed for four months when solids were introduced. She vomited after meals, was given medicine, but "had grown out of it" by the age of 1 year. There was no evidence of early separations or deprivations. The impression I formed of Miranda's mother was that she was considerate, caring, and loving, even "doting." I would like to draw the reader's attention to the central theme of "hands" in Miranda's paintings. I felt that these expressed her precarious hold on the world and, at the same time, a rather steamrolling, grasping, and manipulative relationship with people and things.

When I presented this case 23 years ago at a Tavistock case conference, prior to qualifying in 1972, I commented on the way that Miranda conveyed very little except her niceness, friendliness, obligingness, and "normality" whilst I often felt useless, thoughtless, and futile. Our communication had a flat, one-dimensional quality that seemed to link with her learning difficulties. Yet I also had glimpses of another Miranda: a child who was quite frightened, flustered, easily startled by noises; who felt lonely and left out; and who was often physically ill. Miranda's outer appearance could be disarmingly discrepant with her feelings, which themselves were only detectable in her tummy aches, sore thumbs, and bandaged arms and legs. Using Tustin's terminology, it seemed that Miranda lived in a world that was dominated more by sensation than emotion.

Miranda lived in extremes, and these extremes can be seen in her paintings, which can be divided into black, bare, skeletal paintings and bright, cheerful, light, full paintings. The paintings are expressive, but Miranda was not. Her talk was flat and factual, and her play was highly repetitive, involving endless games of jacks, snakes and ladders, and ball games played against the wall. The games always involved numbers and points, and she would add up long columns of figures to score herself. She regularly reordered and recounted her drawings, putting them into folders and stamping them with her name.

Amassing and possessing made her feel full and in control, whereas talking and associating to the drawings brought up the unknown and unconscious.

After three or four weeks of therapy, I realized that I felt more hopeful and had more sense of a meaningful meeting on Fridays; and, in a different and opposite way, on Wednesdays. On Mondays, we seemed as stuck as ever. The "black Friday" paintings conveyed a rather empty, deathly, lost feeling. The central object—a car, house, cat—was usually surrounded by space, often blue, as if there were no ground, no firmness or support.

In contrast, the Wednesday paintings were bright, even garish. Hands and fingers, steeped in bright colors, stamped heavily across the page, matching the clumping footsteps with which she planted herself in my room. Miranda would close the door with exaggerated firmness and deliberateness, ousting my hands from the door handle. On Wednesdays, she came at six in the evening, whereas on the other four days, she had to come at half past noon during her school lunchtime. She made a slip one day when, referring to a Wednesday session, she said "when I come at the week-end." On Wednesday evenings, the rather untidy school girl in a worn, short, pleated skirt with fawn socks and brown sensible shoes was transformed into a rather tarty girl wearing 18 to 19-year-old black gear, with brassy jewelry, high-heeled patent red and gold shoes, and made up with eye shadow, red lipstick, and nail varnish.

I shall now present excerpts from the first three weeks of the analysis. The therapy was extremely short, and there were no dramatic changes to report. However, as is often the case, students (beggars) can't be choosers! We take whomever we can get to come five times a week. I suggest that the reader think about the first session from the perspective of the cases described in Winnicott's *Therapeutic Consultations in Child Psychiatry* (1971). In these consultations, Winnicott listened and looked for diagnostic and prognostic clues, whilst capitalizing on any opportunity for therapeutic intervention that might reach the "block in development" that "cut across the line of life of the child." Miranda had visited the clinic two to three times before our first session to see a consultant psychiatrist and an educational psychologist. I will give the first session in full.

First Session

Near the door, Miranda says: "The lady told me that when I came, I could do the same things as I did last time." I responded, "You want to do the same things again?" She said, "Yes. She said that I would have some things all to myself." I concurred, "Yes, this is your drawer with your things, you can do what you like with them."

Miranda got out the dolls and the plasticene and said something about the family being at school and how she had left her history class to come here. She commented on the grandparents and children in the doll family set. I said, "You had to leave your family at school, and come here to another family, just as you had to leave the other lady and come now and see me, another new lady." She replied, "Yes, last time when I saw the other lady, I only had one doll—a little boy—not all these." I told her, "Now you have got a whole family to yourself." Miranda added, "And we couldn't use the plasticene because it was too hard, so the lady put it on the heater but it was only soft enough when it was time to go." I said, "It seems you were just getting to know the other lady when it was time to stop, and now you've got to start all over again with me. That's hard, and perhaps you are using the same things as last time to try to keep something the same so I won't feel so new and strange. Maybe you feel you have already seen a few people here, had a lot of changes."

Miranda said, "Yes—well, I only saw Mr. S. and the other lady—and anyway I don't mind, because I like coming here." I then commented on the "family" all sitting down in their chairs. She said, "Yes, or park seats." I then pointed out how they were sitting up very nicely on their clean white seats, and how perhaps she feels she has to be very good and clean here with me and behave well. Miranda smiled and said "Yes." Then she made a pond with "green" around it and placed ducks on it, and she said, "Last time I made a farm and a zoo. Have you got those things you, you know put together, put round animals?" I asked if she meant fences, and commented once more on her wish to find the same things as last time. She responded, saying "These are different fences, they didn't have stands, and they didn't have a gate," and she linked them together.

I commented on her needing to fence these fierce animals in, to be so good and quiet here, to please me—"Yes"—not show me the fierce wild side of her. Miranda replied, "My sister is fierce sometimes, she shouts and gets very angry. And my Dad." I asked, "Which sister?" She clarified, "My elder sister, she's fourteen, my other sister, she's eleven, she's very quiet, doesn't get angry at all."

Then Miranda put the boy doll kneeling by the fierce animals and the girl by the ducks and explained, "The boy can stay and feed the fierce animals because he's a boy like Daddy" I said, "Mm. But the girl just feeds the ducks." She added, "Daddy gets very angry and roars like a lion sometimes." Seeking clarification, I asked, "With you?" and she confirmed this. When I asked *when*, Miranda said, "When I've done something wrong." After a pause, she went on to say, "We can't really put the other animals in the zoo because they're really farm animals. We could put the bears in here," she said, making a green fence. "When I went to the zoo, there was a huge panda, it was gorgeous, huge and fluffy, you just felt like cuddling him."

I said, "You like to cuddle." She replied, "Mm," So I added, "Perhaps you like to cuddle up to Mummy, like you would want me to care for you." She replied, "Mm, on Sunday mornings, I go and make myself coffee and toast or something and—we've got cats and a dog—I take the dog up to my bed. My Mum doesn't like me having the dog on the bed, but I do, and sometimes I have the cats." I said, "And they all cuddle up." Miranda said, "Mm" and then gave a long explanation about the dog, how the dog had been so ill, and wouldn't eat, so they took it to the vet who gave him medicine, but it had made no difference. Then Mummy found another vet and he cured the dog immediately and the dog has been fine ever since. Miranda went on to tell me how her Nan (grandmother) had a dog, a dachshund with a broken foot, and her Mum had taken it to the same doctor, and it got completely better.

I said, "So you and Mummy both like dogs." Miranda confirmed, "We all do, all our family likes dogs. My Mum has a friend and her dog wasn't well and last week it was put to sleep and Mummy cried." I said, "Mummy was very upset. They couldn't make the dog better." She explained, "Well, they didn't take it to the doctor. Yesterday, I had a jumble sale, we sold all my old things to the society for thalidomide children. We made pounds, at my house, me and my friend." Miranda paused and added, "I think I'll do a drawing now. What shall I draw? I don't know." I said, "Maybe you don't know because you are wondering what I think, and you want to please me, and are afraid I won't like you, or like the drawing." Miranda then said, "I like drawing, art at school. I have a nice teacher. I like P.E. and netball, there is a nice teacher."

Drawing #1 (First session)

As she drew, Miranda said, "This one has green curtains, just the front room, these are the two bedrooms, and this is the sitting room and this the kitchen. This one has red round, all have red. Oh, I know I'll put in a yellow sun." I commented on the bright yellow sun, and Miranda continued, "In my bedroom, last night we moved the bed because Mummy was moving my cupboard so my bed was moved out. It was quite fun, the change, but when I woke up this morning, I didn't know where I was." I said that, "Maybe it felt

a bit like coming here to see me, a new room and a new person, but then feeling frightened of feeling lost and strange." She responded, "Mm, because usually my bed is looking out of the window and I can see the two cupboards and the rooftops and the tops of trees and the sky, but today I couldn't and the window was all misty." I said, "Perhaps you wanted it to be a sunny bright day, your first day here, and to find me warm and sunny because you are rather scared coming here for the first time and you hope so much that I will be nice."

Miranda murmured, "Mm" and after a pause, I commented on how her room sounded quite like this room, because here we can look out and see the tops of the houses, and the trees and the sky, though there is no sun today. I also noted how this room looked onto the front, and maybe she felt she had been pushed into the front room away from the rest of her family, the waiting room, the other people and rooms she already knew in the building.

Miranda replied, "If this was my room, my bed would be across there, facing this way, the cupboards would be here." She went back to painting and said, "This is the Mummy cooking. She has got a frying pan in one hand and [?] in the other." I said, "You hoped I would be a nice Mummy who would cook a nice meal for you, and feed you." Miranda said about the Mummy in the picture, "She's making the breakfast," I offered, "Like Mummy makes your breakfast." She said, "Yes, though I don't usually have time for much, toast and tea, because we are up at 7:30 and leave the house at 8:15, it's a rush."

I said, "But this Mummy is making a cooked breakfast, making a real meal." Miranda said, "Mm, I do like bacon. Mummy doesn't have her breakfast with us because it's such a rush. She wants to have it afterwards when she has taken us to school and then she can have it in peace. She doesn't mind, she isn't hungry, she's used to it now." Then Miranda looked at her watch and said, "Now, they'll all be having dinner [school lunch], I expect, just finishing."

I said that her Mum waits for her to eat her breakfast first, but I am a Mummy who doesn't wait for her to have her dinner, I make her come here so she has to go without her dinner. Miranda argued, "No, I will get it, the lady said she would save some for me, keep it hot, she will save it for me every day." I continued, "So I am making you wait to have your dinner by yourself after all the other children," after which Miranda reassured me or herself saying, "I might just get in on the end of the second dinner, I don't mind though."

When I commented on my not fitting into her time, Miranda said something about Daddy, how he works from home and how he smokes a lot. She said, "We keep telling him not to, but he just goes on." I talked about how she can tell Mummy what to do but can't tell Daddy or he might get angry. I then told her it was time, and that we would go on tomorrow. She joined in saying, "Yes, and at six on Wednesday. Next Monday, I will walk here by myself, but this week Mummy says she will take me to get used to it." Then she put her things in her drawer and asked, "Will the other children use these?" I said "No," and she looked around the room and commented wistfully on how the other rooms had looked onto the back, onto the gardens and the trees.

First Supervision Notes

In our first supervision hour, Frances Tustin took up the mutilated, crippled bit of Miranda. This she connected with the little-boy-thrusting creative part of her, which had been cut off so she could only be good and sweet and nice. The angry bit of her, roaring like a lion, she can only be if she's a little boy. This means that a bit of her body is missing, she's crippled. The roaring bit has been cut off. No one will accept it, so it's gone.

Frances also commented on Miranda's fury at having to fit in, how her whole routine has been upset by me, her worry about her dinner, how this upset in her routine is felt in her body. She's been shuffled around and she doesn't know what this will lead to, what will happen. Frances picked up on how Miranda switched from talking about cripples—the thalidomide children—to talking about school, implying "All right, I'll be the good school girl then." This supervision gives an excellent account of the course of the therapy, including the circumstances of its abrupt termination.

In the Friday session, two days after this supervision, after making "a nice house," Miranda asked me whether I ever saw the schoolgirls going past on their way to the playing fields? (You will recall that she had told me that she liked netball, and P.E.) She then got out the cars, confiding, "I am a bit of a tomboy sometimes, although I'm a girl." Then she put the cars in a black house. Here, Miranda's freer and darker side peeped out, confirming Frances Tustin's observations.

Drawing #2 (Monday after 1st weekend)

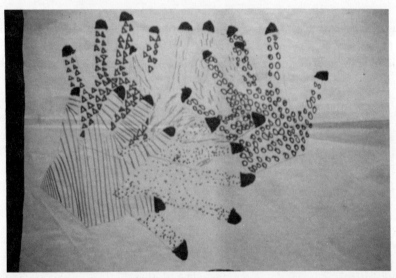

Miranda drew this on the Monday after the first weekend. The five hands are brightly colored, except for one black hand, and they have the red finger nails of the Wednesday evenings. Cleaning up was a central theme during the second week of therapy. Miranda cleaned out her drawer and rearranged her play things each day. She spent much of the session trying to wash out her paints, but as they were wet, they stuck together as soon as she put them away. They then had to be pried apart and cleaned up in the next session.

Drawings #3 and #4 (Friday of 2nd week)

On the Friday before the second weekend, Miranda talked about having her hair done before going to a party and about how much she wanted me to

see it. The party was going to be at a theater, where the audience and actors mix. I talked to her about us being mixed together during the weekend, inside each other's houses, without barriers. She first drew a black boat sailing in a grey sea and sky and then a black car in blue space. At the last minute, she hastily added some yellow clouds, commenting "even the clouds are sunny."

On the Monday of the third week, Miranda opened the passage doors hesitantly, almost going into another room before entering our usual room and hanging up her coat. I commented on how uncertain she seemed after the weekend and that perhaps she felt she had lost her special place with me and that I, like the room, might have become different over the weekend. She smiled sweetly and nodded.

Then she went to her drawer and put her finger in her mouth mumbling, "I don't know what to do." After a bit, I said that perhaps the weekend seemed very long and she felt she had lost touch with me and what we were doing on Friday. She then laughed and spent some time cleaning up the paints, again muttering, "I don't know what to do," and eventually starting Drawing #5.

Drawing #5: "The nice lady" (Monday after 2nd weekend)

First she drew and painted in the hair. She said, "The lady has a bun." I asked, "Like me?" and she answered, "Yes." I commented, "I think this is the picture of me you tried to hold in your mind over the weekend. Perhaps it was difficult to feel that I would still be here on Monday, and you tried to remember me, to feel close when we were apart."

Miranda then painted in the smile, the eye, then the dress, adding the spots, and finally the neckband. I said, "It's a smiling lady with bright blue eyes." And she agreed saying, "Yes, a nice lady." I added, "Perhaps you tried to think of me as a nice smiling lady so as not to feel frightened about losing touch with me, afraid that I might turn into an unkind, frightening lady who left you."

In response to this, Miranda painted the ribbon in the hair, put the red in the cheeks, and added the earring. I commented, "Brightening the lady up, keeps me a warm, smiling Mummy." Miranda then painted in the red all around the figure. I asked her about the red, and she answered, "Just red." On a few occasions, when I tried to make interpretations, she asked me how much time we had left. The atmosphere was sticky. I tried to engage her in talking about Sunday, how long and lonely Sundays can feel, linking this with what she had told me about bringing her dog into bed with her. The mention of the dog did draw an immediate response. She said, "Yes, today is my dog's birthday and I gave him a present of a dish in two parts, one part for food, and one part for water. I think he knew it was his birthday, he was very pleased and wagged his tail."

Drawing #6: "Cartoon lady"

I ask Miranda about this drawing and she said, "Well, its . . . I don't know really." After a while, I commented: "Half the face looks like the lady drawing, and the other half like a dog, and a bit like a bird?" She confirmed, "Yes, it's a cartoon drawing, you know." I added, "And in cartoons, the thing is that you can draw people as you like, half people, half anything, like animals." Miranda said "Yes," so I went on saying, "And they don't have to be like real people. Perhaps at the weekend you would like me to be a doggy person, half like your own dog and then you could go and collect me when you want to and bring me into bed with you to cuddle up and keep warm and you wouldn't have to wait till Monday." Miranda responded by asking, "What time is it?"

I took up the exchanges in this session in terms of Miranda's feelings about waiting over the weekend, not having enough time, and linking me with the dog that she could take away with her at the end of the session. In retrospect, it strikes me that I was hammering on with these weekend separation interpretations and that her asking me about the time might have had more to do with trying to get me to stop this line of interpretation rather than with any anxieties she might have had about not having enough time in the sessions. Perhaps I was already brainwashed by Bowlby and Klein! As some American analysts have noted about the interpretive emphasis on separation of British analysts, "That's all the British talk about, the weekend and after the weekend!"

Miranda looked worried and commented on what she was drawing. She said, "The dog has a red mouth, it's a tongue he's sticking out." Just then, a loud bark could be heard outside, and Miranda listened. I commented on the loud bark, and she said, "It must be a big dog." We talked about her fear of loud barking dogs, and I linked this with the part of her that might get too big and shout over the good, quiet 9-year old girl part. She described the size of her dog: "He's a mongrel, he's the same age as me. He's medium size. What's the time now?"

It was time to pack up and it occurred to me that Miranda might have started to come to sessions by herself, so I asked her how she was going back today. Here I was associating to Miranda's questions about time during the session. Miranda answered uncertainly, "I think by myself, but Mummy might be there." Only then did I find out that Miranda had not been to school that day because she had a sore tooth during the weekend and her mother had taken her to the dentist. The dentist had told her that she had a "bad" tooth, maybe an abscess, and he gave her penicillin tablets. She said, "I have to take four today, then three every day for the next five days." Miranda immediately counted her drawings, looking over what she had done in the three weeks since starting therapy. She remarked, "*Seven* drawings." Then we went to the waiting room to look for her mother, but Mother was not there.

Looking back on my interpretations from today's perspective, one might try to listen with the ears of a late 1960s Kleinian and an attachment theorist. Child psychotherapy students at that time inherited a feud between Esther

Bick and John Bowlby. As noted by one of my fellow-students—an anthropologist who had worked with Margaret Mead in New Guinea—the experience of presenting clinical work to our teachers was like being "caught between two warring parents." So, you can imagine that, while Bowlby picked up on the anxieties linked to separation from the mother, the rest of our tutors—all of whom were Kleinian—focused on Miranda's split-off aggression and the attendant anxieties about her greed as aroused through the transference of the early feeding situation onto the analysis.

If, in addition, we consider the material from the perspective of Tustin's early and later work, clearly Miranda is not a true autistic. Nevertheless, using the diagnostic criteria delineated by Tustin in her first book, Miranda's pathology seems closer to that of the "entangling" ESA (encapsulated secondary autism) or RSA (regressive secondary autism) children. These are the soft, plastic "amoeboid" children that Tustin contrasted with the hard-shelled "crustaceans." My supervisions with Frances coincided with the completion of her first book, published in 1972 and reissued in 1995. Frances saw Miranda as an enmeshed and entangling child. In the book, Tustin states that these children

> seem to have by-passed all awareness of frustration by being compliant and accommodating. . . . They often have a history of normal development but this seems to have been mostly on the basis of compliance—of moulding and being moulded. . . . When threatened with awareness of separateness, [they] reinstate the charmed circle of "nice-me" and no "nasty-not-me." [p. 110]

All these observations seem pertinent to Miranda's way of being. Grey clouds were colored over with sunlight, bright red borders were added to anything ambiguous or odd, and Miranda's most common response to anything "not nice" was "But I don't mind."

Tustin's later thoughts on the "psychotherapy with children who cannot play" (Tustin 1988, p. 97) are relevant not only to autistic children but also to children with inhibitions in learning. Miranda's play was repetitive and often boring. In contrast, her paintings were expressive and spontaneous, although they could not be talked about, we could not "play" with them.

With these points in mind, I shall summarize the sessions leading up to our first separation—a three-week Christmas break—and I will show the reader the paintings from Miranda's last session before the holiday.

First Break in Therapy

Miranda spent December making colored paper chains, Christmas decorations, and Christmas present lists. She gave me the impression of a busy, rushed mother. One week, she brought in a spirograph with a mirror and spent the sessions making "pretty" patterns. She had five spirographs at home. I was to look in the mirror and choose the one I liked. In supervision, Tustin interpreted these as the "spider's web" in which I was enmeshed. Miranda was out of school with tummyaches, and the atmosphere was both monotonous and frenzied. When I commented on her worried preoccupation with her Christmas present lists, Miranda said, "It's all right buying presents when you know what they want—like Daddy wants a key ring—but it's not when you have to *choose*."

As Tustin pointed out, Miranda was worried about pleasing everyone, about making everything fit, and about having to separate people out from one another in order to make choices. In one session, however, she took a break from her lists and paper chains to make a Christmas card for her new baby cousin, who was only a few days old. She said, "I love babies, I haven't seen it yet, but I look forward to it."

I don't have this card but I will describe the diagram I made at the time. On the top left hand corner of the card, Miranda drew a blue balloon. On the top right hand corner, she drew a bottle. She had difficulty with the perspective and the "joins" and told me, "I can do the teat but not the bottle." On the bottom left corner, she drew a "teddy" and then stopped, unable to think of what to draw on the fourth corner.

This enabled me to open up the topic of herself as a baby and her favorite baby things, "Perhaps a bottle?" I suggested. Miranda replied, "I didn't have a bottle. Mummy fed me, and then I had a cup with a special top, you know." Then, with a grey crayon, Miranda colored in the bottle to the half-full mark. She rubbed the grey milk with an eraser to make it lighter.

I would like to think about this card in connection with Drawing #6: the dog-person with the tongue sticking out that seemed to frighten Miranda. Tustin focused on the importance of the tongue in early infantile development: "a bodily organ which has been little discussed in psychoanalytic literature" (Tustin 1995, p. 112). I will quote the passage from Tustin's book as we look again at Drawing #6.

Tustin refers to a paper by Augusta Bonnard (1960), in which Bonnard describes the tongue as the first "major scanner." In this paper, Bonnard presents case material to show the marked improvement and great spurts in intellectual and emotional development that occur in therapy following discussions of the significance of the tongue. Putting together Bonnard's observations with Spitz's (1955) concept of the mouth as "the primal cavity," Tustin notes that:

> Early oral trauma may have been associated with the feeling of the tongue suddenly being "in space" without the lulling continuation of the mother's body afforded by the teat. Many E.S.A [encapsulated secondary autism] children, when they begin to draw, are preoccupied with problems of perspective and the drawing of three-dimensional objects in space . . . to a degree that amounts to an obsession. Awareness of separateness is inseparable from awareness of space and brings with it awareness of outsides and insides . . . Until awareness of "insides" has been achieved, inner life is not possible. [1995, p. 112]

Tustin concludes, because these children blot out awareness of separateness and thus of space inside and outside, "They have no inner life, which accounts for the impression they give of emptiness and vacancy" (p. 113). Tustin also notes that the entangling, amoeboid children are usually very inhibited in the expression of anger. Expressions of anger were markedly absent from Miranda's therapy. She was not vacant like an autistic child, nevertheless her inner life was thin and impoverished. She had difficulty drawing the inside of the bottle, and when she did so, it was half full with grey milk.

When the week before Christmas came, Miranda was in a flurry of activity, bringing in bags of Christmas presents to wrap. She made presents for "the poor children" and told me, "We bought a big tree and we put it in the hall so that other people can see it when they pass by and they can get the joy of Christmas too." On our last day, Miranda told me with great excitement of the Christmas calendar that she and her sister opened every day until the one big day, the 24th. She then drew a flower with petals around a big center. One petal was black. I interpreted the excitement and the letdown after Christmas, wondering about the days after Christmas when she wouldn't be coming here. She said, "Well, there will still be all the things to play with." She then painted a person with a white face on a black bed, Drawing #7. I suggested that this might be herself, ill in bed as she had been during the previous weekend.

Miranda responded by saying, "No, she's waiting for Father Christmas to

Drawing #7: "Dream" (Session before Christmas)

come." She then added a smile to the white face. I said, "She's smiling. I wonder why." Miranda conjectured, "She's probably having a nice dream or something." This enabled me to ask Miranda about her dreams. She replied, "Well, I've had some nice dreams, but I also had some nightmares." When I asked about these, she said: "Last Christmas I had one—I'll never forget—that when I woke up I had no presents. But then when I *did* wake up, Father Christmas or Mummy had brought them after all, so it was all right."

Summary of Sessions Between Christmas and the End of Treatment

Illness continued to be a dominant theme in the sessions that followed this first "exciting" Christmas holiday. Reading over the session material from this next period, I found myself thinking about why Frances had turned to Mahler's work on autism and symbiosis, in particular Mahler's (1958) concept of the "symbiotic love object." Frances had come across Mahler's work, as well as that of other American analysts, during the year she spent at the Putnam Center in Boston. However, back in England, it was heresy for someone trained at the Tavistock to read the work of Anna Freud, and therefore Mahler. Yet, there was no equivalent to Mahler's concept of the "symbiotic love object" in the Kleinian literature at that time. Tustin's use of Mahler's distinction between benign and parasitic symbiosis seemed to fit the deadening, entangling relationship that resulted from the fear of separateness that was shared by both Miranda and, I suspect, her mother.

The following anecdotes express this entwined relationship, and the adhesive identification in the symbiosis. For example, when talking about her illness on return to therapy, Miranda described a memory of the time when she was 4-years old when she, her mother, and her elder sister had all gone to the hospital together to have their tonsils out. Her sister had screamed because she had a "scary, black doctor." He can be seen as the dark one who broke into the nice white symbiotic circle.

The next session, when I linked these fears with anxieties that I might become ill, Miranda told me that only that day she had found out that both she and her mother had been thinking the same thing: What would happen if Miss Hamilton was ill? Would I phone, would the session be canceled, or would she see somebody else? When, on a later date I did have to cancel two sessions because of "flu," Miranda returned with a bandaged hand.

Another example: Following her birthday in February, Miranda described an exchange with her mother in which Miranda had seen a ring on her mother's finger and had said to her mother, "What a lovely ring, I wish I could have it." Her mother said, "Close your eyes," and gave her the ring "as a little extra for [her] birthday." For the next few days, both at home and in sessions, Miranda became very worried about losing the ring. During this time, she also reported sleeping difficulties but made light of these, telling me that her mother let her come into her bed to cuddle. She said, "Daddy doesn't mind, he can look after himself." Again, Frances linked these fears with Miranda's need to maintain the agreeable symbiosis and keep the father out.

Miranda also told me of a recurring nightmare: There were two girls (not her sisters) in a big hall. One person was going round and round with a large black sack. In the dream, Miranda wakes up screaming. Her sisters, mother and father are in the room, but they daren't wake her up in case she gets more frightened. After she did wake up, she burst into tears. Miranda thought the dream had to do with getting lost for hours on a holiday in France and not being able to speak or understand the language. When I suggested that the large black sack might have a body or something dead inside—linking the nightmare with fears of death and feeling left to die—Miranda stated baldly, "No, just a black bag like a large rubbish bag." As usual, there was nowhere to go with this meaningful material.

Some Paintings From This Period

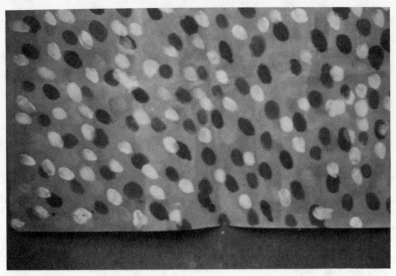

Painting #8

This is a finger painting. Miranda said, "I'll tell Mummy I did a painting without brushes."

Painting #9: "The Matchstick Family" (Session after Christmas)

Painting #10: "Hands"

These three paintings contrast with two paintings Miranda made on two separate occasions following absences when she and I had been ill.

Painting #11: "The pram on the hill" (on her return from an illness)

In this painting the chimney looks as if it is falling down. When I commented that the Mummy had no hands and was not holding onto the pram, Miranda said, "She isn't holding it, but it won't roll down the hill."

Painting #12: "The circus" (painted after I was sick)

The following five paintings were produced on Fridays.

Painting #13: "The black cat"

Painting #14: "A house"

Painting #15: "The lonely soldier"

Painting #16: "A house"

(Note that the customary sun is transformed into a witch monster. In this session Miranda talked about policemen, witches, God, and whether psychologists can tell what you are thinking.)

Painting #17: "The watch"

("My watch doesn't keep the right time [I comment about worries over time]. "It's just a watch," she said.)

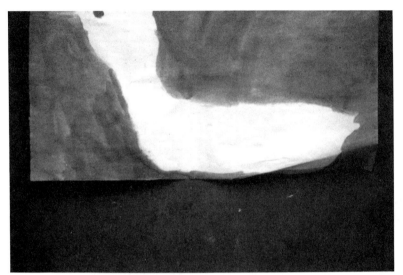

Painting #18: "The swan-duck sitting on black water (no feet)"

When I asked Miranda about the "duck," she said quietly, "It's meant to be a swan." And when I wondered, "Why a swan?" Miranda told me that there was a swan in their French book that day. We then talked about how much she loves baths, the warm scented water all around her, especially if she has bath salts. She particularly liked the blue bath salts she was given for Christmas. It seemed that Miranda wanted to be the white baby-swan that did not have feet but was surrounded and held up by, and floated blissfully on, warm blue soothing water. Here she was telling me about her sensuous self, so much at variance with the literally minded school girl.

Between the Easter holiday and our last session in July, a number of changes occurred. On two occasions there was a mixup over the allocation of rooms at the clinic, and Miranda's parents canceled the last few sessions. I will describe the last session.

Last Session

Miranda arrived ten minutes late to our last session and handed me a box of chocolates and this card:

I think the picture vividly displays Miranda's plight and her image of herself, which she so valiantly had tried to push away. She said, "I'm sorry I haven't been to see you but—well—I've been round so many people, Mummy's taken me to so many places, but she told you, I think, that I'm going to see another lady now for my reading, so I couldn't come here anymore. I brought you these," she said as she handed me the chocolates and the card. I said, "Thank you very much. It must be strange coming back here again now that you're not coming for sessions." Miranda replied reluctantly, "Well, it does a bit, but I wanted to come in and say good-bye, but . . . I just . . . well it's my reading that really matters most, so I just have to."

I said to Miranda, "Perhaps you feel a mixture of feelings coming to say good-bye, glad in some ways that you can just concentrate now on reading, but sad also that you are coming back to say good-bye. Maybe you are frightened about what I might feel about your leaving, would I be upset and angry." She responded. "Well, I like coming here . . . I mean . . . I hadn't thought of *not* coming . . . just that as my reading is the most important thing, I have to do that first and Mummy arranged it all so I just have to do that . . . so well, I have to go."

When I asked Miranda if she could tell me a bit about the reading, she replied: "I have to go and see this lady twice a week and she gives me exercises because one of the things I can't write is vowels, and then the letters after them. I know vowels but just, you know, the letter that comes before or after. So I take these exercises home and I am allowed to ask my sisters or Mummy to get help, and then I take them back, so I'll learn to read."

When I took up her disappointment in me, her feeling let down by me—that I had not helped her to read, that I hadn't held onto her but had left her to be taken by Mummy to so many places and so many people—Miranda said, "Well, I do remember two *au pair* girls who left like that, I liked very much, but, well, they had to leave." Miranda then asked, "Can I take the drawings home?" This was a difficult question. She wanted to have them, but then, of course, she said, "I don't mind, it's up to you to decide." We talked about the drawings in terms of her remembering me and the sessions, and my keeping them so as I would remember her and our times together. She then asked, "Shall we look at the drawings?"

It was fascinating to listen to her assessment and reflections. When she looked at Drawing #5—the one of me with the bun—she said, "Mm, not quite right, the nose is still too long." She didn't like the two Friday drawings that she painted at the beginning of therapy. Most of the drawings that she did not like were "the messy ones." I interpreted that she might feel that I had encouraged her to be messy here, to be more tomboyish, and now she feels she has to be the good schoolgirl who has to get her letters straight. At the end of our resume, Miranda held the drawings against her. We arranged that she would take them home, but when she came to visit me, she would bring them back for us both to see.

References

Anzieu, D. (1985). *The Skin Ego.* New Haven: Yale University Press, 1989.
Bonnard, A. (1960). The primal significance of the tongue. *International Journal of Psycho-Analysis* 41:301–307.
Mahler, M. (1958). Autism and symbiosis: two extreme disturbances of identity. *International Journal of Psycho-Analysis* 39:77–83.
Spitz, R. (1955). The primal cavity: a contribution to the genesis of perception. *Psychoanalytic Study of the Child* 10:215–240.

Stern, D.L. (1985). *The Interpersonal World of the Infant*. New York: Basic Books.

Tennyson, A. (1973). *In Memoriam*. New York & London: W.W. Norton, ed. Robert Ross. Stanza 50, p. 32.

Trevarthan, C. (1979). Instincts for human understanding and for cultural cooperation. In *Human Ethology: Claims and Limits of a New Discipline*. London: Cambridge University Press.

Tustin, F. (1988). *The Protective Shell in Children and Adults*. London: H. Karnac Books.

——— (1995). *Autism and Childhood Psychosis*, 2nd ed. London: H. Karnac Books.

Winnicott, D.W. (1971). *Therapeutic Consultations in Child Psychiatry*. London: Hogarth.

6

Analysis of Hard and Soft: Tustin's Contribution to a Jungian Study of Opposites

JoAnn Culbert-Koehn

Out of this union of hard and soft sensations a new way of functioning is born.

Frances Tustin

As a Jungian analyst, I have found Frances Tustin's work to be particularly helpful in illuminating very primitive reactions to analytic breaks in those patients undergoing Jungian analysis. Tustin's paper "Psychological Birth and Psychological Catastrophe" (1981) has proven useful to me, both in teaching a course on separation dreams for candidates in my Institute, and in my work with patients in my consulting room.

The feeling quality of Tustin's paper—in which she states that trying to understand and talk about such phenomena is like putting "a nightmare under a microscope"—helped me to recognize the extent of the pain of difficult physical and/or psychological birth as well as my own resistance to teaching the material. I often felt like the harbinger of bad news taking such ideas into Jungian seminars. Yet I knew it had to be done, for as Tustin has noted, "not to do so would be a professional dereliction" (1986, p. 310). It became vital for me to teach and write about this material on difficult birth for two reasons: first, because patients find the pain of birth so difficult to bring up and articulate, and second, because not identifying birth pain in the transference/countertransference relationship can lead to certain patients feeling deeply misunderstood and to potential analytic impasse.

Integrating Opposites

A central concept in Jung's description of psychic life—and in Jungian training—is his theory of opposites. Jung viewed the unconscious as a counterpole to consciousness with the capability of serving a compensatory function. Near the end of his life Jung (1963) wrote, "The opposites are the ineradicable and indispensable preconditions of all psychic life" (p. 206). In the index to Jung's *Collected Works* there are over 450 references listed to the opposites.

In *A Critical Dictionary of Jungian Analysis* (1986), Samuels and colleagues state:

> An acquaintance with the principle of opposition is essential to an understanding of [Jung's] point of view. It was a foundation for his scientific endeavors and lay at the root of many of his hypotheses. Jung was expressing the dynamism of the psyche in terms of the first law of thermodynamics, which states that energy demands two opposing forces. At different times he made reference to several philosophical sources for his thesis but none was acknowledged as primary. [p. 102]

Among the salient clinical revelations in Tustin's writing on mismanaged psychological birth is her idea of the importance of integrating the opposites through the baby's experience of the mother's body. While Klein emphasized the good and bad breast, Tustin (1981) particularly emphasizes the opposites of hard and soft:

> In the sense-dominated state of early infancy the infant's primary distinctions are between "comfort" and "discomfort," "pleasure" and "unpleasure." "Soft" sensations are pleasurable and comfortable. "Hard" sensations are unpleasurable and uncomfortable. [p. 185]

Tustin continues:

> When on the basis of a cooperative suckling experience, "hard" entering nipple and tongue are experienced as working together with "soft" receptive mouth and breast, there is a "marriage" between "male" and "female" elements that takes place. Out of this union of hard and soft sensations a new way of functioning is born. [p. 186]

Jung also believed that a third element was produced when the opposites were brought together and contained. He referred to the newborn third as the "transcendent function." Tustin wrote about the third emerging from the infant's integration of hard and soft as the birth of a new way of functioning that is firm, adaptable, resilient, and tough. She states, "This means that reality can be processed and the world will begin to 'make sense'" (1981, p. 186).

After rereading Tustin's words, it occurred to me how often the message patients bring into the consulting room is about how "hard" things are—how hard outer or inner life feels. The soft pole of early experience has not been sufficiently experienced or integrated, or the hard pole has been *so* hard that insufficient softness has been constellated, or adequate containment has not been present. Patients vary greatly in their capacity to integrate the opposites. In Jungian analysis this is expressed in terms of the capacity to integrate shadow qualities, both personal and collective. Are these differences inborn? Are they the product of variabilities in the containing function of caretakers? Perhaps there is a combination of both.

Tustin reminds us repeatedly that we are talking about a complex process that we can infer or intuit from our clinical experience but cannot really see. She also reminds us that in working with such areas of the mind, our words are limited and that we might best rely on metaphor in our communication.

In further describing the early integration of hard and soft, Tustin says:

> The earliest situation is particularly difficult to describe because the sensation-dominated child is in a state of oneness with the mother. In this state he is not likely to be aware of nipple-tongue-mouth-breast as separate entities. To describe as nearly as possible his probable state, we might say that "nipple-tongue" is "hardness" and "mouth-breast" is "softness." In a satisfying suckling experience, sensations of softness and hardness work together to produce a state of well-being. [1981, p. 186]

Tustin cautions us again that there are parallel neuro-physical integrations, and above all that this is a "mysterious process." Part of the brilliance of Tustin's writing is that she expresses her ideas in a clear and focused way yet still conveys the poetry and dark mystery of the unconscious. In this way, her writing itself carries and integrates the opposites of hard and soft.

Although Tustin's article concentrates on her child analysands, my focus will be on my adult patients who, in the course of their analyses, discovered a difficult physical and/or psychological birth experience, as this experience emerged in the transference/countertransference relationship. Each patient whose material is included here was seen four times per week.

Vignette: Mark's Painting

It was tax season in the U.S. as I was writing this chapter. A patient brought in an example of his difficulty in integrating the opposites of hard and soft. In recent months, analysis had helped Mark locate and mobilize an artist-part of himself that, in the beginning of the analysis, had been buried and paralyzed. Recently he had been able to paint at least once a week while managing attacks—from other sectors of his personality—upon his emerging creativity. In a recent session he had been anxious and concerned about how he would continue to paint while working on preparing his taxes.

Painting seemed to represent the soft, personal, world of feeling, color, fluidity, and spontaneous expression. Taxes represented the hard, cold, impersonal world of numbers, thinking, and a rigid, authoritarian masculinity. In Mark's mind, these forces were always at war in a killing way. He was afraid the artist and the child in him would fiercely resent working on taxes and would go on strike. He also thought the practical, rigid father in him— that would emerge to do the taxes—would attack his art and stop the flow of his creativity altogether.

This patient had had a difficult prenatal experience and a difficult birth. Mark's mother was prenatally hypertensive, and he was delivered by cesarean section. He was both physically and psychologically separated from his mother upon the event of his birth because of her need for additional emergency surgery. Mark's beginning was "hard"—there seemed to be no mother available to contain and mediate the opposites of hard and soft.

Mark had dreams in which my office appeared as a neonatal intensive care unit for infants at risk. Tustin writes: "The therapeutic setting acts as a kind of incubator in which the psychological 'preemie' can achieve those basic integrations he did not make in infancy" (1981, p. 195). I was hopeful that the analysis could be used to contain and to continue Mark's work on integrating hard and soft: that the painting could continue and the taxes could be completed; that there might be a bringing together of hard and soft, feeling and thinking, outer and inner, rather than an inner destruction. Mark's conflict also had oedipal layers, however he found most helpful those interpretations focused on the mediation of the opposites of hard and soft.

Case Studies: Judy and Doris

I have selected two case examples that further highlight difficulties of integrating the opposites and illustrate Tustin's ideas about the consequences of mismanaged psychological birth, particularly the presence of catastrophic anxiety at times of transitions and separations. I believe that Judy's analysis reveals how the effects of a mismanaged physical and psychological birth surface at times of potential life transition.

Judy

For Judy, at age 40, moving into a relationship was "hard"—there was a constant pull back toward the womb, which was imagined to be soft and nondemanding. Judy had undergone an induced birth followed by a separation from her mother, who suffered from depression shortly afterward due to the loss of a parent.

During the time in the analysis that I wish to describe, Judy was in a new relationship with the most compatible man since I had known her. In the past she had chosen unavailable men; this new man was bright, available, worked in the same profession, and liked her. Several months prior to the session I will describe, a fourth hour had been added with the idea that if Judy could experience more contact in the analysis, perhaps she would be able to tolerate more intimacy outside the analysis as well.

Judy was excited partly by the prospect of this "new relationship" but also terrified of the feeling, which she described as a horror of being more separate from me and from her parents. In one hour, she told me she was thinking of Alice in Wonderland. She said, "I'm afraid of falling into the rabbit hole. This new relationship feels like falling into a rabbit hole." There was fear and terror in her voice, and she asked, "How could Alice tolerate her adventures?" Judy said that the thoughts of these "adventures" frightened her—things going from big to small, changing sizes, growing, shrinking, the unfamiliar. She seemed to anticipate that a feeling of havoc would be unleashed in her by this new relationship to me, as well as to the boyfriend, if she allowed the "adventure" to continue. She said that Alice has to meet all these strange people (parts of herself, her feelings). "It doesn't feel safe to me. I'm not Alice. I'd want to be with Mom."

Near the end of that hour she told me about a recurring dream from her childhood in which she was going down wooden stairs into the ground:

"Maybe it's the underworld—there's no going back and it's scary going forward, like down the rabbit hole. There's scary stuff in the passage. You have to go through to get out."

In a subsequent session Judy began by saying she had felt angry driving to the appointment. She said that I had pushed her out at the end of the last session after I had said it was time to stop. She had kept talking and I had said, "We really need to stop." This upset her, as she thought it was an especially good session and wanted to savor it. My comment made her feel as if I merely tolerated her and that my office was "just a factory."

Near the end of that hour, having talked about her ambivalence and resistance to her new boyfriend, Judy said, "I just want to be a cute kid, forgiven for everything and allowed to act young. Not a stiff, married, traditional adult." After a pause she added, "I'm over forty and I still want a perfect childhood."

I said that she seemed to be longing for paradise, that maybe she was longing for the womb. Offered the new relationship with Mike and the feelings and anxieties it stirred up, a part of her wanted to go forward into life, while another part wanted to go back (to the paradise of the womb).

In the countertransference, I now had images of her grandmother's home on an East Coast beach, where Judy had remembered the happiest times of her life. The atmosphere in my consulting room seemed very fluid. Then Judy, who often changes the subject quickly after an interpretation, said in an uncharacteristically soft way, "I wonder what my experience in the womb was like, and what my life would have been like if I hadn't been induced." She began to talk about her grandmother's summer house. "The summers in that home were the best part of my life. The grass was soft, and it was a big place with a lot of land and huge trees where I would climb. I was more on my own there than at home. My imagination felt free. I could be on my own and not be discovered. The house was like a castle with secret places. I really felt safe there."

For patients with premature, cesarean, or induced births, the movement from inside the mother's body to the outside world may be felt as a traumatic loss, or as Tustin suggests, a "catastrophe." At the beginning of the first hour of the next week, Judy talked in a highly anxious way, communicating through projective identification an overflow of anxiety about a catastrophe that was about to occur. Michael Paul (1981) has suggested that patients with such birth experiences may feel robbed or ripped off. Breaks in analysis—as well as life transitions requiring separation and loss—activate a desire to remain in the womb as well as the hatred and terror of being born.

The prospect of beginning a relationship with a suitable man seemed to be experienced as a threat to the status quo, a violent birth, a rupture in the relationship to the analyst-mother and her body. It is possible that Judy felt that I was pushing her into the new relationship, as well as pushing her out at the end of the hour. The psychological work necessary to navigate the transition was felt to be too "hard," and she was not sure she could survive all the bewildering and frightening feelings involved.

Perhaps because Judy's birth was induced, followed by only a partial bonding with the mother, she felt that she was not really part of life on this planet, that she was not fully human. She often stayed in an anesthetized state, disconnected from her feelings. She observed other people dealing with loss and could not imagine what equipment they had that allowed them to process such feelings. She conveyed pervasively sad feelings that basic instinctual connections—what Tustin referred to as "primary integrations"—had not been established. The work of relating was felt to be too "hard." There existed a claustrophobic fear of being suffocated in a relationship as well as a fear of being untethered and floating into space.

In a recent session, Judy brought a dream in which she found herself at the campus of the college she had attended:

I felt completely lost. I was supposed to have a date in a cafe, but I was sitting watching another woman chat up a man. I wandered out to the campus but didn't know in which direction to go. I didn't know how to ask people for directions. A compass appeared so I could orient north, south, east, and west, but I still didn't know which direction to take. Nothing looked familiar.

The dream continued:

I was on a bus and got off. I found myself skating on thin ice. I realized I didn't have shoes on. I had left them on the bus. I'd also left my purse. I had no identification but, most upsetting, I'd lost my dog Missy. I was very upset. I went back to my apartment and lay down. I woke up at 10:30 or 11:00.

Among the associations to her dog, Missy, was Judy's fear of losing her. She said she didn't want Missy to experience "what [she] felt when Mom wasn't there to pick [her] up after kindergarten. I think I felt Mom didn't love me.

My Mom would say I shouldn't get so worried because I should know she was coming, but I would get upset anyway."

This dream presented themes and feelings that pervaded Judy's treatment. It was reported a few days after her return from a break, during which time she functioned well at work but had many feelings about the break that emerged in this session. It was as if, as mother-analyst, I had dropped her out of my body and pushed her into life on a college campus for which she was ill-prepared, and she felt she was "skating on thin ice." In fact, Judy did suffer from a serious incapacitating anxiety during her college years. She was a spectator in a world where girls try to relate (chat up guys). She was disoriented, did not know what direction to go in, and—as expressed in a later dream—didn't even know night from day. She was afraid I wouldn't get there on time to pick up on these feelings, like her Mom after kindergarten. She was afraid that her feelings would not be taken seriously and that the vulnerable, soft, Missy-part of herself would be lost, pushed into the "hard" adult world.

Judy said that it was hard for her to describe her distress in the dream at being disoriented and that this made it hard to ask for help. She said, "I was so disoriented I didn't know where I wanted to go. I was very disoriented and trying not to panic." As she talked, I thought about how a newborn baby might not know where it wanted to go (the breast) if its instinctual cycle was disrupted by a chemically induced birth and not repaired or contained by a mother who could bear her daughter's distress.

Doris

Another example of feelings of catastrophic anxiety presenting at a time of transition comes from my patient Doris, another woman in her forties. Doris arrived for her last session before the holiday break and arranged herself in the chair opposite me. In a despondent tone, looking at the floor, she said, "I have a headache and was dizzy driving here. I feel very anxious." After a pause she added, "Forget anxiety. Let's go for terror." I said, "Okay. Forget anxiety. Let's go for terror."

The sense of impending disaster was now palpable in the room, spreading everywhere, radiating outward so that I would feel it and hopefully contain and metabolize it. We had been in this painful separation place before. Doris now remembered a session some months back, when she was going on a business trip in a state of terror about flying. She remembered that talking about her terror at that time had helped.

"Often these feelings come a day or so before a break in our work," she said. "They are here now in this last session. My head aches. I'm dizzy. My throat hurts." I said that part of that terror was probably a "baby part" of herself who fears she can't survive without me: a wrenching sense of physical separation. Doris replied, "It's so hard. When the session ends today, and I walk outside the door and it closes, it will be like an umbilical cord being cut. Will I live or die?"

From the dizziness she mentioned, I had a sense that she feared falling. I asked about this and she answered with some relief. "Yes. Once outside, I won't be held. The terror I feel will just spill out, or maybe I will fall into nothingness." I wondered aloud if, when I went away, Doris felt she was no longer in my thoughts, that I became totally detached, turned my back, and let her "fall." She nodded and said, "No one sees what's happening to me." For a moment she seemed satisfied. Then she said the headache was coming back, that she felt intense pressure on her head, as if she were stuck; that she wanted to "get out" but didn't know how, that she wanted someone to pull her out. "I'm sure I was delivered with forceps," she commented. "Do you remember the dream I had before Thanksgiving? Of a maze I couldn't get into or out of? I wonder if these feelings are why it's hard for me to leave relationships, even after I've outgrown them, and why leaving sets off all these feelings." She said that she hated how this memory always came back, how it affected her life, how strongly she felt it today, all the terror. Then, she added, "But I think it's there in less intense ways a lot of the time."

I asked her what she meant, and she described the terror of leaving a current relationship, saying, "I wish you could pull me out of my relationship with Fred, like an obstetrician would pull a baby from the womb. I don't feel like I can get out of the birth canal. I'm stuck. Nobody knows. Mom was unconscious. She couldn't help me out. She was paralyzed and I was paralyzed. I often look at you before the break to see if you are paralyzed. I worry that my feelings will overwhelm and paralyze you. It scares me when you don't talk. I'm checking you out to see what's happening, to see if you're still functioning." Then Doris asked, "Do you think I want you to be paralyzed and not go away, or not to have any fun while you're away?" I asked what she was thinking, and she answered, "It's okay for you to have a good time, even if I feel jealous and left out. But when you're quiet and I fear you're paralyzed, it makes me feel hopeless. It's really the worst." I said, "I wonder if, in addition to this session, the break itself brings up that paralyzed-mom feeling. During the break, you experience me as paralyzed, anesthetized, unaware of you and what you're experiencing."

"Yes," Doris said. "That's possible. I hate it when you go away. It feels so cold, the winter break especially." As the hour ended Doris looked more relaxed. She said, "I hate having these feelings, but you didn't get paralyzed. You did hear me." As she left, she said she didn't know what the break held in store for her but that she hoped it would be good for me. Where there had been terror, there was now some understanding and gratitude. When she returned from the break, she commented on how bright the morning light had been as she walked outside—how filled with life the street outside my consulting room and the world itself had seemed.

Doris's material, like Judy's, gives us much to discuss. Doris had been in treatment for 5 years at the time of this session. By that time, the consulting room and the analysis itself represented a softer world where many feelings could be safely expressed and received. While the world outside the consulting room and away from the analyst's body—both the inside and outside— was experienced as colder, harder, and rejecting. At the same time, a conscious, listening and *under*-standing mother-analyst seemed to be felt as a firm and "hard" object *in the positive sense,* while the unconscious, paralyzed, in-firm, silent mother was experienced as "soft" and unreliable. Although there was still more work to be done with this patient on integrating all aspects of "hard" and "soft"—on developing the capacity to hold certain opposites— much progress had been made.

Here, I believe the emergence of a difficult physical and psychological birth and the catastrophic anxiety that accompanied it—and, in the analysis, accompanies its reemergence—was being faced. Although at times Doris wished such feelings would just disappear from her psyche, both she and I knew this was not realistic. The issue was integration, not evacuation, building the mental muscle—or in Bion's terms, "alpha function"—to bear such feelings. There was a growing understanding that this was an interpersonal process and that the analyst's function as a firm yet receptive "container" was crucial. Doris repeatedly made the point that she needed me to be alive and present, not anesthetized, so that I could assist her in bearing her terror. Oedipal jealousies may have existed as well, but the deeper layers resolved around her primitive terrors of annihilation and nonexistence.

Doris's hour had begun with physical symptoms (headaches and dizziness) and the subjective sense of a building pressure and an impending catastrophe. Bion (1966), Paul (1981), and Winnicott (1949) have each emphasized this experience of growing pressure in patients with birth anxiety. Doris's sore throat may have been an analog of an imprinted behavioral memory related to the umbilical cord around the neck, and the infant's experience of the umbilical cord as the first object. The separation from the umbilical cord and the fear of death could be linked, suggesting perhaps a near-death in-utero experience. In Doris's case, I had data from previous sessions suggesting this association.

Paul (1981) and Winnicott (1949) both emphasize the terror and intense—almost unendurable—pain of a near-death in-utero experience. Bion (1976) and Bettelheim (1983) have also commented on the long-term effects of this kind of trauma. The fear of falling in this session may be related to an early terror also mentioned by Winnicott (1949). The baby—or the adult patient in analysis—will become unconscious, go mindless, or blank out in order to avoid this original terror. Dizziness and a fear of fainting may then result.

Tustin (1981) refers to the sense of "spilling out" described by my patient, when the mother is not a strong-enough container. This is often the case when the mother has been anesthetized during delivery, as Doris's mother was. The anesthetized mother is experienced as unavailable, oblivious, not able to help with the pain of birth. Doris's mother was also unavailable to hold or soothe her baby after birth, further complicating the problem of integrating the painful transition from the womb to the outside world.

In Doris's case, as in Judy's material, there are feelings of claustrophobia—of being unable to get out of the womb—as well as feelings of agoraphobia—terrors of falling, feeling lost in space, with no anchor or walls to serve as boundaries. These two sets of feelings are often found in patients who have had difficult physical or psychological births and incapacitated or unavailable mothers. Forceps delivery, mentioned by Doris here, can result in feelings of pressure, chronic headaches, a belief in one's helplessness, and a desire to be rescued. The after-birth period, as portrayed in this hour with an "anesthetized mother," is often experienced as cold and hard. The mother is unconscious and the baby, taken to an impersonal nursery, is deprived of any skin contact, and bottlefed. It may also be experienced as "soft" in the negative sense, the mother being experienced as insufficiently supportive, as I was experienced at times in my silences. How is it possible to feel welcomed after birth under such conditions?

The feeling of fear associated with moving from inside the consulting room to outside, mentioned at the end of Doris's hour, has been written about in Paul's work (1981), as noted earlier, as well as in the work of Maizels. Maizels (1985) notes the movement from darkness to light when patients relate birth experiences. He suggests that there is an ongoing conflict in life between those parts of the personality that strive to stay in the womb—in the darkness of the unconscious—and those parts that strive for change, to move forward into the light. This conflict is very present in both Doris's and Judy's material.

Conclusion

In writing about mismanaged birth and psychological catastrophe, I often use the phrase "physical or psychological birth" to encompass both the complex possibilities inherent in birth: The physical process of birth affects the psychological birth process, and the psychological process of either mother, father, or fetus may affect the physical birth. I wonder if the term "birth complex" (Sullivan 1996) might be helpful in capturing this tangle of variables that surrounds this area of psyche common to us all, at the same time "archetypal" yet deeply personal and individual.

Jung described a complex as "a collection of images and ideas clustered round a core derived from one or more archetypes and characterized by a common emotional tone" (Samuels 1986, p. 34). In the case of the "birth complex" the common emotional tone is—when it emerges in analysis— often one of catastrophic anxiety. Complexes are often marked by affect, whether the patient is conscious of it or not. The catastrophic anxiety, embedded in the birth complex, may be somatocized and communicated to the analyst via projective identification.

Tustin's paper, "Psychological Birth and Psychological Catastrophe," (1981) helps us delineate and describe our individual birth complexes. It is my experience that this complex is imprinted in the psyche and deeply affects us at times of life transitions. If one has had a difficult beginning, making this "catastrophe" conscious can affect one's ability to risk change and continue to grow and develop. Tustin makes it clear that the integration of hard and soft is necessary to provide the resilience and faith required to persevere and expand throughout the cycle of life.

References

Bettleheim, B. (1983). Afterword. In *The Words to Say It*, ed. M. Cardinal. Cambridge, MA: Van Vector & Goodheart.

Bion, W. R. (1966). Catastrophic change. *Bulletin of the British Psycho-Analytic Socie y* 5:18–27.

———— (1976). On a quotation from Freud. In *Clinical Seminars and Four Papers*, ed. F. Bion. Abingdon: Fleetwood Press, 1987.

Jung, C. G. (1963). Mysterium coniunctionis: an inquiry into the separation and synthesis of psychic opposites in alchemy. In *Collected Works* 14:89–257. New York: Bollingen Foundation.

Maizels, N. (1985). Self-envy, the womb, and the nature of goodness. *International Journal of Psycho-Analysis* 66:187–194.

Paul, M. (1981). A Mental Atlas of the Process of Psychological Birth. In *Do I Dare Disturb the Universe?* ed. J. Grotstein, pp. 552–570. London: Karnac Books.

Samuels, A. (1986). *A Critical Dictionary of Jungian Analysis*. New York: Routledge and Kegan Paul.

Sullivan, Mark. (1996). Personal communication.

Tustin, F. (1981). Psychological Birth and Psychological Catastrophe. In *Do I Dare Disturb the Universe?* ed., J. Grotstein, pp. 181–196. London: Karnac Books.

———— (1986). *Autistic Barriers in Neurotic Patients*. London: Karnac.

Winnicott, D.W. (1949). Mind and its relation to the psyche-soma. In *Collected Papers: Through Pediatrics to Psycho-Analysis,* pp. 243–254. New York: Basic Books, 1958.

7

Autism as a Defense Against Hopelessness

Isca Wittenberg

People may freeze into paralysis—depressive psychosis, autism, and catatonia are instances of this—as if by stopping themselves, they can stop unchanging time, which has now become the dreadful foe of hope.

Harold Boris, *Envy*

It is many years ago now since I had a little autistic child called John in psychoanalytic treatment, but the experience was so immensely powerful that it left a permanent impact on me. Not only did I continue to worry about this helpless little boy who came to see me when he was 3, but my mental states—experienced during and after the sessions—often come vividly to my mind.

John

John's wild, triumphant twirling around me with the plant he had pulled out of the garden, his interminable bouncing on the couch, the banging of his head against the table without apparent physical pain, his excitement when endlessly letting the water pour out of the tap and run over his hands, raised many questions of technique as well as puzzlement as to what meaning to attach to all these activities. However, it was the despair I felt at not being able to reach him, my inability to break into his ceaseless abandonment to intense manic excitement that I found overwhelming. I would long desperately for his repetitive actions to stop for just a moment, to arrest the bombardment of my senses, and allow me a space for reflection.

When I could no longer bear it, I felt compelled to switch off thinking and feeling or, alternatively, to let my thoughts turn away to matters unconnected with John. Yet when my thoughts strayed from him, his behavior became still more frenetic and it was clear that, far from being out of contact, John was acutely aware of me and at once noticed my absentmindedness. It was indeed frightening to realize how almost uncannily he sensed my physical and mental states. If I had a cold, was feeling tired, depressed, upset, or preoccupied, John's jumping up and down reached fever pitch.

I learned over time that it was important to keep talking, even if it was no more than commenting on what he was doing or wondering aloud how this John-baby was feeling and voicing my wish to understand. It was my attention, my voice—and the interested concern and hope these conveyed—which I believe got through to him, even if he did not understand much of what I said. Singing the words had an especially calming effect on him. On the other hand, the sound of a passing airplane, or the sight of birds flying past, made John immediately stop whatever activity he was engaged in; he would run to the window, get up on the windowsill, hold on desperately to my earlobe, and gaze at the sky, looking quite forlorn. Looking through the windowpane seemed to be equated with looking right into my inside and seeing a daddy or inside babies. These rivals, it seemed, were felt to have taken over the whole of the internal space of this mommy-me.

We came to understand this as evidence of John's experiencing me as a transparent object without firm boundaries to protect it from intrusion. This mommy was felt to be physically and mentally either totally occupied by him or, alternatively, with someone else. In the latter instance, John felt that no space was left for him. I could easily imagine that a young baby could experience a depressed mother, withdrawing her attention from him and preoccupied with her inner world, as having turned to inside babies or an absent daddy. This might cause the baby to feel not only excluded but enormously jealous. I also had learned from infant observation that, when mothers are turning to their inner world in this kind of way, they sometimes are quite oblivious to the baby pushing into their chest, nostrils, and ears. Might this contribute to the child's perception of an easily penetrable object?

When I first met John, I thought what a strong, healthy, attractive little boy he was. Yet he seemed quite lost and helpless as he walked along, held between mother's and the *au-pair* girl's hands. Without looking at me, he literally let himself be handed over to me. There was, at the same time, a great intensity and passion in the way he pushed himself into my lap the moment I sat down in my chair in the consulting room. The combination of his little-boy-lost quality and his loving forcefulness evoked in me a wish to protect him.

In addition, John showed, from quite early on, that he possessed a sense of beauty: He would stop halfway up the stairs to look deeply into the stained glass windows, lovingly exclaiming "roses, roses." He was so absorbed and fascinated by them that it was only when I pulled him by the hand that he could be parted from them. Apart from "roses," his vocabulary consisted of "moose"—said in a gruff voice—which meant milk, "airplane," "gone" and "broken." Later on, "lady"—which was what he called me—and "laby," which I took to mean lady with baby, and a few other words were added to his vocabulary. The range of his play was equally limited and immensely repetitive, needing very careful observation in order to detect the slightest variations.

Although I have described aspects of John's analysis in detail elsewhere, in this paper I want to concentrate particularly on my countertransference feelings. These I see as holding the most important clues to his fundamental problem. I took these feelings evoked in me to be a reflection of the anxieties that were intolerable to him and hence were being projected into me. They caused me almost intolerable pain, so much so that I needed prolonged recovery time after each session. Yet the resonance they found within me left me feeling deeply moved. This resonance made me care very deeply for this child and helped me not to give up trying, in spite of all the agony and despair. The agony was related to the bombardment of my senses, primarily of my eyes, as he bounced up and down continuously or twirled a plant around close to my face. It made me wonder whether this was what he had experienced as a newborn baby: Could having lights impinge on him or having shapes flickering in front of his eyes been that painful and meaningless?

John had spent two days in an incubator. Was this experience being communicated by making me go through a similar one? On the other hand, his fascination and total absorption in the deep-colored roses and the in-touchness with constantly flowing water made me think that he must have had a deep attachment and appreciation of a beautiful, life-giving nipple and breast.

I learned from John's parents that he could not be parted from his baby bottle until the age of 4. He carried it with him everywhere and had refused to eat anything but mashed food. However, such attachment left no space for contact with another person. It left me feeling useless, excluded, unable to find a foothold in his mind. Was he showing me how intolerable it was not to get through to the other person, that the only safeguard was to hold onto an inanimate object, some thing that was under his control? Yet sometimes I could reach John by going back to a point in the session which had happened just before he had felt especially cut off. There were times when, fearing he had exceeded my tolerance, he would collapse on the floor and cry inconsolably. Such crying also occurred at home at the beginning of my holidays. What was the nature of the tragedy that this expressed, which at such times broke through his powerful defenses?

Over time, I was convinced that the hopelessness, which I so often experienced in John's presence, was indeed the primary intolerable feeling that he was trying to keep at bay. Long after he had withdrawn from treatment, it was John's grief and despair, on a primitive level—soma-psychotic, to use Bion's phrase—that I resonated with and that continued to interest me. The experience with John made me more sensitive to such states in ordinary children and adults that I came across, as well as in myself. I shall later bring some material from infant observation and extracts from the analysis of an adult to highlight this. However I want first to show the theoretical framework which helped me to understand John.

I was familiar with Esther Bick's work: her understanding of the survival mechanisms used by infants to hold themselves together when not held physically or emotionally by the parents. She postulated (Bick 1968) that the newborn baby is in a state of unintegration and experiences a terror of falling and spilling out. It is mother's holding arms and lap, the nipple in the mouth, as well as mother's attention that pull the different parts of the infant together and provide a boundary, a psychic skin. When this is temporarily unavailable, babies tend to resort to motor activity, a kind of muscular holding of the self to keep themselves from falling apart. If this becomes a more permanent feature, they develop a tough "second skin"—rather than a psychic skin—as a protective barrier against anxiety.

Joan Symington (1985), in her paper on omnipotence, has spelled out Bick's ideas clearly and has shown how turning to omnipotent self-sufficiency, which we encounter so frequently in child and adult patients, is often used to avoid feelings of helplessness connected with dependence on others. Such ideas seemed very helpful in trying to understand John's behavior.

I was further helped by Donald Meltzer's (1975) understanding of the autistic state as an arrest in development arising from a highly sensitive infant's dismantling of his mental apparatus when mother's attentive and

sensuous contact with the baby becomes unavailable. Bick (1968) pointed out
how the mother's containment leads to the notion of space, both within the
mother and, through introjection, within the baby. Meltzer (1975) showed us
how the autistic child's breaking into the maternal space, through the skin
barrier so to speak, results in a paper-thin, two-dimensional object. Hence the
child can find no safe space within his object, no hiding place from rivals.
Furthermore, Meltzer's working group for child psychotherapists, which I
joined while I was treating John, kept thinking alive and helped me to hold
onto hope. This was essential to my continuing work with John.

Frances Tustin was not a part of this group, but at the same time was
independently developing her groundbreaking ideas on autism (1972). When
I later came to read her moving account of the analytic work with *her* little
patient John, I could see many similarities between him and my John. I was
deeply impressed by Frances's capacity to be in touch with and to verbalize
primitive feelings. The early loss of the experience of closeness to a good
maternal object—the disappointment and grief reactions of these children—
became part of my understanding. Never had the experience of being in the
presence of an autistic child been more poignantly described; I was full of
admiration for Tustin's ability to break through the autistic barrier, her ability
to put a stop to such mindless activity by interpreting simply and meaning-
fully to these children.

Over the years, through infant observation and working with patients, I
have developed some further ideas about autistic defenses and the underlying
anxieties, which I now wish to put forward.[1] While I remain moved by all that
has been written about autistic behavior as a reaction to loss and disappointment in early infancy, I am no longer convinced, as Winnicott and Tustin
were, that this occurred at a stage when the baby was not yet able to experience
the breast of the mother as a separate object.

These authors believed that a too-sudden separation or loss of the breast
was experienced by the baby as the loss of a part of its own body: that tongue
and nipple, mouth and breast were—at this stage of development—felt to be
at-one, fused and confused. Thus, mother's withdrawal was not only felt by
the infant to leave an emptiness but was experienced as if part of the self was
missing. I think that this is in line with Winnicott's belief that "good-enough"
mothering in the early days of the baby's life includes her being available just

---

1. I am concerned with the aetiology and meaning of the underlying depressive
anxieties of one group of patients who manifest autistic states of mind.

as the baby becomes aware of his needs and, in this way, fitting in with the infant's omnipotent phantasy of the breast being part of his body.[2]

My thinking is more influenced by Wilfred Bion's work; and here I am referring specifically to his hypothesis that the infant is born with a preconception of an object that satisfies its own incomplete nature. He defines preconception as a state of expectation, a type of vague *a priori* knowledge to which no experience has as yet given validity. Bion does not state whether this preconception is due to genetic inheritance, or has its origin in the prenatal experience of feeling held and nourished. I suspect that he took it to be the former, for the experience in the womb would more nearly correspond to what he called the realization of a preconception.

When a preconception meets up with a realization, this leads to its becoming a conception: in other words, as I understand it, once the preconceived idea is confirmed by an experience, the two are married and form the basis for further preconceptions, hypotheses in phantasy, and mental constructs. A conception becomes a concept when the infant finds certain elements constantly conjoined. For instance, the preconception of a mother who satisfies his needs, becomes one who is warm, safe, removes or relieves pain, or— through her containment—makes pain more tolerable. All these may eventually be aspects of the concept "mother."

It is the mother's response to the infant's sensual perception and feelings that gives meaning to his experiences, confirming or negating his preconception. This applies to his gratifying as well as to his painful experiences. It would seem to me that the notion of a preconception implies that there exists, in whatever primitive a form, a phantasy of a separate object from birth, if not earlier. This is in line with Klein's concept of mental activity—in the form of unconscious phantasy—as being linked to and concomitant with sensuous experience from the beginning of life.

Nowadays, we are inclined to be curious also about the baby's experiences within the womb and how these shape his expectations. Piontelli's (1985, 1992) followup studies of infants she had observed in utero with the help of ultrasound have demonstrated just how early distinctive character traits develop. I have no experience or strong belief in prebirth experiences being recalled

---

2. In her later writing, Tustin speaks of the baby's "psychological birth," which comes about through Mother's emotional containment. Yet, even this notion, although stressing the infant's mental needs, implies that in earliest infancy there is no perception of Mother as in any way a separate object.

under hypnosis; but it certainly makes this a more plausible possibility if we hypothesize that mental activity begins much earlier than has been assumed hitherto. If primitive mental life already encompasses a preconception of a life-sustaining object, then the first and most profound disappointment and loss is the disconnectedness from this object, which the infant encounters at birth.

Mrs. Bick showed the need for a mother to hold the baby and the survival strategies babies adopt to deal with the breaks in the continuity of being physically and emotionally held by the mother. Bion showed us the need for the mother to take in the infant's distress and, through her mental digestion, clarify the nature of the emotional pain and make it more bearable. This enables the infant to gradually introject a mind capable of containing and thinking about emotional experiences.

What then is the particular anxiety situation that the autistic child is unable to contain and think about and instead attempts to deal with by ceaseless activity? Are we dealing with an intolerance to any frustration or is there a specific emotional pain that cannot be borne? Were these babies hypersensitive and hence especially vulnerable to any discontinuity of attention? Has there been insufficient containment of the baby's distress? Has the infant been disappointed in his preconception of a satisfying object? All these seem possible hypotheses regarding the aetiology of autism, which could also be applied to any number of my patients to a greater or lesser degree.

I asked myself: was there something distinctive about the autistic experience? The only evidence I was left with was my feeling in the countertransference: being deeply moved and nearly overcome by despair. Yet at the same time, I was determined to maintain a lifeline of hope, since the only alternative was simply to give up. Watching the children, it struck me that they were also, in their own way, desperately holding on to life, whether through their own motility or by clinging on to objects that provide nonstop sensuous in-touchness. They were not giving up, not withdrawing into an apathetic state. In fact, their determination not to let go of their way of relating to inanimate objects was that which made it so hard to get into contact with them.

Apart from the feelings evoked in me, the words "gone" and "broken," so frequently used by John and other autistic children, kept reverberating in my mind. Was it the connection to mother that was gone when her attention was unavailable? One might think of this connection as having been broken. However, "broken" also suggested a different line of thought, a damaged object, a mother who was gone *because* she was broken. Was she felt to be broken by the child's demands or his biting? These children were not especially destructive. On the contrary, there was a gentleness in John's and other autistic children's contact with people; was this to protect them from damage? So was it rather that the child was despairing because a depressed mother was felt not to be able to contain worry and depression? This led me to think that John, and others like him, might have sensed very early on that Mother was unable to contain *her own* depressive anxiety about damage and was certainly not able to take the infant's depression on board.

Seen in this light, John's heightened awareness of my physical and mental state could be thought of as a way of constantly checking whether I was intact or broken. Maybe the preconception of a life-hope-breast had not, or not consistently enough, been matched to a realization. Did this mean that the manic excitement was being used as a survival kit in the face of hopelessness about a broken, dying object? Did the turning away from mother and other people arise from a fear that they were too easily breakable and hence that it was safer to hold on to hard, less easily destroyed objects? Maybe these objects also provided a barrier against being flooded by Mother's depression, her internal damage, her fear of death?

What I am putting forward is the possibility that these highly sensitive and intelligent babies, born with a great lust for life and sense of beauty, are overwhelmed by depressive anxiety. In addition, they may attribute their mothers' emotional disturbance to themselves. This may make them wish to protect her, but it also makes them very vulnerable to feeling accused and rejected when her attention is given to others. It would seem to me that such infants cease to trust mother to be the source of hope, that it is this preconception of a life-hope-mother, so essential for survival, which has met with disappointment. This trust may then have been transferred on to a hard object, or self-sufficiency or nonstop activity. All these are means of escape from the terror of hopelessness and the fear of dying.

These ideas had begun to float into my mind when I wrote about John many years ago (Wittenberg 1975), but they only took on a more definite shape when they found an echo in the observation of some infants and in my work with some adult patients. These latter came for analysis for a variety of reasons and, like those Sydney Klein (1980) describes in his paper on autistic phenomena in neurotic patients, were cooperative and appreciative of the analytic work but, at some deep level, lacking in trust. The difficulty arose not so much from the projection of destructiveness but rather from a profound fear. I was felt to be unwilling or not able to tolerate their profound distress. This went along with a dread that, if they were to invest hope in my under-

standing, it was bound eventually to result in disappointment. Instead it was
I who repeatedly felt disappointed when the hope and trust that seemed to
have been established kept being lost from one session to another. It was I who
felt despair when the patients' communications became intellectual and emotionally shallow, frustrated at not being allowed to get in touch with the needy
infantile parts that were so transparently present.

I will here present some excerpts from the analytic work with a young
woman, aged 23, who helped me to understand the nature of the hopelessness
and some of the autistic defenses that might be employed to escape from it.

Stella

Stella was successful and, on the whole, satisfied with work and marriage, but
experienced her emotional life as somewhat superficial. What happened right
at the start of her analysis took both of us by surprise. Far from relating
superficially, she was overwhelmed by misery and cried in session after
session. During weekend breaks, she felt that I was leaving her to die and she
experienced chest pains of such severity that she found it hard to breathe. She
was alarmed by her reactions and reported that she had never felt as bad as this
before.

She had always coped well and had been the one who supported others. She
was said to have been an easy baby who could be put out in the sunshine for
hours on end. She did not cry much and could be passed from one person to
another without protesting. I can well believe this for even now she was
undemanding and uncomplaining, pleasant and cheerful. Yet her reaction to
beginning analysis told a very different story. It revealed some deep pain and
misery as well as a fear of being left to die. It would seem that early in
babyhood she had managed to cut herself off from such catastrophic anxiety,
but at the price of losing the in-touchness with deep feelings. Now that she
had found someone who paid attention to the needy, distressed baby-self, it all
burst forth, and she felt taken over by fear and grief, which she had not known
to be a part of herself.

She told me that she did not want to cry because she was afraid that the
tears would never stop, that everything would spill out and she would just
dissolve. I understood this to mean that she was afraid that there was no
mommy who could absorb her tears and misery, no me to hold this baby
together. I attributed her chest pains to an intense tightening of her muscula-
ture, used to hold herself together in my absence. I felt all the more convinced

of this when I found that sometimes I could hardly get out of my chair after the session because of the painful tightness in my chest. I thought that this arose from my feeling that I needed to hold on to this baby tightly to prevent it from falling into an abyss. Or was my somatic symptom due to an identification with this baby-Stella?

Quite early on in her analysis, Stella brought a dream that was so painful that it made her cry in the retelling. It took place in the morning room, adjoining the kitchen. She would often play there when she was little. In the dream,

> She was looking at a little bird sitting on its perch. She was terribly afraid that it hadn't the strength to hold on; she thought it was about to die and fall off at any moment. She pointed this out to her mother but her reaction— something that mother said and her continuing smile—convinced Stella that she was being told that nothing could be done about it.
>
> Stella left the room, unable to bear watching the little bird die. She remembered clearly shutting the door firmly behind her, feeling its hardness against her back as if it was holding her upright. She was facing the hallway and felt very alone, but somehow that was better than having to watch the death of the bird. She was determined never to return to that room.

The dream clearly shows Stella's concern with death. We might think that she was telling me that she was afraid that I, like the mother in her dream, would manically deny her vulnerability and terror, not pick up and try to contain her fear and grief. Hence she may have felt left on her own with such emotional pain, and that was unbearable. Or is this a screen memory that she has brought to tell me that she feels hopeless because there is no mother in her internal world who can bear to take the fear of death on board? If mother ignores it, makes it a smiling affair, does not acknowledge the seriousness, then it is better to close the door, separate oneself from the experience, never ever to risk going through this again, a kind of determination that gives the illusion of strength.

I believe that Stella's terror was not only for her own safety but, sensing within mother an undigested death constellation, an inability to bear depression. This conveys that "nothing can be done about it," that it is too awful, too hopeless to pick up or hold it in one's mind. The comfort of the hard door supporting Stella's back reminds us of the hard objects which autistic children tend to hold onto to give them backbone. We learn also from the dream about these children's determination not to have the door to the morning/mourning room of depressive pain and fear of dying—within themselves or their objects—opened ever again.

Indeed, Stella shut the door leading to emotional pain firmly during the first analytic holiday. On her return, she was very talkative, reporting all sorts of daily concerns. While it was possible to understand and interpret some of these, they did not evoke much emotional response in me. I was reminded of babies who keep their tongues moving in and out of their mouths when their mothers leave the room. While Stella appeared to be happier and claimed to feel a lot better, I was dissatisfied, depressed at the superficiality of the conversation, which felt like cutting herself off from any depth of feeling in order to escape from pain. The anxieties, so evident in the first analytic term, had completely disappeared.

I considered that my absence, experienced as being left alone with the fears of her death and mine, had made her despair and abandon hope of such anxieties ever being understood and contained. Did my taking a holiday mean that I wanted to escape from such anxieties, that they were too much for me? It was noticeable that her alertness to the state of her surroundings was even more acute than before the holiday. A kind of scanning took place at the start of every session. The freshness of the flowers in the consulting room was always carefully checked: Had they been well tended, watered? Were the little flowers "thrown away prematurely?" Was there enough support for a tall plant or would its stem break? She was equally sensitive to the air in the consulting room: Was it fresh or left stale by the patient I saw before her?

The noise of the heater was registered. It could be felt as intrusive but was more often felt as comforting and something to be absorbed into. I felt that I was dealing with a baby who was quite uncertain that mother had a space for her, doubtful of her readiness to receive her, provide a good lap and fresh milk. It reminded me of John's sensitivity to the state I was in. On the one hand, there was the question of whether there was an available physical and mental space within the maternal object. But in addition, the quality—the freshness and goodness of what mother contained—was clearly crucial. It seemed that it was not a bad object as such that was feared, but a breast-mind that contained some dangerous stuff. The picture that emerged was of a mother who might be unable to deal with her worries, her depression, her fear of death or unable to keep these in a separate department of her mind and body. Hence the baby feared to be infected by contact with such dangerous stuff, or worse still, be used as a repository for it.

In spite of my efforts to put such and other anxieties into words, it took years for Stella to trust me enough to bring her neediness into the transference in a more direct way. Then her deep anxieties gradually began to surface in dreams. In addition, there was a recurring preoccupation with a girl whose kidnapper had left her suspended on a narrow ledge overhanging a deep hole. Stella felt it was much better to give up and die rather than to feel terrified, suspended between life and death. I interpreted that she had given up hope of my coming to rescue this terrified little girl, that I had abandoned her to the fear of dying.

Two other often-repeated themes now came to the fore. One was the doubt whether I would understand if she voiced what was deeply troubling her. The other was the oft-repeated contention that she supposed she was "making a fuss about nothing." Eventually, I was struck by the thought that this phrase needed to be taken literally, that she was complaining about there being nothing, a no-mother, or one unavailable to the baby's distress. I found myself giving constant attention to her fear that I would not see her distress or would not see it quickly enough. I verbalized that she was afraid that she would fall into an abyss of hopelessness if she gave up her self-control and I was not immediately available to hold the frightened Stella. I spoke about her being so afraid to be disappointed that she did not dare to grasp and hold on to the lifeline that I, as a hope-mother, was throwing out to her. Her determination to manage on her own, which she had after all done with considerable success for most of her life, seemed insurmountable. Eventually, she was able to put her deep anxiety into words: "If I said something and you failed to understand it, that would be too terrible. It's a risk I cannot, will not take!"

A few weeks later, she returned from a weekend bringing the following dream:

> There was a baby sitting outside a big building. The building was boarded up. The baby was crying but the mother did not notice this. The baby felt angry with her mother for not registering the distress but the anger did not last for more than a moment. She told herself that she must have been mistaken, that the baby was not really crying, did not really feel awful after all.

I interpreted that when it came to the weekend, she experienced me as putting up a wall, that I was unaware of her great pain, not wishing to know about it, being bored by it, or incapable of understanding how she felt or unable to tolerate the pain. When there was no mother who paid attention to the crying baby, she felt her distress to be unbearable, uncontainable and then said to

herself that her perception was wrong, there was no crying baby, there was
nothing to be upset about.

Stella started to cry. She stopped herself and said that she had a great pain
in her ribcage: There were endless tears pressing on her. The grief—the deep
feelings of loss and being lost and the yearning to be held in understanding—
could be allowed to emerge once more. Yet such trust could only be reached
temporarily. The fear of closeness, and the attraction to the voice that told her
it was preferable to cope on her own, remained.

The dream I have just related shows that when the baby's distress is not
acknowledged and contained by its mother, this leaves the baby with what
Bion called a "nameless dread": an unnamed, unacknowledged, unbounded,
hence dreaded, quantum of anxiety. I think that this kind of nonacceptance or
denial on the part of the mother may result in the baby losing hope of ever
finding the realization of its preconception of a life-hope-sustaining maternal
object being realized. This maternal object is felt to be lacking strength and
tolerance in the face of pain, and thus leaves the child feeling hopeless. The
autistic solution is the denial of pain, toughness, and the dismantling of an
apparatus capable of thinking about pain, becoming mindless. Emotional
pain which cannot be borne by the baby alone is made into "nothing," wiped
out.

I would like to link the above dream to the earlier one I quoted in which the
mother ignored the impending death of the little bird. Was it the baby's fear of
death, or was the mother felt to be unresponsive to such anxiety because she
herself was unable to deal with a dying object, either in the external or her
internal world? In the dream she made it a smiling matter and conveyed that
she could do nothing about it: She did not pick up the bird, did not acknowledge its suffering nor the child's upset about it. It is the bypassing of the mental
anguish, and the child's awareness of a mother's incapacity in the face of such
pain, which leads to the loss of hope, to despair.

I was throughout struck by Stella's concern with whether I was in a good
enough state to receive her but also her quite inordinate protectiveness. I was
struck by her constant anxiety that she might be early, that she might have
mistaken the time or the dates of my holidays, that she might be intruding and
disturbing me. In fact, she never made a mistake. So why did she doubt her
perception and knowledge? When I made a mistake, this could not be
acknowledged by her, it had to be her mistake. This puzzled and worried me
for years.

Only with hindsight did I understand that it was preferable to think herself
to be in the wrong rather than entertain the idea that I was at fault. For that

would have implied that my mind was not intact, was broken. Yet I felt it to be essential to point out to her when she was right and I was wrong. It seemed to me that, as a baby, she did not get such confirmation of her perceptions and this had left her unsure about her own capacities. Moreover, by acknowledging my own mistakes, I believe I was able to bring hope of a mother capable of facing the truth, however painful, and such evidence of my strength brought Stella relief. It is their internal tragedy and their worry about others that makes these patients so appealing and lovable.

I have been speaking throughout about the infantile aspects of the patient because I believe that autistic defenses arise in the first year of life. This may be deduced from the analysis of children and adults but can actually be directly observed when we study infants. At the Tavistock Clinic, regular observation of an infant within his own home is undertaken by all those training to become child-psychotherapists. It has been painful to witness autistic behavior developing in a few of the babies observed. I shall describe an observation of one such baby.

Sylvia

Since the age of 4 months, Sylvia had been content to wake up and play with the toys hanging over her cot for hours on end. When Mother entered the room, Sylvia appeared to take no notice of her. The parents had been married for ten years and then, as mother put it: "We decided after all to have a baby, although we were very worried how this would affect our marriage, which had been such a close one. I have always worked alongside my husband and this has suited me."

The observer, who first met this mother soon after the baby's birth, reported that mother always looked depressed, very quiet and lifeless. She never spoke about the pregnancy or the birth nor did she ever explain why she had decided to bottlefeed the baby. Questions about such matters seemed unwelcome and the observer did not wish to intrude by being inquisitive. While feeding the baby with the bottle, the mother sat absolutely still, closely watching the baby but not saying a word. It looked as if it needed a great deal of effort as well as concentration.

Here is an observation when the baby was 8-months old. Sylvia was sitting in her cot, swinging a rattle in front of her face. Mother commented on how pleased the baby seemed to be to see the observer. She said: "You do nothing and all the same the baby looks and smiles at you. She does not do this for me."

Indeed the baby responded to the observer's "hello" by looking up at her, smiling. Then she went on playing with her toy but from time to time smiled at the observer.

Mother reported that the baby had been sleeping for much of the morning (that she slept so much had been a worry) and only woke up a short time before. Mother gently lifted the baby out of the cot and carried her to the sitting room. She sat her up against a wall, surrounding her with lots of cushions and placed a heap of toys in front of her. Having been seated, Sylvia moved her head forwards and backwards rhythmically; she banged on the toys with both hands and at the same time emitted a strange, long-drawn-out high sound. (The observer remembered that the baby had a toy chicken that made a similar noise.)

Mother went to attend to something in the kitchen. Sylvia watched her leave, stopped for a moment, then took a deep breath in and exhaled deeply. She turned her face towards a mirror that stood to her left, saw her own reflection, and grinned. Suddenly, she discovered the observer's reflection in the mirror. She looked for a long moment, smiled briefly, but appeared confused and shook her head. She looked briefly at the observer but quickly turned back to the mirror and moved her body so that she could not see the observer in the mirror. Her face relaxed and she looked at her toys, again breathing out forcefully. She pushed her hand into the middle of the heap of toys and got hold of a plastic beaker, which she put against her lower lip and used to make loud noises. She now held it tightly with both hands and sucked it. Then she held it a little away from herself and studied it intently, turning it round and round. She lost it, found it again and immediately put it back into her mouth, biting the edge of it, letting it go, biting it some more.

Suddenly, as she blew into the beaker, she made a deep, dark sound. She pulled it away from her mouth; the mouth stayed open and she emitted the same high, long sound as she had done earlier. The beaker dropped onto her lap and rolled onto the floor. Sylvia's eyes turned to a big, furry dog. She grabbed hold of it and poked her fingers into its fur. She laughed and moved her head and upper body to and fro excitedly for some minutes. Mother laughed and commented that the baby was happy. Sylvia saw herself in the mirror and stretched her hands towards her reflection as if to get hold of it. When the sound of the electric mixer mother was using intruded, baby looked tense and sat very still; her breathing was now fast and shallow.

When the noise of the mixer stopped, the baby turned to the toy dog. Mother entered, bringing Sylvia's lunch. She carried the baby to the sofa and placed her on her knee. Sylvia looked towards the bowl of food and kicked her legs, and her whole body began to shake with excitement. She did not look at her mother but fixed her eyes on the spoon and tried to get hold of it. At first, Mother said, "You can't have it." However, she soon gave in, let the baby hold the spoon and fed her with a fork. Sylvia inserted the spoon into her mouth and kept it there throughout the meal. Later, when mother took it away in order to wipe the baby's mouth and chin, Sylvia arched her back and started to scream. She calmed down only when Mother allowed her to have the spoon again; it was quickly put back into her mouth. When Mother stopped feeding her, Sylvia pulled the spoon out of her mouth, examined it, again emitted a high pitched sound, and then laughed continuously. Mother also started laughing loudly.

Here is a baby who, although initially able to respond to the observer's friendly and happy overture, seems to prefer her own company. She turns to her own reflection in the mirror, deliberately excluding the observer. She neither looks nor smiles at her mother. We know from previous observations that Sylvia never cried for help; it was as if there was no expectation of her distress being received. Indeed, when Mother goes out of the room, Sylvia sighs as if it is a relief to get rid of her. She shows great sensual excitement— rather than pleasure and joy—in relation to her furry dog, the food, and the spoon. Her anxiety about doing damage and losing a good, feeding mother emerges at times. It does so, I feel, in the way she studies the beaker after she has sucked and bitten and blown into it. She seems to be afraid of the dark echo it might throw back at her.

I think we see here Sylvia's fear that Mother is not able to stand her strong desire nor her worry of emptying her; worse still, she is afraid of some unfathomable danger lurking within her mother. Sylvia's laughter, when mother stops feeding, seems to be a manic reaction to despair about an emptied mother. Mother readily joins in with the mania, mistaking it for happiness. It would appear that Sylvia's anxieties about her mother have resulted in not wanting to be dependent on a human relationship—and indeed human vocal sounds—and instead she is turning to inanimate objects. Emotions are replaced by sensuous excitement. Yet her ability to respond to the observer indicates that this development could be reversed.

In *Love's Work* the philosopher Gillian Rose (1995), describing her mother's state of mind, wrote:

> The denial and unexamined suffering are two of the main reasons for her all-jovial unhappiness, the unhappiness of one who refuses to dwell in hell and who lives, therefore, in the most static despair. [p. 15]

Such mothers often provide excellent care, but they cannot help their mental state undermining their children's hope that grief can be borne. Such children convey their hopelessness by inducing despair in us. Yet, if we are to reach them, our empathy needs to be sustained by hope.

References

Bick, E. (1968). The experience of the skin in early object-relations. *International Journal of Psycho-Analysis* 49:484–486.

Klein, S. (1980). Autistic phenomena in neurotic patients. *International Journal of Psycho-Analysis* 61(3):395–401.

Meltzer, D. (1975). Dimensionality in mental functioning. In *Explorations in Autism*. Perthshire, Scotland: Clunie Press.

Piontelli, A. (1985). *Backward in Time*. Perthshire, Scotland: Clunie Press.

——— (1992). *From Fetus to Child: an Observational and Psychoanalytic Study*. London: Routledge and Kegan Paul.

Rose, G. (1995). *Love's Work*. London: Chatto & Windus.

Symington, J. (1985). The survival function of primitive omnipotence. *International Journal of Psycho-Analysis* 66:481–488.

Tustin, F. (1972). *Autism and Childhood Psychosis*. London: Hogarth.

Wittenberg, I. (1975). Primal depression in autism. In *Explorations in Autism*. Perthshire, Scotland: Clunie Press.

8

Borderline Autism as a Factor in Somatoform Disorder[1]

Sheila Spensley

One function of the psychosomatic illness seems to be to release and deal with the violence associated with unregulated sensuality, as well as to give form and shape to formless, raw auto-sensual elements.

Frances Tustin, *Autistic States in Children*

It is a tribute to the originality and depth of Frances Tustin's thinking about autistic states in children, that her ideas have already been taken up by theoreticians seeking to integrate her concepts into the tradition of psychoanalytic theory. In this chapter, I shall be drawing on Tustin's innovative concepts in relation to her understanding of the isolation predicament of children with autism as well as on those contemporary developments of her thinking.

This chapter falls into two sections. The first outlines briefly the directions of theoretical growth following the discovery of autism and explores the repercussions of Tustin's insights concerning autistic states with their implications for the psychoanalysis of adult patients. In the second section, I shall relate these advances in understanding to the treatment of a somatoform

---

1. Some sections of this chapter are contained in Frances Tustin, London: Routledge and reprinted by kind permission of Routledge. An earlier version of this chapter was published in *The Bulletin of The British Psychoanalytic Society* 1995.

disorder in a patient whose psychoanalytic inaccessibility has been particularly marked. The patient's symptom involved an eating disorder, although she was not anorexic.

Tustin was greatly interested in the idea of the existence of autistic enclaves in adult pathologies and regularly quoted the work of Sidney Klein on this topic (Klein 1980, Tustin 1990). She considered the intractability of anorexia, in particular, to be attributable to hidden autistic phenomena. A child psychotherapist, Tustin herself rarely saw adult patients, but she wrote of one anorexic adolescent who had formerly been her child patient (Tustin 1986). This was a child whom Tustin had first treated in the hospital when the child had been admitted with severe anorexia nervosa. At the time, it was Sydney Klein who held medical responsibility and they worked closely together in the care and management of this very ill child.

Problems of psychoanalytic inaccessibility are characteristic of the somatoform psychiatric disorders, where projection into the body and out of the mental sphere creates an impasse in intra-psychic as well as interpersonal communication. In this connection, the introduction of a concept of a *borderline autistic disorder* may prove to be clinically helpful and I shall present some material, which I understand from this point of view. First of all, however, it may be instructive to take a historical perspective on the use of the term autism and the course of its clinical applications.

Origins

As far as I am aware, the term "autistic" was first used by Bleuler in 1911 when he specified the diagnostic features of schizophrenia. He used the descriptor "autistic" to indicate the quality of withdrawal he had observed in schizophrenic patients whom he saw as appearing to be absorbed exclusively in their own internal experience. Thirty years later, the same term was used by Kanner to describe a group of children in whom he observed a striking common feature, which was the shutting out or ignoring by the children of anything coming from outside them and which resulted in a state of "extreme aloneness" (Kanner 1943).

When Kanner gave the name "autism" to his syndrome, the term immediately became associated exclusively with that particular diagnostic group and this rather preempted its use in the further investigation of any commonalties between those two distinct and separate observations of withdrawal behavior, which had each prompted the use of the descriptor "autistic." The separation of autism and psychosis that resulted was probably premature, but the division that was established then remains and is still defended with vigor. This contributes, I think, to the continuing controversies and confusions associated with the exploration of both conditions and the investigation of their origins.

Kanner applied the term "infantile autism" to a highly defined syndrome of rare occurrence, but his discovery was followed by a steady movement in the direction of broadening the criteria for autism as it became apparent that features of autistic behavior were to be found in other children falling outside the classical syndrome. By 1979, Wing had selected and defined three core diagnostic criteria for autism and related autistic disorders to which she gave the name the "triad of impairments," that is, the triad of social, language, and behavioral impairment. In a large epidemiological study of a London borough, she showed that the incidence of autistic conditions (i.e., frequency figures for the "triad") was much higher than first suggested for autism (Wing and Gould 1979). On the basis of these findings, Wing introduced the concept of an "autistic continuum" disorder. The London incidence figures have also been replicated in Sweden in a similar study by Gillberg (1988), with the result that autism is increasingly seen now as a spectrum disorder. The classificatory consequences have also been taken up by Gillberg (1990).

In DSM-III-R, the concept of childhood psychosis has disappeared in favor of Pervasive Developmental Disorder. Within that category, autism is placed as a subtype. Gillberg now suggests that the problematic PDD might be replaced by "autistic continuum disorder" and a strong argument in favor of this is that autism, among "all the psychiatric syndromes arising in childhood . . . is much the best validated by empirical research" (Rutter and Schopler 1987, p. 180). In all of this, it is important to notice the subtle and persistent sloughing off both of Kanner's original diagnostic trait "autistic aloneness" and of any association with psychosis. Asperger introduced the concept of "autistic psychopathy" in 1944, but this too has been subsumed in Wing's argument that Asperger's Syndrome is on a spectrum with autism (Wing 1981).

The emphasis is on the continuities of autism, which are thus being thoroughly researched. However, discontinuity with psychosis was accepted without demur ever since it was conclusively established that autism was not a form of early onset schizophrenia (Wolff and Barlow 1979). Although schizophrenia has been found to throw little light on autism, in my view it does not necessarily follow that autism cannot illuminate schizophrenia. My own work with autistic children was preceded by a long experience of working with hospitalized adult psychotic and borderline patients such that I was interested, from the beginning, in making comparisons between the lives of autistic children and the experiences and behaviors of regressed psychotic patients. It is on my thinking about the relationship between the two—and on how the primitivity of autism may help to illuminate psychosis and the psychotic aspects of lesser disturbances—that I have developed in this paper.

The Aloneness of Autism

As early as 1930, Melanie Klein was puzzled by the child "Dick," whom, in the absence of the concept of childhood autism, she could only describe as "largely devoid of affects" and in whom "emotional relations to his environment were almost entirely lacking." She concluded that the child was suffering from an inhibition in development, not a regression. Her speculation was that this might be associated with an excess of early oral sadism which, overwhelming all sources of libidinal pleasure, had created an obstacle to taking in and learning. A powerful sense of aloneness was experienced by a patient whom I shall refer to later in this paper. My patient could feel extremely isolated and alone with her symptom, and that sense of aloneness was also conveyed to me in sessions where the transference experience was one of deadlock.

Obstacles to taking in are highly relevant to the failure in some infants to form the vital human connectedness necessary to the establishment of bonding and the early mother-infant processes of attachment. Not only the failure to internalize but the failure to project is characteristic of autism and was implicit in Kanner's (1943) observations of the "extreme aloneness" of autistic children. Since the development of human bonding follows a biological pattern with adequate instinctual gratification an essential component, it is clear and not surprising that disturbances at this level are detrimental to human attachment and hence to psychic development.

The advances of modern infant research have revealed that the developing infant is predisposed to be aware of self-organizing processes and begins to experience from birth a sense of an "emergent self" (Stern 1985). In the first weeks of life, sensory experiences are paramount; the human infant actively seeks sensory stimulation (Stern 1985). In Tustin's understanding of autistic children, the world of sensory experience is also highly emphasized. She regards the autistic child as arrested at a sensory level of experience, adhering to the reassurances of sensations and trapped alone in a self-centered, self-relieving cycle, this in stark contrast to Stern's image of the normal child's infantile "sense of emergent self."

The theme of sensory experience is prominent in Tustin's work, as is her related concept of "black hole" terrors. Her thinking on these subjects was greatly influenced by the work of Winnicott, whose paper on traumatic early loss was crucial in directing her attention to the possibility of experiential confusions between loss of the object and loss of a part of the self (Winnicott 1958). Winnicott understood that there were terrors more primitive than the fear of madness and that the deepest trauma was associated with threats to the sense of existence; primitive fears of falling endlessly or, as he put it, threats to the sense of "going on being." These are alienating states of privation with a deep and grievous sense of an amputation of life and meaning, which Winnicott saw as characterizing psychotic depression. In Stern's terminology, such states of anxiety can be viewed as threatening to the organization of the "emergent self."

The World of Sensory Experience

Like Mahler (1975) Tustin talks of a "psychological birth," meaning the transitional point at which the human infant enters into a world of mind and a capacity to "mentalize" experience is born. Tustin identifies the cardinal role of sensory experience as the prelude to the inception and development of the psyche. She postulates that the earliest capacities and drives towards differentiation, about which modern infant research has now taught us so much more, that those processes of discrimination need to take place alongside—or perhaps within—a continuing experience of undifferentiation.

Following Winnicott, Tustin saw "flowing over" feelings between mother and infant as precursors to projection and as providing a continuum of experience—an illusion of oneness with the mother, a psychological membrane, helping to bridge the caesura of birth and predating the projection-introjection process. These ideas are also in harmony with Mahler's symbiosis, although Mahler's (1958) concept is associated with a later developmental phase.

Tustin's thinking may also owe something to Bion's (1962) "maternal reverie." As far as the infant's earliest experiencing is concerned, it remains a fine point whether a period of undifferentiation implies absence of projection-introjection, since the very act of perception itself can be considered to comprise these processes. In either case, the disruption of primary existential security or the disruption of the primitive projection-introjection processes constitutes the traumatic event which she believed precipitated autistic aloneness.

Tustin, like Mahler, saw the experience of trauma at the heart of psychosis. She saw autism as a reaction to early primitive trauma—the trauma of a premature and disastrous disruption of the illusory psychological membrane—before the infant had achieved sensory and existential security based on a primary sense of groundedness in its own body. This initial period of sensory dominance was much emphasized by Winnicott, who delineated some critical discriminatory tasks involved in the feeding experience, namely the differentiation of nipple, tongue, breast, and mouth into separate entities.

Tustin took that thinking to a deeper level by introducing the idea of the differentiation and integration of the dichotomies of hardness and softness as a dialectic integral to the experience of feeding and having implications for all subsequent object relationships—soft sensations ultimately becoming associated with receptivity and taking in, and hard sensations with thrusting and entering. An interchange of the two, as in a well-established to and fro cooperation of mouth and nipple in feeding, is the basis of strong, rhythmic, satisfying suckling as it is also the basis of the qualities of resilience and adaptability in enduring personal relationships. Conversely, hardness in physique and/or in personality may be used defensively against the threat of softness and vulnerability.

Tustin's focus on the critical function of the sensory organization in securing a foundation for psychic development contributed a new dimension to the understanding of the genesis of psychic life. Her ideas have already been expanded to lead to suggested extensions of psychoanalytic theory and there is now confirmatory support from developmental psychology for the significance of preverbal subjective life in the infant. Disturbances at preverbal levels of organization produce intrapersonal impairments which are inevitably destructive of subsequent interpersonal development, upon which further psychic growth also depends. In autism, Tustin detected evidence of what she saw as the catastrophic consequences of emotional ingress and the eclipse of these delicate formative processes. I think her "black hole" concept, which represents this eclipse, is also relevant to theories of primitive pathology and therapeutic impasse.

For the study of personality development, in general, the introduction of the importance of sensory security as a prerequisite of psychic development means a shift of focus from the psychological to the biological domain and pushes back the frontiers of psychic development. One might say that the autistic child hasn't so much lost his mind as he has lost his senses. It is "coming to his senses" that is the priority—a prerequisite vital to the processes of bonding and attachment and rooted in physicality.

"Black hole" phenomena signify a discontinuity of consciousness and of the sense of "self" and occur at a point somewhere on that continuum between the biological and the psychological. Defenses are body-centered, like rocking, head-banging, and stereotypic movement in autistic children and self-injurious behavior, or somatoform symptoms, paralysis, depersonalization, amnesia, and so on in other adult pathologies.

In stressing the primacy of the sensory experience, Tustin finds support in Freud's (1923) thinking that "the ego is first and foremost a body-ego" and again in Bion's (1962) view that the "self" is an entity having mental and physical attributes and not a mind in a body. She saw the very sensitive and delicate processes of sensory organization as fundamental to the growth of a sense of being and "going on being," to use Winnicott's phrase (Winnicott 1958) and are essential to a "psychological" birth and the capacity to "mentalize" experience (Mitrani 1992). Sensations carry the *potential* for feelings. With psychological birth, emotional meaning is bestowed on sensory perception so that feeling states, as distinct from sensations, can come into being. Putting this into Bion's terminology, the infant's preconception of a nurturing object must be realized (in the sensory experience) to create the maternal matrix for internalization and the growth of identification.

In other words, any rupturing of this primitive sensory structure destroys the illusory psychological membrane between mother and infant and precipitates premature psychological birth. An "agony of consciousness" is what Tustin saw as the precipitating factor in autism. The infant is left to the experience of feeling both helpless and unbearably exposed, a level of anxiety precipitating organismic and existential distress. Houzel (1989, 1995) proposes the concept "precipitation anxiety" to encompass these primeval fears of falling.

Lacking primary sensual containment (for whatever reason), the sensual containment of enfolding, of rhythmic beat, of sensual hardness and softness, of periodicity—all of which provide a sense of "going-on-being"—the infant experiences being exposed—exposed to weather as it were, a hurricane, or a volcanic eruption. Against such odds, the last resort is a massive withdrawal from the psychic into an auto-sensual anti-thinking world where sensations are turned to as ends in themselves serving the purpose of shutting out awareness of the object and the "not me." This leaves the infant a sense of utter aloneness, as if it has been left in the middle of a desert or a postnuclear wasteland, two images commonly found in the dreams of borderline patients (Spensley 1995).

When the child is exposed to trauma, emotions are experienced "in the raw." That is, the impact of the experience is untransformed by a containing object, to modulate and give meaning. Instead of giving birth to a conception of mental space, which is based on relationship with an object, there is a violent eruption into unbounded endless space, which is perceived as a "black hole." This was Tustin's construction of the early traumatic experience of the autistic and psychotic children she studied. It is a picture composed from an imaginative conjunction of objective clinical observation of the children with a singular quality of sensitivity and empathy, all her own. What I have found striking is that it is a picture regularly presented in the accounts of psychotic, obsessional, and some borderline patients when they try to communicate their view of the world they live in. The image of a black hole is not confined to autism. It is a universal symbol of nihilism, meaninglessness, and despair. In psychotic individuals it is an everpresent threat, often experienced quite concretely.

I have been privileged to learn a great deal from the history of an obsessive-compulsive patient who is now able to tell me about how she experienced a time in her life when she suffered very severe mental illness. An intelligent woman, she first broke down while attending a university, and for a considerable time her early adult life was spent on the streets or in mental hospitals. During that period, she used alcohol and drugs to stave off "black hole" threats to her sense of existence. Because of her disconnectedness from her body, she had no way of protecting herself except to focus on her few possessions, her clothes, and her handbag. It was as if her life depended on *their* existence and she was compelled to keep watch over them. Still severely ill, she has been coming to me for once-weekly psychotherapy for about five years, and she is able to tell me about states of mind which once put her into appalling situations when she was a young woman.

For example, she did not defend herself from rape because it was more important to be sure she did not lose sight of her handbag. The handbag was far more important to her than her body. In her sessions with me she has, at times, felt that she was literally surrounded by "black holes," chasms down which she might be in real danger of falling if she were to get up out of the chair. At such times, the object of security in the room is the chair. At other times, it might be the sight of her coat hanging on the back of the door. Much of her checking behavior seems to be in the service of assuring herself of the reality of her own existence. In the absence of a "felt" self or a "body ego" (Freud 1923), she clings desperately to sensory orientations, in this case to the sensory data provided by the sight of her coat. These derive from inanimate objects and always take precedence over people as a source of reassurance of her being and existence.

Black Holes

Tustin saw the trauma of nothingness associated with the black hole threat as the nadir of human experience. This is the fundamental "nil" experience. Loss of the very matrix of identity, with an inexorable descent into nothingness and meaninglessness, poses the most dreaded human experience; not psychosis, which indeed seems to proffer the final defense against this cataclysm. This was Winnicott's contention in a posthumously published paper, "Fear of Breakdown" (1974). In that paper, he states: "It is wrong to think of psychotic illness as a breakdown, it is a defense organization relative to a primitive agony . . ." (p. 104).

A traumatic invasion of the sensory organization produces organismic panic with feelings of running out or dissolving away. These are feelings which reach a depth of terror beyond neurotic and psychotic fears so that "fate" rather than "guilt" becomes the overriding dread. The greater threat to the psyche, then, is not from the destructive eruption of primitive instinctual impulses into the ego, as in psychosis, but from an impending threat of dissolution of the self, identity, and objects into chaos and meaninglessness. The "black hole" metaphor represents a catastrophic discontinuity in the experience of "self," with loss of meaning, predictability, and the sense of being alive: The black hole psychotic depression consumes or engulfs the personality with feelings of dissolution and of losing the very floor of one's existence.

Such chaotic disruption of the sense of being obtains at a biological as well as a psychological level. It is the precursor of psychosis and it may or may not be capable of psychotic transformation. If the disruption is not mentalized and not psychically transformed in psychosis, a state of autistic isolation and powerlessness ensues. Elements of the primitive self survive, but in a deadened state where feeling is obliterated. Mahler (1961) noted this when she spoke of the psychotic break with reality being "ushered in" by a deep depression.

Tustin was not the first to draw attention to ontological insecurity and existential terror, but she writes evocatively of such experiences that—since they are primitive and essentially preverbal—are at the frontiers of communicability. She illuminates some of the obscurities of existing writings and theory by her introduction of the importance of sensory contributions to primitive mentation and the growth of the psyche. Above all, however, her writing has stimulated new theory to advance the thinking about thinking, its origins, its development, and its pathology. I'd like now to turn to that interface to see where new ideas correspond and how they might be aligned with existing theory.

Theoretical Implications

Two psychoanalysts in particular have been stimulated by Tustin's imagery to develop their own thinking about psychoanalytic theory. They are James Grotstein and Thomas Ogden, who have each taken Tustin's ideas a stage further by considering their place in the scale of present psychoanalytic understanding. Tustin's writing has a ready appeal to clinical and personal experience. Her work is widely read and understood by the parents of autistic children and by those charged with their care and education. She did not concern herself greatly with theory and said often that she had difficulty understanding much of her analyst's (Bion's) writings. However, her work does complement that of Bion, often illuminating some of his formulations in a way which makes them more accessible. For example, her black hole imagery portrays a striking impression of the desolate half-life lying beyond Bion's psychological catastrophe.

Tustin, Grotstein, and Ogden are all concerned to move psychoanalytic inquiry to the very frontiers of human experience. In close agreement with Tustin about the significance of sensory modes of experience, Ogden (1989) argues that the paranoid-schizoid position can no longer be regarded as the most primitive level of personality organization, and he proposes what he terms an "autistic-contiguous position" to represent the human being's most primitive mode of experiencing a sense of "self." This emphasizes the fundamental importance of body-centered experience, which is essentially pre-psychic but a vital precursor to psychic life and mentation, a level of activity which Bion (1962) called "proto-mental."

Ogden's clarification of the position of the sensory modes of experience in human mental development suggests an extension of psychoanalytic theory in which human experience may be understood in terms of the interplay of three

rather than two modes of psychological organization. The three bring suc-
ceeding advances in integrative capacity but retain the distinctive patterns of
anxiety characteristic of each level of organization. These three patterns of
anxiety are determined by the characteristics of the disruption occurring
within each mode of experience. In the "depressive position," feelings are at an
interpersonal level, with fears of harming or of being harmed by the object. — ?
"Paranoid-schizoid" anxiety concerns fears of fragmentation and disintegration of the self and objects. In the "autistic-contiguous position," the disruption is to the sense of existence with fears of dissolving, disappearing, or falling
forever. Primitive object relationships are therefore threatened by fear of
engulfment by or fusion with the object, while whole- and part-object relationships are disturbed by confusion with the object.

What is now proposed in Ogden's formulation is a level of understanding
which identifies fears emanating from unspeakable existential terrors and
which are communicated predominantly in autistic nonverbal and preverbal
form. Paralysis of thinking, fears of having reached a dead end in understanding, and states of seeming incomprehension, as in the case I shall discuss
later, are some of the clinical manifestations in adult patients.

Grotstein (1987, 1989) has written extensively about these black hole fears
in adult patients with primitive mental disorders, and he too acknowledges
the stimulus of Tustin's work in furthering his thinking. Complementing
Ogden's autistic contiguous position, Grotstein seeks to add a new paradigm
of "powerlessness" to psychoanalytic theory traditionally based on mental
conflict and power. Following Tustin and Bion, he sees sensory stability as a
prerequisite of the interpersonal emotional interactions which lead to mental
growth. He proposes a new dynamic of self-regulation which accounts for
stabilization at this biopsychological level. When distress is extreme, but its
nature cannot be recognized, the turbulence is modulated by autosensory and
motor attempts at self-soothing. Activities such as rocking, head-banging,
and stereotypy, which are common among autistic children, are by no means
confined to children nor to those with a diagnosis of autism. Autistic behavior
is not mediated by an object and is not meaningful, except as attempts to
self-regulate—through rhythm and action—the dread of falling endlessly,
of dissolving away, or evanescing. It is a desperate, mindless attempt to hold
on to some kind of order and substantially in a world of rapidly diminishing
meaning and predictability. Obsessional behavior has a similar dynamic in the
compulsion to find substantiality and authenticity in sensory reassurances
pertaining to physical and not to mental experience.

These terrors of nothingness and meaninglessness, which characterize autism, are also to be found with greater or lesser predominance in other adult psychopathologies. Somatoform and eating disorders are particularly associated with autistic-like blockages, where not only is the symptom felt by the patient to be beyond understanding—in that it pertains to physical and not mental experience—but frequently, a strong sense of helplessness and impotence prevails, along with a rigid attachment to a meaningless state of affairs. This has a significance which is central. Treatment impasses may be interpreted in object-related ways as an indication of unconscious envious attacks on thinking or projections of hostility, but in the case I now wish to discuss, the impasse seemed to result not from an attacking state of mind but a defeated one—defeated, I have come to think, not in conflict with the object, but in conflict with the self.

In this case, unable to stand unbearable pain, the strangulation of such feelings seems to have been experienced concretely as a constriction in the throat. In her state of desperation, regulation of the patient's sense of "self" was restored at the price of her feelings, which reverted to physical sensations. Consequently, in the absence of her feelings, she lacked, as she herself said "the equipment for thinking." It was in this sense that I understood her dilemma from the perspective of a borderline autistic state. A recurring image in the phantasies and dreams of this patient was of being imprisoned in a high-walled yet open structure from where there seemed no direct way of making contact with life on the outside, the existence of which she had some awareness. A cognitive deficit was thus brought about as a result of an emotional loss, which had held the potential for meaning. As another patient said of not being able to think, she "knew where she was" when she started to feel tension in her body.

Clinical Example[2]

The patient had a rare eating disorder: as a child, she had always been very self-contained and had never been considered difficult or disturbed. It was not until adulthood, and after the onset of her symptom, that her life came to be characterized by a feeling of emptiness and meaninglessness, from which she rarely found relief. In the countertransference, I came to experience her

---

2. I am most grateful for the careful thinking of Dr. Robin Anderson who supervised the first two years of my work with this patient.

self-containment as being intimately linked with the need to preserve a static world of self-sufficiency. Any "good" experience was treated like a kind of random bonus, whether experienced within the session or outside of it, and its effects soon evaporated. Seen as unpredictable and unreliable, these positive experiences were given little meaning or value and so held no potential for change or hope for the future.

The patient was an educated, highly intelligent, and sensitively gifted young woman in her twenties. From the beginning, she was articulate in talking about herself and seemed tireless in her efforts to understand her predicament, which was an unusual eating disorder that, at times, reached life-threatening proportions. Her giftedness and apparent insight seemed to be an advantage, which should have contributed to the psychoanalytic work. However, from my first meeting with her I also experienced a certain disjointedness in our relationship. Something of a contradictory nature in her gave rise to marked awkwardness and discomfort.

She was very frightened and desperate to find help when I first met her, yet I constantly suspected that she might give up and abandon her treatment. She would often repeat her honest appraisal of her dilemma: She had felt driven to seek help because of the fear and desperation engendered by her symptom, yet she was convinced that she could not be helped. She could see no meaningfulness in her symptom nor any connection between it and her state of mind, yet she was also certain that it was not an organic abnormality, and, of course, this had been extensively investigated.

The patient had a severe but sporadic inhibition of swallowing. She was not anorexic but shared some of the personality characteristics of the anorexic. Cool and detached, she found her symptom quite incomprehensible. Any anxiety or frustration she did express was focused not on the severe limitations placed on her life by the symptom, but rather on her bafflement at not being able to enlist others to agree to her helplessness and her powerlessness to effect any change in her behavior.

During her first years in psychotherapy, she was appreciative of my efforts to help her and many times seemed to find certain interpretations interesting and helpful. She brought plenty of material: memories, dreams, anecdotes, self-observations, and observations of relationships she had witnessed. All of it was helpful in providing paradigms of her own emotional predicament and usually led to apparently sensitive and creative thinking. Yet, every time I felt we had achieved some feeling of satisfaction in a session, she would, in contrast, return the next day filled again with the familiar hopelessness and futility, talking as if what had been of interest on the previous day now held little meaning. This frustrating state of affairs continued for a considerable time before there was any experience of something having been gained and sufficiently retained for her to be able to notice that she had actually taken something in from me. The following excerpt records one such insight.

She said she had gone away the day before feeling confident and had thought about the whole session, what she had said, and what I had said. She found two points I'd made of particular interest. Those were that she was guarding her emptiness and that she continued to feel empty because she did not let any new thought in. She said that this had suddenly seemed like a new way of looking at her symptom. She said she recognized that I must have made this point many times before, but that it was quite different for her this time because she had started to think that I must be trying to get something into her.

She said she realized that this idea had come from me, but that it had seemed revolutionary. She described how she had always taken the view that she came to talk and she knew, too, that she could get upset, confused, or frustrated. Some shift of attitude might take place, but she had always put that down to her having let things out. This was the reason why she could not see how any real change could ever come about. She had never thought of my contributing anything or giving something to her, although she recognized that each time she had gone off feeling more confident and hopeful it had been when I had said something she had not thought of and she'd been given something new to think about. This had never before been equated in her mind with an idea of taking something in. She said the idea of taking in was such a revolutionary thought, it seemed almost too big to grasp and too much to go on thinking about just then.

I said that she needed time to consider the implications of such a change of perspective and this was then followed by her recalling being rushed by a close friend the minute he saw an improvement in her symptom. She was shocked to observe how angry and stubborn she could become, refusing categorically to try to follow up the improvement. I related this to fears of engulfment, which had also appeared in a recent dream. I thought she felt she had no way of regulating relationships so she had to switch off arbitrarily. She replied that the sessions had always felt like that. She switched off at the end and on again the next day.

Her fear of engulfment related to one aspect of the symptom, and I distinguished between "letting" something in and "taking" something in, where choice would be included. She said she had never felt she had any control and that the idea of choice was revolutionary too. She seemed to have to behave as if she were either passive and helpless or ruthlessly controlling through her defiant and obdurate refusals.

A brief excerpt from another session illuminates the state of powerlessness in this patient, a feeling which I too had strongly experienced at the beginning of the therapy. This session had included memories of a time when she had been full of anger and resentment about not being looked after properly when she was becoming very ill (not connected with her symptom). She had been totally unable to voice her need to seek medical help, but felt others should have seen and known she needed a doctor without being told and should have taken responsibility for finding one. In addition, there was a reference to a dream where she had been barely able to walk and had struggled to drag herself through deep mud. I drew her attention to a similar sense of powerlessness in the session where it seemed that it was entirely up to me to make some contribution if there was to be any movement in the session. She was presenting herself as helpless and not to be expected to take any responsibility for change. Indeed, the idea that she could have any capacity to think or act on her own behalf seemed incomprehensible to her.

My patient agreed and said it seemed so babyish. I said a little baby could not be expected to tell mother what was needed; mother has to know or discover what is wanted. She expected me to know and indeed felt I did know (as she had often said) but felt I chose, for reasons of my own, to keep things back from her rather than that there should be any part of her to play or that she should have to take any responsibility for contributing to the work. At that, she began to shed very painful tears, saying that it was hardly believable. It made her physically shudder.

She said she could hardly bring herself to say that she did recognize that she thought like that. She thought she only had a faint awareness of it but knew it to be true that she didn't feel any responsibility for herself. "It's too much to be able to hold on to this thought—I only get a glimpse. It's like a shadow. I've kept this image for a long time, never knew what to do with it." Describing the image, she said, "After Hiroshima, there was a place with a shadow of a body, where a woman had been. . . ."

I think this image vividly conveyed the catastrophe that had befallen this patient's thinking. There was only a shadow of it left and it is little wonder that she felt she did not have the "equipment" to think or that she experienced the therapeutic task as incomprehensible. These excerpts may help to communicate the qualities of devastation, deadness, and paralysis of thinking which underpinned my relationship with this patient and which eventually explained the disjointed and lifeless feelings that characterized the therapeutic relationship for a considerable time.

A gifted and articulate woman, she was capable of engaging in relevant discussion of her problems, bringing more and more intuitive and perceptive material which one might have thought could hardly fail to produce insight. That it did not and could not was so easily camouflaged by her earnest and genuine efforts to understand. It was only when all the apparent cooperation and support of the therapeutic alliance was discounted and an underlying vise-like grip on helplessness and futility was exposed as functioning like an autistic stronghold, defending her against the very recognition of object qualities, that the patient came to experience feelings of hope that change might be possible.

Following that session, she could begin to want something and to experience a longing to be free of her symptom. She could begin to want something of the therapy instead of feeling suspended in a meaningless endeavor related predominantly to staving off the terror of getting worse. To want began a process of bringing back into awareness feelings of need and dependence, which had previously been experienced as past enduring. A further exchange between us illustrates the subtlety of the dynamic.

She had returned from the summer break referring to a difficult and beleaguered time but said that more recently, towards the end of the holiday, she had been thinking about coming back with some excitement and an exhilarating feeling that she must change. She must have a different dialogue, although she wasn't sure that "dialogue" was the correct word. Approaching the house and the consulting room, however, she felt pulled back into the same familiar attitude: Everything looked the same, so she began to think nothing would ever change. She continued with some meticulous examination of her own lamentable lack of motivation and how easily she gives up.

I spoke of the way she had looked around on arrival and that I had been seen as part of the furniture, taken for granted, having little to do with dialogue. She agreed and said she did feel that she "shut her ears" to me. I then took up the "beleaguered" feeling of the holiday, of which nothing more had been said. She then said she had had fears of going completely out of control and of having to be taken to the hospital again. However, she was sustained by a conviction that she could prevent this. Her symptom had gotten worse, but she felt confident it would go no further. Now it's a question of "thus far and no further." During the previous session, she added, she was full of tension all over her body. Now, today, she had a headache. I noted how much her relationship with me was conducted in the same way, "thus far and no further." She had not, for example, mentioned the physical tension at the time. I thought "Thus far and no further" meant not only that she would not get worse but she would not get better either.

On Monday, she said that was a remark which had unsettled her all weekend but she then went on to talk to some familiar themes relating to a friend's symptoms and how much easier a life he had, not being dominated by one single symptom like she was. I drew her attention to the fate of the "unsettled" feeling she had first spoken of and how it was now being buried under settled thoughts we'd heard before.

After a pause, she replied that she had been faintly aware of a feeling that she was not really contributing to thinking but was seeking to round off any discussion and bring it to an end. She was, I said, shutting me up in a way which sounded like she was being exploratory. With a familiar soft little gasp, she agreed. This tiny indicator of acceptance and "taking in" held a signifi-cance which for a long time I had not recognized or appreciated. In this barely articulated utterance was displayed all the hesitation and apprehension about "swallowing" a new point of view, as was mirrored in her symptom.

Conclusion

In this chapter, I have tried to convey the extent of some of the developments in psychoanalytic thinking now beginning to emerge from Tustin's work in autism. Her ideas derived from a dedicated interest in trying to understand what remains the most enigmatic of mental disturbances, notwithstanding its being the most researched and the best validated psychiatric syndrome arising in childhood. I have chosen to emphasize the relevance of Tustin's thinking to the broader field of adult mental illness where failure to mentalize, so promi-nent a feature in autism, may also be found to be a significant factor. Tustin herself had begun to draw attention to the possibilities of autistic enclaves in the neurotic personality (Tustin 1986, 1990).

It is less well-recognized that the phenomena of autism do not belong exclusively to a rare and severe form of infantile psychopathology. Head banging, self-rocking, and other body-directed activities are to be found in adult patients with obsessional and psychotic disturbances. The significance of the nonverbal and nonmental forms of communication within a psycho-analytic session is already well-recognized, and such communication is used in the processes of therapeutic transformation. Often, however, actual autistic

"mentalize" —what is that ?

behaviors are indulged in secretly, and the perpetuation of such extreme activities comes to light only in the course of psychoanalytic work.

In the examples I have given, it is not the content of the verbal communications of the patient which is critical to moving the therapeutic work forward. Despite her intelligence, sensitivity, and fluency—which was formidable—it was the detection of the patient's covertly ruthless adherence to helplessness and incomprehension and the exposure of an obdurate belief in the futility of all our efforts at understanding which finally allowed a little movement in her thinking.

In this case, the body and the physical symptom seemed to short-circuit mental states, and the resultant incomprehension, emptiness, and meaninglessness created an autistic fortress in which the patient felt impotent. A protective maneuver, which depends on the isolation of the subject and prohibits contact with the object, paralyzes thinking. The resulting therapeutic impasse does not yield to object-related interpretations because the autistic fortress functions primarily not to obviate or attack relationship with the object but to protect the self from existential threat. Unmediated by an object, my patient's terror was regulated instead by her body and her symptom.

In this patient, the autistic enclave was exceptionally difficult to detect because of her seeming interest in self-exploration and her high-level of motivation. She presented richly intuitive material which we could investigate and analyze together in a quite convincing way. I think now that most of her material presented her dilemma, but the impasse itself could not begin to be tackled until the existence of the autistic enclave began to be exposed as a consuming "black hole." Its "black hole" nature was continually being experienced by me in such a way that good work seemed regularly to disappear overnight.

Until it was recognized that the patient had a facility for "distance" communication, for broadcasting from within her stronghold, her very real alienation escaped notice. Dreams and phantasy images of being in a keep or a fortress added confirmation to the impression that her experience was of disconnectedness with and nonattachment to the object and in this respect approximated the distinguishing characteristics of autism.

References

Bleuler, E. (1911). *Dementia Praecox* or *The Group of Schizophrenias*. New York: International Universities Press.

Bion, W.R. (1962). *Learning from Experience*. London: Heinemann.

DSM (1987). *Diagnosis and Statistical Manual III*. Washington, DC: American Psychiatric Association.

Freud, S. (1923). The ego and the id. *Standard Edition* 19:3–63.

Gillberg, C. (1988). The neurobiology of infantile autism. *Journal of Child Psychology and Psychiatry*, 29(3):257–266.

———— (1990). Autism and pervasive developmental disorder. *Journal of Child Psychology and Psychiatry* 31(1):99–119.

Grotstein, J.S. (1987). Borderline as a disorder of self-regulation. In *The Borderline Patient: Emerging Concepts in Diagnosis, Psychodynamics and Treatment*, ed. J. Grotstein, M. Solomon, and J. Lang. New Jersey: Analytic Press.

———— (1989). The "black hole" as the basic psychotic experience: some newer psychoanalytic and neuroscience perspectives on psychosis. *Journal of the American Academy of Psychoanalysis* 6(3):253–275.

Houzel, D. (1989). Precipitation anxiety and the dawn of aesthetic feelings. *Journal of Child Psychotherapy* 13(2):65–78.

———— (1995). Precipitation anxiety. *Journal of Child Psychotherapy* 21(1):65–78.

Kanner, L. (1943). Autistic disturbances of affective contact. *Nervous Child* 2:217–250.

Klein, M. (1930). The importance of symbol formation in the development of the ego. In *Contributions to Psycho-Analysis*, pp. 236–250. London: Hogarth.

Klein, S. (1980). Autistic phenomena in neurotic patients. *International Journal of Psycho-Analysis* 61(3):395–401.

Mahler, M. (1958). Autism and symbiosis: two extreme disturbances of identity. *International Journal of Psycho-Analysis* 39:77–83.

———— (1961). On sadness and grief in infancy and childhood: loss and restoration of the symbiotic love object. *Psychoanalytic Study of the Child* 17:332–351.

Mahler, M., Bergman A., and Pine F. (1975). *The Psychological Birth of the Human Infant*. New York: Basic Books.

Mitrani, J. (1992). On the survival function of autistic manoeuvres in adult patients. *International Journal of Psycho-Analysis* 73(2):549–559.

Ogden, T.H. (1989). *The Primitive Edge of Experience*. New Jersey: Jason Aronson.

Rutter, M. (1983). Cognitive deficits in the pathogenesis of autism. Journal of *Child Psychology and Psychiatry* 24(4):513–531.

Rutter, M. and Schopler, E. (1987). Autism and pervasive developmental disorders: concepts and diagnostic issues. *Journal of Autism and Developmental Disorders* 17:159–186.

Rutter, M. and Schopler, E., eds. (1978). *Autism: A Reappraisal of Concepts and Treatment*. New York and London: Plenum.

⊳ Spensley, S. (1995). *Frances Tustin*. London: Routledge.

Stern, D. (1985). *The Interpersonal World of the Infant*. New York: Basic Books.

Tustin, F. (1981). *Autistic States in Children*. London and Boston: Routledge and Kegan Paul.

———— (1986). *Autistic Barriers in Neurotic Patients*. New Haven and London: Yale University Press.

———— (1990). *The Protective Shell in Children and Adults*. London: Karnac Books.

Wing, L. (1981). Asperger syndrome: a clinical account. *Psychological Medicine* 11:115–129.

Wing, L. and Gould, J. (1979). Severe impairments of social interaction and associated abnormalities in children: epidemiology and classification. *Journal of Autism and Developmental Disorders* 9:11–29.

Winnicott, D. (1958). The capacity to be alone. In *The Maturational Process and the Facilitating Environment*. London: Hogarth.

———— (1974). Fear of breakdown. *The International Review of Psycho-Analysis* 1:103–107.

Wolff, S. and Barlow, A. (1979). Schizoid personality in childhood: a comparative study of schizoid autistic and normal children. *Journal of Child Psychology and Psychiatry* 20:29–46.

9

Understanding Varieties of Autistic Encapsulation: a Homage to Frances Tustin

David Rosenfeld

Autistic encapsulation seems to be an elemental concretized forerunner of "repression", of denial and of forgetting. I see it as a psycho-physical protective reaction rather than as a psycho-dynamic defense mechanism.

Frances Tustin, "The Autistic Capsule In Neurotic Adults"

I am very pleased to have this opportunity to honor the great teacher, Frances Tustin. Tustin was a *real* teacher, proposing ideas and reexamining rigid perceptions, just like Galileo, who asked us to look through a telescope to discover that we were just one of a number of satellites turning around the sun and that we were not, as we had formerly imagined, the center of the universe. Tustin's work and her legacy have directed us towards new discoveries and faraway worlds. Her work concerned autism and psychotic patients. However, influenced by her, we have been given a telescope through which to have a more comprehensive basis for observing and understanding other disturbances. Tustin has influenced my own work with child patients who move from autism to psychosis; drug addicted patients who demonstrate some autistic features during childhood; some psychosomatic cases; and those survivors of the Nazi Holocaust who have used autistic mechanisms as a way of preserving their childhood memories and identity.

Additionally, I would like to present to the reader a new problem: We are just now receiving cases in psychoanalytic practice of people who have under-

gone vital organ transplants and who have consequently developed a hypochondria—and, at times, a psychosis and psychosomatic illnesses—based on
a specific psychodynamic mechanism. This group of patients with psychosomatic disturbances generally present with autistic mechanisms. Like autistic
children, these patients are enveloped in a world of bodily and tactile sensations. Their psychosomatic symptoms give this type of patient a "sense of
being" which is similar to the bodily sensations autistic children attempt to
achieve by pressing a part of their body against a "hard" object. This use of
bodily sensations makes these patients difficult to cure; the disappearance of
the psychosomatic disturbance means the disappearance or annihilation of a
primitive identity. Even in patients who seem to make use of more "healthy"
or neurotic mechanisms, it can be very useful to look for autistic pockets. It is
also interesting to observe how these very primitive autistic pockets are
hidden by apparent sexual or neurotic behavior (Tustin 1986, 1990).

As Tustin points out (1988), autistic patients are fearful, despite having this
"protective shell," because they feel there is a hole in it. She also states that even
parts of their bodies can be used by these children as "autistic objects," which
create a cluster of sensations that provide them with the illusion of being
impenetrable, all-powerful, safe, and protected. I think today that the "holes"
in the body that adult patients experience might be filled with psychosomatic
disturbances. Just as the autistic children described by Tustin cover over the
"holes" through the use of autistic mechanisms, psychosomatic symptoms
with bodily sensations might be used to provoke a "sense of being," a very
primitive experience of identity.

To illustrate, I will here present a short vignette: the case of a patient I will
call Clarisse. This patient tried to maintain a tenuous "sense of being" and a
primitive sense of identity by provoking bodily sensations. I believe that this
was the only way she was able to feel that she existed.

Clarisse

Clarisse was 24 years old when she was sent to me by a colleague for psychoanalytic treatment. She arrived in my office looking so untidy that she gave
the impression that she was psychotic. She told me she was under psychiatric
treatment and that she was receiving medication since a transient psychosis,
which had begun when she was undergoing treatment at a weight loss clinic.
Her father came with her to the first interview, and he told to me that Clarisse
had a delusion in which she felt that men were following her. In the clinic, she

had felt that one of the male nurses was pursuing her. Both Clarisse and her father also mentioned that she frequently wet her bed at night.

Clarisse was black and, when she started treatment, she explained to me that her biological mother was black and from another country. Clarisse had been adopted by a white family. Her adoptive parents were divorced when she was 14, thus she now lived with her father in Buenos Aires. When she was 11, something very important happened to her. She moved from a quite distant province to Buenos Aires, leaving behind her beloved adoptive maternal grandmother.

During our work together, Clarisse often repeated comments which other therapists had told her during previous treatments, as if these were slogans. For example, on one occasion the patient told me that she masturbated with urine. I was never sure if she was saying this because it was something she actually did or rather because it was something other people had said to her.

The patient started to recover memories which I had asked her to bring to the sessions. She remembered how, during her first year of life, she was absolutely immobile, rigid, and silent. She told me that she had weighed 5 pounds at birth and that her adoptive mother was so afraid of hurting such a "tiny thing" that she would never touch her with her bare hands but only with cotton wool. She never dared to pick up Clarisse. Members of her family remembered Clarisse as lying absolutely rigid and immobile in her cot. She was always silent, with her little arms crossed in front of her chest. It seemed to me that Clarisse had formed a rigid shell in order to protect herself. I interpreted in the session the times when I felt that she was doing the same thing with me in the transference, and I pointed out to her how she always arrived at the sessions absolutely enveloped in a large shawl which she would never take off.

In another session she spoke about the person she loved most in her life: her adoptive grandmother from whom she was separated at the age of 11 when her family moved to Buenos Aires. At the time of this session, the grandmother was still alive. The grandmother was very affectionate—she had contained Clarisse when she was a child and had held her very close to her in her arms. She always caressed Clarisse. She had been the one to help her get dressed, to help her with her school homework, and to take her for walks. Clarisse repeatedly said: "I love her deeply." I discovered in this session that the patient had felt absolutely empty and that she had suffered a terrible affective catastrophe and loss when she moved to the city, losing daily contact with her adoptive grandmother. As we recovered these events during the session, Clarisse said, "I feel a hole in my soul."

Two months later, Clarisse brought a dream at the beginning of the session. The dream was of a white geography teacher at Clarisse's primary school. Clarisse had been the only black child in her school in Buenos Aires. She remembered that this teacher was the only one in whom she could confide, especially with respect to her feelings of loneliness. In her dream, the teacher had black skin, just as Clarisse does, and not white skin like her adoptive family or her beloved grandmother. Based on her associations, I told her that in the dream she seemed to transform her grandmother—who was alive at the time, although old and ill—into a young woman with whom she could talk easily, just as she had been able to do before she was 11 (the age at which she moved to Buenos Aires).

I asked her to remember that in the dream she is a young girl at primary school, before she moved to the city. However, I also interpreted that the teacher could also be her biological mother, represented by the black skin, which was the same color as Clarisse's own. I added that perhaps the dream appeared today for two reasons: one, because the grandmother was more ill than before, and second, because she felt that she had found—in the therapist—a person to whom she could confide her feelings and emotions.

Since moving to Buenos Aires, the patient had started to provoke sensations within her own body as a way of feeling that she was full rather than empty. She achieved this by compulsive eating and by retaining great quantities of urine in her bladder. After a couple of months, I began to understand that her bed wetting was not of the typical variety—that is, due to loss of control of her bladder—but that she would withhold urine for as long as she could stand it in order to have the sensation of being completely full. Only when she was full and about to burst would she run to the toilet. Often, she would wet her bed in her scramble to get to the bathroom.

In that same session she told me that, during her psychotic episode, she had put on fifty pounds. I interpreted that it was very important for her to feel that she was full up and not empty by retaining urine until she was full to bursting and by eating compulsively in order to feel full. I did not take these actions at a sexual/masturbatory level, but at their most primitive level: to be empty or not empty, full up or not, therefore to exist and to have a "sense of being" or to be annihilated. The patient quickly replied that she also retained feces and then asked me if this might be for the same reason. I replied that I thought it was and that she had probably been doing this since she was a little girl in order to feel that she was complete.

In the following session, Clarisse began to recount more of her experience of the loss of her grandmother. She cried inconsolably throughout the session.

She said, in her own words, that she now understood that this loss was the reason why she ate so much and held her urine. I added: "If you don't obtain this sensation in your body, you suppose that you will lose your sense of being, and you will cease to exist."

At the same time, I thought something which I did not mention to the patient: that the bulimia was a way of searching for sensorial experiences. As I write these lines, I am thinking that these bodily sensations are similar to those which autistic children have in early childhood, that this patient was doing the same, although she was an adult. Although an autistic child will actually insert something hard or metallic in the mouth, ear, or anus, as an adult this patient was able to create the same sensations by retaining feces or urine or by eating. This was, in my view, her way of provoking sensorial feelings inside her body. On the more primitive level, this patient was trying to survive terrible and painful losses by obtaining a primary sense of identity.

As for Clarisse's psychotic delusion, that men were persecuting her, I believe that this delusion was also related to her attempts at survival. In her delusion, she is the center of the world, the center of attention of all the men around her. For her, it was better to be the center of persecution than to feel she had been abandoned to solitude—as a little girl by her biological mother, by her adoptive grandmother, and by the adoptive mother who would not touch her.

Clarisse was trying to obtain a very powerful sensation and a sense of omnipotence. Tustin suggested that this state of omnipotence differs from that usually referred to by psychoanalysts. In this case, the patient used part of her own body as an autistic object, which provided the sensation of hardness. An autistic child in the same situation feels invulnerable, impenetrable, armored, and safe. The "holes" are filled by a cluster of subsensations—the autistic shape—and these are comforting and tranquilizing. This is what I believe happened to Clarisse: She used her own body and bodily substances as autistic objects and to create sensation shapes, to feel that she was utterly impenetrable and invulnerable and that nothing could destroy her.

When we treat these adult patients, they gradually develop more of a sense of their own existence and their terrors are mitigated. Using this concept, we can begin to understand many psychosomatic disturbances in a very different way.

Drug Addicts

In my book *The Psychotic Aspects of the Personality* (1992), I proposed a classification of different types of drug addicts that may be useful for the evaluation of the clinical and prognostic status of these patients as well as the therapeutic approach.

Type A

This group is composed of patients who seek a feeling of being enfolded in the sensations that the drug produces in them. They seem to be in search of an envelope or a skin substitute. In these patients we generally find less pathological mourning than in other cases. Provided they are in therapy, their prognosis is generally more favorable.

Patients classified as type A usually have a more neurotic adaptation to reality than other types. Many of these cases are triggered by internal factors reinforced by real situations of mourning. They generally accept analytic treatment.

Type B

This type is composed of patients in whom we find a pathological mourning process, because they identify with a dead object from whom they cannot differentiate. These patients have no concept of danger; they have no perception of risk. Their minds lack this concept because they feel dead. Therefore, they expose themselves to high-risk situations in which their lives are in danger. At the most perilous point, they defy death, and if they survive, they feel as if they have been remarkably resuscitated.

It is very difficult for us, as psychoanalysts, to realize that we are faced with a dead person, an individual who feels dead (a patient totally identified and bonded to a dead object, because of a pathological mourning process), and sometimes it is hard for us to understand that everything the patient does— when he defies death—is really aimed at feeling alive for a short while. In such cases, the whole technique of interpretation must be reconsidered. Countertransference is the key for understanding this type of patient. Boyer, another great teacher, taught us to understand severely regressed patients through the use of the countertransference (Boyer 1983).

Type C

In this category of addicts I find patients who, as children, had some autistic features and who survived by creating their own world of sensations and feelings. Autistic "sensations" are self-generated and are of preeminent importance to such children. About these children Tustin (1990) said:

> Their excessive concentration on sensations engendered by their own body makes them unaware of sensations with more normal objective relevance. [p. 17]

To come back to our adult addicts, type C patients are confined within a paradox, because if they do not achieve those autistic "sensations," they believe they will disappear or die, and if they resort to drugs to achieve them, they may actually die of an overdose. This is a pragmatic paradox. These are extremely serious cases, with scant probability of a cure. These patients differ from type B cases in that they often are reticent to express themselves. They are rarely involved in promiscuous sex or acting-out, and their everyday behavior displays little violence or exuberance.

Into this third category I would put those kinds of patients for whom it is most difficult to effect a change for the better and for whom it is unusual to expect a lessening in drug-taking. The psychopathological structure of these patients is different from that of the others. They are people who, in their early childhood, had mothers with severe depressive episodes. One of my patients, Mr. A, had a mother who suffered from a severe postpartum depressive state. She also had another depressive state after the death of her father, the grandfather of my patient, when Mr. A was 5 years old.

During the first interview with him and one member of his family, it came to my patient's attention and to mine that the grandfather had committed suicide. During the treatment, in one session, Mr. A showed me a photograph album. The photographs exhibited the mental state of the mother very clearly. In one we could see the mother lying on the floor in a depressive state, looking at nothing, while a 3-year-old Mr. A tried with one hand to reach his father, who is standing behind her.

In another case, discussed in a clinical seminar, a 5-year-old girl, diagnosed as autistic, provoked bodily sensations by pressing her tongue around her lips. As she repeated this constantly, her lips became very sore, and it was difficult for her to eat. She had to be put in an intensive care unit. She also refused to eat because she preferred her own bodily sensations, with which she felt protected from dangers in the outside world.

In general, patients in category C are children with autistic features who survive by creating their own sensation-dominated world. However, the adaptation of these patients is very fragile. Faced with any kind of external or internal catastrophe, they try to repeat their early autistic functioning by means of drug consumption or other corporeal activities that provoke bodily sensations.

In the case of Mr. A, his mother died when he was 12 years old. One year later, he began to experiment with drugs, apparently in an effort to deny this unbearably painful situation but also to find, in the drugs, his bodily sensations and to live inside them, as in his early childhood. I see this kind of patient not just as a drug-addict, but as a *survivor*.

Even with good treatment and some hospitalization, one cannot always be successful with these patients. They are prisoners of a pragmatic paradox: They use drugs to obtain very primitive autistic sensations which seem necessary for them to survive and be protected, as in a "shell." They fear that if they cannot obtain these sensations through drugs, they will lose all sense of identity and will disappear. However, if they continue with their level of drug consumption, they become more intoxicated each day, and finally they may die. This is the real pragmatic paradox: Whatever they may decide, whether to abandon drug use or to continue with it, will always be wrong for them.

Survivors of the Nazi Holocaust

I would like to introduce the use of the concept of autistic encapsulation in the treatment of survivors of the Nazi Holocaust. These are patients who used autistic mechanisms as a way of preserving childhood memories and identity. I will present a summary of one case to show how Tustin's theory applies.

The patient, Mario, who was over 40-years old, looked younger than his years. He was tall, dark-haired, athletic-looking, in spite of which his fear, anxiety, and withdrawal were obvious. In the first interview, he spoke about his problem: A stomach pain had returned. His physician had diagnosed gastric ulcer and advised him to start psychoanalytic treatment, which Mario did. He was a typical representative of the Jewish-Spanish Sephardic community of the Bulgarian city in which they were born. Roustchouk, on the Lower Danube, was a wonderful city for a child. People of very different origins lived there together and spoke seven or eight different languages. When asked about his father, Mario said he was a gentle, affectionate man whom everybody loved and who frequently used to play with him. He also remembered that his father used to make fun of him when he could not pronounce certain words correctly.

His first memories concerning fear dated back to his eighth year of life, at which time the Germans had bombed Roustchouk. Mario recalled blood, mutilated bodies, death, and terror. The Nazis were looking for his father, but Mario and he left the city disguised as Moslems. They reached the Dalmatian coast, but Mario's father was arrested there. Luckily, he fell into the hands of the Italian army and was set free. The Italians and Italy had since then become an admired symbol. Mario and his father ran away to Trieste, where the "men in black" tied them with chains and took them to the city of Turin, where they were released and then lodged. After that, Mario lived alone in an orphanage. Those months were like long years for him.

Some time after that, he arrived in Buenos Aires, where a relative secured a job for him in a small factory. In the meantime, he learned that his grandparents and two of his mother's brothers had been killed in Bulgaria. He was over 30-years old when he had his first sexual relationship.

During his first three years of analysis, the patient preserved his apparent formal adjustment, his pseudo-identity, and his narrative-obsessive linguistic style describing real facts and speaking about his commitment to his job. While I supervised this case, Mario's therapist and I attempted various hypotheses on technical approaches in order to get in touch with the encapsulated or supposedly dissociated areas. One of these approaches was to suggest that, since one of the following sessions coincided with the most important Jewish religious festivity—Atonement Day or Yom Kippur—the therapist might make it clear that if the patient did not want to come to his session, he did not have to. That is, his therapist would respect his being a Jew and that he did not have to hide again.

Three sessions later, something completely new happened: The material brought by the patient showed how important his Jewish identity was for him. This had not become manifest before; it seemed to have been encapsulated and kept away, preserved by the patient, as well as he could, within his self. In this session, he remembered the time when he used to ride on his grandfather's shoulders and was filled by the peculiar smell of his grandfather's hair. He went as far as to say: "I seem to smell it in the session." Then he told the therapist he had watched "Holocaust" on television and described an episode in which the father of the family in the film met a brother, and they both walked together along the railway tracks.

At that moment, the patient stopped. His mind seemed to go blank, he remained silent, he skipped the next scene, and he started speaking about another part of the film. The therapist, who had seen "Holocaust," pointed out his mistake to him, saying that he had stopped, remained silent, and then gone on talking after skipping a whole scene in which the father walked with a man called Moses. The patient's tone of voice suffered an abrupt change and, deeply impressed, he said: "Doctor, you're right. I've just remembered my name *is* Moses." The patient had lived in Argentina for more than 30 years, during which time that name had never reached his consciousness nor had he ever spoken about it or mentioned it at home. He was 14 when he arrived, and it was as if, ever since then, part of his identity had remained encapsulated; now, after that long hibernation, it had emerged again, well preserved, in the course of a session. Deeply moved and trying to overcome his own surprise, his therapist asked: "But then, your name isn't Mario but Moses?" "Doctor, I have just remembered they used to call me Misha, as a diminutive of Moshe."

In another session, the patient reported that he had attended an important event in the Jewish tradition: the celebration, known as Bar Mitzvah, of his partner's 13-year old son. Obviously moved, the patient said he had found himself crying at the Synagogue. He added that he had felt frightened and that, like in his dreams, he was suddenly filled with emotions and memories: Roustchouk, voices calling him Misha, an image of himself on his grandfather's shoulders, the strong smell of his grandfather's hair.

Then he told the therapist: "I will never recover that name, because the registrar's office where my true name is written down was destroyed, burned down by a bomb." The patient remained overwhelmed by deep emotions for the rest of the session. Childhood feelings and memories connected with his father, prior to the Nazi persecution, also began to emerge. This made it possible to deal with the mourning over his father's death from another perspective, for instance the memory of some mischief. When he was a child, Mario had drawn away the chair on which his father was about to sit down so that he would fall. The 1982 war between Argentina and Great Britain over the Falkland Islands aroused feelings of exacerbated terror in Mario-Moshe. Although in the course of the session he said, "This is too much for a child," it was our belief that he now had new and better resources to face this war as well as the kidnapping and abduction of people in the streets of Buenos Aires during the military regime, which always reminded him of the day his father was taken away and sent to jail.

Very early childhood memories cropped up suddenly and in a disorderly way. The patient himself realized that there was a "hole," a gap, in his earliest childhood. One day he asked his mother what had happened in his early years in the town of Roustchouk. The mother told him facts and anecdotes, among them, one in which a neighbor gave him a present. The patient, in a deeply regressed state during the session, unwittingly spoke in Italian. In this way he expressed, in a very concrete manner, the linguistic regression he allowed himself. And, as the poet says:

> Est parvenu maintenant au terme de sa route, il se
> devoile et eclaire
> les vingt annees de mutisme ecoulees dans son ombre.
> Il ne pourrait pas
> autant reveler s'il ne s'etait tu si longtemps . . .
> (Elias Canetti, *Territoire de l'homme*)

> He has now reached the end of his journey, he takes
> off his veils and
> clarifies the twenty years of silence elapsed under his
> own shadow. He could
> not have revealed so much if he had not remained
> silent for so long . . .
> (translation mine)

Psychosis and Cardiac Transplant

In my book *The Psychotic Aspects of the Personality* (Rosenfeld 1992), I presented the case of a heart transplant patient about which I now have new thoughts. I would like to establish clearly two aspects that are evident in the following clinical case: the transference psychosis and delusions (expressed in the transference-countertransference interplay), and the role of the father in the evolution of this patient. These two elements, within the framework of the sessions, allowed the therapist to detect the rejection of the transplanted organ.

In the clinical material, we will see how the patient sometimes became his own father; he imitated his voice, his accent, and his mannerisms. At other times, he became his own son, who died at the age of 19. He believed that he was resurrecting him, as he carried inside himself the transplanted heart of a young man of the same age. At one point during the treatment, he played the father taking care of his son, and it was then that he best took care of the heart of the young man he fantasized to be his own son, and for whom he was caring.

The patient, whom we shall call Hamlet, was 51-years of age and had sought psychoanalytic treatment after being told that he had to undergo cardiac surgery, with an indication for a heart transplant. He was in a state of extreme anxiety and despair, and in this condition he began treatment. He appeared to be an intelligent, tuned-in, thinking person, with sensitive feelings. He had divorced and remarried, and he had a 10-year old daughter. One of Hamlet's sons had died a few years earlier, at the age of 19; before that, Hamlet's father had died as well. His mother had died when he was 2. She had been very ill for a year after the birth of his younger brother.

Hamlet was prepared for cardiac surgery; he was waiting for the moment when a donor heart was obtained for transplant. The donor turned out to be a young athlete who had died in a car accident. After surgery, Hamlet resumed analysis when he was authorized to leave the special care unit. In one of the sessions, the patient greeted the analyst in his hospital room, shouting: "Out, you intruder! I want no intruders, you're invading me!" During this episode the patient was in a state of delusion, in which the analyst was one of the intruders who invaded him.

Let it be clear that this delusion did not appear on the day following the transplant nor immediately upon leaving the intensive care unit but rather when he was about to be discharged from the hospital. The analyst had been seeing Hamlet every day, and, when Hamlet was near his recovery and discharge, he suddenly and surprisingly received the therapist in this state of delusion, which enhanced the impact on the therapist. (The therapist made a note after the session to the effect that he believed that this delusion might indicate a rejection of the therapist in the transference and that he feared that it might presage or indicate Hamlet's rejection of the graft.)

I believe that the patient was projecting into the external space—into the hospital room or the consulting room—and into the transference the unfolding of his inner world, something that in a persecutory or delusional way was felt to have gotten into his body. The room seemed to represent his body, in which the alien heart or the analyst were intruders (Searles 1966). It is in this space that we suppose he rejects the therapist. Could it be possible that he is also rejecting the introjection of the primitive protecting figures of his childhood, possibly his mother-the-breast, and his father? Is it the specter, the ghost? Who comes in as an intruder, the ghost of his mother or that of his son? Is it Hamlet's ghost that is reappearing?

In addition, we believe that he was reacting to this very special situation in the same way that he experienced his childhood bonds or introjections. The following day, a routine heart biopsy showed signs of rejection, and the cardiologist asked the therapist to prepare the patient psychologically to receive the news of the rejection, which implied that his discharge would be delayed. (We are not stating here that psychoanalysis can always detect transplant rejections. We are only presenting an experience interpreted as a hypothesis that the patient was rejecting a part of himself, of his new identity, or something coming from outside, which was very dangerous and was invading him.)

The following session began as follows: The patient said that in the hospital, with the doctors and the nurses, he felt that he was being taken care of, since they came rushing as soon as he called. Using the same words as the analyst, he added that the prospect of going home made him feel helpless, unprotected, and in danger. The therapist interpreted that the prospect of going home also meant that he was well and getting better, that he would rejoin his family environment, and, above all, that he would be reunited with his small daughter, whom he missed very much.

In another part of the session, the therapist interpreted that the small daughter represented the infantile part of the patient which had been left unprotected. The patient went on to say that "the intruder was inside him and that he had to perform mental immobilization exercises and send messages from his mind to his sick heart in order to attain harmony between his mind and his heart." (The similarities with some phases of the Shreber case are remarkable.) The therapist told him that the intruding heart was the healthy heart.

After a period of recovery, the patient was discharged. From October onward he was able to go out, walk, and attend the consulting room. The insomnia that had afflicted him became less serious. Sometimes he came: (1) with the more adult part of his self; (2) as a trembling (2-year-old) child, as he had come during the beginning of his treatment; (3) as another part of the patient with his omnipotent self; (4) with his adolescent part; (5) confused with his adolescent son, whom he brought back to life and resurrected inside himself, as he carried inside him the heart of a young man whom he believed to be his son, or the heart of his son; (6) looking like his father, when he imitated his voice, his accent, and his verbal mannerisms; or (7) as the mother, in the transferential dynamics, projected into the therapist, who thus assumed the role of the mother (or of the grandmother, who had lovingly taken care of him as a child).

It was at this time that the material about the patient's feminine aspects, which he mistook for homosexuality, became clearer: This was a total or narcissistic early identification with his mother, which became more intense two years later when she died. We could see that for him, searching for and being with his mother was in fact like becoming and being the mother-feminine-woman. In moments of regression, this was the way in which he could find his mother, though at the expense of feeling tied up and confused with a woman. His defense before this consisted in: (1) promiscuous sexual escapades (particularly some years before) to prove to himself that he had a penis and that he was a man for many women; and (2) appearing as a child with an omnipotent self—trying to prove that he needed nothing from anyone (the breast, the mother, the therapist). All this was mixed up with an intense homosexual panic.

As I said before, I have revised my ideas on this case. I believe that, with the revolutionary surgical breakthroughs of the last years, patients do in reality lose very vital parts of their own bodies. To cover up this loss the patient creates a "protective shell," just as autistic children do, to cover up the "black hole" left after the event of the loss. As a consequence, patients with transplants often present hypochondriacal symptoms. My thought today, after treating and supervising a number of cases of organ transplant patients, is that these patients repeat the same evolution and mechanisms as described by Francis Tustin in her studies of cases of infantile autism. Autistic children suffer a terrible depression after their birth, because they have the sensation that they have lost a vital part of their bodies, and that vital part which has been lost is represented as a "black hole." The "black hole" is so terrifying that it needs to be covered with a "protective shell."

When an adult undergoes a vital organ transplant, he consequently needs to cover the loss, and he does so by developing a hypochondria, the hypochondria being a sort of mental protective covering which will keep the mind occupied with rumination and repetition on what has happened to the bodily part which has been separated. If this covering of the hole is not successful, then these patients will become psychotic and delusional. My conclusion is that these transplant patients seem to repeat the same defensive maneuvers and mechanisms as autistic children who move from autism to psychosis.

References

Boyer, B. (1983). *The Regressed Patient*. New York and London: Jason Aronson.

Rosenfeld, D. (1992). *The Psychotic Aspects of the Personality*. London: Karnac Books.

Searles, H. (1966). *The Non Human Environment in Personal Development and Schizophrenia*. New York: International Universities Press.

Tustin, F. (1986). *Autistic Barriers in Children and Adults*. London: Karnac Books.

———— (1988). "To be or not to be": a study of autism. *Winnicott Studies* 3:43–55.

———— (1990). *The Protective Shell in Children and Adults*. London: Karnac Books.

10

Some Theoretical Comments on Personal Isolation[1]

Thomas H. Ogden

> *It remains to learn in what delicate, exquisite region of Being we shall encounter that Being which is its own Nothingness.*
>
> Jean-Paul Sartre, "Being and Nothingness"

In the course of the past decade, I have come to view the concept of personal isolation as central to an understanding of human development. My own conception of personal isolation is based upon ideas derived from the psychoanalytic study of autistic phenomena by Frances Tustin and others, as well as Winnicott's conception of isolation as a necessary condition for psychological health.

Winnicott's work will be taken as a starting point for the understanding of personal isolation as an essential facet of the experience of being alive. I shall then attempt to describe a primitive form of isolation that involves the disconnection of the individual not only from the mother as object but also from the very fabric of the human interpersonal matrix.

The idea that there is an aspect of experience in which the individual must be insulated from being in the world has its origins in Freud's (1920) concept of the stimulus barrier (*Reizschutz*). Freud believed that the preservation of

---

1. An earlier version of this paper was published in 1991 in *Psychoanalytic Dialogues*.

the organism is as much dependent upon the capacity not to perceive as it is upon the capacity to register internal and external stimuli:

> [the organism] would be killed . . . if it were not provided with a protective shield against stimuli. It acquires the shield in this way: its outermost surface ceases to have the structure proper to living matter, becomes to some degree inorganic and thenceforward functions as a special envelope or membrane resistant to stimuli. . . . By its death, the outer layer has saved all the deeper ones from a similar fate. . . . [p. 27]

In this chapter, I shall make use of concepts emanating from the psychoanalytic study of autistic phenomena to further develop the idea that the experience of being alive as a human being is safeguarded by forms of suspension of being.

Winnicott's Conceptions of Isolation

The discussion of personal isolation must begin with the study of Winnicott's seminal contributions to this area of thought. Winnicott (1963) viewed the individual as (in part) "an isolate, permanently unknown, in fact unfound" (p. 183). He believed that the isolation of the infant from the object objectively perceived is an essential experiential context for the development of a sense of realness and spontaneity of the self. The concept of isolation is an idea that evolved over the entire span of Winnicott's writing. It overlaps and is intertwined with such ideas as the holding environment, relatedness to transitional objects, the capacity to be alone, the experience of playing, and the development of the True and False Self.

In the present discussion, I shall focus on what I understand to be Winnicott's two principal conceptions of isolation. Although the two "forms" of isolation that will be discussed can be understood as having a sequential, developmental relationship to one another, they must at the same time be thought of as coexisting facets or qualities of a single, dynamic phenomenon: the experience of personal isolation.

The developmentally earlier form of isolation described by Winnicott involves the insulation of the infant from premature awareness of the separateness of self and object. This insulation is provided by the mother-as-environment as she meets the infant's need before it becomes desire (Winnicott 1945, 1951, 1952, 1956, 1971a). In so doing, there is a postponement of awareness of the separate existence of the object of desire. As importantly, the infant is protected (isolated) from the awareness of desire itself, and therefore, of the separate existence of the self. The reliability of the mother-as-environment renders her (and the infant) invisible. The nonself-reflective state of being that occurs within the context of the mother-as-environment is termed by Winnicott (1963) a state of *going on being* (p. 183). The phrase, "going on being" is particularly apt in that it names a state of aliveness without reference to either subject or object.

The developmentally later form of isolation that Winnicott (1958, 1962, 1963, 1968) discussed is that of relatedness to objects that are created and not found. Such objects are termed *subjective objects.* The mother-as-environment provides the infant a form of isolation from externality by means of an illusion of "omnipotence" (1963, p. 182). The mother creates this illusion by providing the breast when and in the way that it is needed and desired by the infant. Winnicott's term *omnipotence* is a bit of a misnomer, since there is no experience of power over, or domination of, the object. In fact, the infant's experience of himself as powerful would reflect a breakdown of the infant's unself-conscious illusion that the world is simply a reflection of himself. The infant need not control the object: the heart of this illusion is the infant's sense that the object could not be otherwise. In this way, the infant begins to apprehend the qualities of his own individuality as he sees himself reflected in the world that he has "created." From an outside observer's point of view, the mother substantiates—and gives observable, palpable form to—the infant's internal state through the way in which she responds to him. For example, the infant's curiosity is reflected (given observable shape) in the mother's tone of voice, facial expressions, tempo of motion, and so on: "The mother is looking at the baby and what *she looks like is related to what she sees there*" (Winnicott 1967, p. 112).

The subjective object—created through this form of interaction with the mother—is therefore both a creation of and reflection of the evolving self. Subjective objects are internal objects that are derived from this form of early mother-infant interaction. Communication with subjective objects is a "cul-de-sac communication" (Winnicott 1963, p. 184), a communication that is not addressed to external objects and therefore entails an isolation of the self from the necessity to be responsive to objects objectively perceived.[2] Communica-

---

2. This form of isolation (relatedness to subjective objects) becomes one pole of a dialectic that underlies the creation of transitional phenomena (Winnicott 1951,

tion with subjective objects is, from an outsider's point of view, "futile" (p. 184) and yet "carries all the sense of real" (p. 184). Isolation of this sort is experientially related to a sense of privacy as opposed to a feeling of loneliness.

In summary, Winnicott has developed conceptions of two forms of isolation, each of which facilitates the development of the self and each of which paradoxically involves a disconnection from the mother as object that is achieved within the (invisible) mother-as-environment.

Autism and Multiplicity of Forms of Consciousness

Before presenting my own conception of a type of isolation more primitive than those described by Winnicott, I would like to briefly comment on the Mahlerian notion of an early phase of autism and to introduce the idea of coexisting forms of consciousness.

For decades, Margaret Mahler's (1968) conception of a normal early phase of autism followed by a "hatching" subphase represented an important organizing concept for psychoanalytic developmental theory.[3] However, there is, by now, general consensus among analytic thinkers (supported by neonatal observational studies and the application of ethological models to psychoanalysis) that the infant at birth is already a psychological entity engaged in a complex set of interpersonal interactions with the mother. There is little if any evidence to support the notion of an early stage or phase of development in which the infant exists in a cocoonlike state that is preliminary to primitive relatedness to human beings. At present, such a position seems untenable. The work of Bower (1977), Brazelton (1981), Eimas (1975), Sander (1964), Stern (1977), Trevarthan (1979), and many others has provided powerful evidence for the notion that from the first moments of extra-uterine life, the infant is

---

1971b). Relatedness to subjective objects and communication with objects objectively perceived coexist in dialectical tension in the creation of transitional objects. Such objects are both created and discovered: The question as to which is the case never arises.

3. At the end of her life, Mahler reportedly modified her position with regard to her idea that in the earliest months of life, the infant lives in a "closed monadic system, self-sufficient in its hallucinatory wish fulfillment," (1968, p. 7) and began to integrate the findings of neonatal observational studies concerning the infant's responsiveness to his human and nonhuman environment (cf. Stern 1985).

constitutionally equipped to perceive and enter into a reciprocal dialogue with the mother or other caregiver.

The debate concerning the question of whether the infant is in the beginning at one with the mother (and therefore unaware of her separate existence and his own), or whether the infant is capable of recognizing the difference between himself and the Other, is a more complex matter. It seems to me that it is no longer necessary or advisable to construct our questions about infantile experience in such a way as to force us to choose between the notion of the infant being at one with the mother or separate from her. Instead, if we view infantile experience (and human experience in general) as the outcome of a dialectical process involving multiple forms of consciousness (each coexisting with the others), it is no longer necessary to cast our questions in terms of mutually exclusive oppositions (Grotstein 1981, Stern 1983).

The question of whether the infant is at one with the mother or is separate from her becomes a question of the nature of the interplay between simultaneous experiences of at-one-ment and of separateness. These forms of experience are not viewed as entering into a compromise formation or a mutually diluting (averaging) interaction; rather, the different forms of consciousness are understood to coexist dialectically in a way that is comparable to the relationship of conscious and unconscious experience (Ogden 1986, 1988). Each provides a negating and preserving context for the other. The experience of at-one-ment does not dilute the experience of separateness any more than the experience of consciousness dilutes unconsciousness. Each form of consciousness maintains its own qualities that have meaning that is, in large part, created by its relationship to that which it is not.

The Sensation Matrix

As further background for the understanding of primitive isolation, I would now like to briefly present a group of concepts emanating from the psychoanalytic investigation of autistic phenomena. The primitive type of isolation that will be discussed involves an isolation of the individual in a self-generated sensation matrix (which substitutes for the interpersonal matrix). In what follows, I shall attempt to provide a vocabulary for thinking about the notion of auto-sensuous isolation.

In previous papers (Ogden 1988, 1989a, 1989b, 1991), I have introduced the idea that there exists a psychological organization more primitive than those addressed by Klein's (1946, 1958) concepts of the paranoid-schizoid and depressive positions. I have designated this psychological organization the *autistic-contiguous position*[4] and conceive of it as standing in dialectical tension with the paranoid-schizoid and depressive positions. It must be borne in mind that the term *autistic* is used in this context to refer to specific features of a universal mode of generating experience and not to a severe form of child-hood psychopathology or its sequelae. It would be as absurd to conceive of the autistic-contiguous position as a phase of infantile autism as it would be to conceive of the paranoid-schizoid position as a phase of infantile paranoid schizophrenia or the depressive position as a universal period of childhood depression.

The autistic-contiguous position is characterized by its own distinctive form of relatedness to objects in which the object is a sensation experience (particularly at the skin surface). Such sensory experience is an experience of *being-in-sensation*. Within this sensation dominated realm, the experience of objects is predominantly in the form of relatedness to "autistic shapes" (Tustin 1984) and "autistic objects" (Tustin 1980). Autistic shapes are "felt shapes" (Tustin 1984, p. 280) that arise from the soft touching of surfaces that make sensory impressions at our skin surface. These are not experiences of the "thingness" of an object; rather, they are the experience of the feel of the object held softly against one's skin. This shape is idiosyncratic to each of us and represents the beginnings of the experience of place.

For example, the breast is not experienced as a part of the mother's body that has a particular (visually perceived) shape, softness, texture, warmth, and so forth. Instead, (or more accurately, in dialectical tension with the experi-ence of the breast as a visually perceived object), the breast as autistic shape is the experience of being a place (an area of sensation of a soothing sort) that is created (for example) as the infant's cheek rests against the mother's breast. The contiguity of skin surfaces creates an idiosyncratic shape *that is the infant at that moment*. In other words, the infant's being is in this way given sensory definition and a sense of locale.

The experience of autistic objects represents quite a different sensory event

---

4. In proposing the concept of an autistic-contiguous position, I have attempted to integrate and extend the pioneering work of Bick (1968, 1986), Meltzer (Meltzer 1986, Meltzer, et al. 1975), and Tustin (1972, 1980, 1981, 1984, 1986), as well as that of Anthony (1958), Anzieu (1985), Fordham (1977), E. Gaddini (1969, 1987), R. Gaddini (1978, 1987), Grotstein (1978), Kanner (1944), S. Klein (1980), Mahler (1952, 1968), Rosenfeld (1984), Searles (1960) and others.

from the experience of autistic shapes. Autistic objects are sensory experiences that have a quality of hardness and/or edgedness and serve to create a feeling of protectedness against nameless, formless dread. Such sensations might arise from the pressing of a stone hard into the palm of one's hand. As with autistic shapes, it is not the visually perceived thingness of the object that is experienced; rather, the experience of an autistic object is one of *being a hard shell or crust*. It must be emphasized that the use of autistic shapes and objects is by no means a phenomenon exclusively associated with severe psychological illness. Relatedness to autistic shapes constitutes a part of normal infantile, childhood, and adult development.

For example, the comfort that an infant experiences in thumb-sucking is not only derived from the representational value of the thumb as stand-in for the breast; in addition, there is a dimension of thumb sucking that can be understood as involving a relationship to an autistic shape through which a sense of self-as-sensory-surface is generated.

Similarly, relationships to autistic objects represent an aspect of psychological life of healthy individuals from infancy onward. For example, "pushing oneself to one's limits" intellectually and/or physically generates a psychological state in which the individual feels fully engrossed, not only in meeting specific ego ideals, entering into competition (unconsciously phantasied as a battle), and so forth. In addition, such activity often involves a dimension of relatedness to an autistic object through which one creates a palpable sensory "edge" that helps provide a sense of boundedness of self.

Relations with autistic shapes and objects are "perfect" in that they lie outside of the unpredictability of relations with human beings. Autistic shapes and objects (for example, hair twirling and biting down on the inner surface of one's cheek) are sensory experiences that can be replicated in precisely the same way whenever they are needed. These "felt shapes" and "felt-objects" exist outside of time and place.

I would like to focus for illustrative purposes on rumination as a use of ideation as an autistic shape. Rumination is a form of mental activity that can be called upon instantaneously as a sensory medium in which one can immerse oneself. The repetitive thoughts are associated with a rhythmic set of "physical-mental" sensations, that is, a state of mind that has a palpable, sensory quality. The individual and the sensation-thought are one. To a large degree, there is simply a sensation-thought in the absence of a thinker. This absence of subjectivity is akin to Bion's (1977) notion of a "thought without a thinker." Rumination can be compared to a flawlessly operating machine.

Nothing in the world (of object relations) can begin to compete with its reliability.

Primitive Isolation

With the background provided by the foregoing discussion of (1) Winnicott's conceptions of personal isolation; (2) the notion of a dialectical interplay among a multiplicity of forms of consciousness; and (3) the concept of relatedness to autistic shapes and objects, it is now possible to offer some comments on a type of isolation that involves a more radical disconnection from human beings and yet is no less life-sustaining than those forms of isolation previously described.

The isolation associated with experience of an autistic-contiguous sort involves a more thorough detachment from the world of human beings than either of the two forms of isolation described by Winnicott. Isolation of an autistic-contiguous sort involves *to some degree* the act of substituting a self-generated sensation environment for the mother-as-environment. The mental activity involved in the creation of this sensation-environment has the effect of suspending the individual somewhat precariously between the land of the living and the land of the (psychologically) dead. Coming alive as a human being involves the act of being held by and within the matrix of the physical and psychological aliveness of the mother (initially the mother-as-environment and later the mother-as-object). This aspect of normal development, including the necessary isolation of the individual from premature awareness of the externality of the object (and the separateness of self and object), has been described above.

What I would like to add to this conception of early development is the notion that psychological life does not unfold exclusively within the context of the mother-as-environment. I am proposing that from the beginning of psychological life (and continuing throughout life), there exists a form of experience in which the mother as psychological matrix is replaced by an autonomous sensory matrix. In replacing the environmental mother with an autonomous sensation matrix, the infant creates an essential respite from the strain (and intermittent terror)[5] inherent in the process of coming to life in the realm of living human beings.

---

5. Failure of the mother to provide a good enough holding environment (whether primarily the result of the inadequacy of the mother or a reflection of the hypersen-

It is essential to bear in mind that the autistic-contiguous dimension of isolation that I am describing constitutes a universal dimension of human experience and is an essential part of the overall process of coming alive as a human being. It represents a necessary resting point or sanctuary within the process of becoming (and being) human.[6] Autistic-contiguous isolation stands in contrast to the stable, impenetrable solipsism of pathological autism. The primitive isolation that I am describing represents a sensation-dominated form of insulation that serves to protect the individual against the continuous strain that is an inescapable part of living in the unpredictable matrix of human object relations. It provides a temporary suspension of being alive within the mother-as-environment as opposed to a permanent negation of being or irrevocable renunciation of the maternal matrix. The capacity to suspend being in the mother-as-environment exists in dialectical tension with the capacity to tolerate the strain (and terror) of being alive in the human interpersonal context.

The suspension of the uncertainties and unpredictability of being in the realm of the human is achieved through a shift in the balance of coexisting forms of being. The living human environment is replaced by relationships with perfectly reliable sensory experiences of an autistic-contiguous sort. Such autistic-contiguous "relationships" are machine-like in their precision and therefore can be thought of as a replacement of the human world with a nonhuman one (Searles 1960). However, the nonhuman is not synonymous with the dead; rather, nonhuman (machinelike) sensation shapes and objects provide a context that is free of the inexplicable, unpredictable ripples and gaps that are an inevitable part of the texture of living human relationships. The type of isolation I have in mind is not a form of psychological death. (Death, conceived of as inert nothingness, cannot constitute a pole of a dialectical process.) What I am attempting to describe is a suspension of life in the world of the living and the replacement of that world with an autonomous world of "perfect" sensation "relationships."

The well-timed, periodic letting go of and retrieval of the infant from this

---

sitivity of the infant) is experienced by the infant as the terror of impending annihilation (Winnicott 1952). An important dimension of this feeling of terror is the sensation of falling or leaking into boundless, shapeless space (Bick 1968, Rosenfeld 1984).

6. Perhaps the non-REM portion of sleep (dreamless sleep devoid of both dream objects and "the dream screen" [Lewin 1950]) represents a form of being that is isolated from both the mother-as-object and the mother-as-environment.

form of isolation is an essential part of the early rhythmicity of human development. In the process of letting go of the infant, the mother must allow the infant to replace her, to exclude her (to obliterate her existence both as object and as environment). Very often, one of the most difficult facets of being a mother is the pain entailed in not being allowed to be a mother. The mother must tolerate the experience of not existing for her infant without becoming overwhelmed by feelings of depression, fear, or anger. Instead, she must be able to wait while her being-as-mother is suspended (she must allow the infant his sanctuary).[7] Fain (1971) has described mothers who are unable to let go of their infants in this way. The result is a type of infantile insomnia wherein the infant can only sleep while being physically held by the mother.

It is equally important that the mother be able to "compete" (Tustin, 1986) with the perfection of the infant's sensation-dominated sanctuary in her attempts to retrieve the infant and return him to the land of the living. Such efforts at competing with autistic phenomena require considerable confidence and feelings of self-worth on the part of the mother (Ogden 1991, Tustin 1986).

I have come to view pathological autism as representing a failure of the mother-infant dyad to negotiate this delicate balance between being in the mother-as-environment and the suspension of that form of being. A depressed mother may mistakenly experience this form of primitive isolation as a categorical rejection of her as a mother. This may set in motion a vicious cycle of mutual withdrawal: The infant's withdrawal from the mother leads her to become despondent and overwhelmed by feelings of worthlessness

---

7. An analysand who had recently given birth to a healthy infant experienced a state of panic when the infant slept, fearing that he was dead. Anxiety of this type (although usually of lesser intensity) is not uncommon and often leads the mother to be unable to sleep when the infant sleeps for fear that she will awaken to find that her baby has died. We as analysts are familiar with such anxiety and have tended to understand it in terms of universal unconscious murderous wishes as well as the projection of the mother's own sense of inner deadness. It seems to me that such understandings must be supplemented by an appreciation of an additional component of the early mother-infant relationship. I have come to view such anxiety as reflecting the mother's response to her actual experience that the infant at times has been lost to her and each time has somehow been retrieved. That is, the mother has in fact experienced the loss of her infant in the course of the infant's periodic isolation of himself in his own sensory matrix and she is terrified that this experience of "near death" will be repeated (this time irreversibly).

which in turn leads the infant to seek deeper refuge in his auto-sensuous sanctuary. Eventually, this spiral of disconnection of mother and infant reaches a point of no return. At this juncture, there is a collapse of the normal periodicity of withdrawal into auto-sensuality and retrieval into the realm of the human. This collapse represents a psychological catastrophe of the greatest magnitude—the infant moves beyond the "gravitational pull" of human relatedness and "floats off" into a realm of impenetrable, uninterrupted nonbeing. The crossing of this "line" represents the transformation of normal auto-sensuous isolation into pathological autism.

Concluding Comments

In this chapter, I have attempted to expand the concept of personal isolation to include a form of isolation in which the infant replaces the mother-as-environment with his own sensation matrix. The creation of such a self-generated sensation matrix stands in contrast to Winnicott's concept of the early illusion of at-one-ment with the mother and his concept of relations to subjective objects since both of the types of isolation described by Winnicott are mediated by a relationship to the mother-as-environment. The type of isolation that I have described involves a more radical withdrawal from human beings; it entails a withdrawal from the mother-as-environment as well as from mother-as-object.

Withdrawal from the mother (both as object and as environment) into a world of relations to autistic shapes and objects is viewed as a feature of normal early development. Relations to autistic shapes and objects are machinelike in their reliability and in their capacity to be endlessly replicated outside of time and place. This form of experience is not conceived of as representing an early phase or stage of development prior to object relatedness; rather, it is viewed as an ongoing facet of all human experience that serves as a form of buffer against the continual strain of being alive in the world of human beings. It provides a rim of suspended being that makes bearable the uncertainty and pain of human relations. In the absence of this facet of experience—this form of not being in the human world—we are skinless and unbearably exposed. Physiologically, it is essential that one's skin be continually generating a layer of dead tissue that serves as a life-preserving outermost layer of the body. In this way, as in Freud's concept of the stimulus barrier, human life is physiologically encapsulated by death. I have suggested that psychological life is from the beginning similarly safeguarded by the sanctuary provided by the experience of not being in the "land of the living."

References

Anthony, J. (1958). An experimental approach to the psychopathology of childhood: autism. *British Journal of Medical Psychology* 31:211–225.

Anzieu, D. (1985). *The Skin Ego.* Madison, CT: International Universities Press.

Bick, E. (1968). The experience of the skin in early object relations. *International Journal of Psycho-Analysis* 49:484–486.

——— (1986). Further considerations on the function of the skin in early object relations. *British Journal of Psychotherapy* 2:292–299.

Bion, W.R. (1977). Unpublished presentation at Children's Hospital, San Francisco, CA, February.

Bower, T.G.R. (1977). The object in the world of the infant. *Scientific American* 225:30–48.

Brazelton, T.B. (1981). *On Becoming a Family: The Growth of Attachment.* New York: Delta/Seymour Lawrence.

Eimas, P. (1975). Speech perception in early infancy. In *Infant Perception: From Sensation to Cognition*, vol. 2, ed. L.B. Cohen and P. Salapatek, pp. 193–228. New York: Academic Press.

Fain, M. (1971). Prélude a la vie fantasmatique. *Revue Française Psychanalyse* 35:291–364.

Fordham, M. (1977). *Autism and the Self.* London: Heinemann.

Freud, S. (1920). Beyond the Pleasure Principle. *Standard Edition* 18:3–66.

Gaddini, E. (1969). On imitation. *International Journal of Psycho-Analysis* 50:275–484.

——— (1987). Notes on the mind-body question. *International Journal of Psycho-Analysis* 68:315–330.

Gaddini, R. (1978). Transitional object origins and the psycho-somatic symptom. In *Between Reality and Fantasy*, ed. S.E. Grolnick, L. Barkin, and W. Munsterberge, pp. 109–131. New York: Jason Aronson.

——— (1987). Early care and the roots of internalization. *International Review of Psycho-Analysis* 14:321–334.

Grotstein, J.S. (1978). Inner space: its dimensions and its coordinates. *International Journal of Psycho-Analysis* 59:55–61.

———— (1981). *Splitting and Projective Identification.* New York: Jason Aronson.

Kanner, L. (1944). Early infantile autism. *Journal of Pediatrics* 25:211–217.

Klein, M. (1946). Notes on some schizoid mechanisms. In *Envy and Gratitude and Other Works, 1946–1963*, pp. 1–24. New York: Delacorte, 1975.

———— (1958). On the development of mental functioning. In *Envy and Gratitude and Other Works, 1946–1963*, pp. 236–246. New York: Delacorte, 1975.

Klein, S. (1980). Autistic Phenomena in neurotic patients. *International Journal of Psycho-Analysis* 61:395–401.

Lewin, B. (1950). *The Psychoanalysis of Elation.* New York: The Psychoanalytic Quarterly Press.

Mahler, M. (1952). On childhood psychoses and schizophrenia: autistic and symbiotic infantile psychoses. *The Psychoanalytic Study of the Child* 7:286–305.

———— (1968). *On Human Symbiosis and the Vicissitudes of Individuation, vol. I.* New York: International Universities Press.

Meltzer, D. (1986). Discussion of Esther Bick's paper, "Further considerations on the function of the skin in early object relations." *British Journal of Psychotherapy* 2:300–301.

Meltzer, D., Bremmer, J., Hoxter, S., Weddell, D., and Wittenberg, I. (1975). *Explorations in Autism.* Perthshire, Scotland: Clunie Press.

Ogden, T. (1985). On potential space, *International Journal of Psycho-Analysis* 66:129–141.

———— (1986). *The Matrix of the Mind: Object Relations and the Psychoanalytic Dialogue.* New Jersey: Jason Aronson.

———— (1988). On the dialectical structure of experience: some clinical and theoretical implications. *Contemporary Psychoanalysis*, 24:17–45.

———— (1989a). On the concept of an autistic-contiguous position. *International Journal of Psycho-Analysis* 70:127–149.

———— (1989b). *The Primitive Edge of Experience.* New Jersey: Jason Aronson.

———— (1991). Analyzing the matrix of transference. *International Journal of Psycho-Analysis*, 72:593–605.

Rosenfeld, D. (1984). Hypochondrias, somatic delusion and body scheme in psycho-analytic practice. *International Journal of Psycho-Analysis* 65:377–388.

Sander, L. (1964). Adaptive relations in early mother–child interactions. *Journal of the American Academy of Child Psychiatry* 3:231–264.

Sartre, J.P. (1943). *Being and Nothingness.* Trans. H. Barnes. New York: Philosophical Library, 1956.

Searles, H. (1960). *The Nonhuman Environment.* New York: International Universities Press.

Stern, D. (1977). *The First Relationship: Infant and Mother.* Cambridge, Mass. Harvard University Press.

———— (1983). The early development of schemas of self, other and "self with other." In *Reflections on Self Psychology,* ed. J. Lichtenberg and S. Kaplan, pp. 49–84. New Jersey: Analytic Press.

———— (1985). *The Interpersonal World of the Infant.* New York: Basic Books.

Trevarthan, C. (1979). Communication and cooperation in early infancy: a description of primary intersubjectivity. In *Before Speech,* ed. M. Bellowa. Cambridge: Cambridge University Press.

Tustin, F. (1972). *Autism and Childhood Psychosis.* London: Hogarth.

———— (1980). Autistic objects. *International Review of Psycho-Analysis* 7:27–40.

———— (1981). *Autistic States in Children.* London: Routledge and Kegan Paul.

———— (1984). Autistic shapes. *International Review of Psycho-Analysis,* 11:279–290.

———— (1986). *Autistic Barriers in Neurotic Patients.* New Haven: Yale University Press, 1987.

Winnicott, D. W. (1945). Primitive emotional development. In *Through Paediatrics to Psycho-Analysis,* pp. 145–156. New York: Basic Books, 1975.

———— (1951). Transitional objects and transitional phenomena. In *Through Paediatrics to Psycho-Analysis,* pp. 229–242. New York: Basic Books, 1975.

———— (1952). Psychoses and child care. In *Through Paediatrics to Psycho-Analysis,* pp. 219–228. New York: Basic Books, 1975.

———— (1956). Primary maternal preoccupation. In *Through Paediatrics to Psycho-Analysis,* pp. 300–305. New York: Basic Books, 1975.

———— (1958). The capacity to be alone. In *The Maturational Processes and the Facilitating Environment,* pp. 29–36. New York: International Universities Press, 1965.

———— (1962). Ego integration in child development. In *The Maturational Processes and the Facilitating Environment,* pp. 56–63. New York: International Universities Press, 1965.

———— (1963). Communicating and not communicating leading to a study of certain opposites. In *The Maturational Processes and the Facilitating*

Environment, pp. 179–192. New York: International Universities Press, 1965.

——— (1967). Mirror role of mother and family in child development. In *Playing and Reality*, pp. 111–118. New York: Basic Books, 1971.

——— (1968). The use of an object and relating through cross identifications. In *Playing and Reality*, pp. 86–94. New York: Basic Books, 1971.

——— (1971a). Creativity and its origins. In *Playing and Reality*, pp. 65–85. New York: Basic Books, 1971.

——— (1971b). *Playing and Reality*. New York: Basic Books, 1971.

11

Themes of Being and Non-Being in the Work of Frances Tustin and Jacques Lacan

Jane Van Buren

When autistic children are studied in the psychotherapeutic situation, we find that they are in a state of limbo, teetering between 'being' and 'not-being'. . . . [this because] . . . their early sense of going-on being, as Winnicott so well called it, has been put in jeopardy.

Frances Tustin, "To Be or Not To Be"

Psychoanalysis in England, France, and Germany in the late 1920s and early 1930s took a turn away from an exclusive adherence to Freud. New themes were mapped out by such key figures as Klein, Winnicott, and later Lacan, although there were others as well. Freud had been attempting to work in the conscious/unconscious dichotomy, but held his theory firmly within a positivist framework. Although he theorized brilliantly about the dream work as the "royal road to the unconscious" and as an opening for interpretation of deep experience, Freud was firmly convinced that the basic fuel for the construction of dreams and symptoms was the need to find libidinal satisfaction.

Lacan's departure is somewhat more radical than other followers of Freud. He was deeply influenced and affected by Freud's notion of decentered consciousness and felt that Freud's dream work was the essence of psychoanalysis. Lacan, writing in the 1940s and 1950s, began to emphasize the role of signification, and as he deepened his theory, he felt that the motive for the creation of psychological structures was the realization of human vulnerabil-

195

ity and "lack" (Lacan 1949, 1953). In the era in which Lacan wrote, the final blows were delivered to the cultural conviction that there were laws and principles that predetermined the creation of meaning.

Freud had employed the logical positivism of the Nineteenth Century to develop a theory for his notions of the function of the mind. Lacan was not moved by biological determinism, and he emphasized language and signification as the determinants of mental life. The first important shift within psychoanalysis, as well as in culture, was made known through questioning the validity of earlier beliefs while at the same time reckoning with the realization that meaning is created out of the workings of the mind, not from the workings of ideal powers. The second profound realization was that language, symbols, and signs do not reflect either a particular reality or truth but instead these are part of a human armamentarium of inborn capacities of the mind, implemented to protect and enhance human life.

At their deepest roots, signs are the means of signaling distress; the infant cries to enlist aid as later (s)he will employ more organized vocal signs to communicate both joyous and painful feelings. Primitive signs and symbols, then, are the vehicle for communicating states of mind, and as Bion has described, primitive signs grow out of somatic experience and are part of the somatosensory vocabulary. They are eventually transformed by the mothering adult's function of "reverie," which imparts patterns of meaning and the means to tolerate the upheaval of vital patterns of being. However, these processes may be aborted not only by the lack of a mother capable of containing, but also by deficits in the infant, which bar the way for the development of attachment processes including communication (Grotstein 1996).

Tustin, writing in the 1970s, began to realize that the infant–mother connections may be disturbed by many factors. One factor that she emphasized was the trauma of losing the maternal connection too soon, or the unfortunate appearance of states of mind in the mothering-one that seem to curse the infant's arrival into differentiation, leaving a hole or wound in the surface of the infant's forming skin ego (Anzieu 1989).[1] For Tustin, the existence of such a profound conviction of a hole or a wound in the skin of the infant's forming skin-ego produces several responses which importantly are dangerous to the development of a lively sensual and later mental experience.

Painters, writers, and poets have led us into such states found in tombs and

---

1. See Anzieu's *The Skin Ego* for another explanation of the development of psychic skin.

crypts of dark meaninglessness. Recall Poe's crypts in *The Fall of the House of Usher*. These are felt to be enclaves or dwellings for the living dead, where neither life nor death intervenes directly. In this image, we find a schizoid twilight, or what Tustin has designated "psychogenic autism." Tustin was a poet of serious withdrawal, aborted meaning, shutting out, and sealing off. A superb clinician and writer, Tustin described the phenomenology of the threat to "going-on-being," and of the invention of shells, barriers, enclaves, and confusional states, all of which are atrophied and throttle the vitality and aliveness of early affectual-sensory experiences.

Tustin meticulously appreciated the differences between organic difficulties and what she came to call psychogenic autism, a condition which shut down sensory life, but nevertheless was felt to be amenable to therapy. She discovered shells, crypts, and crusts which relentlessly thickened over time, separating the subject from the aspects of mental life that make up the beginning elements of attachment, communication, and the creation of protosigns, instead deanimating the rhythms, pulses, and messages of normal auto-sensuality.[2]

The fundamental psycho-sensual narrative that Tustin posited was the journey from the "ecstasy of at-onement" to the "tantruming of two-ness." Tustin thought that passing from the womb to a post-natal at-onement in the mind of the mothering-one allowed the infant to again find closeness through sensual feeling and touching, which both stimulated and gratified the infant recently shorn of a watery medium and faced with the phenomenon of gaps. Leaving the ecstasy of the touching and feeling mother's presence is challenged by some awareness of differentiation leading to fear and anxiety, the tantrum of two-ness. In both these circumstances, ecstasy and tantrum, Tustin posited that the mothering-one must hold the overflow of these passions in order for their intensity and force to stay alive. Tustin explained that "overflow" is a pre-projective mechanism, which uses the mother's body and emotional presence to hold overstimulating, exciting, and despairing experiences. She called this the "stuff" of early mental life (Tustin 1981).

It was at this point that Tustin found the need for shells, enclaves, and crypts. Her explanation centered around the pain and the dreadfulness of the hole or wound, which must be covered at any cost in order to bind a self in

---

2. Tustin rethought the concept of "normal" autism and constructed the concept of auto-sensuality as the threads or corridors through which contact and meaning could be lived out.

danger of flowing out or disappearing. Another technique for binding the wounds that Tustin emphasized was the confusional state, which leads to sticky, adhesive relationships and a deep overlapping between the two subjects involved (Mitrani 1992, 1994, Tustin 1981). Following on Tustin, Mitrani emphasized the ruination of sensory exchange. Sticking onto the skin of the mothering-one prohibits any intersubjective exchange. Also, in this way of closing down space, messages arriving from the body and from perceptions are blocked off.

Tustin also discussed a sense of fragile "going-on-being" and its relationship to primary depression (Tustin 1972, 1981, 1986). In her way of thinking about the growth of meaning, signification, and communication, interruption or prevention of the bonding experience brings about a sense of a terrible black hole or a wound in the skin boundary of the subject, both of which leave a profound lithograph on the psyche of the person in the sense of bringing about closure of the 'ordinary' pathways of lively signification. Autosensual elements are misused under these conditions to shut down mental life, thus preventing further mental growth.

For Tustin, primary depression was a crucial factor in the abruption of significance. Primary depression is associated with disruptive forces and factors, perhaps a deficit in the infant or in the holding environment, which is so painful and overwhelming that the temptation to shut down normal autosensual expression is powerful, and parts of the personality are locked away or banished into some kind of cryptlike or living death situation, finally separated from the body's sensory messages. Thus, the prisoner dwells in a state of numbness, darkness, and emptiness.

Grotstein (1990a, 1990b, 1991) explains that the abruption of bonding leads to a psychotic state of chaos, meaninglessness and nothingness. He suggests that either a neurobiological difficulty—as in schizophrenia—or in a borderline condition or a poor holding environment states of undifferentiation and randomness prevail while meaningfulness, a sense of mattering and "ongoing-being" are overwhelmed.

Grotstein points out that Winnicott had already noticed that the infant is born with a conception of something which can be called primary chaos (undifferentiated and unorganized states). The impossibility of developing organization and a sense of meaningfulness seriously interferes with a vigorous sense of "going-on-being." The pulses of being that bring together the rhythm of "going-on-being" are stilled, as are faith in being and in the "background presence" (Grotstein 1990a, 1990b, 1991, 1996). In this situation, the infant feels him or herself to be floating in a universe of infinite space or a sea of nothingness.

In this chapter, I will discuss adult patients who suffer from some of these difficulties with contact and communication, nonverbal and verbal. While treating such patients, I found myself immersed in nonverbal countertransference states that were strange and puzzling (Tustin 1986). I found these people very challenging to work with, in that almost all of the usual aspects of human relating were absent in the analytic encounter. After many sessions of bewilderment and fury at what seemed to be a lack of interest and great sadness at being rejected, I began to experience states of terror and utter despair; these seemed in turn to evolve into feelings of falling forever into a void—disappearing or shrinking. I also felt trapped, with no means of calling out. After some reflection I was able to begin to read these visceral responses. It seemed to me that I was experiencing both a leak in my membrane of being and at the same time feeling a desperate effort to seal off the hole (Anzieu 1989, Tustin 1981).[3]

Tustin thought that there were two main techniques for attending to the hole or wound and shoring up the tenuous sense of going-on-being. She explained that a radical separation of hard and soft sensations into "me" and "not-me" was integrally connected to a crisis in being and the felt belief in the need for a shell structure, which stops up sensual exchange while that which lies behind the shell or fortress walls is cut off from the "not-me" to the degree that mental growth is impeded or stopped.

In her work, Tustin demonstrates the great disturbances these "shell children" display (Tustin, 1981, 1990). Playing with others and toys requires a flow from inside to outside and the reverse. The shell children are imprisoned inside a barrier, and without new stimulation they begin to drift off into a nether world of no stimulation and no mental objects or lively feelings with which to create aspects of representation, including language and other symbols. Recall Tustin's ideas about autistic objects and shapes. These are set against the gathering of meaning and are used to block the felt-hole in being

---

3. Anzieu (1989) proposes the utter importance of sensory feedback loops to provide a surround for the infant and to create a flexible boundary that allows for information to move back and forth through the various sensory channels. Anzieu states that the sensory loops develop into envelopes that foster mutuality. Otherwise, the infant feels isolated, overwhelmed, flayed, and without life. See particularly Chapters 2, 5, and 7.

at the cost, however, of playing out internal dilemmas to the extent that they cannot be understood through images, phantasies, and stories. Thus, a metal truck has no meaning but is used as a cork to stop up the felt holes in the body and skin. The contents of the anus are not manipulated to triumph over a powerful other but to prevent any awareness of movement or flowing ongoing experience.

Similar purposes are found to be related to Tustin's second major technique of covering over rips or tears in the skin of being: confusional states, which she understands as ways of shutting out any awareness of inside and outside or any space internal or external. These infants may be already at risk for psychosis, but lack of differentiation through fusing and merging intensifies feelings of chaos, randomness, nothingness, and non-being. Within the confusional technique, autosensual elements are employed to entangle, enmesh, and thus strangle the roots of communication, symbols, or thought (Bion 1962/1967, 1962/1977, Grotstein 1996, Tustin 1981, 1986, 1990). Tustin suggested that infantile confusional states might be the precursor for psychosis and schizophrenia. The countertransference is felt as physical states of confusion, disassociation, suffocation (claustrophobia), loss of the sense of time and space, in a limbo or a fog, with no possible way to maintain awareness, let alone communication.

In analytic work with adult patients with autistic enclaves, I found that these subjects experienced themselves as buried alive in an eternal crypt, with no hope of forming flexible boundaries. I came to think that these were enduring states of profound sensory deprivation. Gradually, over many sessions, I began to recognize these states as emanating from the tomb. Following on Grotstein (1994), I thought of the other side of projective identification, of the aspect of the subject that shrinks away and is severed from body experience—due to withdrawal from the conductors of perceptions, the skin, eyes, ears—and feels deadened and entrapped. At the same time, another aspect of the subject remains hooked up to body experience and feels hollowed out and barely present, and is vulnerable to disappearing inside another's body (Klein 1955).

Molly

One female analysand, Molly, has taught me a great deal about the disappearing subject. I first came to know her through long silences in the sessions. I felt the nonverbal emanations moving from her to me were expressive of the emergence of states of mind or aspects of her that were buried alive. The silences were felt to be not only tedious in their emptiness but gradually exuded terror. I knew that I must not break the silence because of my own need to make contact, but I found that such restraint became torture. I felt that Molly pulled me into her void or crypt, not out of malice, but out of a need to communicate her dilemma.

Another difficult aspect of making contact with Molly was related to her inability to hold on to her thoughts and images when they did break through the barriers. At times I would say to her, "What are you thinking?" Her response was often, "I forgot," or, "It slipped away, I don't know where." In these moments my thoughts were paralyzed. When I recovered, I wondered what agency or will had taken over my normal ability to think and to be able to communicate her states of burial or her feelings of nothingness. I tried to resonate with the experiences of nothingness and the unknown. Within the silences Molly seemed to sink deeper into deathlike states, but eventually life stirred behind the autistic barrier and the walls of the enclave softened to the extent that the silences took on a feeling of contact. I thought perhaps my attempts to resonate with her as a live subject despite dominant states of "nothingness" (Grotstein 1990a, 1990b, 1991) had begun to set growth in process. I also felt that there had always been a subject waiting to be enlivened by the mothers' body and mind.[4]

Thus, there came a period in which Molly began to see images structured in small vignettes. A St. Bernard appeared in a snowy setting, complete with flask. Eventually words were used to decipher the image. Other images depicted her mental capacities as problematic. In one vignette, Molly as a boy was blind and had the wrong operation. Later, with the use of halting phrases, we were able to provide some meaning to the blindness and to the surgery. The blindness referred to an infantile catastrophe in which Molly fragmented and could no longer bear to "see" or to know (Bion 1957/1967). I was inclined to think that her holding environment had been deficient in warmth, receptivity and spontaneity but also that as an infant she may have been prone to fragmentation and driven to hold herself together through withdrawal behind a shell-skin.

---

4. Grotstein (1990, 1991) offers a theory of the development of malignant nothingness. He proposes the absence of significant bonding experiences in the sense that holding, containing functions or the *background presence* (the sum of all the dimensions of bonding and attachment) leave the helpless infant without a skin envelope, a sense of regulation, and ultimately without hope and faith.

The surgery seemed to signify a castration ceremony. Molly believed that parts of her mind and body had been cut away. This belief served as an explanation for her massive sense of damage and deficiency. Gender differences served as an explanation as well. Molly both valorized women as morally superior to males and idealized men and the sign of maleness—the penis—as a carrier of privilege. She believed that she had lost her mark of superiority and entitlement benefits through the *wrong operation*.

After five years of silence and utmost depression, Molly spoke to me in the sessions. The long silences had subsided, emotional liveliness colored her speech, but at the same time she rarely spoke of personal relationships, and the potential feelings that might be evoked in relationships rarely surfaced. I remained a background presence rather than a stimulating, desired other, though she slowly emerged from her crypt-like states. To be evoked too quickly or too powerfully was still felt to be a mortal threat.

I propose that adult patients with autistic barriers and confined within autistic enclaves need to be thought about in terms of an interrupted sense of being. Molly's situation attests to that reading: so thoroughly buried inside her sealed crypt in deathlike states that her sense of being is not only faint but incapable of feeling life with no possibility for change. Though Molly purports to carry out the business of living, much of her remains behind in the crypt.

Her associations in the sessions cannot yet be read in terms of metaphors or metonymies. The existence of a referent seems off in the future. Molly dwells in a concrete prerepresentational stage of communication. Nevertheless, the buds of a lively subjectivity have sprung up in the sessions, having made their way through the doors of the crypt.

Marjorie

Another patient entered analysis for acute anxiety and fluctuating moods. From the beginning of the analysis, Marjorie spoke very rapidly. Her delivery stimulated in me a sense of being pounded by a rapid fire of meaningless bits (Bion 1957/1967, 1962/1967). Furthermore, I felt reduced to a useless person who was unable to follow any patterns of expression.

When I attempted to give meaning to her excited states, Marjorie either ignored me completely or became argumentative and hostile. Her prickly attacking responses evoked terror in me. I felt deeply that our efforts at making meaning out of chaotic forces were cursed. The image of a chained wild animal—snarling and baring its teeth—came to my mind during these encounters. I thought of the film *A Cry in the Dark*, based on the true story of an infant who was kidnapped by a dingo and who was never to be seen again.

Marjorie's words conveyed some meaning, unlike Molly's discourse, which was barely intelligible. However, once again I experienced frustration as I struggled to understand an alternative meaning that was as yet unavailable or had not been fertilized through continuous intersubjective intercourse. I am referring to an interaction that Bion described as the container-contained; the infant's raw data of psychosomatic experiential bits is caught by the mothering-one, who digests them and returns them in assimilable form to the infant, who then is not only supported and calmed but is introduced to the process of signification (Bion 1967, Grotstein 1994, Tustin 1981). However, we are also beginning to realize that the processes of intrasubjectivity are begun in less familiar ways. Along these lines Piontelli (1992) has made some interesting forays into the differences in temperament revealed in ultrasound studies in utero.

I considered Steiner's (1993) and Meltzer's (1992) theories of split-off aspects of the personality dominated by a highly organized pathological group or gang. I then realized that Tustin's idea of autistic enclaves needed to be applied to the "wild animal" who both resists any interference from another but who is also severely caged behind the autistic barriers. Marjorie had encountered the "wild animal" at birth when her head became stuck in the birth canal. She was in terrible danger of dying inside her mother's body when a pair of forceps was applied. These efforts to save her broke her collarbone and she was casted even before her first external meeting with her mother. This version of her birth trauma was not only hearsay from members of her family but was mirrored in her dreams.

Shortly after her birth, Marjorie developed severe eczema, which lasted throughout her first three years. I felt that on the one hand she developed the eczema as a hard shell by which she was protected from brute experience of "the real." Lacan explains the latter as an encounter with that which cannot be signified (digested), when the experience is presented before the infant can manage it at all. On the other hand, Marjorie longed for a skin container that was present and adequate. The truth was that she felt her skin remained undernourished and distant due to her shell enclosure. As I interpreted her dilemma, Marjorie became calmer. Later she also told me that when they uncasted her it left a terrible rip in her underlying flesh.

Over many sessions, this particular panic abated with the development of some sense of an unmutilated and more resilient skin. However, there remained the matter of the "wild animal" breaking out to guard her from the me who was felt to threaten the "shell" and the infant within: that part of her that had been cut off from care due to her autistic enclaves, the shells that were felt to be cruel to her. These forces were projected into a father-me and returned as the murderer. Marjorie spoke often of her night terror—like nightmares—the content of which was a person who broke in and murdered her. After the birth of her son, Marjorie included him in her nightmares and developed a generalized anxiety about his differentiation. She was so terrified in these nightmares that she awakened to find herself screaming and traveling across the room. Her husband confirmed her description, adding that she screamed, "Oh no, not me!" and, "He's trying to murder me!"

As discussed above, there were many levels on which Marjorie's terrors could be interpreted. Nevertheless, I want to stress that without Tustin's notion of autistic barriers and enclaves, an understanding of her terrors would be limited. The idea that a part of the ego breaks off and comes under the rule of the death instinct, and manifests in malignant narcissism (Meltzer 1992, Steiner 1993), is highly applicable here. However the notion that the failure of early overflow and ecstasy experiences, for whatever reasons—the infant's deficits, the mothering environment or both—had caused such autistic barriers to be set in place seems more to the point. Here instead of the overflow and ecstasy with integration of sensual elements and free-floating exchange, normal autosensuality is commandeered to construct hard, lifeless, impenetrable barriers.

Recently Marjorie dreamed that someone was hunting her down and was attempting to enter her bedroom. This night terror occurred on the eve of a departure for a weekend trip but also a few days before a longer trip. As usual, she had several fits of frustration, anger, and blaming that previewed or accompanied her trips. She became irritable, paranoid that everyone was letting her down deliberately and she could not find anyone to help her. The dream contained images of being stuck inside a long opening, darkness, suffocation, and a horrible attack. Marjorie's associations led me to say, "You seem to be describing a difficult, even dangerous birth." She responded quickly and with conviction. Her shell seemed to melt, a phenomenon rarely occurring in our sessions.

Marjorie then was beginning to put together the horrors which had lain dead beneath the shell of meaningless words. She combined sensual memories with meaningful assessment of the events of her birth and early months. From a more balanced binocular vertex, Marjorie realized that her birth was almost a death. She had isolated herself behind a sea of words. Her language was not only exclusively focused on surface narrative, but was used to wall off and conceal her interior world. My counter-projective experience was that of two aspects of her: the aspect of her that wanted to share and experience her internal world and the feelings that are trapped, distorted, and stripped of aliveness there, and the presence of the autistic "wild animal" that attacked my mind and feelings to preserve the status quo. Often I felt exhausted and battered by the two conflictual projective identifications coming at me, particularly the battering that the wild animal put me through when I attempted to decode the significance of her words and the feelings that were frozen inside.

I want to emphasize here that this aggression may be deconstructed as an effort to keep me from offering human contact and penetrating her thick walls. In Marjorie's case the shell or barrier was angry and dangerous. We might note the difference between her aggressive stance and Molly's deadened one.

Conclusion

Lacan's response to the pain and danger of non-being and a sense of lack was centered around the search for the primary object of identification, or the narcissistic object. The lost object, designated *petit object a,* signifies differentiation and interruption in being for the newly forming subject (Lacan 1953, 1958), but it is Tustin's genius to grasp the real crater that prevents the subject from developing. Lacan, like Freud, was not able to image the earliest mother-infant relationship, and in this way it plays no role in his theory of the growth of the infant's mind. Instead, Lacan followed the philosophical fathers. He believed the problem of being and nothingness arose from man's faith in self-knowledge. Tustin, guided and inspired by Bion—her analyst and mentor—and nourished by the contemporary child analytic movement in England, penetrated into primitive states of mind and found there the possibility of the critical failure of attachment to the mother's body and to life, and the consequent onset of severe withdrawal and mental death. Thus, Tustin provided for us the excruciating phenomenology of living and dying internally.

Tustin was a key figure in pursuing and defining the dangers of the "black hole." Her theories on the gathering of meaning and of the etiology of intrasubjective and intersubjective lines of communication (Tustin 1981) suggested that all significance evolves out of several momentous realizations; that we are separate from the great sources of power and protection in the universe; that neither are we omnipotent; that we will always be faced with loss of the object of primary identification and that the realization of loss and a sense of limitation is among the great tasks of our human life; that we can never *know* the full meaning or significance of our lives and that we are only able to develop a fullness of being through our faith that we are alive and present and in the presence of others to whom we matter.

all broken, only a few fragments allowed

References

Anzieu, D. (1989). *The Skin Ego*. New Haven: Yale University Press.

Bion, W. (1957). Differentiation between the psychotic and the non-psychotic part of the personality. In *Second Thoughts*. New York: Jason Aronson, 1967.

—— (1962). Theory of thinking. In *Second Thoughts*. New York: Jason Aronson, 1967.

—— (1962). Learning from experience. In *Seven Servants*. New York: Jason Aronson, 1977.

Grotstein, J. (1990a). Nothingness, meaninglessness, chaos, and the "black hole": Part I. *Contemporary Psychoanalysis* 26(2):257–290.

—— (1990b). Nothingness, meaninglessness, chaos, and the "black hole": Part II. *Contemporary Psychoanalysis*, 26(3):377–407.

—— (1991). Nothingness, meaninglessness, chaos, and the "black hole": Part III. *Contemporary Psychoanalysis*, 27(1):1–33.

—— (1994). Projective identification: a reappraisal. *Contemporary Psychoanalysis*, 30(4):708–746.

—— (1996). One pilgrim's progress: notes on Frances Tustin's contributions to the psychoanalytic conception of autism. (This publication.)

Klein, M. (1955). On identification. In *Envy and Gratitude & Other Works 1946–1963*. New York: Delacorte Press, 1975.

Lacan, J. (1949). The mirror stage as formative of the function of the I as revealed in psychoanalytic experience. In *Ecrits*, pp. 1–7. London: Tavistock, 1977.

—— (1953). The function and field of speech and language in psychoanalysis. In *Ecrits*, pp. 30–113. London: Tavistock, 1977.

—— (1958). The signification of the phallus. In *Ecrits*, pp. 281–291. London: Tavistock, 1977.

Meltzer, D. (1992). *The Claustrum*. London: Cluny Press.

Mitrani, J. (1992). The survival function of autistic maneuvers in adult patients. *International Journal of Psycho-Analysis* 73:549–559.

———— (1994). On adhesive pseudo-object relations, Part I: Theory. *Contemporary Psychoanalysis* 30, 2:348–366.

Piontelli, A. (1992). *From Fetus to Child: An Observational and Psychoanalytic Study*. London: Routledge.

Steiner, J. (1993). *Psychic Retreats*. London: Routledge and Kegan Paul.

Tustin, F. (1972). *Autism and Childhood Psychosis*. London: Hogarth.

———— (1981). *Autistic States in Children*. London: Routledge and Kegan Paul.

———— (1986). *Autistic Barriers in Neurotic Adults*. London: Karnac Books.

———— (1990). *The Protective Shell in Children and Adults*. London: Karnac Books.

12

A Scientific Turn of Mind:
a Tribute to Frances Tustin

Susanna Isaacs Elmhirst

Science is nothing but trained and organized common sense, differing from the latter only as a veteran may differ from a raw recruit; and its methods differ from those of common sense only as far as the guardsman's cut and thrust differ from the manner in which a savage wields his club.

T.H. Huxley, "The Method of Zadig"

Frances Tustin and I were friends for over forty-five years. That is a long time, so it should be easy to write about her; but it isn't at all a simple task, just because she has done so much for, and been so much to, so many people. Her abundance makes it hard to choose what to put into such a piece and, even more difficult, what to leave out. A celebration of someone's life and work is usually made in, and nearly always associated with, obituaries or "eulogies," as they are so often called in the United States. This present piece is developed out of one written in 1989 for Edition No. 4 of *Winnicott Studies*, published by the Squiggle Foundation of London during Frances' lifetime.

What I and others wrote then was intended to tell Frances herself, as well as many others, something of why we loved and admired her. I did not discuss in advance with Frances what I was going to say, but I knew her well enough to know that she was pleased and relieved by this contribution, among others, as well as delighted by the whole concept of a vital and honest memorial tribute to her work while she was still able to be interested in her characteristic way, combining enthusiasm with quietly concentrated attention.

The focus of my past and present contribution is Frances' truly scientific turn of mind. From time to time, I had for years tried to tell her of my perception of that quality in her approach to her own work and that of others. We rarely managed to fit a tête-à-tête, or even a telephone conversation, into our bilaterally busy lives, so I particularly welcomed the original invitation from the Squiggle Foundation.

So, how did we meet? Actually this first encounter set the scene for my interest in Frances' original and—at core—scientific approach to human beings, young and old, in emotional health and turbulence. My first babies, twin boys, were being observed by a colleague of Frances' in the Tavistock Clinic Psychotherapy Training, the late Dina Rosenbluth. One day Dina asked if she could bring a fellow trainee for just one visit so that they could observe the twins and me from different visual, and presumably intellectual and emotional, vantage points. Frances' memory of that happening was much more detailed than mine is, but I do vividly and gratefully remember that it was not at all an intrusive or persecutory experience.

Indeed I have sometimes wondered whether Dina and Frances together, or perhaps Frances alone, might have made more impact than Dina did on Esther Bick's tendency to idealize me as a mother, an attitude which caused me considerable amazement and perturbation at times. We shall never know. What I am convinced of is that the scientific approach in psychological matters should be nonpersecutory in intent and in reality, so far as is compatible with the existence of the unconscious mind in both observed and observer.

Science is about studying with an open mind. Inevitably every mind must be to some degree selectively open if it is to go beyond the ordinary into areas of unknown experience. One cannot do detailed original psychoanalysis and research into analytical chemistry simultaneously. Practitioners of psychodynamically oriented studies of the minds of others have to have their initial openmindedness released and expanded for personal cultivation and use by involvement as an object of such study themselves. To be an openminded student of psychodynamic process in living human beings necessitates the experience of being the subject of an observer-observed psychodynamic relationship. Maintaining creative openmindedness in such studies is a lifelong, and difficult task; but it was one Frances could be relied on to carry out courageously.

First and foremost in her work she concentrated her well-honed capacities on the struggles of children trying to develop minds of their own. Her particular interest and concentration was focused on those children who appear to be mindless and feeling-less. Her discoveries about these cut-off and cutting-off "autistic" children—revealed in her writings, her seminars, and lectures about the outcomes of her work—have helped innumerable people, all over the world, who want to develop her sort of binocular vision.

My favorite of Frances' many poems—"The Growth of Understanding: a Personal Statement"—was first published in 1984 in the French journal *Patio*. A revised version of that paper forms Chapter Two of her book *Autistic Barriers in Neurotic Patients* (1986). I liked and still like this paper because of its intelligent, honest and unmocking use of Peter Medawar's *Advice to a Young Scientist* (1979). Frances correctly applied its clearly set-out principles to her young patients, to their minds and her own. Although she was around 70-years old, she creatively closed a blind eye to Medawar's apparently un-abashed, vehement, inability to take his own advice about the relevance of his core attitude to the study of human psychology.

Another reason I especially like Frances' paper is that in it she describes how and why she changed her mind, from believing that there is a normal autistic phase in infant development to the view she held for the rest of her life, which is that

> In *normal* early infantile development, there is an awareness of separate-ness which is made bearable by auto-sensuous activities such as sucking and bodily interactions with other people, particularly with the mother (Tustin 1986, p. 43).

For Frances it was a life's work to apply her principles to herself, to "practice what she preached" without preaching. In this area, Medawar tended to preach lambastically, but in the area of human psychodynamics, he didn't practice the honesty of ignorance.

Of course, I also like that particular change in Frances' mind because it meant that we became more—not less—in agreement as colleagues than we had been. But I am glad that our friendship would have survived and thrived anyway, whatever our scientific disagreements, because we both agreed with Peter Medawar (as quoted by Frances) when he wrote, "a senior scientist is much more flattered by finding that his views are the subject of serious criticism than by sycophantic and sometimes obviously stimulated respect."

In the late 1980s Frances was regretfully unable, because of ill-health, to attend a paper on autism to which she knew I was going. She asked me to convey her apologies and inform the meeting that her main contribution to the discussion would have been to confirm that she did indeed adhere to the change of view I have quoted above. This I did, with the comment that I found it "very encouraging." This produced a laugh, not of mockery but of appreciation—a joyous laugh expressing feelings in which I shared and in which I rejoice now as then, despite the loss of Frances in our external lives.

References

Tustin, F. (1986). The growth of understanding: a personal statement. In *Autistic Barriers in Neurotic Patients*, pp. 33–47. London: Karnac Books, 1986. Originally published in *Patio*, 3:109–121, 1984.

Medawar, P. (1979). *Advice to a Young Scientist*. London: Pan.

13

From Fear of Change to Mourning[1]

Renata de Benedetti Gaddini

In natural science, the subject is the mobile body which has within itself the logos of continuity, thus containing the logos of infinity.[2]

Dante, *Convivio* II, XIII, 17

While for years the main problem in psychoanalysis had been the relationship between technique and theory,[3] theoretical interest in the change patients undergo during treatment—and how it is experienced, and often dreadfully opposed (E. Gaddini 1982)—has become an issue of interest only in recent years. There appear to be two main kinds of loss that the patient protects himself from with his defenses.[4] One is self loss, of the type the young child

---

1. This paper has been presented in part at the 37th IPA Congress, Buenos Aires, 1991.

2. "Ne la scienza natura è subbietto lo corpo mobile, lo quale corpo mobile ha in sé ragione di continuitade, e questo ha in sé ragione di numero infinito." Dante, *Convivio* II, III, 17.

3. This topic was debated in various psychoanalytical Congresses. Among others, at the 7th IPA Congress, Berlin, 1922, where the subject was "The relations between analytic technique and analytic theory," and also at the Congress for the celebration of the 50th Anniversary of the Italian Psychoanalytic Society (1983), where the main topic was "Terapia e conoscenza in psicoanalisi."

4. Naturally, since "natura non facit saltus," a number of intermediary situations may be found.

213

encounters when confronted with separation before he has acquired a capacity for mental representation. The suffering in this case is 'agonic,' because it is unthinkable, and the mind is not yet able to come to the rescue. This suffering is related to primary omnipotence which implies total dependence: the subject magically becomes the object. To face this anxiety, imitation is probably the self's earliest defense.

Another type of suffering has a different nature, and is typical of those conditions where loss and mourning have been worked through and a need for reparation may ensue, both taking place through symbolic operations that belong to mental processes. The type of omnipotence we find here is instinctual and not as magical as the former, since the subject is compelled to recognize the object and cope with the anxiety of a real dependency in order to survive.

Many authors, including Anna Freud, Klein, Mahler and Winnicott, have investigated change met by children in the course of real time development. Natural change differs in character from that promoted during analysis, because the latter can probably be compared to the violation of the unconscious by the analyst *qua* "brave robber who dared to defy the taboos of religion and myths, and rob the treasures hidden in a spot which was guarded by evil and dangerous spirits" (Bion 1973, p. 20). It is specifically on the fear of change—be it part of the natural process of growth or analytically induced— that I wish to concentrate on this paper.

The Method for the Study of Human Development

There has been a great debate concerning the most appropriate method of studying change during natural development, the alternatives being direct observation suggested by Freud (1917), a very specialized method as described by Bick (1964),[5] or the "experimental" method called "infant observation"

---

5. Bick (1964) developed her own way of teaching infant observation, which has become a classic in the formation of psychoanalysts in many institutions. What Bick values in the analyst's formation, as far as infants and mothers are concerned, is the thorough observation and description of the mother-neonate dyad prior to any interpretation. She also stresses the observation of the neonate with the mother within the family as a way of capturing the familiar and unique communication which takes place in every human couple. The latter seemed particularly valuable to Bick for those trainees who did not have previous opportunities of learning from these basic expe-

(Stern 1985). In this last method, I believe that the specificity of psychoanalysis is scarcely considered.

In a letter to Jung, Freud (1911) mentioned that one of his highest aims was to succeed in thinking inductively rather than intuitively. Freud, in fact, had a very high opinion of direct observation, as may be argued from this statement: "What we inferred from these analyses (of symptoms) in adults was later confirmed point by point by the direct observation of children." (1911, p. 310). Eugenio Gaddini (1984) also stressed the importance of observation, however, he always considered the "inherently experiential" situation of the psychoanalytic process far more valuable than the "experimental" one.

In 1981, the Helsinki IPA Congress concluded that only in analysis is it possible to fully recapture the early mental processes related to the self's primary sense of being—as well as those sensations of discontinuity—lying at the basis of the arrests and distortions of natural growth, which inevitably lead to psychopathology. During the last decades, various models for the study of child development have tended to confirm one of the earlier hypotheses of psychoanalysis: that is, that on the basis of an original central core, (differently denominated by the various authors), an autonomous state of being emerges in the course of the dynamic process from fusion to individuation. When differentiation occurs—around the second semester of life—the child faces loss and experiences what Klein (1952) called the "depressive position." Winnicott considered the maturational aspect of the process more important than the loss and called this period the "age of concern."

The child is now confronted with two paradoxically opposite tendencies. On the one hand, he tends to continue being at-one with the mother in a state of fusion. On the other hand, and at the very same time, he exists as a separate person, outside and even against her. In my opinion, here lies the essence of human drama, implied by growth as the child moves towards autonomy. This paradox has troubled the minds of many researchers who seem uneasy and even incapable of coping with ambiguous and contradictory situations. I agree with Sander (1984) that a great part of our difficulties in conceptualizing individuation derives from our avoiding to accept the fact that paradoxically opposite processes are ubiquitous (Freud 1915), and that the creative process is

---

riences (Bick 1964). It is on the basis of her suggested infant observation within the family as well as her psychoanalytical work with children, that she has developed her theories of bi-dimensionality, adhesive identification (1968) and also the concept of a "second skin" (1968) as defense from "no-way-down" or "falling-forever" (1964).

endlessly contained between these two extremes: to be fused or to separate. The capacity to bear these uncertain and intermediate situations is crucial in order to accept and facilitate growth.

As I have pointed out elsewhere (1987) this theme is well illustrated by Goethe's (1793) comment on Correggio's painting "La Madonna del Latte": It represents a mother with her child, just when the latter is hesitating between the beast and a few pears offered him by an angel. It is the weaning of Christ.[6]

Continuity

During the late 1960s, I was in search of an indicator to help me explore the infant's steps towards individuation and relating by direct observation, and I studied nonnutritional consolers, which I called *precursors* (of the transitional object).[7] The transitional object is the first bridge between me and not-me, where the symbolization of reunion occurs (Winnicott 1963). The precursor object (PO) on the other hand, be it a thumb or a pacifier or any nipple-like object, *is me* (or the breast), as me and breast are the same thing for the baby at this early stage (R. Gaddini 1971).[8]

Through my observations, I became convinced that sucking as well as skin contact are the main consolers, constituting the physical basis upon which feeling and thinking take place. Ideally, the basic consoler is the breast-nipple; when this is unavailable, the sucking of a substitute, a nipple-like object— such as a thumb or a pacifier or something similar—will take its place and apparently produce the same effect. It is as if together, nipple and mouth saturate the valence left open by separation at birth, thus reestablishing continuity and cohesion.

According to Bion's developmental model, thought is produced when a preconception meets with a realization (Bion 1962, 1968). A preconception is

---

6. These very elements of attachment and dependence, on the one hand, and of separation and moving towards an object, on the other, were emblematically expressed by Hermann (1929).

7. In this presentation, I shall refer to precursors as PO's and transitional objects as TO's.

8. Circa the genesis of the TO, my studies suggested that prolonged maternal symbiotic ties to the baby interfere with the symbolization of re-union with her after loss. Children do not represent their re-union with her symbolically if the mother is physically available.

the innate expectation of the breast, the open valence as I represent the idea for myself. When the infant is brought in contact with a breast, the preconception becomes a conception, insofar as he takes a realization for granted. Concepts are therefore associated with the emotional experience of satisfaction. Development of thought, on the other hand, is tied to frustration with a nonbreast. At first, this nonbreast is experienced as a bad object and expelled by the infant's omnipotent phantasy. He may, however, have acquired sufficient tolerance towards frustration to the point of not expelling this bad object immediately. With time, he may come to realize that the bad thing he has inside him is a product of his own mind, that it is not real. When he succeeds in this, a transformation has taken place. Thus Bion concludes "without breast, therefore thought" (Bion 1962).

Here, we have an indication that "evolution" and "evolutionary changes" (changes for Bion, though catastrophic, were always evolutionary) are seen as a way out from frustration. The crucial element of this "getting to know" is the infant's disposition to modify himself (therefore evolving) or, as an alternative, to evade frustration. The strategies used by infants and young children to maintain continuity are multiple and vary along their developmental process. In this context, through the study of the mother–infant relationship at the breast, aggression appears as the initial manifestation of a positive developmental force—the fierceness of search and of expanding maturity— not of hostility.

Modes of Functioning

Different modes of functioning may be illustrated by Antonio's case history. He is now a grown man; I saw him when he was a child because of rumination. He was the premature second-born of an elderly couple. From the very beginning, his mother's nipple cracked; thus, after two weeks of "battling" with a bleeding breast ("he regurgitated all my bloody milk"), Antonio was weaned. Cow's milk in various forms was then forced into him and, when regurgitated, was patiently fed again into the struggling baby. These forced feedings went on during Antonio's first year, and by the end of it, he had become a ruminator, acquiring the capacity to bring the ingested food back into his mouth and then slowly reinvesting and swallowing it in a reiterative way.

At the age of 2, he began to talk, repeating his mother's songs and his elder sister's counting: 2–4–6. His parents reported that his speech did not progress because he was only capable of imitating sounds. At the age of 4 years, he spoke "obsessively" in front of a mirror and in general—his repetitive capacities seemed astonishing. At 11 years of age he resumed ruminating. This happened when he went from elementary school in Calabria to a high school in Perugia. His school performance, despite his obsessive brooding 24-hours a day, continued to be good. But he felt persecuted by his companions and teachers and had persecutory ideas of being genitally attacked by his schoolmates—of being teased and made the brunt of their jokes. He felt clumsy and his attempts to rule his mind versus his nonintegrated sense of body–self did not seem successful at the time.

Rumination continued on and off for two years and was now an occasional symptom, limiting itself to fluids. Another symptom appeared when he was 14 and his parents brought him back to me for analysis. He had become aggressive with his mother and could not stand the sight of "naked women." He appeared obsessively religious, and life events were inscribed in compulsive rituals. He played the piano as compulsively as he did his schoolwork, claiming that "he had to realize himself," meaning—as it appeared to me in the brief analytical experience—that he wanted to *be*, as a protective maneuver against breaking down.

There was an extreme tendency to idealize the sources of life—the sun, God, Mother—and a painful sense of betrayal (Rosenfeld 1971). Instinctual excitement was experienced as a threat causing panic, as it seemed to mobilize primary agonies and fears of self loss. Defensively, he kept away from body excitement and moved towards religion and music in a most ritualistic and stereotypical fashion. His "learning through imitation" gave his cognitive processes a quick grasping character rather than one of reflective assimilation.

In his thinking there was no personal point of view. Instead he kept reproducing mother, teacher, books, outside world. Imitation allowed him "to be" what he imitated, although with an element of deep rivalry and defiance. His being-the-other (never losing contact) seemed to form the basis of his speedy, compulsive, nonconstructive learning (both manual and verbal), and of his giving symbols a concrete character in the same way as his ruminated food used to be a perpetually self-enacted image of his feeding and refeeding mother.

In analysis we came to realize that separateness was so terrifying just when the good and bad aspects of the object were becoming more clearly visible as the patient started to emerge from total fusion with the object–mother (Rosenfeld 1971). His retreat to living inside the object—previously adopted and which interfered with all sorts of relations—appeared essentially as a retreat to a world of omnipotence where reality need not be faced and where he could be at one with it (subjective object).

The functional levels I have attempted to describe are basic in that they occur during the earliest period of life. They are extremely arduous to study and understand because, as Frances Tustin so aptly says, "it is difficult to conceptualize what for the child was unconceptualized" and, I would add, unthinkable. It is also difficult but essential to distinguish the normal process from pathology. The succession of "normal" phenomena at a determined stage of development may be understood only in process. Only *within* this context can variations from normality to pathology be fully captured.

Bearing this in mind, we can trace the earliest beginnings of life back to the individual's genetic endowment which interacts with earliest experience commencing with the process of birth (perhaps earlier). This interaction within a continuum leads to growth, but also to later conflicts.

The PO's model is the baby's "illusion" (Winnicott 1951) that he is mother and mother is baby. We are now in the realm of fantasies *inside* the body (E. Gaddini 1982), that are imageless and closer to physical sensations and functioning than to thinking (Freud 1923, p. 21). Based on body sensations, these fantasies are necessarily fragmentary in essence. From a developmental point of view, the PO belongs to a stage when there is no differentiation of inner and outer. In fact it operates defensively against this differentiation, as it seems to reinforce the infant's sensation of being-at-one with mother, protecting him from disillusions. These disillusions will come anyway, as part of growth, but it is the incidence of these painful experiences—their timing and how they succeed each other—that matters. They may constructively promote self structure with its own defensive organization, or give way to panic caused by self-finding, leading to relating. With no frustrations, learning from experience is impaired, and in this type of situation, the individual is forced to learn only from his own body (R. Gaddini and E. Gaddini 1959). When the maturational process is fixed on learning from one's own body, and does not come to its mental representations, we meet with a developmental failure.

Infants who ruminate in order to be (*to be* the feeding mother) have all been breastfed at least a fortnight and all have had, at least for this short time, the experience of *being* the feeding mother. Because the need-satisfying experience of breastfeeding was lost at a time when he was unable to represent it in any mental way, the baby who ruminates lives his fantasy of continuity inside his own body. In the mind of the young infant, the mental parallel of his biological functioning stands for a skin-mucosal contact through which support for the sense of being takes place and is continually furthered. When the mother–substitute takes him over and gives him back his lost sense of continuity, he stops ruminating, and his learning emerges from the limits of self-learning towards mental representation. (R. Gaddini and E. Gaddini 1959).

Another example of the search for continuity may be found in the case of a premature infant who had been kept in an incubator for forty days. Brought home, this baby, who had not experienced oneness with mother, rebelled at being held and rocked. The baby rejected those comforts out of a fear of change. This baby was a good example of the pleasure/unpleasure principle (Freud 1917) where change is unpleasure. The incubator *was* the unconscious mother for this baby and she rejected any change, which was experienced as catastrophic (Bion 1966). The same may be true for the autistic child who has missed early human care—and thus a sense of continuity—and who consequently perceives the object-outside world as a frightening change.

The way in which institutionalized mental patients protect themselves from change, including discharge—no matter how ghastly life in the institution is for them—is quite similar to those reactions to the terror of change manifested by the premature child who cannot accept mother's care and rocking. The fear of change, which was emblematically expressed by hospitalized mental patients, may be found with similar characteristics in all therapeutic situations where severe illness is involved.[9]

The analyst, or therapist, is a precursor for such patients, as most of them have never reached the stage of using an object. They hang on to him since they are incapable of using the outside world as a space for growth, just as the child who pulls hair or plays with his feces to deny separation. Drugs, overeating and obsessive ideas are also "precursors of thought" (only slightly more evolved than pulling hair or manipulating feces) for very ill patients. Our task is to actively adapt to their needs, to allow regression and work towards a capacity to meet the losses they deny.

In these patients, the ego had to organize itself for survival in a primitive way. Their ego ailments are the expression of the limits within which they were allowed to move between the urgent needs of the self and the demands of the outside world. The notion that the analyst functions as an active container for the patient's developmental process is also the view Menzies-Lyth (1988) proposes in her studies of social institutions.

---

9. In Italy, with a 1978 law, open structures such as day hospitals and therapeutic communities are gradually taking the place of the old mental hospitals.

Need

Need is a state/process in course of action: the fear experienced by the young infant when mother turns her head and he loses eye contact with her pertains to the loss of self, which is also the loss of his illusion of *being* (mother). Concern and mental pain occur in growth within this illusion/disillusion and so does fear of change. This fear may later appear in the form of fantasying or fixed ideas or in psychosomatic manifestations, all of which interfere with true living and learning, and do not promote growth. In all these pathological conditions, the patient is trapped in this percursorship of relating and thinking, just as he used to depend on a thumb or pacifier in order to be. His quest is saturated and no exploration or learning from experience takes place.

We should consider that if a precursor's (pre-object or phenomenon) loss has such a massive impact on the nature of learning, as well as on that of suffering, the significance of this loss must be relevant along the entire growth process. For the young child, the precursor's loss is in fact far more important than that of a transitional object and, at times, even of the caring person, both in immediate manifestations as well as in distant consequences, because the infant's sense of being lies *in the precursor,* whereas only a sense of relating is implied by the transitional object.

Young children are frightened by both kinds of loss, but the loss of the PO means a loss of physical continuity based on concrete senses, when cohesion and its mental representation have not yet developed. The eyes-into-eyes continuity of the young infant is also a precursor of the symbolic representation of continuity. The relative evolution and mode of dealing with loss determine the nature of relations the child will be able to sustain after separation. Difficulties at the precursor-level may, in fact, produce dysfunctions in symbolization and thinking, as the development of cohesion and its mental functioning (concepts) are strictly connected with early emotional experiences of satisfaction and the mother's capacity to hold her infant's nascent fragments together.

In the past, we used to think that the child's auxiliary ego was the mother's ego functioning for him until his own was properly structured. The two concepts—auxiliary ego and mother's functioning mind—are equivalent; both are functions that hold the infant's fragmentary sensations together and bring them to cohesion and maturity, thus permitting the child's autonomous mental functioning to emerge.

His fantasies operate differently according to the maturational level attained (E. Gaddini 1982). Just as frustrations are necessary to promote thought (R. Gaddini and E. Gaddini 1984), they may also be annihilating if experienced in excess or at the wrong time. The amount of frustration—in excess or in defect—which a child faces during infancy may interfere with the outcome of his maturational process. There are many children who never attain the use of growth-promoting fantasy, and who—terrified by early situations experienced as threatening—withdraw instead into fantasizing and reverie. Many are those who will never succeed in incorporating and introjecting, and who therefore will never reach individuation and a mature identity. They continue depending, and when their "precursor" is lost, they are totally bereft.

At times, the loss is acknowledged only in part, as an element of self is retained and, with it, the trend to reestablish the lost fragmentary functioning (E. Gaddini 1982). This attempt may be sufficient to prevent anxiety caused by the original catastrophic change if the child's mind is able to conceive of the catastrophe as something belonging to the past, which has already taken place (Winnicott 1974).

Mourning

Differentiation of self from object and acknowledgment of reality of loss are critical achievements that enable mourning to take place. The separation of self from object cannot occur until the object is loved and its loss can be felt as a whole. If projective identification and narcissistic organization (Rosenfeld 1971)—along with early defenses from object-loss or even earlier imitation (a defense against self-loss)—are rigidly fixed, it is impossible to differentiate loss of object from loss of self. Only in the transference (E. Gaddini 1982) may we get a clear idea of what is happening in our patient's mind and obtain his help in deepening the investigation of the vicissitudes of the "precursor" or "illusion."

Change always retains its dramatic evolutionary significance pertaining to the patient's early defensive fantasies as they emerge during the psychoanalytical process. The patient's acceptance and use of change can, at times, render the analyst's work extremely arduous.

Defense Against Change

A clinical vignette comes to mind in the context of this discussion of defense against separateness. A 14-year-old girl was seen in consultation because—

after having viewed a TV program—she was afraid of becoming a boy. Returning years later at the age of 22 to begin analysis, she was in agony due to rigidly fixed ideas of being in love with women and was "physically " unable to have intercourse with her boyfriend. The anxieties underlying this defensive organization, which we were able to recapture in dreams, had to do with self-loss and disintegration dating back to her early protective maneuvres in search of a sense of continuity between self and mother. A total split of body–mind experiences, and an idealized state of fusion with her parents, gave her a profoundly painful sense of betrayal, as if the patient felt that she "was promised a perfect object and the reality of disappointment seems unfair and unbearable" (Rosenfeld 1971).

In E. Gaddini's view (1969), the search for continuity and the struggle against separateness comprise the basic core of the early defenses based on preobjective imageless fantasies.[10] These take place before the fantasy is visualized and can be represented in the mind. Imitation—in order to be— (the basis of psychophysical syndromes) is the earliest functional organization of defense that the young infant is able to mobilize in order to protect himself from loss. This type of defense stems only from bodily sensations because, at this early age, a mind which can elaborate sensations into thoughts does not yet exist. E. Gaddini suggests that the young baby's compulsion to repeat is an attempt to relive and endlessly reenact the sensory experiences of early being. Occasionally this type of organization is a part of normal growth, but more typically, it is found in young infants who undergo sudden loss. Rosenfeld used this concept of early defense when suggesting that narcissistic organizations protect the patient from the experience of separateness. In both concepts, the reality of what belongs to the self and what belongs to the object is obscured.

"Flowing-over-at-oneness" (Hermann 1929), associated by Tustin with imitation (E. Gaddini 1969), "is the process by which the illusion of 'primal unity' is maintained" (Tustin 1981, p. 80) along with continuity, and it implies rivalry (although not envy yet). Imitation, however, is earlier than projection and identification, "which imply some sense of bodily separateness between mother and infant" (Tustin 1981, p. 80).

Tustin pays great attention to imitation as an early defensive fantasy and uses it largely in her work. She wrote (1981):

---

10. Boyer (1990) suggests the term "proto-thoughts" for these experiences.

In his paper on imitation, Eugenio Gaddini (1969) tried to clear our ideas on the psychoanalytic use of terms for early developmental situations and also to clarify for us the order in which early developmental processes occur . . . he sees primitive rivalry as being even earlier than the primitive envy described by both Klein (1957) and Jacobson (1964). This confirms my own experience. Children whose womb-like oceanic feeling is unduly disturbed seem to be faced by death-dealing "rivals" who could never exist in reality and whose threats are worse than death. Even "annihilation anxiety" seems too mild a term to describe the state of terror which either paralyzes these children or causes them to behave in an impulsively irrational way, like rushing out of the consulting room or refusing to go to school. The threat is of a cataclysmic catastrophe which they feel they have already experienced, a repetition of which must be avoided at all costs (this needs detailed clinical material to make it meaningful to workers who have not experienced these elemental states) (p. 89).

Such detailed clinical material is presented in full in Chapter 9 of her book *The Protective Shell in Children and Adults* (1990). Here, Tustin attempts to conceptualize these primitive rivals as "a mouthful of sucklings," "a breast of babies," or "a swarm of stinging rivals."

In imitation, which could develop into narcissistic organization, E. Gaddini (1984) saw a quest for protection against death. For the young infant, death is separation and the distinction between self and object, which gives him an unbearable sensation of loss. Rivalry, at most, is the sensation upon which imitation is based at this early stage. Envy, in its various expressions, including projective identification, may take place only later.

From these formulations on early rivalry, E. Gaddini derives the concept that early learning implies *learning in one's own body inside a sensation-based process*. As perceptions do not exist at this stage of growth, there can hardly be any form of introjection with its mental working-through mechanisms. This view is not in agreement with psychoanalytic developmentalists (e.g., Emde, Stern, Osofsky, etc.) who do not distinguish perceptions from sensory data, not even in the frame of reference of the maturational process, where sensory data are the basis on which perceptions and feelings and thinking later develop.

In the earliest stages, sensory data are not experienced as such, but rather as bodily modifications. It is only at the end of the third month that perceptions develop in the infant's mind. In terms of mental development, the appearance of perceptions coincides with an obscure sense of non-self accompanied by the precursors of the process known as separation, which implies an early *objective recognition* of one's own separate being.

Eugenio Gaddini differentiated the "inner world" from the "interior world," as well as the "exterior world" from the "external (outside) world." The differences between exterior world and external world is determined by the subjective use that the individual is capable of making of objective reality.

We may say that exterior reality is less objective than the external reality, to a degree which varies between a maximum and a minimum of objectivation. Internal and external worlds therefore exist in an unending interaction, which may vary from a minimum to a maximum possibility of distinction between one and the other. E. Gaddini's concept of imitation typically refers to a period when this distinction has not yet taken place (the first few months of postnatal life) whereas defensive narcissistic organizations imply ego structure and a mind able to perceive the good qualities of an object; in this case, envy can be introjected.

In describing these two phases of development, Winnicott (1962) noticed that during the former, the infant had not reached the stage of emotional development which could provide the equipment for dealing with loss. He suggests that the same loss of the mother, a few months later, would be a loss of object without this added element of loss of parts of the subject.

Because of the equation early=severe in psychopathology, pathology based on a premature loss of the object is particularly severe: We may find perversions (particularly fetishism), fixed ideas, compulsions, and convictions of the reality of an imaginary companion as an outcome of this developmental failure. The sense of loss experienced by the child who has been deprived of his transitional object is, we know, closer to mourning than to disintegration and self-loss. It seems to me that E. Gaddini's idea of "integration anxiety" (1982)—seen as an arrest in the development, which occurs during analysis when the process is experienced by the patient as a particularly threatening and painful loss—comes very close to Bion's idea of catastrophic change (Bion 1966).[11]

---

11. For Bion, change (in the analytic process) is—at the same time—evolution and disaster, as it implies learning through "elaboration" a process which brings forward new products and new states on the basis of data acquired during the infant's (or patient's) previous experience. In this light, knowledge and learning may be seen as a sort of biological adaptation similar to any other adaptation, except for the fact

In his early months, the young child goes from holding (or containment)—which gives emotional meaning to things and events and makes it possible for early sensations to gradually grow into affects and thoughts—to differentiation. The complex mental operations of later stages will follow on the basis of sense data gathered during the phase of containment. If things don't go well—in a gradual and smooth way—it is possible that instead of being-at-one with mother, where a sense of self is still only sketchy, the infant suddenly finds himself in front of a not-me, an unthinkable experience where elaboration from sensations towards perceptions cannot take place properly. If he does not reach the necessary maturation for this stage of growth, and is therefore not mentally capable of such an operation, primary terrors (cosmic in character) may be experienced. A good example is the sense of loss the young child experiences the moment mother turns her head away from him, which I have referred to above. Here disillusion takes the place of the previous illusion, and the child experiences a sudden sense of self-loss.

Self-Loss Anxiety

The concept of self-loss anxiety (E. Gaddini 1982) was used to describe what happens in the course of growth when fear of integration takes the place of the tendency toward individuation (p. 344). The integrative process grows out of unintegration and occurs in the fragmentary organization which preludes the formation of the self and reflects the way in which separation has been experienced.

In the pathology of separation, this anxiety may reach unbearable levels and the integrative processes may be experienced as the threat of a new and final catastrophe, a menace to survival. The psychophysical syndrome, a frequent early defense from this agony, is the only auto-protective operation the fragmentary self can muster up. With this in mind, it is to be hopefully expected that the study of imitative phenomena, on which these syndromes are based, long neglected by psychoanalysis, may find a new impetus.

In the beginning, in fact, the child is all body: entirely physical. In the course of growth, he passes from the physical dimension to the mental—from

---

that we are dealing with the mind and with thinking, where conflict between the subjective and objective soon begins.

body to mind—and gradually the mind takes the place of what was originally only physical.[12] The child learns about himself through his own senses, but sense data are not yet perceptions: They do not pass through the mind. True, the mind builds itself on the basis of physical senses, particularly ". . . those springing from the surface of the body" (Freud 1923, p. 26). Through physical sensations, we come to perceptions and then to introjections and to the construction of an inner world.[13] Feeling and thinking have their basis in all this and are achieved at the end of the first year.

We may say that in each session, Bion, with his concept of not fostering memory, started out from the origins. Origins, for him—as for those of us who have studied early defensive fantasies as mental processes (E. Gaddini 1982)—mean departing from sense data as they are relived in the analytic setting.

Conclusion

My intent was to investigate the function of early defenses as one meets them in the psychoanalytic process. At attempt has been made to describe the defenses of the self as distinct from those of the ego, built on the former. When, on the basis of fear of separateness, nonintegration is organized as a mental defense, then "can we say that the psycho physical syndrome is closer to self-loss than non-integration" (E. Gaddini 1987, p. 327).

The capacity to feel dependent—acquired only if the mother–infant dyad was good enough, and if the mother was able to actively adapt to the infant's needs—is essential to the formation of a true Self capable of facing loss. The possible relationship between negative therapeutic reaction defenses and organization of the self still remains an open question.

---

12. Evidence that feeling and thinking have their basis in sense data may be found in the observation that children born in summer have cool transitional objects, while those born in winter have warm woolly soft ones. That means that the symbol of reunion, implied in the TO, had its basis in the early sensations of the time when the infant was fused at his mother's breast.

13. Eccles (1988) also pays particular attention to the inner-outer world distinction, and to the moment in which a connection is established between the former and the latter in the child's mind.

References

Bick, E. (1968). The experience of the skin in early object relation. *International Journal of Psycho-Analysis* 49:484–487.

———— (1964). Personal communication.

Bion, W. R. (1962). A theory of thinking. *International Journal of Psycho-Analysis* 43:108–117.

———— (1966). Catastrophic change. *Bulletin of the British Psycho-Analytic Society* 5:18–27.

———— (1968). On concept-formation. *International Journal of Psycho-Analysis* 49:692–693.

———— (1973). *Brazilian Lectures I*. Sao Paul, Brazil: Imago Editora.

Bleger, J. (1967). Simbiosi y Ambiguedad. *Estudio Psicoanalitico*. Buenos Aires: Editorial Paidos, 1972.

Boyer, B. L. (1990). Introduction. In *Master Clinicians in Treating the Regressed Patient*, p. 10. New Jersey: Jason Aronson.

Eccles, J. (1988). Brain research and the body-mind problem. In *Brain Research and the Mind–Body Problem: Epistemological and Metaphysical Issues*. Vatican City State: Pontificia Academia Scientiarum.

Erikson, E. (1956). The problem of ego identity. *Journal of the American Psychoanalytic Association* 4:56–121.

Freud, S. (1911). Letter to Jung, Dec. 17, 1911. In *Freud-Jung Letters*, W. Mac Guire, ed. New Jersey: Princeton University Press, pp. 472–474.

———— (1915). Letter to Abraham, April 5, 1945. In *A Psychoanalytic Dialogue. The Letters of Sigmund Freud and Karl Abraham*, ed. Hilda Abraham and Ernst L. Freud. London: Hogarth.

———— (1917). The sexual life of human beings. *Standard Edition* 16:310–323.

———— (1917). The development of the libido. *Standard Edition*, 16:324–349.

———— (1922). 7th IPA Congress, Berlin, Germany, August.

———— (1923). The ego and the id. *Standard Edition* 19:3–63. (footnote added in 1927.)

Gaddini, E. (1969). On imitation. *International Journal of Psycho-Analysis* 50:475–484.

———— (1982). Early defensive fantasies and the psychoanalytic process. *International Journal of Psycho-Analysis* 63:369.

———— (1984). Changes in psychoanalytic patients up to the present days. *IPA Monograph Series N* 4:6–39.

——— (1985). La maschera e il cerchio. In *Scritti (1953–1985)*, ed. A. Cortina, pp. 731–744. 1989.

——— (1987). Notes on the mind–body question. *International Journal of Psycho-Analysis* 68:315–329.

Gaddini, R. (1971). Transitional objects and the process of individuation. *Journal of the American Academy of Child Psychiatry*, 9:347–365.

——— (1975). The concept of the transitional object. *Journal of American Academy of Child Psychiatry*, 14:731–736.

Gaddini, R., and Gaddini, E. (1959). Rumination in infancy. In *Dynamic Psychopathology in Childhood*, ed. J. Pavendstedt and L. Jessner, pp. 166–185. New York: Grune and Stratton.

——— (1984). La frustrazione come fattore di crescita normale e patologica. In *Scritti*, pp. 603–617. Crescita, 6 Genn. 1984.

Goethe, W. (1793). Italienische Reiser. *Berliner Ausgabe Werker*, Vol. 14, pp. 388–422.

Greenacre, P. (1971). *Emotional Growth. vol. I.* New York: International Universities Press.

Hermann, I. (1929). Das ich und das dekken. *Imago* 15:89–110.

Jacobson, E. (1964). *The Self and the Object World*. London: Hogarth.

Klein, M. (1952). *Developments in Psychoanalysis*. London: Karnac Books, reprinted, 1989.

——— (1957). *Envy and Gratitude*. London: Tavistock.

Mahler, M. S., Pine, F., and Bergman, A. (1975). *The Psychological Birth of the Human Infant*. New York: Basic Books.

Menzies-Lyth, I. (1988). *Containing Anxieties in Institutions and the Dynamics of the Social*. London: Free Association.

Rosenfeld, H. (1971). A clinical approach to the psychoanalytic theory of the life and death instincts: an investigation into the aggressive aspects of narcissism. *International Journal of Psycho-Analysis* 52:169–178.

Sander, L. (1984). Personal communication.

Segal, H., and Laufer, M. (1979). What is Psychoanalysis? Statement for the Pre-Congress of the 31st IPA Congress, New York, July.

Steiner, J. (1990). The defensive function of pathological organization. In *Master Clinicians in Treating the Regressed Patients*, ed. B. Boyer and P. Giovacchini. New Jersey: Jason Aronson.

Stern, D. (1985). *The Interpersonal World of the Infant*. New York: Basic Books.

Tustin, F. (1981). *Autistic States in Children*. London: Routledge and Kegan Paul.

———— (1990). *The Autistic Shell in Children and Adults*. London: Karnac Books.

Winnicott, D. W. (1951). Transitional objects and transitional phenomena. In *Through Paediatrics to Psycho-Analysis*, pp. 229–242. London: Hogarth Press, 1958.

———— (1962). Ego integration in child development. In *MPFE*. London: Hogarth, 1965, pp. 56–63.

———— (1963). The mentally ill in your caseload. In *The Maturational Processes and the Facilitating Environment*, p. 222. London: Hogarth, 1965.

———— (1966). Somatic illness in its positive and negative aspects. *International Journal of Psycho-Analysis* 47:510–516.

———— (1974). Fear of Breakdown. *International Review of Psycho-Analysis* 1:103–110.

14

Verbal Rituals in Autism: The Concept of the Autistic Object and the Countertransference[1]

Anne Alvarez

Ritual or ceremonial magic is aimed at the control of the spirit world by various means, from short spells and charms to lengthy and highly elaborate ceremonies including prayers and invocations.

Wilfred Bion, *Cogitations*

One of the greatest of Frances Tustin's theoretical achievements was the development of the concept of the *autistic object*. Her paper on the subject was first published in 1980, but she sent me the manuscript some time before. It was an absolute revelation to those of us trying vainly to find meaning in the repetitive preoccupations of our autistic patients. It gave us permission to use the countertransference to which we should have been attending: a countertransference often of absolute meaninglessness.

Tustin made it clear that many of the toys, tin cats, teddies, and boxes that the child with autism carried around with him needed to be sharply distinguished from Winnicott's *transitional objects*. Winnicott (1958) had placed the

---

1. An earlier version of this paper appeared in Alvarez, A. A. (1992) *Live Company: Psychoanalytic Psychotherapy with Autistic, Borderline, Deprived, and Abused Children*. Routledge, London.

transitional object halfway between the true symbol and the symbolic equation, as outlined by Hanna Segal (1957). None of these three authors was writing about actual teddies or actual toys. They were discussing the different ways in which any object may be used. Tustin showed how the toy Austin car—which her patient carried around—did not, as she had previously thought, stand for herself—Tustin in the transference—as the same car used in a real symbolic manner would. She showed that, like Segal's symbolic equation, an autistic object was felt to be equal (if not superior) to the primary object (i.e., breast, mother, or maternal function in the transference).

Transitional objects and symbolic objects, on the other hand, are filled with meaning and phantasy, and—in the case of true symbolic objects—open to new and creative meanings; symbolic equations are rigid and limited. Tustin identified autistic objects with symbolic equations, but at times she implied that autistic objects were even more limited and empty. One might also add that the fetishistic use of objects, to which she also referred, also goes well beyond the level of a symbolic equation. Something else seems to have been added to twist, complicate, and escalate the situation. My patient described in this chapter no longer used physical objects repetitively: As he entered adolescence and his language improved, the ritualistic habits began to invade his rapidly elaborating and expanding speech. Excitement about the pleasures of communication could easily go over into something else.

The Countertransference Used for Purposes of Description

There is no doubt that autism is a condition which provokes extremely powerful reactions in its students. Perhaps it is the depth and profundity of the withdrawal, and the seemingly immovable determination to stay withdrawn (or undrawn), that is so unnerving and which calls forth these extreme reactions. In the diagnostician, it is sometimes a reaction which a clinician would regard as excessively—possibly even defensively—detached. In the clinician, at least in my own case in the early years, it was a reaction that led to too great an engagement, in the sense of a determination and insistence on finding meanings where meaningless so clearly ruled.

In the literature on autism, there have been major differences, not only over aetiology but in the language of description. Kanner's (1944) description of the first major symptom as one of "extreme aloneness from the beginning of life" has become Wing's (1981) "severe social impairment." The second symptom, that of impairment in communication, has changed little in its description.

But the differences between Kanner and Wing over the description and definition of the third major symptom in the autistic triad are even more dramatic than in their differences over the first symptom. Kanner's "anxiety obsessive desire for sameness" becomes, in Wing's hands, "the absence of imaginative and pretend play, with the substitution of repetitive behavior." The latter description seems careful to eschew Kanner's assumptions of human motivation, desire, and human meaning.

However, a purely behavioral description leaves out important features. One may question whether repetitive behavior is simply repetitive behavior, or can we allow ourselves the freedom to see the deadliness in it, the emptiness, and possibly something even worse? Do the emotive adjectives necessarily involve a reading in, or should they perhaps be a careful part of the description of the behavior? For what is left out—even in Kanner's somewhat more emotive account—is the horror, disbelief and tormenting boredom engendered in the mind of anyone who is willing to *sit for long enough* with an autistic child engaged in his particular autistic ritual, to attend fully to what this feels like, and to examine reflectively both the quality of the child's behavior, and the feeling states engendered in himself by such behavior. These emotions in the countertransference towards the autistic child may, of course, lead the clinician astray. He may, for example, be tempted to read meanings into meaninglessness. But used properly and circumspectly, they may be not only the lifeblood of the psychotherapy, but a vital instrument for the accurate and detailed *observation* of autistic sympotomatology (Kanner 1944, Wing and Gould 1979).

I shall therefore include the emotive language in my descriptions, partly because I am aware that it was only when I allowed myself to feel my profound boredom in the face of the repetitive behavior of Robbie—one of my first and most severely impaired patients with autism—and to acknowledge the full horror I had been denying about Robbie's own lack of boredom and lack of urgency about the passage of time, that I got anywhere at all, first in understanding his state of mind, and second, in helping him to come to life. Neither scientific detachment, nor pseudoneutrality, nor even receptive containment, in its more passive forms, were adequate. Is our normal human desire for and expectation of aliveness and novelty, and the reaction of horror at the deadness and boring quality of the rituals, necessarily a "reading in," or is the sense of human alarm and urgency essential to lend our statements adequate descriptive power?

There are further reasons why a more emotive clinician's language is appropriate for purposes of accurate description. It has to do with the clinician's perceptions of the qualitative nature of the rituals themselves at each moment; that is, the perception of some very disturbing and unpleasant qualities attached to the rituals. These have little in common with the more respectable motives that clinicians originally looked for, such as avoidance of anxiety. I am thinking instead of the perverse excitements, the bathing in thrills and frenzies, and also of some of the more sadistic and destructive motives which may attach themselves to the rituals and may play a large part in their perpetuation.

I suspect that the real insanity of autism is at times so disturbing that diagnosticians and clinicians all search for single explanations or causes which are sufficiently separate from the psychological *being* of the child to spare the onlooker the task of looking too closely. Perverse or addictive motives do not always accompany the rituals, but most clinicians consider it a more worrying prognostic sign for the therapy than when the rituals are more purely compensatory and also not too fixed, or even desultory. But even without these perverse elements, the *degree* of withdrawal (or undrawal), the degree of refusal or inability to respond to our overtures, evokes powerful feelings of rejection, incomprehension, despair, and also rage. Many professionals prefer to view such a "black hole" in a mind from a great professional distance. Others, in their desire to get close, may neglect the importance of the conditions under which such distances can be bridged.

If Hobson (1993) is correct in asserting that autism should be counted a social-affective deficit which derives from faulty empathic interactions with others, then the instrument for study may need to be not only a scientific description of quantifiable units of behavior, but a study of the method of empathic interaction itself. To examine the autistic child while ignoring the interpersonal dimension *between us* is like listening to music while tone deaf or comparing the scent of two roses without a sense of smell. The musician buying a new cello insists on playing it first in order to assess its tone and resonances. To judge its responsiveness to his playing he has to engage with his instrument in a highly skilled way. Hamlet, mocking Guildenstern for imagining he can play *him*, says of himself, "and there is much music, excellent voice, in this little organ, yet cannot you make it speak."

The psychoanalytic observer of autism studies not only the child's responses to him in the transference but his own countertransference responses to the child and then the child's responses to his responses. He studies responses *in the context of their relationship and in sequence* and how changing contexts affect responses from moment to moment. What is studied is a relationship: a duet, not a solo. Two of my autistic patients do certain things only when my attention has wandered for a moment, never when my attention is fully on them. I have to monitor my responses as well as theirs. Intersubjective analysts in the United States have pointed out that if an archaeologist unknowingly dropped a wristwatch into a dig, it would be dangerous to assume that everything found in the dig must have been there beforehand. As Stolorow and colleagues (1987) put it, psychoanalysis is unique among the sciences in that the observer is also the observed.

This attention on the part of the therapist/observer to changes in the state of his own mind can shed much light on the autistic child's apparent lack of interest in other people. Frith (1989) stresses that this is not a lack of awareness of other *people,* but rather of other minds. Frith goes on to discuss the autistic child's lack of interest in creating shared attention: for example, Curcio (1978) has shown that young autistic children tend not to have used proto-declarative pointing. I once heard Trevarthen give a wonderful example of the effectiveness of this for "social referencing" in a 10-month old baby girl who was brought into his experimental lab by her mother for the first time. She apparently pointed with astonishment—and a somewhat agitatedly curious "uh!?"—at the video camera up on its stand. Her mother replied confidently and reassuringly, "That's a video camera, dear," and the baby gave a satisfied "uh," and turned her attention elsewhere. The baby clearly did not understand the words "video camera," but she did understand that her mother felt that strange contraption was a knowable thing. Frith takes Curcio's finding to be evidence of an (innate) inability to recognize other minds. But suppose we specify, instead, a *developed deficit* (a development beginning in the early days and weeks of life) *in the ability and/or will to recognize other mindful minds, that is, minds sufficiently able to share in delighted recognitions and capable of attending to and attuning to oneself.*

My own clinical experience with autistic children leads me to think that, although they do not *declare* an interest and invite one to share it in normal open ways, they do find their own methods of *eliciting* interest and attention, and not always interest and attention of a purely need-satisfying type; that is, they seem to elicit *mindful* attention.

One autistic patient, Mark, could go on engaging in his repetitive rubbing of the table, walking in circles, rubbing the table, walking in circles again for half an hour at the far end of the room while my gaze was on him. The minute, probably the second, my mind and probably my gaze wandered away from him, or the quality of my gaze changed, the circle changed to an oval. This brought him into my field of vision and he got my attention back. Then, and only then, did he return to his circle. If I was only studying his behavior, and not also monitoring my own state of mind, I would miss this connection and miss his responsiveness to my lack of responsiveness.

Robbie, even from his position on the couch where he could not see me at all, always seemed to know the moment my attention wandered, and sometimes he would then introduce one of his most annoying verbal rituals, a permanently effective way of drawing anyone's full attention to him. Asperger, who identified what many people regard as a higher-level sub-type of autism, thought that these children seemed to take things in with short peripheral glances (Frith 1989). I suspect this is true of some of the more ill autistic children as well. The problem is that the child may be using his apparently most un-object-related symptom—a stereotyped ritual—in highly indirect, but nevertheless powerfully object-related ways. I shall illustrate this later.

Explanations for the Rituals

I will here review some of the ways in which other authors have discussed the problem of stereotypy, or repetitive behavior. To begin with, Dawson's and Lewy's (1989) thought that the explanation for the autistic children's lack of habituation could be found in their inability to modulate states of arousal. This is an interesting observation, but not necessarily a causal explanation. Kanner (1944) himself did refer to actions and rhythmic movements and noted that the accompanying ecstatic fervor strongly indicated the presence of masturbatory gratification, but this observation has, to my knowledge, never appeared again in the organicist literature. The understanding of perverse sexual acts, or perverse fantasies with perverse content, has a long history in psychoanalysis, but the understanding that perverse fantasies may express themselves more indirectly not through the content but through the *form* of verbal presentation is a relatively recent formulation.[2]

My own experience with Robbie suggests that a particular repetitive preoccupation could begin as a way of managing some state of disturbance or of emptiness, or, sometime later in his treatment, even as an object of genuine fresh interest. But the fuel, which afterwards kept it going, was neither the disturbance, nor the emptiness, nor the novel interest, but something else.

---

2. See Betty Joseph's observations on "chuntering" in "Addiction to near-death" (1982).

Perversions and addictions have a way, like bronze, of keeping their shape even after the cast is removed. The building agents, once the mold is cast, may be of another order altogether and tend not to be amendable to being analyzed away by simple explanatory interpretations referring to whatever causal agent may set the activity in motion in the first place.

Dawson (1989) discusses psychophysiological evidence that autistic children have abnormalities of attention: that is, they do not habituate. The clinician treating these children may feel she is on the edge of death from boredom at witnessing a repetitive activity for the hundredth or thousandth time, but the child never seems to get bored! It is my impression, in fact, that a very close study, both of the moments when the therapist gets bored— which can alert her to the fact that the child perhaps should also be getting bored by now—and of the subtle qualitative changes in the child's repetitive activity, may reveal that he actually does seem to be getting bored but does not show this in any obvious way. Sometimes he goes on because he doesn't know how to stop. Sometimes he forces himself to go on because he cannot imagine doing anything else. Sometimes he is driven to go on, sometimes he goes on because he likes producing boredom in us; and sometimes he goes on in a kind of frenzy because he finds this particular brand of stereotypy thrilling. He may go on mindlessly in a desultory way, but *he goes on*. The lack of habituation needs, I suggest, to be studied in far more detail.

Dawson (1989) points out that autistic children also fail to turn to a new stimulus even when they do habituate. Those moments when the child is suddenly tired of a stereotypy pose difficult but crucial technical problems for the therapist. Such moments—which, as I have said, are difficult to detect because the child often does not know what else to do with his attention—are gone before the therapist can get in quickly enough to make use of them to help the child see that he might find some other object of interest. A lot depends on whether the child has simply lost heart or whether he is more coldly determined in his refusal to find new objects of interest. Dawson argues that the autistic individual suffers from difficulty in modulating his states of arousal and that this directly influences his capacity to attend to and comprehend both social and non-social information, and ultimately to function adaptively in both of these spheres. Her research on therapeutic interventions shows that autistic children's attention to other people can be increased by sensitive interactive strategies that provide simplified, predictable, and highly contingent responses and allow the children to control and regulate the amount of stimulation. This seems to me a promising area of thinking and of treatment and sounds close, in certain respects, to the developments in psychotherapy I have described elsewhere. (Alvarez 1992, 1966, Dawson and Lewy 1989).[3]

Much work has now been done on the way in which the modulation of arousal is achieved and laid down in the early months of life in millions of repetitions of minute rhythmic and cyclical interactions between the baby and his living, human, responding caretaker. Stern and others have shown (Stern 1985), for example, that the maternal gaze and the constellation of vocal and facial behaviors that may accompany it exert a strong effect on both eliciting and holding the infant's gaze. Attention, as Meltzer (1975) said, has to be "paid" to—as Klaus and Kennel (1982) put it—the face and voice and breast of the mother, which acts as the "magnet which lines up the iron filings." Later, once such experiences are internalized, the magnet's attraction is internalized and represented inside, so the normal child is drawn to seek contact with a living object that can produce novelty and that he now expects to find. In other words, it is *attraction*—emanating from a living object—which combats distractibility. Until researchers consider the effect of these early interactions in relation to and together with the factor of neurological dysfunction, their assumption of basic impairment in the brain—as the only causative factor in autism—has to be seen to be extremely partial. Dawson's theory suffers from the same problem as Frith's "central cohesive force." Both derive from a one-person psychology. Surely it is the mother—in her *focusing function* (Lisa Miller, personal communication)—that plays a major part both in the central cohesive organizing function, and in modulating arousal. Much comes from the baby, but much also comes from the caregiver as well.

Frith's explanation of the repetitive behavior differs, suggesting that it is a result of the child's lack of symbolization and his problems in processing sensations. She believes that both the terrifying power of sensations, and the repetitiveness in autism, are two sides of the same coin—the coin being the impairment in the central cohesive force. At one point she mentions the slow habituation to novel stimuli and adds that although some research suggests that stereotypies occur among normal people in stressful situations in order to reduce the level of arousal, an extensive review shows that stereotypies often *increase* arousal. Again, this would not be difficult for the clinician to explain. A symptom may begin as a reaction to stress and therefore would lower arousal; it may add secondary gains where it neither decreases nor increases

---

3. See the interesting broadening in the behavioral methods used by Howlin and Rutter in their home-based treatment of autistic children (1987).

arousal; and eventually it may even gather perverse motivations to itself, thus increasing arousal.

Years of observation of the changing use of a single symptom make the simple notion of a primary function, or even of secondary gain, far too simplistic. The symptom may gather countless new motivations to itself. I have felt, with some of Robbie's symptoms, that almost the whole of his personality, and a huge range of quite complex feeling, could be caught up in a single repetitive series of phrases. Oliver Sacks (1985) quotes Richard Woll- $<$ heim, who—in *The Thread of Life*—makes an absolute distinction between calculations and what he calls "iconic" mental states (p. 195). Sacks goes on to discuss the idiot savant calculating twins: "They do not seem to 'operate' on numbers, non-iconically, like a calculator; they 'see' them, directly, as a vast natural scene" (p. 195). Robbie's icons were far more limited, but he did seem to experience a synaesthesia similar to Luria's (1968) famous mnemonist, and sometimes, when Robbie repeated some of his favorite phrases or described someone who had "a bright green velvety voice;" his face would light up with joy. So the rituals were by no means always dead or always perverse, particularly at their inception.

Robbie's Rituals: The Need for Multiple Explanations

I have described elsewhere (Alvarez 1992) how the wall-touching and hand-flapping rituals, which Robbie used as a child, were gradually replaced by repetitive narrative accounts of things that had happened to him long before. These repetitions went through what finally became, for me, a familiar series of stages. At first they seemed to involve a reaction to anxiety, or an agitated but excited interest, and an inadequate attempt to control and get hold of and process such an experience. On one occasion, for example, long before Robbie could manage to cross streets and travel about London by himself, he escaped from his mother's car and arrived 15-minutes early for his session. I knew he had no idea of road safety and I couldn't imagine how he had arrived alone so early in this excited state. He was too disturbed and impaired in those days to be able to explain what had happened, so I had to remain in ignorance until, eventually, his frantic mother arrived. In the meantime, my voice clearly betrayed the anxiety I felt for him (and for his mother) when I said, "It's a bit too early, Robbie, could you wait for a while in the waiting room?" For years afterwards, he never entered my door without saying, "It's a bit too early." I am certain that on the day of the incident he picked up my shock, and for the next day or so was trying to come to terms with it—and also of course, with his own. But for years, I went on trying to understand what I saw as its meaning when, in fact, the sentence had become ritualized. I thought his words told something about the fact he had sensed I wasn't ready for him and that there was a deeper sense in which he felt the world hadn't been ready for him. This may well have been the meaning in the first few days. But later the situation changed. Had I used my countertransference honestly and acknowledged the terrible weariness I felt when I opened the door years later and he still uttered this dead phrase in a dead manner, I might have succeeded in not being as autistic with him as he was with me. Tustin's work on the autistic object was, unfortunately, still to come. I might have also been able to show him what we learned together years later, that somewhere he did know that this dead dullard's way of talking to people made them feel very unwelcoming and unreceptive to him.

There were many other verbal rituals which, if responded to too passively, would never have outlived their usefulness and become digested and processed in the natural way. After the first genuine use, they tended to go into a stale dead period where they seemed to have no meaning or life or motivation attached to them at all. Later, once I became alert to this, I interpreted it more vigilantly, and he became less repetitive—or else he used his repetitiveness for provocative, irritating, but certainly very alive and hopeful motives. By then, the rituals were never desultory. But it is in relation to the desultory periods that I think Frith's observation is instructive: she insists that "what is needed by a central agency is switching off, not switching on." Frith, of course, thinks this is done in the brain, but it may be that it is also partly learned in the early days and weeks of life in interaction with a caregiver who helps the baby to switch *on* to new objects of interest by the animation of her face, voice, and breast.

The problem was that if a symptom escaped my attention—or that of Robbie's parents, as they too became alert to this problem—it tended to go into a stage that was addictive, or even perverse and fetishistic. These are the rituals which may overlap closely with the iconic states described by Wollheim and Sacks, but they are far narrower in emotional scope. Robbie, in anxious moments, could lick the inside of his lower lip apparently for purposes of self-soothing; but at other times, he gave himself over to it, doing it with a masturbatory and highly sensual pleasure, and the expression on his face was sly, perverse, unpleasantly lascivious, and somehow lewd and triumphant. Tustin (1981) and Meltzer (1973, 1975), both writing from a psychoanalytic perspective, are the only authors after Kanner who refer to fetishism and perversion in autism. Meltzer (1975) refers to the autistic child's favorite toy or ritual as a "fetishistic plaything" (p. 28).

Frith and Dawson give clear—if unemotive—descriptions of the lack of symbolization in autism, but it is to the psychoanalytic clinicians one must turn for close observations of the ways in which, and conditions under which, the autistic child may move back and forth from the concrete to a more symbolic mode. Tustin, in hypothesizing about the infancy of such children, described the processes by which a child's sucking of the inside of his cheek may become more and more deviant and perverse. Winnicott is clear that a transitional object may degenerate into something perverse, but Meltzer (1973) seems to suspect that the transitional object is itself fetishistic. Meltzer's preference for making clear distinctions between the paranoid-schizoid position and the depressive position sometimes leads him to an either-or attitude which discounts the possibility of gradualism and transitional developments from one to the other. Yet Meltzer himself elsewhere points out that defense mechanisms may be modulating devices deployed for development (1975).

Meltzer has an additional explanation for the obsessive repetitive behavior in autism. He sees it as resulting from a process of "dismantling the sensory apparatus into its component parts." As a result, the senses attach themselves to the most stimulating object of the moment.

> The essential mode of activity is aimed at rendering an incipient experience meaningless by dismantling it to a state of simplicity below the level of "common sense" so that it cannot function as a "symbolic form" to contain emotional significance, but can only, in its various parts, find articulation of a random and mechanical sort. [Meltzer 1975, p. 217]

Note the activity and intentionality in the notion of dismantling and rendering experience meaningless. I have certainly witnessed such active assaults on meaning by autistic children, but I would not feel this could be offered as the single explanation for their concreteness. It is my impression that their experience is also often "unmantled"; sometimes some of the fragments have simply never been put together.

Meltzer has some interesting things to say about what he calls the "autistic state proper" as opposed to the autistic residues. He describes this as a state of withdrawal which interrupts the transferential object-relations much as static on the radio interrupts—but does not destroy—the flow. Such interruptions, he says, are reversible, and the living relationship can continue as though it had never been interrupted. He describes how, if we cancel out the interruptions, we may see something consecutive is happening, similar to the time-lapse photography of the blossoming of flowers (Meltzer 1975, p. 6). This helps one understand the excessively delayed reactions and touching recognitions of which these children are capable. I still remember my astonishment at Robbie's first comment on his return after the ten-month break: "Where's the ticket?" The purity, however, of these apparent "islets of ability" (Frith) are not, as Frith points out, a sign of special ability. They are a sign of dysfunction in the sense that something *should* have happened to Robbie's memory. Powerful flashbacks apart, the mind has to engage in processes of forgetting in order for new and present experience to make its impact. Memories need to take their proper place on the back bench of the mind. Robbie found it almost impossible to forget, and unfortunately, my early technique of persisting in trying to understand persistent material colluded with his addiction to the past.

The professional mnemonist studied by Luria also eventually ran into the problem of being unable to forget and erase images he no longer needed: great charts of numbers and sums from past performances, from decades before, began to clog his mind. In his concrete way, he tried to imagine himself erasing the blackboard; he also tried writing the sums down and burning the notes. But nothing worked until one day he discovered that a particular chart of numbers was not turning up in his mind because *he didn't want it* to. He said, "Aha! That means if I don't want the chart to show up it won't. And all it took was for me to realize this."

In Bunuel's film "The Exterminating Angel," the desperate starving guests believe themselves to be imprisoned in the house where they have attended a dinner party. Suddenly, after days of horror, they discover that all they have to do if they wish to leave is leave! Similarly, and equally slowly, Robbie and I came to learn that he *could* forget. He could get rid of the apparently compulsive thoughts and sentences that seemed to dominate and fill his mind. He could, that is, when he *wanted* to and when he decided something else was worth putting there.

As he learned that he could exercise agency over his own mind—be a subject rather than the helpless object of his thoughts—and also as he began to achieve some differentiation between one part of his mind and another (he had seemed to have had very little ego) he often *chose* to indulge in his verbal rituals. But this was a very different activity from the past when *they* ruled him. Now he could choose to be sane. We could have whole sessions where he, albeit somewhat slowly, could remain in full contact with me and himself throughout. But by now he had developed some sense of himself as possessing agency, potency, and a will which he could exercise over his own thoughts. In a way, he seemed to experience his mind as possessing some muscularity and power and to be finally his own. It no longer had to be the flaccid, helpless, and titillated medium for whatever thoughts happened to be passing through it at the time.

So far I have been trying to distinguish between motives for the rituals, which involved attempts to manage anxiety or excitement, and motives that were more clearly perverse or morbid. Yet, as in all *real* as opposed to *ideal* and theoretical situations, the motives were often very mixed, and it was sometimes difficult to tell—especially as Robbie's personality became richer and more complex—which was dominant and which was worth most discussion at any moment. For example, he would occasionally arrive in a clearly agitated state and tell me that someone at work had shouted at him. He would repeat this over and over.

We had by now understood together for some years that he was not simply telling an upsetting and frightening story. He also was turned on in a perverse way by the experience and the idea of someone being angry with him. He was both frightened and excited, or, to be precise, he was frightened/excited. Sometimes he even had an erection as he repeated the story over and over. But it was not simply the content of the story or the idea that was disturbing and exciting him. It was also the way in which *he was living out this sadomasochistic phantasy in the telling of it to me.* He would be half glaring, a bit frightened of me, but also frenzied and thrilled by the way his repetitions were so cruelly penetrating into my mind.

It was necessary to show him that although it was true that he was in part trying desperately to communicate his upset, he was not simply desperate, and he was by no means simply engaged in a communication. He was, instead, engaged in a highly perverted form of conversation designed both to excite and enrage the listener so that he could get the irritability to begin all over again in someone else. If I missed the excitement and simply betrayed irritation, a highly sensual grin would show me I'd gone wrong and had played my part in the perverse game.

An object relations perspective on the third symptom—where the observer uses both her feeling-ful perceptions of qualitative features of the ritualistic behavior and also her countertransference feelings and responses to the behavior—means, I believe, that the symptom receives a fuller definition and a fuller description. I suspect that over the years—of variations in the motives for and mood of Robbie's rituals—I have seen examples of everything from Kanner's "anxiously obsessive desire for sameness," to Wing's "repetitive behavior," to Meltzer's more active "dismantling of meaning." At other times, I have seen Tustin's "autistic object used to shut out meaning and life," and Joseph's "addictive and perverted chuntering." We may need not one but several explanations for this symptom, which is so threatening to normal psychological life and development.

Technical Problems in the Treatment of Stereotypy: Robbie in his Thirties

The therapist of an autistic child who has developed rituals seems to be faced with two major technical problems: that of helping the child to give up his rituals and that of helping him to discover that life may be worthwhile without them. Of course, the situation is in fact far more complicated because as the child becomes more alive, the rituals themselves may be used in quite lively ways. So the problem becomes more one of helping him to learn to prefer interaction with a live object rather than with a totally controllable dead autistic one. But this is very different from work with an obsessional neurotic patient who has at least a part of his personality that wishes to be free of his rituals.

Many authors have noted the similarity between autistic repetitive behavior and obsessional behavior in neurotic patients. Freud (1909) referred to the repression and prohibition involved in obsessive-compulsive neurosis. However, as Tustin has pointed out, a major problem with autism is that it is a relatively conflict-free state. Clearly, the obsessive-compulsive neurotic suffers; he complains about his symptoms. The autistic child seems at times to be thoroughly enjoying his symptom and absolutely content, if not ecstatic. Meltzer has described their sensuality and "the joy and triumph of possession" (1975, p. 10). The joy, of course, is by no means always innocent. Sometimes it is sadistic, but in any case it is invariably ego-syntonic. The autistic person may not complain, but his companions do.

Tustin believes that the child has to experience firm restraint on his idiosyncratic activities to bring about the type of conflict and repression which is characteristic of normal healthy growth. She is therefore against abreaction and cathartic measures and warns that much individual psychotherapy with psychotic children has been "too permissive and too passive" (1981, p. 154). Reid (personal communication) takes a similar view. Both Tustin and Reid argue that the restraint has to be carried out with skill and sensitivity. Tustin says that to stop these activities in a clumsy, insensitive way is as harmful as letting them continue, perhaps more so: "The overriding aim should be to help the child feel 'held' in firm and understanding hands so that inner structures can begin to develop" (1981, p. 155).

Barrows goes even further. Influenced by Tustin's work, she believes that the Asperger's children she treats in California do have an organic deficit. There is, she says, a substantial difference between her approach and that of traditional nondirective play therapy:

> Whereas in the latter it is essential that the therapist take her cues from the child, the perseverative and non-relational aspects of the play of an Asperger's child demand that the therapist actively intervene to draw the child out. Often at the risk of what, in traditional therapy, would seem intrusive, I have had to structure my patient's play so as to introduce symbolic or reciprocal content where she would have persisted in ritualistic behavior (Barrows 1988, p. 149).

Since I have been treating Robbie for almost the whole of my working life as a psychotherapist, he has had to experience the whole gamut of my developing ideas. Although his intensive treatment did not start until he was 13, my work with him in the late 1960s and early 1970s was, I think, far too permissive and passive. Tustin's work on the autistic object (1985) had not been published, nor had Joseph's on addictive "chuntering" (1982). Later, the parallels between Tustin's young patients' use of toys and Robbie's use of repetitive stories became obvious. I began to understand the appropriateness of my countertransference feelings of terrible impatience. I think what happened during those early years—when I was not permitting myself to use my countertransference and was repressing or denying my boredom and resentment—was that my feelings sometimes erupted in a clumsy and hurtful way. I would suddenly, to my own surprise as well as Robbie's, raise my voice and tell him to stop talking about that or to stop rushing back and forth and to sit down.

I now think that it is only rarely necessary to actively stop the patient. A vigilant use of the countertransference, as well as of one's perceptions of what is going on in the patient, can usually ensure that the interpretation gets made early enough and firmly enough. Once the excitement has managed to escalate, it is much more difficult to get the patient back into contact.

However, effective vigilance depends on how much work the therapist has done on processing the boredom and the feelings of distaste about the shallow thrills that the patient is indulging in. In the early years, these were very private to Robbie, but as his attachment to me and others grew, we became included in his phantasy life so that he assumed, quite delusionally if fixedly, that I shared in the excitement of talking about what, to me, were the same old subjects but what, to him, were a form of mutual verbal masturbation. I had to learn not to repeat certain phrases of his and to make myself put things in a fresh way. Such work demands constant supervision of one's own autistic laziness of mind. At his most crazy moments, it was sometimes better if I said nothing at all for a few minutes, for he heard my words, no matter how soberly they were spoken, as collusion and permission to go on. Yet sometimes, at those moments, he did seem to hear the silence. I also found that I never got away with the least trace of self-congratulatory eagerness in my voice, when, for example, I thought we were really on the edge of understanding something. That too would send him over the top.

There were other problems to do with language and its usual capacity to carry implication. It was not enough, for example, to say to Robbie in one of his high states, "I think you feel you are in bed with me today," although he clearly did feel just that. Unlike a sane person, he would hear that as a confirmation. So I had to turn the sentence round and say, "It seems difficult for you to realize that I'm actually a few feet away from you over here on my chair simply talking to you and trying to understand you." The temptation—as his licking gaze swept over me and his confidence in his delusions led him into ever more sensuous writhings—was to brush him off psychologically or, to be more honest, to scrape him off myself.[4] I had to do a great deal of work on myself to avoid rejecting him, either openly or subtly, and, instead, to try to get in touch with a part of him capable of a close warm contact that was not so slippery and sensual. I also had to get myself to be capable of inviting such a part when there was often so little evidence of its existence.

With other autistic children of a different type, this evidence is not so hard to find. In Robbie's case, it really seemed as if a mind had to grow and that I had to show him that a nonperverted form of pleasurable interaction with another person was a possibility. I also had to adjust my technique constantly to the level on which he was functioning at any given moment. When he was in a state of real and desperate confusion, and thus muddled about his "I's"

---

4. Robbie rarely actually touched me, but the intrusiveness of his gaze was so sensually unpleasant that he had, on at least two occasions, been attacked in public places by outraged strangers.

and "you's," it seemed better simply to do my best to understand. When he was in a calmer state—able to think yet getting away with the old undifferentiated way of talking—it was important to help him to make differentiations.

If he began the session by talking about something that had happened at "this" house, it was necessary to show him his reluctance to bother to make the distinction between "this" and "that," between his house and mine. This casually neglectful attitude to thought was very different from the real confusions of identity and place that occurred more in the earlier phases of treatment.

All these differentiations on my part helped, I think, to push Robbie back on his own resources and to give him a stronger and more focused sense of his own identity and of the sense of his own "bone" and "muscle" that he had spoken of so many years before when he had begun to discover a new, more vital sense of identity. But this somewhat depriving element in the work had to be balanced with interpretations which were alert to the moments not only when he tried to be sane and to talk sanely with me in order to please me, but also to note the occasional moments when he himself enjoyed talking to me in an ordinary way. And, just as it was important to show him when he had clearly sensed my distaste for the perverted talk and my consequent dislike of him, it was also vital to show him that he felt I liked him much better when he made an effort to speak to me in a straightforward way.[5]

In his late twenties, Robbie began to have moments when, instead of just parroting an old phrase such as "I want to grow and catch up," he showed real sadness and regret for his missed development and spoke of "missing being a man." Naturally, this too got ritualized, but more and more often the mood of regret was genuine. By now he was no longer an amoeboid single-celled psychological being; his mind was differentiated and had some structure. He had a sane self to struggle with the mad self. As his sane self gradually became able to take some pleasure in contact with a live mind, he became able tentatively at first to use his imagination and to be capable of the beginnings of symbolic activity, "the other side of the coin of repetitive activity," that Frith speaks of.

One of the consequences of his problem with symbol formation was that Robbie's grammar was very strange. He always spoke either in the present

---

5. There are some interesting parallels here between work with psychopathic or sexually abused children and children with autism.

tense or the simple past. He had never used what in Latin languages would require the subjunctive mood. That is, he could never manage to describe, or probably even conceive of, hypothetical situations. He had rarely even said "I want to have . . ." and it was years before he could manage the future tense, because time simply was not differentiated out into a past, a present, and a future. At first, there was only a something like a brief dot. Later, there was only the past pushing out the present, the past dragged remorselessly and relentlessly into every conversation. Finally, he became able to narrate a simple event, but I thought he would never manage to say "I wish that I could" or "I hope that I can" or "I would like to. . . ."

One day in October at the age of 29, he suddenly managed something that seemed finally to involve the move from an autistic object to transitional and even symbolic object use. Around this time his mother had told me that he had started calling her by her first name, a sort of playful trying-on of his father's identity and an attempt to see his mother from his father's perspective. This "binocular vision" (Bion 1950, p. 18–19) tends to be impossible for autistic people, and Reid (personal communication) has pointed out the importance of the development of a dual perspective and its implications for symbol development when it finally comes.[6]

One day Robbie began talking without waiting for me to ask him anything—an unusual start. He said, "I'm *looking forward* to seeing Laurel and Hardy on the TV tonight" (my italics). He said he had seen a film about a man who had "jumped in the river and been scared but had gone to the hospital and been bandaged." I said that he himself was a bit like the man because he had "taken the plunge" by starting talking first today. Perhaps he'd been scared to do it, but he felt that he and his words had arrived safely into my mind and he had managed to tell me some things.

At this moment, some footsteps could be heard further up in my house (the consulting room is on the lower ground floor). Robbie went immediately into one of his stereotyped repetitive announcements, which consisted of the apparent confession, "I've been running back and forth at home." It is a complicated matter to explain this. The running back and forth was a very early autistic ritual of his. He would run back and forth shaking his hands, as though to rid himself of something. I had not seen him do this for years and he

---

6. Also see Bruner's work on "two-trackedness" and its link with the capacity to "think in parentheses."

had told me he no longer did it in public places. The problem, however, was that what replaced the running was a newer ritual: the confession itself.

The confession had become a subtle way of achieving several purposes. Sometimes it was designed to annoy the listener, presumably his parents, who knew he had mostly given up the running long ago. However, they would also have been alarmed to hear that it had happened again, since on one occasion he had been arrested for behaving in this "crazy way" in the middle of the street. So, no doubt, he had managed to get a rise out of his parents on a few occasions. Sometimes, it was a way of getting someone to pay attention to him when he actually needed some contact, but neither did he know how to get it in more "normal" ways nor did he even really know that this was what he wanted. I felt, on this occasion, that there was a bit more to it, in that it was probably directly related to the noise of the sound of footsteps upstairs. So I said that I thought he was trying to annoy me with this statement but that actually *he* had been annoyed that someone upstairs was walking back and forth.

Here, then, is an example of a "stereotypy"—an apparently meaningless opposite of an object-related contact—being used in, what I would maintain, was an object-related way. First, it was, I think, responsive—however instantaneously and invisibly—to something other people were doing within his range of hearing; and second, it was being used to produce some sort of effect on me and in me, that is, for purposes of projection and avoidance of anxiety. In fact, I think it was nothing like so perverted a use of the ritualistic confessions as it had been in the past.

Robbie seemed to attend quietly to what I said, and the confession didn't get repeated nor did it escalate into one of his more excited outpourings. I asked what he was thinking and he said, "I'm thinking of the stars in the evening." I hadn't heard about this for years, not since the days of his telling about a terrible hallucination/nightmare of falling off a cliff "into the evening." He went on: "The sky . . . is dark, . . . and the moon is lovely. I want to be up there . . . I want to be up here." I suddenly realized how rare it was for him to say that he wanted to *be* somewhere else. There were no "somewhere elses" when he was in his ecstatic states; he didn't have to want to be there, because he usually felt he already *was* there. But on this occasion, in spite of the confusional use of the word "here," there was also a concept of a place where he wanted to be and where he felt he was not. Then he went on: "I want to live . . . here." I said that I thought he wanted to live here with me and be able to go upstairs like a member of my family. He replied, happily but not excitedly, "I want to live on the moon. It's bright there." I said he seemed to be enjoying being able to talk about these feelings and ideas.

I was struck by the way in which he seemed like a very young child enjoying experimenting with phantasy and enjoying the experience of sharing the phantasies with someone. I tried to show him that in a way he had got up on the moon just now because he'd felt so free to use his imagination and was enjoying sharing it with me (a transitional, not autistic moment). At this point, he did not become more excited. He agreed with me, sounding alert and interested, and then came the use of the conditional. He said, "I'd like to fly up there in a plane—in a spaceship—I'd like to fly to Spain and France." (Probably this was a rare moment of real symbolic functioning).

At that point, I made another transference interpretation, somehow feeling I should not, but not quite understanding why at that point. What I said was something about his wish to be with me on the weekend. He started to rise into a very high state, and I realized that there were two problems: first, he had heard this not as a description of a wish but as a sort of collusive confirmation and gratification of a wish, sending him back to symbolic equations and autistic objects. My interpretation should have included the understanding that he was aware that Spain was a place *elsewhere*, or that he knew he could *not* be with me on the weekend. Alternatively, I could have enabled him to go on with the experience of exploring the places he would like to go in his imagination called "Spain and France."

Winnicott's stress on the importance of respecting the transitional space is relevant here, as are Tustin's warnings on the dangers of the possibly intrusive effect of transference interpretations on the confusional autistic patient (Tustin 1981). As Robbie's mood began to rise into a highly sensual and perverse state, I said quickly and soberly that he knew by now that he did not spend his weekends with me but that what he had just been doing here at this moment was enjoying talking with me and using his imagination. He calmed down, but without deflating into despair as he might have years before, and said, playfully but not crazily, "The policeman would arrest me! I'd like it if they would fly after me!" I said he felt I'd had to police him just then, but I was also very struck by his use of the conditional and the sense of his being able to play with ideas and to inhabit a hypothetical world.

In a session later that year, a very old theme of falling emerged again in a different way. In the earlier version, he had fallen down forever into a very deep pit; but this later version was far less desperate. He had started the session in a very mad state—repeating one of the old refrains—but I had managed, with his help, to get him out of it. He then told me he'd seen a film about a man who had fallen down a pit. "The man was not dead. He climbed back up on the rope." He said this with unusual strength and determination in his voice, and I pointed out that perhaps he felt he was rather like the man because in fact he had started the session down in the pit of mindlessness but had managed to climb back up out of the madness and make contact with me, and perhaps he was proud of himself. It had been unusual to hear strength in his voice, which even when sane usually had a light, thin, uncertain quality to it. He always seemed to be feeling his way. No single word sounded rooted, partly, I suppose, because he was never sure where his thoughts were coming from or where they were going. But this was different. He agreed with me, and he remained sane and talkative for the rest of the session.

Two years later, when Robbie was 31, the image of falling into perversion appeared again, although by now in a far more animated and feeling way, and it seemed he had not so far to fall. He had come late but had managed by himself, without any pressure from me, not to go into a mad, agitated state about his lateness. Later, he announced proudly, "I kept my mind clean, I told the dirty thoughts to get lost!" At the end of the session he exhaled and mused, "There, I didn't slip over . . . into the gutter . . . into the *slippery gutter!*" He said this with real contempt and revulsion in his voice, and added "I stayed alive!" It was interesting that he no longer seemed to have quite so far to fall; the problem was no longer despair and a headlong fall out of control, but a slip. I was struck even more by the animation in his voice and the fact that instead of having to parrot or even to use respectfully but emptily one of my metaphors, he was able to use his own.

What these last two sessions demonstrate, I think, is that there are signs of the establishment of some ego, some capacity to think for himself and even to think feelingly about the value of sanity. It would be difficult to claim that there was much evidence of that in Robbie's sessions in previous years. In those days, it seemed that it was up to me to carry the ego functions of judgment and discrimination and also to do the necessary "policing." But now Robbie seemed to have internalized some of this—originally in a rather pious way but by that last session, he really gave the impression of speaking with his own voice on behalf of something that could finally be called his *self*.

A few months later, he surprised himself, I think, and astonished me by discovering that he could criticize me for endangering his still fragile mental balance. The session had started sane, but about halfway through I had interpreted some eagerness of his and had done so in what I suspected was a somewhat too eager tone: My voice had lifted a bit. He immediately started his unpleasant grinning and licking of his lips. Sometimes asking him what he is thinking helps to evoke a more reflecting part of him, but at other times it only exacerbates the situation. I decided to ask what was happening, and he replied, "Oh, forget it! . . . It's none of your business!" This is a phrase which he had used previously, not exactly in an echolalic manner but in a parroty way and for self-scolding, when he felt some inner figure was objecting to his intrusiveness. He had also sometimes used it in a very stereotyped and perverse manner. But it came out of his mouth with some feeling and a note of impatience. He stopped short, seeming to have surprised himself, as if considering the astonishing fact that he'd said it to me, not to himself. Then he seemed to register that it was actually appropriate to direct the phrase in my direction.

He had been turning around on the couch and looking at me a great deal in this session in a clear and direct manner. He looked again, as though checking that the phrase fit, and then repeated it, his voice gathering force, "It's none of your business . . . it's . . . private!" Then he added persuasively, but kindly, "*You* don't want to know." Amazed by such a direct communication and feeling that I had nearly weakened his resolve with my question, I agreed that he was right. Agreement over the simplest of things has often carried the risk of overexciting him, and he started to giggle but calmed down, and began: "When I was a little boy, Mrs. James (a teacher he loved, now dead), and Mrs. C. (the speech therapist). . . ." Here my heart sank because these figures play a major part in his ritualistic talk and when they do, his voice usually takes on the singsong perverse quality. But I realized his tone was, indeed, rather moved and quiet. He finished. "They helped me . . . they asked me questions. They helped me find out . . . things."

What is interesting is not only that Robbie was relating to me as a real person in the session but he seemed now to have achieved some degree of identification with a sane discriminating figure who has feelings about what is worth knowing and what is not. He discovered that he could have the power to tell *me* what I should and shouldn't want to know.

The next day, I wanted to give him the dates of my Christmas holidays. I suspected that he was perhaps not concentrating fully nor was he off on one of his highs, so I decided to try. In the distant past, of course, he could take in nothing like that, but in the middle years of his treatment, if he had failed to take something in, he would try to force me to give it to him again. He would make wild guesses which often forced people to correct him and thus repeat themselves. In other words, he made manipulative use of his mindlessness and passivity, and I had to watch this carefully. He would try to read the expression in my eyes to see if he had guessed right or wrong, and he was good at this.

But this was dramatically different. He did repeat the dates correctly, but in an absentminded automatic way, and then he must have suddenly realized they had not gone in, because he shouted in panic, "Help! I've dropped them! I'm falling off the cliff! I need help! I've let go of the rock! I'm falling onto the railway tracks! I've lost the dates. I'm . . . it's . . . I'm . . . dangerous."

Robbie had lately started referring to danger but he was muddled about how to distinguish between the object or situation which was dangerous and the person who was in danger. But this was unimportant compared to the fact that, I think for the first time ever, he had really cried for help and really understood something about the tragedy of his mindlessness and of the great chasms and canyons in which his thoughts could get irretrievably lost. I said that he did feel in great danger when he didn't hang on to his sanity and memory and his contact with live people, and that he knew it was dangerous when he let this happen. I repeated the dates, and he, with his mind apparently back in place, worked out immediately how many sessions he would miss.

Robbie is now in his thirties, so this account of his shockingly long treatment and the beginning of the growth of a mind is not a success story. Clinicians nowadays prefer to begin the treatment of autistic children in the preschool years where possible, whereas Robbie's intensive treatment did not begin until he was 13. Although the diagnosis of his autism has been confirmed on many occasions, he started with much less mental equipment than the shell-type autistic children described by Tustin (1972). His passivity and amoeboid floppiness were so extreme that in a way I seemed to be starting from scratch in the attempt to help him become a person. Robbie taught me that I had much to learn about deficit.

Robbie's parents, however, report that he is more alert and interested these days and positively pleasant to be with. He has stopped his insistent repetitive talk, and he has even shown some interest in his parents as people. He has joined a drama group, which is good for his newfound—but still very childish—ability to play with ideas. He has apparently played his parts with gusto and has even contributed an occasional witty improvisation. He has shown, particularly in recent years, some development of real initiative. He can now look after the family house on his own for the occasional weekend. Recently he was robbed on the street, and instead of panicking helplessly, he went straight to the police and then dealt resourcefully with the consequent delays in an already complicated set of arrangements for that particular day. He came to his session explaining perfectly coherently why he was late and also why he had to leave early to go to a football match. When he left, he reminded me, politely but firmly, not to forget to ring his mother and explain why he might be a little late.

As for me, I have learned a lot by working with him, and I think that some of what I have learned has helped him, however belatedly, to begin to use his mind. It is a source of great sadness to me that I did not know at the beginning of Robbie's treatment what I came to understand later. Certainly, the lessons I have learned with him—and from the more modern developments in psychoanalytic thinking about autism and perversion provided by authors such as Tustin and Joseph—have helped other younger autistic and border-line patients—my own and the patients of therapists whose work I have been privileged to supervise—to improve much more quickly. We all owe a great debt to the patients and their families who permit us to learn with them—and on them—as much as we can about this mysterious and devastatingly debili-tating condition.

It perhaps needs to be said that this chapter describes only a very limited aspect of the psychotherapy of patients with complex communication disor-ders. Techniques with other aspects of their tragic symptomatology has gone unmentioned in this paper[7] as well as the very necessary work with the families of these patients.[8]

References

Alvarez, A. A. (1992). *Live Company: Psychoanalytic Psychotherapy with Autis-tic, Borderline, Deprived and Abused Children.* London: Routledge and Kegan Paul.

———— (1996). Addressing the element of deficit in autism: psychotherapy which is both psychoanalytically and developmentally informed. *Clinical Child Psychology and Psychiatry* 1(3). In press.

Barrows, A. (1988). *Asperger's Syndrome: a Theoretical and Clinical Account.* Unpublished doctoral dissertation, Wright Institute Graduate School of Psychology.

---

7. See Alvarez 1996, in press.

8. See Reid, S. and Alvarez, A. *The Autistic Child as a Person* (in process). I would just mention here that Robbie's family worked to great effort to discourage his attempts to involve them in repetitive conversations and to provide more interesting dialogues and activities for him.

Bion, W. R. (1950). The imaginary twin. In *Second Thoughts*. London: Heinemann, 1967.

Bruner, J. S. (1968). *Processes of Cognitive Growth: Infancy*. New York: Clark ←— University Press.

Curcio, F. (1978). Sensorimotor functioning and communication in mute autistic children. *Journal of Autism and Childhood Schizophrenia*, 8:202–215.

Dawson, G. and Lewy, A. (1989). Arousal, attention, and the socioemotional impairments of individuals with autism. In *Autism. Nature, Diagnosis, and Treatment*, ed. G. Dawson. New York: Guilford.

Freud, S. (1909). Notes upon a case of obsessional neurosis. *Standard Edition* 10.

Frith, U. (1989). *Autism: Explaining the Enigma*. Oxford: Blackwell.

Hobson, P. (1993). *Autism and the Development of Mind*. Hove. Sussex: Lawrence Erlbaum.

Howlin, P., and Rutter, M. (1987). *Treatment of Autistic Children*. Chichester: John Wiley and Sons.

Joseph, B. (1982). Addiction to near death. In *Psychic Equilibrium and Psychic Change*, ed., M. Feldman and E. Spillius, London: Routledge and Kegan Paul, 1989.

Kanner, L. (1944). Early infantile autism. *Journal of Paediatrics* 25, (3):122–138.

Klaus, M. H., and Kennell, J. H. (1982). *Parent-Infant Bonding*. London: C. H. Mosby.

Luria, A. R. (1968). *The Mind of a Mnemonist*. New York: Basic Books.

Meltzer, D. (1973). The origins of the fetishistic plaything of sexual perversions. In *Sexual States of Mind*. Perthshire, Scotland: Clunie Press.

Meltzer, D., et al. (1975). *Explorations in Autism: a Psycho-Analytical Study*. Perthshire, Scotland: Clunie Press.

Miller, L. (1995). Personal communication.

Reid, S. Personal communication.

Sacks, O. (1985). *The Man Who Mistook his Wife for a Hat*. London: Picador.

Segal, H. (1957). Notes on Symbol Formation. *International Journal of Psycho-Analysis*, 38:391–397.

Stern, D. (1985). The *Interpersonal World of the Infant*. NY: Basic.

Stolorow, R. D., Brandschaft, B., and Atwood, G. E. (1987). *Psychoanalytic Treatment: An Intersubjective Approach*. New Jersey: Analytic Press.

Tustin, F. (1972). *Autism and Childhood Psychosis*. London: Hogarth.

———— (1981). *Autistic States in Children*. London: Routledge and Kegan Paul.

———— (1985). Autistic shapes and adult pathology. *Topique*. 14:9–23.

Wing, L. (1981). Language, soul and cognitive impairments in autism and severe mental retardation. *Journal of Autism and Development Disorders*, 11(1):31–44.

Wing, L. and Gould, J. (1979). Severe impairments of social interaction and associated abnormalities in children: epidemiology and classification. *Journal of Autism and Developmental Disorders* 9:11–29.

Winnicott, D. (1958). Transitional objects and transitional phenomena. In *Collected Papers*. London: Tavistock.

Wollheim, R. (1984). *The Thread of Life*. Cambridge: Cambridge University Press.

15

One Pilgrim's Progress: Notes on Frances Tustin's Contributions to the Psychoanalytic Conception of Autism

James S. Grotstein

For the modern pilgrim, the final goal is not the Heaven which Bunyan envisaged, but a step into the unknown which Bion so eloquently and disturbingly placed before us.

Frances Tustin, "A Modern Pilgrim's Progress"

Frances Daisy Vickers was born in the North of England on October 15, 1913, the only child of deeply religious parents. Her mother was a deaconess and her father a lay reader in the Church of England. Her father lost his faith, however, because of experiences in World War I. It might be hypothesized that Frances took his apostasy as a model for her own courage, demonstrating her extraordinary clinical talent and her challenge to both the analytic and the psychiatric establishment of the time. When Frances was 13, her mother abruptly left her father, and, according to Spensley (1995), Frances never really recovered from this sudden shock. After a brief marriage that ended in divorce in 1946, she met Arnold Tustin, an academic engineer who, during World War II, had participated in the Manhattan Project.

Tustin trained as a child psychotherapist at the Tavistock Clinic under the tutelage of Esther Bick, the founder of Kleinian infant observation, and John

Bowlby, who originated the concepts of attachment and bonding. At this time, there was a deep rift in the British psychoanalytic establishment between the orthodox/classical Freudians—who swore allegiance to Anna Freud—and the Kleinians. This polarization could not have been better exemplified than in the views of Esther Bick, who speculated about the inner world of internalized phantasmal objects, and John Bowlby, the psychoanalyst/ethologist who valorized the importance of the external object. From our many private conversations, I believe I could infer that Tustin's own thinking came down on the side of what she believed were the more "infant-accepting" ideas of the Independent School, particularly Bowlby and Winnicott in the main, as contrasted to the Kleinian view. I believe that her inclination toward the ideas of the Independents became central to her theoretical stance in conceptualizing her autistic patients' illness.

A graceful woman without rancor or tendentiousness, Tustin frequently expressed her appreciation of Klein's contributions, but I always felt that she believed she was dealing with patients who were significantly different from those with whom Klein was dealing. It was my impression that she believed that her patients' early primal depression had thrust them into a virtually objectless state characterized by a primary deficit, from the object relations (Independent School) point of view. If so, concepts such as "unconscious phantasy," "persecutory anxiety," "paranoid-schizoid position," "projective identification," and so forth would not be apposite to these patients.

As is the policy with candidates at Tavistock, Esther Bick assigned Tustin to an analyst: Wilfred Bion. Frances did not like Bion at first, finding him distant, cool, and forbidding. Later, however, she came to appreciate him and to respect his kindness and regard for truth. With some interruptions, she remained in analysis with Bion for over fourteen years, and always at an unusually low fee because of her restricted income and his generosity. She was grateful to him for his patience, kindness, and understanding, and she used concepts of his that she felt applied to her patients, especially that of "infantile catastrophe." She later came under the influence of Donald Meltzer and participated in the seminars and research studies that Meltzer and his group (including Hoxter, Bremner, Weddell, and Wittenberg) conducted (Meltzer et al., 1975).

During those projects, she met Marianne Putnam, who first fired Frances' interest in autism. This was nine years after Kanner's (1943) first contribution on autism, which brought it to the attention of the mental health public. This phase of Tustin's development was interrupted by an opportunity to travel on a sabbatical with her husband to Boston, and she studied at the James Jackson

Putnam Treatment Center between 1954 and 1955. There she met Margaret Mahler, Selma Fraiberg, and others and became immersed in the New American school of developmental psychoanalysis, an offshoot of ego psychology.

While at the Putnam Center, she spent time in the homes of autistic children, giving their parents a respite. She gained much clinical experience about the home life of autistics and their families, and she developed a deep respect towards parents who have autistic children. Tustin respected Bruno Bettelheim and his work at the Orthogenic School in Chicago. In *The Empty Fortress* (1967) Bettelheim had expressed a belief that the autistic child withdrew from life at a critical point before the child had discovered his essential humanity. Tustin disagreed with Kanner's (1943) concept of the "refrigerator mother" and placed a great deal of emphasis on the infant's fear of separation instead. She did modify this view in her later work in favor of the *folie a deux* of a pathogenic mother and a pathogenic infant.

After two miscarriages, Tustin realized that she would be childless, and she sublimated her disappointment by throwing herself into her psychotherapeutic work. Her first book, *Autism and Childhood Psychosis*, came out in 1972. This work reveals the beginnings of observations on the phenomenology of the autistic child. Tustin believed that the autistic child inhabits a godless world in which the autistic shell is the last refuge. She saw early infantile autism as a pathological barrier created by fixation at a sensation-dominated, prethinking stage of infantile psychological development. She saw this as an arrest rather than a regression. She believed that the block to and deviation from ongoing psychological development arose as a result of the shock of the *traumatic awareness in infancy of bodily separateness from the mothering person*. By this she means that the experience of separations was *premature and traumatic*, and the autistic withdrawal is the ultimate defense against psychotic depression. She invoked the concept of the "black hole" and associated it with Winnicott's (1958) notion of "falling forever."

At first, Tustin used the term "autism" as a normal stage of development in deference to Margaret Mahler. Like Mahler, she later abrogated that notion as emerging research in infant development dispelled Freud's (1914) theories of normal primary narcissism and his (1920) concept of the stimulus barrier. Some examples of her thinking in 1972 include:

It is important to make the point that the normal healthy infant who starts life by being out of touch with reality is not psychotic. But he *is* autistic. [1972, p. 10]

Later, on the same page, she states:

As the thesis of the book develops, it will be suggested that these normal primary autistic processes are in the nature of sensations arising from inbuilt dispositions which as yet do not constitute apprehension but which, given facilitating conditions, will lead on to this. . . . Without, or unable to make sufficient use of nurture, the child remains in or regresses to a sensation-dominated state. Thus, emotional and cognitive developments are either halted or deteriorate. It will be suggested that in this state of inanition, primary autistic processes perseverate or are reinstated. These become over-developed and rigidly maintained. The term *pathological autism* will be used to describe this state. . . . It might be said that normal autism is a state of *pre*-thinking, whereas pathological autism is a state of *anti*-thinking. [1972, p. 10]

On the next page, she states:

Pathological autism develops to deal with . . . depression. Winnicott's term *psychotic depression* will be used to refer to it. [1972, p. 11]

Tustin later changes her mind about the terms she is using, but her acumen in clinical detailing is—and remained—astute. She seems here to be trying to establish a new *sensation-dominated psychology*, which she will later call *autosensuality*. Following Mahler and other classical analytic infant investigators, she considers "autism" as a normal stage of development that can be regressively reinstalled pathologically and that will be manifested by the use of "autistic defenses." Her ideas here seem to reflect the ideas of Bowlby and Winnicott in terms of bonding, attachment, and the holding environment and of Mahler in terms of the protocol of infant development. She establishes the state of a skin-sensation psychology as occurring earlier than Klein's paranoid-schizoid position. However, when she says that normal autism is a state of *pre-thinking*, whereas pathological autism is a state of *anti*-thinking, her concept of "anti-thinking" does not include Bion's ideas of attacks against links, reversal of alpha function, and other psychotic anti-thought processes (Bion 1957, 1959, 1962). Tustin did not employ these concepts, I believe, because she conceived of pathological autism as an *ego-defect*, not a *conflict* illness.

Tustin demonstrated her technique in her first book, describing John, who was 3-and-one-half years old when he began treatment. She writes about her attempt to overcome his dismissal of her:

> He went passed me as if I did not exist. The moment when this was not so occurred in the consulting room when he pulled my hands toward the top which I spun for him. At this, he became very flushed and leaned forward to watch it spin. As he did so, he rotated his penis through his trousers while his other hand played around his mouth in circular spinning movements. This suggested to me that he made little differentiation between the movements of the top and those of his own body. It convinced me of the importance of maintaining the analytic setting and interpretative procedure if I were to be gradually distinguished from his primitive illusions, and do my work as a therapist who helped him to come to terms with the feelings aroused by disillusionment. From now on, I kept to a bare minimum my compliance with the actions he pressed me to do. I made simple interpretations, interspersing them with the few words the parents had told me he might understand. . . . I was then able to interpret to him his disillusionment arising from the fact that I could be "gone," both in the sense of not attending to him and in the actual bodily sense of being separated from him. [1972, p. 18]

She helped him distinguish between animate and inanimate objects, that is, between toys and people. She facilitated the development of an infantile transference where the anxieties were contained. She spoke of John's catastrophic anxiety:

> The crux of the grief-provoking situation was starkly expressed in his first words of "gone!", "broken!", and "oh dear!" These ejaculations seem to express evocations from his infancy when the loss and destruction of the "button" left a "black hole with a nasty prick." This was John's own formulation for the previously unformulated, intolerable experience from which his autistic withdrawal had served as a protection . . . Being pre-verbal, it is difficult to discuss in words; evocative rather than theoretic language seems most appropriate. [1972, p. 26–27]

She then states,

> It seems feasible that John's illusion of the "button," arising in the state when bodily parts were scarcely differentiated, would be formed and

maintained by sensations from nipple-like objects of the mouth and other bodily "holes". . . . In my experience an important source of the "button" illusion seems to be the teat-tongue combination. . . . The "button" also seems to arise from an inbuilt nipple-seeking pattern which took shape again during treatment. [1972, p. 28–29]

In this touching clinical commentary, we see Tustin the theorist blended seamlessly with Tustin the empathic yet unflappably rigorous analytic clinician, a trend which remained her hallmark. When she says, "He passed me as if I did not exist," one thinks of negative hallucination and derealization of the object, common phantasies in primitive mental disorders. When she refers to her patient's "illusions," she not only invokes Winnicott's (1971) work in that area, she also enfranchises Klein's concept of phantasies, from which she seemed to shy away conceptually when considering the autistic mind. On the same page, in another example of her clinical genius, she says:

> Years of intensive work with autistic children has led me to think that such inbuilt instinctual responses are experienced by the child as extrusions of body stuff, as a kind of pseudopodia[1] which reach out into the outside world and mould and are moulded by it. The term "innate forms" is suggested to describe them. These innate forms would seem to be the bodily fore-runners of later thoughts and phantasies. . . . When an innate form seems to coincide with a correspondence in the outside world, the child has the illusion that everything is synonymous and continuous with his own body stuff. [1972, p. 29]

This passage provides a beautiful description of archaic projective identification, where a correspondence (confusion) develops between an object in the outside world and its innate form. Tustin continues:

> In these early days, when the fact of his separateness from me was forced upon him, words seemed to be experienced by him as solid objects. . . . These separations seem to be experienced quite concretely as broken things put into his body. . . . He did not "think" about these things; he felt he

---

1. "Pseudopodia" reminds one of the Imre Hermann's (1936) concept of the "flowing-over" experience in the infant and how it presages what is later to be called projective identification.

took them into his body. When the "button" was gone, anxieties rushed in as uncontrolled physical things. The pain of loss seemed to be experienced as bodily rather than mental pain. [1972, p. 30]

She cited Rank and McNaughton's (1950) report on an "atypical" child who, lying in her therapist's arms after a tantrum-like explosion of panic and rage, sobbed, "A piece fell out! A piece fell out!" (1972, p. 31). She suggests:

John's material suggests that panic and rage, expressed in bodily explosions were responsible for the hole being a "black hole." It also seems to suggest that, because subject and object were scarcely differentiated from each other, as he "annihilated" the "naughty" object he felt threatened with "annihilation" himself. . . . [1972, p. 31–32]

This passage suggests a new way of understanding Klein's concept of projective identification. Klein seems to presuppose that a differentiation between the infant and its part-object mother exists from the very beginning, but Tustin seems to lean on Winnicott's concept of an initial nondifferentiation followed by partial differentiation. From this perspective, the infant's projective identifications would be translocated into an aspect of itself that is still *felt to be* primally fused with its object (in unconscious phantasy) whereas another aspect is felt paradoxically to be separate. When John (the patient) refers to "black holes," he seems to be talking about a phantasy in vivid sensory language. His "annihilation of the 'naughty' object" with resultant fear of his own annihilation certainly recalls Klein's concept of persecutory anxiety and attendant unconscious phantasies of projective retaliation.

In the "controversial discussions" (King & Steiner 1992) between Melanie Klein, Anna Freud, and their followers, one of the key points of dissension concerned the validity of the concept of *primary narcissism*. Klein disavowed this concept because she believed that the infant was capable of relating to the object from the very beginning. The conflict centering around *primary narcissism* versus *primary object choice* dominated psychoanalytic thinking until recently, when findings from infant development research confirmed Klein. On the other hand, two of Klein's followers—Esther Bick and Donald Meltzer—concluded in their studies of autistic children that these patients suffered from a defect in their primary narcissism, thus their propensity toward *adhesive identification* allegedly resulted from the incompleteness of their individuation and their seeming obliviousness to the object except for leaning up against it. Meltzer and colleagues (1975) went so far as to state that autistic patients could not use projective identification because they were stuck in the second dimension of flatness, as were their objects, so that they could not conceive that the object could contain their projections.

In my opinion, these patients *do* avail themselves of projective identification. For instance, how does an autistic know that the object is flat if not through projective identification of the patient's own flatness into the image of it? What appears to be primary narcissism in these cases results from the autistic's inability to *demonstrate* the inchoate object-relatedness. I reject Bick's and Meltzer's fundamental premise when they suggest anything that would differ from the primacy of the paranoid-schizoid position. Similarly Ogden's concept of the autistic-contiguous position is admirable, but I believe that he has only articulated a more inchoate horizon of the paranoid-schizoid landscape.

Tustin did not appear (at least to me) to be sanguine about applying Kleinian formulations to her theoretical constructions of autistic psychopathology. She seemed to feel that thinking about autism in terms of a defect precluded a conflict-based formulation. She seemed to believe that the etiology of clinical autism was different from and occurred earlier than other conditions. She seemed to have disallowed the idea of unconscious phantasies, projective identification, splitting, attacks against objects and links, persecutory anxiety, manic defenses, and so forth. Nevertheless, careful reading of her clinical work reveals that the results of her work substantiate Kleinian thinking.

It seems to me that another reason for this discrepancy may involve the question of whether autism has a biological basis. When Bick and Meltzer began working with autistic children, they did not seem to consider that their autistic patients might be victims of a constitutional pervasive abnormal developmental agenda. Thus, when they discussed their concepts of *adhesive identification* (later "adhesive identity"), they thought of it as an aberrance of *psychological* development on a spectrum of normalcy. They believed that their cases represented exceptions that revealed a new rule highlighting a stage or position occurring earlier and/or deeper than the paranoid-schizoid position, thus they were launching a new psychology around this inchoate stage of development.

It is my belief that this premise represents a fundamental misunderstanding or misconception. The patients that Bick, Meltzer, and Tustin treated probably suffered from a *primary* abnormality of development that may *seem* to have momentarily eclipsed or forestalled the clinical appearance of more familiar patterns of persecutory anxiety. For instance, when Bick (1968) correlated the motor activities of her autistic patients with the sense of their acquisition of a "second skin," I believe she was, in effect, designating a phantasy. It is my impression that Tustin's clinical material clearly reveals the persecutory anxieties and schizoid mechanisms that Klein assigned to the paranoid-schizoid position. It may be difficult to recognize these mechanisms if one does not understand that sensory phenomena, including normal and pathological auto-sensuality, are both represented as phantasy and constitute the anlage of perception (Isaacs 1952). Put another way, the paranoid-schizoid position is activated as soon as the infant is aware of the object, from the very beginning—if not *before* the beginning—of life. This process occurs, to the best of my knowledge, in all infantile disorders, even mental retardation.

An environmental orientation runs through all of Tustin's works. While she is sympathetic toward mothers of autistic children, she—along with Meltzer and his group—implicates them in the genesis of autism. She states:

Tischler read her moving paper at the Sixth International Congress of Psycho-Therapy concerning some of these mothers' heart-broken attempts to get in touch with their inaccessible children. Meltzer (1963) writes that these children are usually born "in a period of parental separation and turmoil particularly characterized by depression in the mother." My experience confirms this. [1972, p. 32–33]

Later she states,

In regard to John's mother . . . she may have had the post-partum depression, the feeling that in giving birth to her infant she had lost a part of her body. . . . A breakdown in the holding situation means that the naive infant is left to bear intolerable anxieties alone. Continuing to use his own body as if it were the mother's, and the mother's body as if it were his own, gives him the protection of the illusion of continuity, but he remains undifferentiated from her or confused with her. [1972, p. 35]

In 1972, Tustin formulated secondary autism as a defense against psychotic depression. She used the term "black hole" frequently in discussing autistic patients as well as Bion's concept of "nameless dread" and Winnicott's "psychotic depression." I have posited that the "black hole" is a term given to the representation of an unconscious phantasy that was described by Freud (1917) and Klein (1940) as melancholia (Grotstein 1990a, 1990b, 1990c, 1991). The infant suffers a concrete sense of loss of its ego when it is forced to experience the loss of an object from which it feels incompletely separated. When this happens, the infant reverts regressively to narcissism to avoid the recognition of the loss ("black hole").

In her second major work, *Autistic States in Children* (1981), Tustin continued to contrast the concept of normal autism with the autism of childhood psychosis. She hinted for the first time at the presence of pathological autistic elements in neurotic disorders. She also developed the concept of autistic states of encapsulation versus confusional psychotic states and dealt with autistic objects and confusional objects and the asymbolic nature of autistic states. Encountering an encapsulation in the autistic children, Tustin immediately correlated it with Esther Bick's concept of "second skin" as well as Winnicott's concept of the "false self" and Helena Deutsch's (1942/1934) concept of the "as if personality," all of which are examples of phantasies made possible by the use of dissociative splitting.

The clinical phenomenon of encapsulation is one of Tustin's brilliant clinical discoveries. However, for the autistic child or adult to feel encapsulated, an unconscious defensive phantasy has to be in place to counteract the return of projected identifications that had earlier been translocated into the object on the other side of the encapsulation. Furthermore, the experience of encapsulation constitutes yet another unconscious phantasy: that the encapsulation is an omnipotently protective object.

Autistic children seem to protect themselves from the predatory "not-me" world by encapsulation or "shell formation," whereas psychotic children seem to employ confusional or entanglement techniques in relating to their objects. Another differentiation is in their respective uses of nonhuman objects. The autistic child uses hard objects (keys, sticks, etc.) in order metaphorically (i.e., in phantasy) to "plug their holes." Confusional children, on the contrary, prefer soft objects in order to "mop up their wounds," according to Tustin.

In her 1981 work she also talks about the absence of primal bonding:

Thus they have never developed the sense of having a working simulation experienced as "something integrating inside." The encapsulated child has experienced bodily separateness from the mother precociously. . . . A traumatic experience of bodily separateness has caused him to recoil from this awareness and has produced massive inhibition in all spheres of development. . . . Thus therapy with encapsulated autistic states is different from the psychoanalytic treatment of neurotic states and confusional ones, because the child has to be given "bonding" experiences which will form the basis for relationships with people. . . . The encapsulated psychotic child repeats with the therapist pre-verbal elemental early situations which are normally left unconscious and are not "recollected." Such a child has to "recollect" that which is not a part of normal recollection. In addition, first of all, he has to develop the capacity for recollection. [1981, p. 164–165]

A vignette shows how Tustin dealt therapeutically with these patients:

In psychotherapy, activities arise which can be equivalent to "bonding" experiences. For example, the container for the child's toys often becomes the fount from which good things come. In these activities, the child is firmly helped to co-operate with another human being who has an orderly, yet flexible mind, and who demonstrates effortful behavior towards him and insists on the need for effort on his part. His evasive tricks and time-wasting activities are discouraged. At the same time, insights are given about how his growing up is impeded by them. It is a relief to find that, even in these very withdrawn children, there is a part of them that is waiting to be helped "to grow up properly" and to commit themselves to an attachment to a parent figure. [1981, p. 165–166]

Later, in discussing the infantile transferences, Tustin states,

The conclusion I have reached after thirty years of working with such children is that the transference situation cannot be established by the use of interpretation alone. Other, more active measures need to be employed but, in doing this, we need to be aware of allowing these active measures to take the place of interpretative therapy. The need to be constantly developing insights which are transmitted by interpretation must be paramount, and activity on our part needs to be combined with reflective communication to the child about why it is being done. [1981, p. 169]

Still later she concludes, "Thus, when working with patients functioning at these elemental levels, transference and countertransference cannot be clearly delineated" (1981, p. 170).

In these citations, we can see Tustin, the master therapist, at work. It is clear that something extra must be added to the treatment before a working alliance can take place. That extra something seems to be an active form of Winnicott's holding environment plus firm encouragement of the child to play and to cooperate. Therapists who use behavior modification techniques for autistics have claimed great success, and perhaps Tustin, while not using frank behavior modification, did work from a stance that beneficently included some aspects of those techniques but within psychoanalytic psychotherapeutic bounds for child therapy. She is both innovative and careful of boundaries. Her statement that activity "needs to be combined with reflective communication to the child" gets to the heart of the importance of encouraging autistic children (who suffer from a primary lack of self-reflection and reflection about the mindedness of others) to attain the capacity for reflection.

When Tustin states, "transference and countertransference cannot be clearly delineated," she seems to refer to a beneficial rebirthing of the patient in the context of at least a transitory, benign "*folie a deux*" (Mason 1990) that serves as a facilitating scaffolding. Later, in discussing the reversal of pathological autism, she says,

> Over the years I have come to realize that this "fracture-dislocation" has caused in-built neuro-mental structures, which are pre-programmed to emerge in an orderly fashion, to come into operation precociously and out of phase. As the result of the "fracture," they become impacted and compressed together. . . . To orient oneself in this disorder, it is necessary to realize that we need to begin at the beginning and to concentrate on oral elements, and to avoid being side-tracked by anal and phallic elements. Work with psychotic children needs to be particularly orderly or else we become as overwhelmed as was the child by having more to process and organize than is humanly possible. [1981, p. 174]

This stance correlates with Klein's ideas of projective identification and with Bion's elaboration of it in terms of the "container/contained." Tustin's statement that "they become impacted and compressed together" reminds one of Bion's concept of "alpha function in reverse." She continues,

> In all states of childhood psychosis in which psychogenic elements predominate, the patient needs to be helped to sort out compressed, impacted sensuous dispositions. [1981, p. 175]

And later, in discussing the "psychotic child's experience of bodily holes," she states,

> The psychotic child does not pay attention to the things we ask him to attend to but, without seeming to do so, is aware of much of which we are unconscious. [1981, p. 177]

This observation is reminiscent of Bion's concept of reversible perspectives. Still later she states that "It will be seen that in some states it is not that the psychotic child is unresponsive, but that he is over-responsive" (1981, p. 178). This—the concept of hyper-irritability, whether inherent (inherited or congenital) or traumatically acquired—is one of her most profound observations about autistic children and others within the spectrum of "primitive mental disorders." Parallel concepts include Bick's (1968) and Meltzer's (1975) adhesive identification (later "adhesive identity"), Anzieu's (1985, 1990, 1993) concepts of the "skin ego" and the "psychic envelope," Marcelli's (1983) concept of the autistic position, Ogden's (1989) autistic-contiguous position, and Stone's (1988) conception of the organizing role of hyper-irritability in the etiology of borderlines.

In the same section, Tustin develops a new psychoanalytic entity, prey-predator anxiety. She states:

> In addition, atavistic in-built fears of predators become associated with these leakages and the child feels threatened by predatory monsters or wild beasts. These "nameless dreads," as Bion terms them, have not been modified by the civilizing and protective influences of parental nurturing, which in most cases was available. This is the tragedy of the psychotic child and his parents. In most cases it is not that the parents have been neglectful, but that the traumatized child could not allow their nurturing to play upon him. [1981, p. 170]

Tustin's ideas can be compared to Bowlby's (1958, 1960a, 1960b, 1969, 1973, 1980, 1983) conception of inherent prey-predator anxiety and Bion's (1962, 1963, 1965, 1970, 1992) general theory of inherent preconceptions. Meltzer, et al. (1975) anticipated Tustin in this regard in their clinical work with autistic children.

Later on she makes a fascinating existential statement:

> The essential quality of any method used for psychotic children should be to help them towards humanness. For most of the time, they feel that they are God's animals or things. The ordinariness of being a human being is not available to them. [1981, p. 179]

This clinical observation parallels much recent empirical work with autistics around the concept of "mind blindness" or a deficit in the capacity for intersubjectivity or social competence.

In the same book she dealt with the concept of *autistic objects*, hard objects that serve as reassuring "plugs" to the autistic child's black-hole vulnerability. According to Tustin, autistic objects are not associated with any fantasy.[2] Autism is a sensation-dominated state in which sensation-dominated objects correspond. Thus, the patient's use of autistic objects testifies to their *pathological autosensuality*, a significant characteristic of autistic illness. Tustin here formalizes her belief that childhood autism begins with the experience of a cataclysmic depression secondary perhaps to a constitutional hypersensitivity of the inchoate sensory system. As a result, autistic children are caught in a "no man's land" between their inability to tolerate sensuous contact with the object and their paradoxical inability to bear separation from the object since separation is felt as a tearing away of parts of their own bodies, leading to the "black hole" experience of their mouths in particular. In other words, when the breast-mother departs, it is as if she rips apart her infant's mouth and takes it away with her. Why does this happen? Tustin's proposed answer is clear, but she neglects the probability that this somatic belief on the child's part is the result of a concrete unconscious phantasy of delusional connection to mother's body so that, when disabused of that phantasy by reality, the child develops another phantasy, that of the "black hole."

In 1986, Tustin published *Autistic Barriers in Neurotic Patients*, a work that extended her ideas far from their origins in formally diagnosed autistic children to the higher level of relatively well-adjusted individuals. It is with this work that her contributions became known to a wider readership in the mental health field. Following her colleague Sidney Klein (1980), she proposed that "autistic enclaves" occur in neurotics. She also proffered the idea of "a significant element in the development of psychogenic autism." After referring to an elemental depression that heralds autistic illness in children and referring to the works of Rank and Putnam (1953), Bibring (1953), Winnicott (1958), and Mahler (1958), she says,

My own work has confirmed that this elemental depression has been crucial in the massive arrest of emotional and cognitive development which afflicts psychogenic autistic children. [1986, p. 67]

---

2. I have already argued this point. Sensation is one of the most basic aspects of phantasy, according to Isaacs (1954). If the hard object is effective in "plugging up the 'black hole'" (which itself is a phantasy), it constitutes yet another phantasy.

She again emphasized the concept of *autistic objects*, which she defined as parts of the child's own body as well as parts of the outside world experienced by the child as if they were his body. She had already distinguished autistic objects from transitional objects and from the "soft objects." Soft objects, characteristically used by psychotic children as opposed to autistic patients, serve to "mop up their woundedness," according to Tustin. Transitional objects, on the other hand, differ from hard and soft objects as they are used to maintain connections to real objects, whereas the hard and soft objects serve to replace them.

Tustin described how autistic children dismantle[3] the desired aspects of mother's body (e.g., breasts) and imbue their own sensory organs with them via introjective identification in order to be able to deny any need for the object thereafter. Tustin refers to this as the "teat-tongue combination" (1986, pp. 82, 295). Mildred Creak, who referred most of the autistic patients to Tustin, believed that there may be a ". . . 'built-in failure to incorporate a system of response to stimuli.' I think she was closest to the truth" (Tustin 1972, p. 138). This concept would explain some of the perverseness in their ways of relating to objects, including dismantling. Failing to be able to incorporate the *experience* with the object, they may feel obliged to incorporate the object's attributes themselves. Later in that same chapter Tustin states:

This chapter . . . has been an attempt to get in touch with the elemental feelings which have provoked the psychogenic autism. In reality, what happened to the children was in the nature of a sensuous mishap, but in the hypersensitized, illusion-dominated state of early infancy, it had become exaggerated to seem like a catastrophe. But the feelings associated with this illusion had been traumatizing. [1986, pp. 92–93]

Here for the first time she describes the phenomenon of *autistic shapes*,[4] the negative counterparts of autistic objects—the after-impressions on the autistic's autosensory skin surface that seem to give a child a sense of sensory definition and containment—and therefore safety. Unlike the shapes made by normal children, the patterns chosen by autistic children have an idiosyncratic, repetitive, ritualized self-sameness.

---

3. This is yet another example of the activity of an unconscious phantasy that has been detailed by Klein as that of "scooping out the breast" and owning it for oneself, and what Bollas (1987) later termed *extractive identification*.

4. These too are phantasies.

Another contribution in her 1986 work is the concept of *the rhythm of safety*. Rocking movements are soothing to all infants since they convey a predictable rhythm of holding over time. Similarly Bick (1968) suggested the equation between muscular movements and *second skin*. Compulsive rocking, spinning, and other motoric activities seem to be hyper-compensations by autistic children to achieve a sense of an autistic holding environment for themselves. In a 1991 contribution, Tustin revised some of her earlier thinking.

After many years working with a certain type of autistic child, and after attempts to digest this experience by writing books and papers, I have come to the conclusion that I made a mistake in following the general trend of psychoanalytical writers in using the term autism for an early stage of infantile development, as well as for a specific pathology. I now realize that it is more correct . . . if the term *autism* is solely reserved for certain specific pathological conditions in which there is an absence of human relationships and gross impoverishment of mental and emotional life; these impairments being the result of the blocking of awareness by an early aberrant development of autistic procedures. . . . The crux of these revised understandings is that autism is an early developmental deviation in the service of dealing with unmitigated terror. [1991, p. 585]

* * * * *

Since autistic states are not relationship oriented, and since there is little inner life, such states are outside the scope of most psychoanalytic formulations. Autistic states are *psychochemical* in nature mostly with surface manifestations. As is exemplified in the references, both neuropsychiatrists and psychoanalysts have contributed to their descriptions and formulations. [1991, p. 589, italic mine]

The first statement—that "the absence of human relationships . . . being the result of the blocking of awareness by an early aberrant development of autistic procedures"—speaks to the recent research findings in autism and the concept of *mind blindness*. The issue specifically is whether this nonhumanizing trait in autistics is autochthonously (natively) inherent to them as an inborn defect, which the research findings seem to indicate, or is it a regressively elaborated psychological defense against the pain of separateness and of its corollary, relatedness to objects? In other words, is it primary or is it akin to Freud's (1917) concept of the narcissist's melancholic defense against object loss by regressing to secondary narcissism? Tustin seems to imply both but leans toward the latter. Put another way, is autism a tropism directed toward the child's becoming defensively nonhuman (depersonalization) along with an accompanying tropism toward the derealization and dehumanization of experience with objects (as things) or are autistics, from the beginning, victims of what Janet (1893) calls *maladie faiblesse*, a weakness of the brain, an inability to support the demanding tension of socialization and humanness? If they withdraw, do they withdraw to their outer defense perimeter of inwardly experienced tolerability?

Tustin also raises the "psychochemical" issue. This seems to be her first formal acknowledgment of the fundamentally constitutional nature of autism. When she said, ". . . such states are outside the scope of most psychoanalytic formulations . . . ," did she mean even of her own technique? Does she mean, and I hope that she did, *that the psychoanalyst and psychoanalytically informed psychotherapist can only treat the individual who is suffering from autism, not the autism per se, as with schizophrenia* (Grotstein 1995a, 1995b)? Until this time Tustin had alluded to neurobiological factors in autism and had always emphasized her lack of medical training. Most of her early patients had been referred by Dr. Mildred Creak, the director of Great Ormond Street Hospital and a psychiatric expert on autism. Tustin assumed that her own patients were higher-order autistics, ones who had "psychogenic autism." Tustin had already demonstrated her graciousness and flexibility when new evidence would come to the fore, and she was well aware of some of the more organic aspects of autism. She often spoke of their tendency to walk on their toes, to have difficulties with personal pronouns, and to be startle-alert. In that regard, she cited empirical studies, including mention of Asperger's syndrome, the "theory of mind" phenomena by Frith and colleagues (1985). Hobson's (1986) notion that autistics do not properly appraise emotions in others, Trevarthen's (1979a) studies on the origins of intersubjectivity and cultural cooperation, and the concept of Wolff and colleagues (1979, 1980, 1986) of the schizoid personality in childhood. Nevertheless, she returned to her theory of "psychogenic autism" in 1993 and thereafter.

In a 1993 contribution, Tustin revealed her later thinking about autism:

I have come to realize that autism—the freezing of ongoing psychological development, the retraction of interest in people, the addiction to inanimate objects—is a reaction that is specific to the pain of a particular trauma . . . autism is a reaction to an infantile trauma associated with unbearably painful awareness of bodily separatedness from the suckling mother. [1993, p. 35]

* * * * *

My psychotherapeutic work with young autistic children has indicated that in early infancy they have been overly close to the suckling mother (or primary caregiver). I term this *adhesive equation*.[5] Mother and child feel stuck to each other and "at one." There is no space between them for identification. [1993, pp. 35–36]

* * * * *

The trouble with autistic patients is that they have "bottled up" their distressed feelings because, for various reasons they have felt that they had no one to turn to for help. . . . As the autism is lifted, waves of destructive rage are let loose. It is like a finger coming out of a hole in a dam. . . . The autism has been a kind of strait-jacket to keep this violence in check. [1993, pp. 39–40]

Tustin's Contributions in Perspective

By confining her observations to autism, Tustin helped bring it into psychoanalytic understanding in a unique way and to establish a genre for herself. Her contributions to the study of its phenomenology are as remarkable as her technical procedures for its treatment. Yet, in limiting herself to autism so exclusively, she may have done herself an inadvertent injustice in not recognizing what I believe to be the larger picture of the syndrome she explored: that is, that encapsulation and confusion/entanglement may be parts of a more generalized pattern inherent in other infantile and childhood syndromes as well as those associated with severe infantile and childhood trauma.

In my estimation, Tustin's genre transcends autism. Parallel concepts outside of autism include Engel and Schmale's (1972) "conservation-withdrawal," Fraiberg's (1982) "freezing," schizoid detachment, and dissociation, and Grotstein's (1995a, 1995b) concept of "orphans of the Real" (changelings). Entanglement/confusion phenomena can be associated with anaclitic depression, adhesive identity, moulding, "second-skin," and so forth.

I believe that Tustin's work brilliantly highlights a span of syndromes covering the spectrum of *primitive psychological disorders of infancy* and *early*

---

5. "I believe that 'adhesive equation' constitutes a phantasy of contiguity with mother's body."

childhood, of which the autistic spectrum disorders are a part (formal autism, higher order autism, Asperger syndrome, schizoid personality, Rett syndrome). Autistic encapsulation, sensory shapes, "premature psychological birth," and hard and/or soft autistic objects—and their differences from transitional objects—remain among Tustin's unique clinical discoveries, although these are frequently found in other disorders. Even though I believe she put the cart before the horse in considering autism as a defense against depression, I also believe that her clinical phenomenology is apposite to other entities, such as primary anaclitic depression, primary panic, and phobic disorders of infancy, infantile trauma, and so forth, conditions that are never autistic *per se*. I believe that Tustin may have innocently erred in her conceptualization of "psychogenic autism" instead of postulating autism due to pervasively abnormal development with psychological sequellae. Sheila Spensley[6] agreed in a personal communication:

I too think that Frances' elucidation of the world of autistic experience has a relevance to the understanding of mental functioning which reaches far beyond the narrow boundaries of that syndrome. However, one of the most extraordinary things about Frances is that she never understood this herself! No matter how often I would point to the important links particularly with your own and Ogden's work, she seemed interested only in that which supported her way of understanding autistic children. In fact, I think her way of understanding these children will be found to be less important in terms of their treatment (which remains highly problematical) than her contributions to the broadening of our understanding of the growth of mind and its pathology. [Personal communication, November 4, 1995]

Autistics *seem* to approximate the traditional idea of the primary narcissistic state insofar as they appear to be objectless. Tustin's clinical vision gives another picture, one that I would describe as the autistic's defensively enacting a concrete phantasy of nondifferentiation by assuming their phantasied encapsulating "shell" to be a mythical shielding object that imitates the illusion of primary (objectless) narcissism (no separation) and by skillfully manipulating the external object to reinforce the phantasy of the shield. This skillful

---

6. I am grateful to Sheila Spensley for her kind permission to quote this portion of her personal letter to me.

manipulation is beautifully portrayed by Tustin in the example of the autistic child's propensity to grab hold of mother's wrist to negotiate her opening door knobs. Forced to do it alone, the autistic has to come out of the shell.

Tustin's treatment techniques with autistics are remarkable. Believing that her patients suffered from autistic defenses against a catastrophic depression due to "premature psychological birth," she established what I described as a dialectic between a frameless frame (holding environment with encouragement) and a rigorous psychoanalytic frame in which the phenomenon of separateness and the patient's stark responses to it could be observed and interpreted, analogous to formal psychoanalytic technique (Grotstein 1993). She metaphorically reached in and pulled the autistic out of the shell—and helped them stay out. It worked! Whether, in retrospect, the patients were "educated" by this procedure or were "conditioned" is moot. Tustin proved that psychological understanding was transformative in autistics. Contributors such as Fraiberg (1982), Alvarez (1992), Mitrani (1992, 1996), Kilchenstein and Schuerholz (1995) and others have studied autistic defenses both in autism proper and in other primitive mental disorders. They agree with Tustin that these defenses are lifesaving measures that avoid the perils of separation from the object and its consequences. That they are lifesaving, or at least mind-saving, defenses is indisputable. My critique is directed toward their being alienated from the rest of the schizoid techniques that Klein uncovered.

Some of the Empirical Studies in Autism[7]

In a personal communication, Justin Call—an authority on infant development and childhood autism—summarized the current nosological situation:

My own clinical experience with many cases has taught me that these infants with autism, and infants who have pervasive developmental disorder with autistic traits do, indeed, many of them, respond very clearly to dynamically oriented psychotherapy of child with the family involved. So there may or may not be an underlying biological basis for the autistic syndrome as formally defined in DSM-IV, but it is clear that even when

---

7. I am grateful to Dr. Allen Schore for placing the empirical research data on autism at my disposal.

there is an underlying "organic etiology, considerable change cannot be ruled out given favorable circumstances. . . . So we are left with an old and familiar term, psychobiology, and that should be no surprise to any of us who have become aware of the extremely dynamic way in which the brain develops and how susceptible the early development of brain is to environmental events (favorable and unfavorable), especially those that shape the organization of affective life. Autism, I believe, should be considered an affective disorder of infancy, in fact, the most important and most prototypic of all affective disorders in infancy, rising above even that of anaclitic depression. . . . The deeper psychological and psychobiological aspects of autism and its various degrees of severity and the highly individualistic way in which children become autistic is not at all considered in DSM-IV. And, of course, that is where the action is for us in psychoanalysis. Your common "psychological autism" may probably be a misnomer for those conditions which are predominantly psychological in origin (maltreatment) and correspond to what you choose to call "schizoid syndrome of infancy and childhood," I think is correct. The idea of psychological autism makes a certain amount of sense if you use the term autism in the old and traditional sense put forward by Bleuler and as a part of the syndrome of schizophrenia. It is purely descriptive in that sense rather than as a syndrome. Your term, "schizoid syndrome of infancy and childhood," would be covered in DSM-IV, I believe, as pervasive developmental disorder with some autistic features since schizoid and autism are so closely related, and, if you wanted to favor a connection with the official nomenclature, I think you would perhaps want to use their term, pervasive developmental disorder with autistic features. [January 8, 1996]

Fein and colleagues (1985), Goodman (1989), Gillberg (1989), and Gillberg and Gillberg (1988) deal with the nosology of autism and Asperger's syndrome, and Szatmari and colleagues (1990) consider the neurocognitive aspects of autism as well. Some investigators have differentiated between autism and schizoid personality disorder of childhood. Wolff and Barlow (1979) state:

Children with schizoid personality disorder are distinct from autistic children on the one hand and from normal children on the other. In all cognitive, language and memory tests the schizoid children were more distractible than the normal group. In language function they show similar disabilities to the autistic group, though to a lesser extent. Unlike autistic children, they were not perseverative. On two tests of affect, the schizoid group used even fewer emotional constructs when describing people than did the autistics. [pp. 43–44]

Ciaranello and Ciaranello (1995) hypothesize:

Classical or typical autism is the most severe expression of a broader phenotype that includes Asperger's syndrome, schizoid personality disorder, and perhaps even cognitive deficits occurring in conjunction with deficits in reciprocal social interaction. [p. 104]

They divide the etiological basis of autism into nongenetic and genetic categories. Genetic etiologies include frank hereditary factors, and nongenetic etiologies include congenital womb influences, such as viral infections. Both ultimately result in either failure of a normal developmental progression or derailment of an otherwise normal one. They also state, "Although a popular notion exists that autism is associated with prenatal, perinatal, or neonatal trauma, there is in fact relatively little evidence to support this view" (p. 109).

Piven and colleagues (1995) studied the brains of autistic patients using magnetic resonance imaging (MRI) and found an overall enlargement as well as enlargement of the ventricles. They speculated that the excessive brain tissue may be due to either an increased growth rate or a lowered death rate (proptosis) of neurons early in life or overproduction of glial (support) cells or blood vessels in the brain. EEG studies by Gianotti and di Astis (1978) have been supplanted by an awesome array of brain imaging techniques that seem to demonstrate midline deformity of the cerebellum as well as hypofrontality and fronto-rostral reversal (Ciaranello and Ciaranello 1995). High blood serotonin seems also to be a verified finding (Schain and Freedman 1961), as does the undersynthesis of and increased degradation of brain membranes (Minshew, et al. 1993). Ritvo and colleagues (1985, 1989) established chromosomal/genetic linkages in autism in their Salt Lake City Study. Cummings (1996) and Mega and Cummings (1994) believe that autistic patients suffer from an orbito-frontal neurocircuitry disorder or syndrome. Neurobiological and neuropsychological findings in autism have been summarized by Bauman and Kemper (1994).

Minshew and colleagues (1993) investigated brain high-energy phosphate and membrane phospholipid metabolism in the dorsal prefrontal cortex in high-functioning autistic adolescent and young adult men. They found:

A common pattern of correlations was observed across measures in the autistic group, but not in the control group. . . . This pilot study provides tentative evidence of alterations in brain energy and phospholipid metabolism in autism that correlate with the neuropsychological and language deficits. The findings are consistent with a hypermetabolic energy state and undersynthesis of brain membranes and may relate to the neuropsychological and neuroanatomic abnormalities in autism. [p. 762]

In a similar tone, Minshew and Goldstein (1992) and Minshew and Payton (1988a, 1988b) postulated a distributed neural network deficit in autism. Novick and colleagues (1979) posit a defective information storage in autism, whereas Novick and colleagues (1980) found electrophysiological evidence for auditory processing deficits. Ornitz (1989), Ornitz and Ritvo (1968), and Ritvo and colleagues (1969) found evidence of anatomic abnormalities in the cerebellum in autism. Raymond, et al. (1989) found evidence of defects in the structure of the hippocampus. Skoff and colleagues (1980), Student and Sohmer (1978), and Tanguay and colleagues (1982) found evidence for prolonged brain-stem transmission time.

Epidemiological studies (Jorde et al. 1991, Minton et al. 1982, Ritvo et al. 1989, Rutter 1967, Rutter and Bartak, 1971, Smalley et al. 1988) and studies of twins (Folstein and Rutter 1977, 1978, Ritvo et al. 1985, Steffenberg et al. 1989) seem unanimous in regard to genetic linkages in autism, as do family studies (Bolton and Rutter, 1990, Folstein and Piven, 1991, Folstein and Rutter 1978, Minton et al. 1982, Smalley and Asarnow 1990).

In their summary of the neuropathology of autism, Ciaranello and Ciaranello (1995) conclude that autism is a developmental disorder of the central nervous system. These studies reveal that autism is primarily a severe disorder of neuronal development, particularly of the cerebellum and prefrontal and frontal areas of the cerebral cortex, which causes an impairment of the autistic's capacity to use attachment/bonding techniques (especially internalization of experiences with objects) for relating to the object and for *transitionalizing* across gaps of separation. These deficits lead to "mindblindedness," not being able to reflect on their own thinking or to comprehend that others have a sentient, subjective mind, and to not being able to locate their bodies or even themselves in motion or in space. Their ability to assimilate and accommodate and to organize and integrate interpersonal affect schemata are fundamentally impaired in *statu nascendi*. A considerable literature has developed in both empirical and psychoanalytic studies regarding the concept of "theory of mind" (Baron-Cohen et al. 1994, Brothers 1990, Duck 1973, Johnson-Laird 1983, Leslie 1987, Premack and Woodruff 1978).

The concept of "theory of mind" speaks to the ability not only to have feelings and thoughts but also to be able to *know* that one has them and can *think* about them (self-reflection). Further, it designates the capacity to be mindful that other individuals have autonomous minds as well. Ozonoff and colleagues (1991) argue that Asperger's syndrome and higher-functioning autistics are separate disorders and can be differentiated by the intactness of "theory of mind" in Asperger cases and its absence in higher-functioning autistics. In retrospect, Tustin's patients and those of others who successfully treated allegedly "autistic" children may have been examples of Asperger syndrome.

Much of the research emphasis in autism currently focuses on the concept of mind blindness. Cummings (1996) and Mega and Cummings (1994) conclude that an orbito-frontal neuro-circuitry disorder of autistics clinically presents as a deficit in the capacity for intersubjectivity, that is, the inability to attribute subjectivity to oneself and to the other. This deficit may account for a certain clinical phenomenon, that is, the tendency of autistics to call themselves "it" rather than "I" and their belief that they live in a nonhuman world. The concept of mind blindness can be connected to the alexithymic, linguistic, and attachment difficulties autistic children experience. It is as if they lack the "hardwired" instrumentation with which to experience their humanness and the humanness of the others, to attach to others, to know the meaningfulness of others for them, and to be able to internalize the meaning and significance of them. They seem to suffer from a coarctation of internal fantasy life, thus the observation that they behave like robots or are from Mars (Sacks 1994).

There is now substantial evidence that psychoanalytically informed psychotherapy alone has been of substantial value in the treatment of many conditions that may have had a biological base, for example, schizophrenia, unipolar and bipolar illness, panic disorder, and obsessive-compulsive disorder, as well as certain forms of autism and other developmental disorders. How is this possible?

The neonatal brain is plastic for the first several years of life; it evolves in a predetermined pattern before *and* after birth but is also subject to the transformative influence of the principal caretaker's ministrations (Schore 1994). Not only does brain affect mind, but mind can also affect brain. Baxter and colleagues (1992) demonstrated with positron emission tomography (PET) images that behavior modification therapy compared effectively with clomipramine in the treatment of obsessive-compulsive disorder. Neuronal lesions were significantly changed with each form of treatment. Obviously, some neuronal synaptic pathology is amenable to remediation and most is not. A number of mechanisms may make this transformation by psychotherapy possible. The brain may have a compensatory mechanism analogous to collateral circulation where there is a vascular block, thus allowing a metaphoric "bypass" to occur. Healthy (unaffected) portions of the personality may exist that are capable of sufficient maturation with therapy to become progressively enabled to contain and mediate the autistic aspects; Katan (1954) and Bion (1957) independently conceived of a differentiation between the psychotic and nonpsychotic personalities in schizophrenic patients. There is also some evidence of spontaneous remissions of autistic and schizophrenic illnesses as maturation into adulthood takes place.

We have to ask some questions. What kind of environmental trauma produces or reproduces the neuropathology that now seems specific for autism, and in what developmental time windows must it occur? If autism is fundamentally a neuropathological entity, what factors allow for psychoanalytic remediation? Perhaps intelligence may make the difference. The concept of the psychotherapy of schizophrenia has come full circle. Originally considered to be a dementia and then a psychological and later a biopsychosocial illness, the concept of it as a form of dementia is currently revived by recent neuropathological findings. Nonetheless, psychoanalytically informed psychotherapy is often of great help. Autism, I believe, can be considered a "dementia of development," mainly affecting the affective and relational modalities (alexithymia, mind blindness, failure of bonding and attachment, and failure of intersubjectivity and empathy). Can we conclude that some (but certainly not all) neurobiological conditions are amenable to psychological intervention, notwithstanding—or even *with*-standing—their biological foundations, or can we alternatively conclude that psychological intervention may participate in the amelioration of the strictly psychological aspects of the disorder that occurs parallel with but orthogonal to the biological condition? As Bion (1975) would sometimes say, "The answer is an embarrassment to the question."

Concluding Comments

Frances Tustin's clinical work with "autistic" children became a milestone in the history of treating children—and adults—who suffer from an inchoate need-fear dilemma of closeness to their needed objects. She painstakingly elaborated the phenomenology of those children and was able effectively to intervene psychotherapeutically in ways that facilitated their being able to come out of their shell-like encapsulation and their being able to allow themselves to long for and to accept their need for the object and to tolerate its absence. It is my belief that her work was probably as effective as it was not only because of her unusual talent and skill but also because of the possibility that she may have worked largely if not entirely with Asperger cases or at least higher-level autistic children. The legacy she left us is a rich and honorable one and will stand the test of time.

I have questioned two aspects of Tustin's theory about autism: the idea of "psychogenic autism"—a concept that I believe, in light of empirical research findings, is more and more problematic—and the idea of the traumatic origin of autism, which is equally if not even more problematic. It is my belief that autism basically is a nontraumatic disorder of development and that the impairments that result from it, particularly "mind blindness," makes these victims more prone to being traumatized in attempting maturation.

The irony is that Tustin rushed in where more knowledgeable angels feared to tread. Yet by rigorously applying psychoanalytic technique to treatment of this disorder, because she thought it was psychogenic in origin, she inadvertently pioneered the enlightened *rehabilitation* of what seems to me to be a predominantly neurobiological disorder. In so doing she helped break the spell about its untreatability in selected cases. Consequently, I think Tustin may deserve credit for instituting what I would call "rehabilitative" or "remedial" psychoanalytic psychotherapy. Along with Tustin, I believe that, when treating patients suffering from constitutional disorders, we should not shirk from the challenge of the analytic task they present, but we should also humbly and realistically respect the enormity of the handicap that brain pathology presents.

Finally, I must acknowledge my profound indebtedness to Frances Tustin for her friendship and her abundant sharing of ideas with me across the years.

References

Alvarez, A. (1992). *Live Company*. London: Routledge.

Anzieu, D. (1985). *The Skin Ego*. Madison, Connecticut: International Universities Press. [(English Trans.) C. Turner. New Haven and London: Yale University Press, 1989.]

——— (1990). Formal signifiers and the ego-skin. In *Psychic Envelopes*, ed. D. Anzieu. London: Karnac, pp. 1–26.

Baron-Cohen, S., Ring, H., Moriarty, J., Schmitz, B., Costa, D., and Ell, P. (1994). Recognition of mental state terms: clinical findings in children with autism and a functional neuroimaging study for normal adults. *British Journal of Psychiatry* 165:640–649.

Bauman, M. L., and Kemper, T. L., eds. (1994). *The Neurobiology of Autism*. Baltimore: Johns Hopkins University Press.

Baxter, L. R., Jr. (1992). Positron emission tomography studies of cerebral glucose metabolism in obsessive compulsive disorder. *Journal of Clinical Psychiatry* 55 Supple.: 54–59.

Bettelheim, B. (1967). *The Empty Fortress: Infantile Autism and the Birth of the Self*. New York: Free Press. London: Collier/Macmillan.

Bibring, E. (1953). The mechanism of depression. In *Affective Disorders*, ed. P. Greenacre. New York: International Universities Press.

Bick, E. (1968). The experience of the skin in early object relations. *International Journal of Psycho-Analysis* 49:484–486.

Bion, W. R. (1957). Differentiation of the psychotic from the non-psychotic personalities. *International Journal of Psycho-Analysis* 38:266–275.

——— (1959). Attacks on linking. In *Second Thoughts*, pp. 93–109. London: Heinemann, 1967.

——— (1962). *Learning From Experience*. London: Heinemann.

——— (1963). *Element of Psychoanalysis*. London: Heinemann.

——— (1965). *Transformations*. London: Heinemann.

——— (1967). *Second Thoughts*. London: Heinemann.

——— (1970). *Attention and Interpretation*. London: Tavistock.

——— (1975). Personal Communication, Jan. 4.

——— (1992). *Cogitations*. London: Karnac.

Bollas, C. (1987). *The Shadow of the Object: Psychoanalysis of the Unthought Known*. New York: International Universities Press.

Bolton, R., and Rutter, M. (1990). Genetic influences in autism. *International Review of Psycho-Analysis* 2:67–80.

Bowlby, J. (1958). The nature of the child's tie to his mother. *International Journal of Psycho-Analysis* 39:350–373.

——— (1960a). Separation Anxiety. *International Journal of Psycho-Analysis* 41:80–113.

——— (1960b). Grief and mourning in infancy and early childhood. *Psychoanalytic Study of the Child* 15:43–52.

———— (1969). *Attachment and Loss. Vol. I: Attachment.* New York: Basic Books.

———— (1973). *Attachment and Loss. Vol. II: Separation: Anxiety and Anger.* New York: Basic Books.

———— (1980). *Attachment and Loss. Vol. III: Loss: Sadness and Depression.* New York: Basic Books.

Brothers, L. (1990). The social brain: a project for integrating primate behavior and neurophysiology in a new domain. *Concepts in Neuroscience* 1:27–51.

Call, J. (1996). Personal communication, letter to J. Grotstein, Jan. 8.

Ciaranello, A. L., and Ciaranello, R. D. (1995). The neurobiology of infantile autism. *Annual Review of Neuroscience* 18:101–128.

Cummings, J. (1996). Frontal-subcortical circuits: pathways of judgment, affect and behavior. Lecture presented to the Los Angeles Psychoanalytic Society and Institute under the auspices of the Neuroscience and Extension Division, Los Angeles, CA, March.

Deutsch, H. (1942 [1934]). Some forms of emotional disturbances and their relationship to schizophrenia. In *Neuroses and Character Types*, pp. 262–281. New York: IUP, 1963.

Duck, S. W. (1973). *Personal Relationships and Personal Constructs.* New York: John Wiley.

Engel, G., and Schmale, A. H. (1972). Conservation-withdrawal: A primary regulatory process for organismic homeostastis. In *Physiology, Emotion, and Psychosomatic Illness*, vol. VIII pp. 57–85. Ciba Foundation Symposium.

Fein, D., Waterhouse, L., Lucci, D., and Snyder, D. (1985). Cognitive subtypes in developmentally delayed children: a pilot study. *Journal of Autism and Developmental Disorders* 15:77–95.

Folstein, S., and Rutter, M. (1977). Infantile autism: a genetic study of 21 twin pairs. *Journal of Child Psychology and Psychiatry* 18:297–321.

———— (1978). A twin study of individuals with infantile autism. In *Autism: A Reappraisal of Concepts and Treatment*, ed. M. Rutter and E. Schopler, pp. 219–242. New York: Plenum.

Folstein, S., and Piven, J. (1991). Etiology of autism: genetic influences. *Pediatrics* 87(5):767–773.

Fraiberg, S. (1982). Pathological defenses in infancy. *Psychoanalytic Quarterly* 51:621–635.

Freud, S. (1914). On narcissism: an introduction. *Standard Edition* 14:67–104. London: Hogarth, 1957.

———— (1917). Mourning and melancholia. *Standard Edition* 14:237–260. London: Hogarth, 1957.

———— (1920). Beyond the pleasure principle. *Standard Edition* 18:3–66. London: Hogarth and the Institute of Psycho-Analysis, 1955.

Frith, U. (1985). Does the autistic child have a theory of mind? *Cognition* 21:37–46.

Gianotti, A., and di Astis, G. (1978). Early infantile autism: considerations regarding its psychopathology and the therapeutic process. Paper presented at the Eighth National Congress of the Italian Society of Infantile Neuropsychiatry, Florence, Italy.

Gillberg, C. (1989). Asperger Syndrome in 23 Swedish children. *Developmental Medicine and Child Neurology* 31:520–531.

Gillberg, C., and Gillberg, C. (1988). Asperger Syndrome—some epidemiological considerations: a research note. *Journal of Psychoanalysis and Psychiatry* 30:631–638.

Goodman, R. (1989). Infantile autism: a syndrome of multiple primary deficits? *Journal of Autism and Developmental Disorders* 19:409–424.

Grotstein, J. (1990a). The "black hole" as the basic psychotic experience: some newer psychoanalytic and neuroscience perspectives on psychosis. *Journal of the American Academy of Psychoanalysis* 18(1):29–46.

———— (1990b). Nothingness, meaninglessness, chaos and the "black hole": The importance of nothingness, meaninglessness, and chaos in psychoanalysis. Part I. *Contemporary Psychoanalysis* 26(2):257–290.

———— (1990c). Nothingness, meaninglessness, chaos, and the "black hole." II. The black hole. *Contemporary Psychoanalysis* 26(3):377–407.

———— (1991). Nothingness, meaninglessness, chaos, and the "black hole." III. Self regulation and the background presence of primary identification. *Contemporary Psychoanalysis* 27(1):1–33.

———— (1993). Boundary difficulties in borderline patients. In *Master Clinicians on Treating the Regressed Patient*, ed. L. B. Boyer and P. Giovacchini, pp. 107–142. New Jersey: Jason Aronson.

———— (1995a). Orphans of the "Real": I. some modern and post-modern perspectives on the neurobiological and psychosocial dimensions of psychosis and primitive mental disorders. *Bulletin of the Menninger Clinic* 59:287–311.

———— (1995b). Orphans of the "Real": II. The future of object relations theory in the treatment of psychoses and other primitive mental disorders. *Bulletin of the Menninger Clinic* 59:312–332.

Hermann, I. (1936). Clinging-going-in-search: a contrasting pair of instincts and their relation to sadism and masochism. *Psychoanalytic Quarterly* (1976), 45:5–36.

Hobson, R. P. (1986). The autistic child's appraisal of expressions of emotions. *Journal Child Psychological Psychiatry* 27:321–342.

Isaacs, S. (1952). The nature and function of phantasy. In *Developments in Psycho-Analysis*, ed. M. Klein, S. Isaacs, and J. Riviere, pp. 67–121. London: Hogarth.

Janet, P. (1893). Quelques définitions l'activité de l'hystérie. *Archives de Neurologie* 25:417–438; 26:1–29.

Johnson-Laird, P. N. (1983). *Mental Models: Towards a Cognitive Science of Language, Inference, and Consciousness*. Cambridge: Harvard University Press.

Jorde, L. B., Hasstedt, S. E., Ritvo, E. R., Mason-Brothers, A., Freeman, B. J., et al. (1991). Complex segregation analysis of autism. *American Journal of Human Genetics*, 49:932–938.

Kanner, L. (1943). Autistic disturbances of affective contact. *Nervous Child* 2:217–250.

Katan, M. (1954). The importance of the non-psychotic part of the personality in schizophrenia. *International Journal of Psycho-Analysis* 35:119–128.

Kilchenstein, M. W., and Schuerholz, L. (1995). Autistic defenses and the impairment of cognitive development. *Bulletin of the Menninger Clinic* 59:443–459.

King, P., and Steiner, R. (1992). *The Freud-Klein Controversies, 1941–1945*. London: Karnac Books.

Klein, M. (1940). Mourning and its relationship to manic-depressive states. In *Contributions to Psycho-Analysis 1921–1945*, pp. 311–338. London: Hogarth, 1950.

Klein, S. (1980). Autistic phenomena in neurotic patients. *International Journal of Psycho-Analysis* 61:395–401.

Leslie, A. (1987). Pretense and representation: the origins of "Theory of Mind." *Psychological Review* 94:412–426.

Mahler, M. S. (1958). Autism and symbiosis: two extreme disturbances of identity. *International Journal of Psycho-Analysis* 39:77–83.

Marcelli, D. (1983). La position autistique. Hypothèses psychopathologiques et ontogénétiques. *Psychiatrie enfant* 24(1):5–55.

Mason, A. (1990). A psychoanalyst looks at a hypnotist: or, where the elephant-skin boy took me. Presented at the Scientific Meeting of the Psychoanalytic Center of California, January. Los Angeles, CA.

Mega, M., and Cummings, J. (1994). Frontal-subcortical circuits and neuro-psychiatric disturbances. *Journal of Neuropsychiatry and Clinical Neuroscience* 6:358–370.

Meltzer, D. (1963). Autism, schizophrenia and psychotic adjustment. Unpublished paper.

——— (1975). Adhesive identification. *Contemporary Psychoanalysis*, 11:289–310.

Meltzer, D. W., Bremner, J., Hoxter, S., Wedell, H., Wittenberg, I. (1975). *Explorations in Autism*. Strath Tay, Perthshire, Scotland: Clunie Press.

Minshew, N. J., and Goldstein, G. (1992). Autism: A distributed neutral network deficit? *Journal of Clinical and Experimental Neuropsychology*, 15:56.

Minshew, N. J., and Payton, J. B. (1988a). New perspectives in autism, part I: the clinical spectrum of autism. *Current Problems in Pediatrics* 18:561–610.

——— (1988b). New perspectives in autism, part II: The differential diagnosis and neurobiology of autism. *Current Problems in Pediatrics* 18:613–694.

Minshew, N. J., Goldstein, G., Dombrowski, S. M., Panchalingham, K., and Pettigrew, J. W. (1993). A preliminary 31P MRS study of autism: evidence for undersynthesis and increased degradation of brain membranes. *Society of Biological Psychiatry* 33:762–773.

Minton, J., Campbell, M., Green, W. H., Jennings, S., and Samit, C. (1982). Cognitive assessment of siblings of autistic children. *Journal of the American Academy of Child Psychiatry* 21:256–261.

Mitrani, J. L. (1992). On the survival function of autistic maneuvers in adult patients. *International Journal of Psycho-Analysis* 73:549–559.

——— (1996). *A Framework for the Imaginary: Clinical Explorations in Primitive States of Being*. New Jersey and London: Jason Aronson.

Novick, B., Kurtzberg, D., and Vaughan, H. G., Jr. (1979). An electrophysiologic indication of defective information storage in childhood autism. *Psychiatry Research* 3:101–108.

Novick, B., Vaughan, H. G., Jr., Kurtzberg, D., and Simson, R. (1980). An electrophysiologic indication of auditory processing defects in autism. *Psychiatry Research* 3:107–114.

Ogden, T. (1989). On the concept of the autistic-contiguous position. *International Journal of Psycho-Analysis* 70:127–140.

Ornitz, E. M. (1989). Autism at the interface between sensory and information processing. In *Autism: Nature, diagnosis, and treatment*, ed. Geraldine Dawson, pp. 174–207. Guilford: New York.

Ornitz, E. M., and Ritvo, E. R. (1968). Perceptual inconstancy in early infantile autism. *Archives of General Psychiatry* 18:76–98.

Ozonoff, S., Rogers, S., and Pennington, B. (1991). Asperger's syndrome: evidence for an empirical distinction from high-functioning autism. *Journal of Child Psychology and Psychiatry* 32:1107–1122.

Piven, J., Arndt, S., and Bailey, J. (1995). An MRI study of brain size in autism. *American Journal of Psychiatry* 152:1145–1149.

Premack, D., and Woodruff, G. (1978). Does the chimpanzee have a theory of mind? *Behavioral Brain Sciences* 4:515–526.

Rank, B., and McNaughton, D. (1950). A clinical contribution to ego development. *Psychoanalytic Study of the Child,* 5:53–65.

Rank, B., and Putnam, M. (1953). James Jackson Putnam Children's Center. Unpublished research report. Cited in Tustin (1986), p. 67, *Autistic Barriers in Neurotic Patients*. London: Karnac.

Raymond, G., Bauman, M., and Kemper, T. (1989). The hypocampus in autism: Golgi analysis. *Annual of Neurology*, 26:483–484.

Ritvo, E. R., Jorde, L. B., Mason-Brothers, A., Freeman, B. J., Pingree, C., et al. (1989). The UCLA-University of Utah Epidemiological Survey of Autism: recurrence risk estimates and genetic counseling. *American Journal of Psychiatry* 146(8):1032–1036.

Ritvo, E. R., Ornitz, E. M., Eviatar, A., Markham, D. H., Brown, M. B., and Mason, A. (1969). Decreased postrotatory nystagmus in early infantile autism. *Neurology* 19:653–658.

Ritvo, E. R., Spence, M. A., Freeman, B. J., Mason-Brothers, A., Mo, A., and Marazita, M. L. (1985). Evidence for autosomal recessive inheritance in 46 families with multiple incidence of autism. *American Journal of Psychiatry* 142:187–192.

Rutter, M. (1967). Psychotic disorders in early childhood. In *Recent Developments in Schizophrenia, British Journal of Psychiatry*, ed. A. Coppen and A. Walk. Special Publication 1:133–158.

Rutter, M., and Bartak, L. (1971). Causes of infantile autism: some considerations from recent research. *Journal of Autism and Childhood Schizophrenia* 1:20–32.

Sacks, O. (1994). An anthropologist on Mars. *New Yorker,* December 27, pp. 106–125.

Schain, R., and Freedman, F. (1961). Studies of 5-hydroxyindole metabolism in autistic and other mentally retarded children. *Journal of Pediatrics* 58:315–320.

Schore, A. (1994). *Affect Regulation and the Origin of the Self: The Neurobiology of Emotional Development*. New Jersey: Lawrence Erlbaum.

Skoff, B. F., Mirsky, A. F., and Turner, D. (1980). Prolonged transmission time in autism. *Psychiatry Research* 2:157–166.

Smalley, S. L., Asarnow, R. F., & Spense, A. (1988). Autism and genetics. *Archives of General Psychiatry* 45:953–961.

Spensley, S. (1995). *Frances Tustin*. London and New York: Routledge.

Steffenburg, S., Gillberg, C., Hellgren, L., Anderson, L. C., et al. (1989). A twin study of autism in Denmark, Finland, Iceland, Norway, and Sweden. *Journal of Child Psychology and Psychiatry*, 30(3):405–516.

Stone, M. H. (1988). Toward a psychobiological theory on borderline personality disorder: Is irritability the red thread that runs through borderline conditions? *Dissociations* 1(2):2–15.

Student, M., and Sohmer, H. (1978). Evidence from auditory nerve and brainstem evoked responses for an organic brain lesion in children with autistic traits. *Journal of Autism and Childhood Schizophrenia* 8:13–20.

Szatmari, P., Tuff, L., Finlayson, A. J., and Bartolucci, J. (1990). Asperger's syndrome and autism: neurocognitive aspects. *Journal of the American Academy of Child and Adolescent Psychiatry* 29:130–136.

Tanguay, P. E., Edwards, R. M., Buchwald, J., Schwafel, J., and Allen, V. (1982). Auditory brainstem evoked responses in autistic children. *Archives of General Psychiatry* 39:174–180.

Trevarthen, C. (1979a). Communication and cooperation in early infancy: a description of primary intersubjectivity. In *Before Speech: The Beginning of Interpersonal Communication*, ed. M. Bullowa, pp. 321–347. Cambridge: Cambridge University Press.

——— (1979b). Instincts for human understanding and for cultural cooperation: their development in infancy. In *Human Ethology: Claims and Limits of a New Discipline*. London: Cambridge University Press.

Tustin, F. (1972). *Autism and Childhood Psychosis*. London: Hogarth.

——— (1981). *Autistic States in Children*. London and Boston: Routledge and Kegan Paul.

——— (1984). Autistic shapes. *International Review of Psycho-Analysis* 11:279–290.

——— (1986). *Autistic Barriers in Neurotic Patients*. London: Karnac Books.

——— (1988). Psychotherapy with children who cannot play. *International Review of Psycho-Analysis* 15:93–106.

———— (1989). The black hole—a significant element in autism. *Free Associations* 11:36–50.

———— (1990). *The Protective Shell in Children and Adults*. London: Karnac Books.

———— (1991). Revised understandings of psychogenic autism. *International Journal of Psycho-Analysis* 72:585–591.

———— (1993). On psychogenic autism. *Psychoanalytic Inquiry* 13:34–41.

Winnicott, D. W. (1958). The capacity to be alone. In *The Maturational Processes and the Facilitating Environment*, pp. 29–36. New York: International Universities Press, 1965.

———— (1971). *Playing and Reality*. London and New York: Tavistock.

Wolff, S., and Barlow, A. (1979). Schizoid personality in childhood: a comparative study of schizoid, autistic, and normal children. *Journal of Child Psychology and Psychiatry*, 20:29–46.

Wolff, S., and Chick, J. (1980). Schizoid personality in childhood: a controlled follow-up study. *Psychological Medicine* 10:85–100.

Wolff, S., and Cuth, A. (1986). Schizoid personality and anti-social conduct: a retrospective case note study. *Psychological Medicine* 16:677–687.

16

Beginning the Search for an Identity: Analysis of a Young Woman with Autistic Features as Supervised by Frances Tustin[1]

Maria Pozzi

The basic sense of being rooted sets the scene for the development of a sense of identity, security, and self confidence.

Frances Tustin, *Autistic States in Children*

In February, 1995, a memorial for Frances Tustin was held at the Tavistock Clinic in London. I began my personal tribute to Tustin by saying something which was also very appropriate for the Memorial in Los Angeles—the City of the Angels—in which I also participated: I like to imagine that Tustin is here with us, but not just in our thoughts and memories of her or with her ideas that continue in our therapeutic work with patients, but that she is here as a *real presence*—perhaps as an angel or a good fairy—fluttering her wings above us.

---

1. A version of this chapter was read at the Frances Tustin Memorial Tribute, held in October 1995 in Los Angeles, CA. The original case material has been disguised to preserve confidentiality.

How It All Began

This chapter is born out of the death of my former supervisor—and later close friend—Frances Tustin. When Tustin died on November 11, 1994—a deep loss for me as for many of those who have met her, loved her, and grown through association with her—I was left with deep pain and sorrow and a desire to be linked with her. I thought this needed to be done in a new way and I became aware that, if I wrote about my work with her on the patient she had supervised for a year, it would be one way to begin to mourn her. This stemmed from the depth of my feelings for Tustin, so I began.

When Tustin agreed to supervise me on the patient here presented, she suggested we met at Amersham tube station. She was going to pick me up to show me the way to her bungalow. On that occasion, she offered me a double time as she wanted to get to know me, to be able to tune in better with my patient, as she put it. That was not the only time that she was so generous and available.

Supervision with Frances Tustin

My supervisions with Tustin gave me an enriching experience as well as a soothing time in my week, and I always looked forward to seeing her. While we drank cups of tea, she would listen to my accounts of Tamara's sessions. Tamara was a young woman nearly 24 years old when she was sent to me for intensive psychotherapy. She seemed to me to fit well with Tustin's description of neurotic patients with an autistic capsule. In her book *Autistic Barriers in Neurotic Patients* (1986) Tustin writes:

> Certain neurotic patients have much in common with autistic children. . . . Such patients feel that they are unreal and that "life is just a dream." On deeper investigation it becomes clear that their sense of existing as a person is tenuous. In such patients, cognitive and affective development seems to have taken place by bi-passing a "blind spot" of arrested development which then becomes a capsule of autism in the depth of their personality. In this capsule, as in the overall encapsulation of autistic children, there are all the potentials for the development of self, but secure and authentic self-representation has never been satisfactorily achieved. [p. 215]

In supervision, Tustin would quickly pick up something of the presented material—that may have seemed insignificant to me—and she would anticipate a theme that was to be confirmed and expanded by the patient in the following week. Tustin was clearly relying on her longstanding clinical experience and acumen to be able to see such concealed matters. She helped me to see and to connect with a deeply rooted sense of void and nonexistence in this girl.

Tustin would point me in the direction of the autistic parts of Tamara's personality and would call my attention to the barriers Tamara used for protection. For example, for a long time Tamara would not address me by name, but as "the Tavistock," thus rendering impersonal and detached a relationship which would have otherwise been felt as engulfing, frightening, and threatening to her fragile self. As she could not think of herself as a person, she projected that onto me.

Taking her coat off and lying on the couch was experienced as an excessive and frightening exposure on Tamara's part. Tustin was soon able to help me to understand that Tamara's mother may have had a symbiotic relationship with Tamara, as I will describe further on, and also that the father figure had not been strong enough in this patient's life to foster sufficient separation between the infant Tamara and her mother.

Tustin used to say to me, as we talked of many things, that too many analyses do not address enough, or not at all, the autistic parts in neurotic patients, thus leaving these patients with autistic pockets that, sooner or later, affect their lives. I found that what we understood about Tamara also applied to many other patients of mine.

Occasionally, Tustin would give me what sounded like charming, grandmotherly advice. For example she once said to me: "You must tell the patient—in a light way—not to use you as a stick to beat her mother with." I also remember the day when, in a panic, I telephoned Tustin just before seeing Tamara. Something unforeseeable had happened, such that I could only see Tamara for a part of her session. Tustin—always available at home and on such occasions—said, in an alive, reassuring and matter-of-fact way: "Oh but don't worry! You just tell her that you need to stop earlier, and then you analyze what comes up!"

After Tustin's death, I reread *Autistic Barriers in Neurotic Patients* (1986) and others of her books. It has been sweet and moving to find there many of her thoughts, similar to those I had jotted down during supervisions with her. Rereading her words, I could almost hear her lively, expressive, and capturing voice, and I could also "see" her mimes and gestures as she recounted many of her experiences and memories.

Tamara

Tamara had many years of intensive treatment with me and the wealth of material recorded on this treatment is enormous. Therefore I will concentrate on a single theme: that of the *experience of separation within the building up of the patient's sense of identity*. I will focus in particular on three moments in Tamara's therapy: the first year, when Frances Tustin supervised me weekly, thus giving me a good grasp on Tamara's autistic parts and on her internal world. Next, a dream, which occurred in her sixth year of treatment, which was rather telling with regard to her struggle to construe her sense of self. And finally, her last phase of treatment, which had presented interesting questions concerning her true identity, her direction in life, and her professional choices.

The Beginning

Tamara came into therapy with an enormous identity problem. It was not so much that she was confused or lost in a psychotic or schizophrenic sense but rather that she was living her life *through* other people, influenced excessively by the flow of events and people. She would take on their choices and personality traits, but deep down she did not know what to do with her own life. At that time she was living with a childhood friend and the friend's parents, who had said it was like having two identical twins in the house, so much was Tamara a shadow of her friend.

In a desperate moment of unhappiness, following her parents' separation, Tamara had attempted to take her life. She was the second of four children and described her mother as being totally dedicated to family life, often with an unhealthy attitude towards the children. She doted on Tamara, and—as it emerged during therapy—treated her as an appendage of herself. Tamara's father was described as a cool, somewhat schizoid, disinterested man, given to occasional outbursts of rage and physical violence. Tamara had felt persecuted by and terrified of him during her childhood. She had had great difficulty when she started school, nearly developing a school phobia at the time of her parents' separation. She felt this as a wrench from which she had never recovered, and she failed to establish herself both socially and academically. Finally, Tamara went to live with her friend's family to escape from her own parents. Her present life and difficulties were spilled out during a very detailed, extensive, and emotional assessment with an experienced therapist, who had subsequently referred Tamara to me for treatment.

However, when the treatment began, Tamara felt empty, with nothing else to say, not knowing how to begin with me, feeling suspicious of my young age. She felt cold and lonely. Tustin pointed out that this situation seemed to be a reenactment of an early separation from the mother, which must have also pre-dated the birth of Tamara's younger sibling, for whom she had always harbored an intense jealousy. After having had such a warm and positive connection with the referring therapist, Tamara had experienced being transferred to me as a repetition of this very premature and wrenching separation from the "suckling mother." As Tustin would say to me, Tamara's merger with the referring clinician—and later on with me—was Tamara's way of avoiding endings and separations.

Tustin also suggested to me that, in this young woman's early infancy, there might not have been a "creative breast"—a coupled Mother and Father—to interact with the baby and to help her heal the loss of the nipple and the breast. Rather, she was left all alone, rocking and banging her head in her cot, while the parents were felt to be absent.

Tustin spoke of the experience of an autistic, automatic breast when she would hear of how Tamara would pour out her story into people (the referring therapist, myself, her friends, etc.). Then Tamara would feel the emptiness, the void, a sense of death, and an inability to have a dialogue with the object. I was then also expected to immediately pour it all back into her; thus, silences were not tolerable for her.

Pattern of Response at Break Times

As Tustin pointed out to me, the first week of therapy was already clouded by the end of the assessment, which had made Tamara feel so special. Although she could not yet be with me emotionally, she had felt almost incredulous upon beginning psychotherapy at last, as well as bewildered at the number of sessions offered, which was more than she had anticipated. She was pleased but worried. Her friend had asked, "Was she so 'disturbed' as to need so much?" Yet Tamara told me herself, in our first session, that she had an identity problem: She did not know what was herself and what was her friend.

Throughout the first week, she became engaged in our work. However, by Friday, she felt "very cool," rational, distant, in a "black mood," and silent. She said she "never felt so bad this week." Her associations were about feeling alone, always alone in the end, "no parents to go to," unlike her friend. She also feared my "assessment" and possible rejection were she to be in a "black mood" with me.

By Monday, she was pleased to be back. She had had an eventful weekend and the issue of couples, her rivalry with mother's new partner, and her feeling of being squashed between siblings emerged vividly. However, the depression, the lack of thought, and a sense of void fell on her by Tuesday, and she no longer knew what to say. This pattern of response at times of separation would, in time, seem to apply also to sessions or to a good experience within one session. Tamara was able to have and to enjoy a good experience, but when this was interrupted or finished and was not long enough, she cut off, like her father, or wrapped herself up in her protection. Tustin helped me to notice how she accomplished this by denial, keeping busy, or using intellectual arguments as an autistic barrier. Afterward, the black depression, the sullen feelings, and a sense of void would follow.

Tustin showed me Tamara's autistic reaction to the first holiday break. During the holiday, Tamara's beloved garden tree was cut down. It had provided her with special comfort in her childhood. She used to talk to the tree and to cry to it when she was low and had problems. "It may sound silly that I didn't turn to people but to a tree," she said. In the session, she cried and was able to be a little sad about the tree, but she had no reaction to the holiday. "Nothing happened in those three or four weeks of therapy [five in reality] prior to the holiday," she said. She had not thought of the therapy since the last session before the break. Depression and blackness followed on the next day. Tustin pointed out to me the negation that therapy had had any impact on Tamara; for her, therapy did not exist so it could not die. This was the core of her autistic bit. When Tustin spoke in these terms, it resonated meanings inside me: I had felt totally canceled out, not seen, negated by the patient. Her early childhood experience was being relived in the transference. Tamara's mother and other important human beings were canceled out and Tamara turned to inanimate objects for comfort.

In supervision, Tustin also spoke of Tamara's liability to commit suicide once she would feel remorse, because her sense of void and emptiness had been caused unconsciously by her annihilation of the other. Indeed, the theme of suicide was to become a *leitmotif* in this patient's psychic and external life. The sense of void and denial—that anything had happened in those few weeks of therapy—was also increased by her grudges: She was left with nothing. I went on holiday at the wrong time, too late for her traveling plans.

If she was eight minutes late to her session because of a travel delay, the session was wasted in her mind. Tustin used to say that she could no longer make any good use of the "good breast," that is, the time left, in this case. Everything was gone and spoiled.

One year into her therapy, I was finally able to offer Tamara a different time for a session, as she had requested. Yet the change put her in a state of confusion and she missed that session. She came back saying that she "felt lost in space" and could only see what was lost, not the gain. Tustin explained that both the feeling of being "spaced out" and of holding on to "the hole"—that is, to the negative, to the missed session—were a typical autistic reaction that she had met with in the autistic children she had treated. Tustin also spoke of the meaning of changes for Tamara: I was a separate person and a very primitive rhythm was broken. It was as if the mother's heartthrob for the baby in the womb—which had given Tamara a sense of continuity of being—was interrupted, and life had stopped. Also the change of time brought about anxiety dreams of being chased by a woman and being raped. Tustin said that the change being like a rape linked up, in the patient's unconscious, with having witnessed the primal scene too early. This precocious experience of bodily separateness was evacuated into me.

Again Tamara's dreams about weekend separations were extremely vivid and rich, filled with dramatic and pictorial images of: (1) rapists and children invading her sessions, pushing her out; (2) foreign food being dished out to her and turning out to be "her dog cooked on a plate"; (3) a French man who gives her group-therapy and does not speak to her but to other patients in a foreign language (Italian); (4) myself talking to her friend and not to her; and (5) I cut her session in half and give it to another woman; Tamara wants to run away but a man is there to chase and castrate her. We could see that I was present in many of her dreams as the mother of her infancy, the mother who did not protect and support the baby-Tamara. Tustin spoke of the "shock-absorber" mother or the mother-stomach-mind—trustworthy and helpful—which Tamara did not have. This mother is able to contain and digest, by her alpha function, the baby's beta elements, that is, the raw sensory experience, the tantrum and the ecstasy, the rivalry and the envy.

In Tamara's therapy, we also began to see a shift from an autistic sense of annihilation and void to persecutory images, dreams, and rage which were there in the absence of the sessions. As I reread my notes, taken during those supervisions, I can understand much better many of Tustin's ideas, which have informed my work with Tamara all along. Having never dealt with the feeling of bodily separateness from her mother, from me, from her friend, and so forth, Tamara always looked for replacements as soon as there was a separation, a weekend break, or a holiday. Her psychical torment was unbearable. During breaks, she would fill up her times with plans, actions, and people—and later on with sexual relationships—to avoid feeling the dangerous gap.

A large part of my work with Tamara was about the experience of loss—of "missing" me and her therapy without feeling it as a catastrophic loss or a black hole—as well as helping her to mourn and to get on with her own life and creativity.

The Dream

By her sixth year of psychotherapy, Tamara had graduated in European History with top grades. At that time she had a very interesting and enlightening dream, a landmark of her unconscious mind which provided us with food for thought up to the end of her therapy. The dream was produced in the context of an unexpected long break, which I had to take. Until then, my absences had been very rare. At the same time, a close friend of Tamara's had committed suicide following the death of her partner. Tamara had also been exploring once again the issue of her own future. She had felt unable to decide her future, as she had felt too "tied up by being a patient" and by deeper issues of adhesive and projective identification with me as well as by destructive envy. In this dream:

> Tamara and "a therapist" were watching a TV program about Marilyn Monroe's suicide; Tamara's cousin was there in the background. Tamara and the therapist were wearing similar white dressing-gowns and Tamara crossed her legs, just like the therapist. Then she realized that she was too similar to the therapist and decided to cross them in the other way. The therapist stood up and turned the TV off. Tamara got angry as *she* still wanted to watch television. The therapist apologized and Tamara woke up.

She told me that her mother always turned the TV off when she wanted to go to bed, and she was totally oblivious to Tamara's presence in the room. She acted as if Tamara were a part of herself. Tamara was anxious in recounting this dream, as she feared that I would say that she was "stealing from me." We had previously spoken at length of her tendency to buy for herself what other people had, to "borrow" their identities, choices, possessions, when she felt she could not build things up for herself. She told me that she had bought the same white dressing gown as her dearest friend. Through her associations, it also emerged that she was projecting her rage at being different and separate from her object, that is, myself in the transference. For example, in the dream, she orchestrated an interruption by me of the TV program—that is, the treatment—when she was different from me, crossing her legs in a different way. The relationship with the object—based on being identical to the object or being a nonseparate appendage of it or merged with it—was clearly confirmed by the patient's associations about her mother acting as if Tamara were not in the room watching TV with her. In the transference relationship, Tamara was wearing the same clothes as me (the white gown of a doctor), sitting exactly like me, and being aware of copying, stealing, or recycling my therapeutic hat. This had been an ongoing theme in the past, when she had switched from being the poor, deranged, suicidal girl, to becoming a "mock" therapist with her mother, her friends, and others. She also spoke of a girlfriend who had become psychotic and committed suicide after the death of her husband. In the dream, we both watched the suicidal part of her being projected into Marilyn Monroe. This had to do with being in a symbiotic relationship with the object, then feeling destroyed, and then destroying when separation occurred. Tustin called this "imitative fusion."

Tamara's sense of identity was so dependent on others—vanishing so easily when a separation occurred and fusion ceased—that nothing was felt to be left of her. Tustin used to talk of Tamara's fear of not existing at all. This fear was very deep and went beyond the fear of death. She stressed the difference between dying—which implies having existed and having had a body—and not existing at all when nothing is left behind, not even a memory of oneself. Tustin also used to say that autism is a form of suicide and also the murder of all human efforts and care. She wrote:

> This potentiality for cruelty is often turned against themselves in that they will cut and hurt themselves, bring their creative endeavour to an abortive halt or, at worst, kill themselves. [1987, p. 299]

In some aspect of their being, these patients have rejected the "breast-mother," violently turning away from her.

> All possible healing overtures from her . . . have been rebuffed, just as, in their early painful awareness of separation from her, they felt that they had been. [p. 300]

As well as fusing with the object, Tamara would also "steal" the identity of the object in a manic way, thus becoming the object. This would happen particularly during breaks. I remember once that she played to the hilt the role of being an actress, and on her return to therapy she swore to me that she had finally found out what she wanted to be and do in her life. After some weeks of therapy, her plan disintegrated and she blamed me for having destroyed her future plans and her identity.

At the time of the dream, Tamara had once again been debating whether to become like Peter Smith, an academic lecturer whom she had been attracted to and also admired professionally, or to become like me or a well-known doctor she had met. Her tendency to be like one of these characters—without doing enough work in the real world of experience—had been partially modified in the course of her therapy, but it still posed some questions as we approached the end of our work together.

Last Stage of Treatment

In the last stage of her therapy, Tamara continued exploring both her plans for the future, her relationship with her boyfriend, and people in general as well as the ending of our work together. For the first time ever, she had returned from the summer holiday feeling that she had been able to enjoy her newly acquired feminine charm with men. She had started to go out with a young man, to enjoy her sexuality, and also—although with great difficulty—to think seriously of giving up her clerical job and to work in a "caring profession." However, she soon contracted various ailments that placed her physical life at risk. The themes of self-destructiveness, lack of both proper care and thoughtfulness, acting-out, and so forth, were paramount and became linked with the prospect of ending treatment. This had been an almost unspeakable topic for Tamara. We understood that her liferisking actions were an unconscious suicidal attempt caused by guilt and self-punishment, at a time when her life was blossoming and therapy could soon come to an end. She could not face ending, it was better to act out her own death as this would have allowed her treatment to continue. Also, ending was clearly experienced by the patient as the death-by-murder of the therapist.

Tamara's choice—to work in the psychosocial field—was partly dictated by a genuine, caring interest, but mainly by the intellectual excitement and a filling-up function that knowledge performed for her. Also, the extreme anxiety, panic, persecution, and terror that she experienced, as the reality of ending therapy became imminent, were somehow acted out in this way. The feeling of reparation in her new psychosocial activities was not well established in Tamara, who still seemed to be driven by envy, rivalry, competition, triumph, superiority, and a sense of persecution vis-à-vis her therapist. In her unconscious, the deeply rooted feeling that there cannot be space for two— that is, Tamara and the therapist, herself and her younger sister in her mother's mind during Tamara's infancy, and herself and her dearest friend both having partners, and so forth—was still very real for Tamara.

One aspect of her work in therapy—and possibly one of its flaws—was her deep difficulty in giving her therapist a life of her own when they were not together. She could take away and think of the analytic ideas of the sessions and apply them to herself, life, friends, and work, but somehow the therapist ceased to exist once the session was over. This narcissistic trait had also been pointed out to her by one of her most skilled senior colleagues.

Ending therapy was an enormous task for Tamara, and we had to analyze at length the violence and destructiveness of her impulses, which were more easily recognized in the people she was working with rather than in herself. However, she was also aware of her determination to do things properly and to manage a good ending: this meant to be able to also feel sad and to share and talk with me about such feelings rather then splitting, rejecting, and projecting them at work.

Before one of the last therapy holidays, she came to a session ten minutes late because of a bus delay. She reported having run all the way from the bus stop and feeling the same panic as many years earlier if she was late for her session. I spoke of that unmodified bit of her that still experienced being late and missing a few minutes as a catastrophic loss, a fall into a black hole (Tustin 1972) and a total destruction of her therapy and life. She responded to this interpretation with silence and feeling persecuted, as she would later admit. In the past, she would have lashed out verbally and mercilessly at me.

In feeling persecuted by me, she was still perceiving me as a critical figure and not as someone who was trying to understand and help her. Then she admitted to feeling that I was sweeping away nine years of work together, all her efforts and good progress. She had projected into me that bit of herself— unmodified and rather entrenched—that destroyed everything and then felt destroyed, dropped into a black hole and annihilated when either a gap or lost minute of a session or separateness occurred.

Ending therapy was also linked in Tamara's associations with: (1) losing a precious, special and lifegiving link with the therapist; (2) sinking in minutes, just as the Swedish boat <u>Estonia</u> had on that same day, killing 825 people (by then Tamara had had about 895 sessions!); (3) her feeling that I was no longer willing to tolerate her psychological, destructive violence towards me and was no longer giving her subsidized therapy; (4) in a dream a pretty and elegant woman of Anglo-Spanish origin was also an excellent social worker and Tamara envied her so much that she had to break off contact (The direct transference translation to me could also hide her anxiety that I had stopped her treatment because I was so fed up with her often-verbalized envious attacks on me, and on our good work together); and (5) ending reminded her of when she first came to see me many years earlier: every end of session, week, and term was like "stepping into void, was like death, catastrophic."

Tamara was also able to feel more connected with a sense of loss and sadness, although this was still based on splitting and projection: She was left with the excruciating pain, loneliness, and memory of the therapy while I went off happily and thoughtless about her and her pain. This was the way she had acted when she canceled sessions for social commitments. All went well and no thoughts were spent for the therapy but only relief: "A therapy-free week," as she put it when she came back.

The analytic struggle continued till the very end, and the question of whether she was ready to finish therapy, to "leave the nest," as Tustin would say, loomed in my mind as I was aware of both her good progress and also her need for more work. Tustin wrote:

> Patients who have become addicted to the lunacy of an autistic way of life, even if it is only a part of their being, need a firm and resolute push at the right time to help them. . . . If we are able to help them in a compassionate way, we need to be well attuned to the griefs and terrors that have beset them and kept them "hide-bound" or "nest-bound," as Christopher Logue (1981) implies in the following poem:

> Come to the edge.
> We might fall.
> Come to the edge.
> It's too high.
> Come to the edge.
> And they came,
> And he pushed them,
> And they flew.

But this happy event only occurs after much preparatory work has been done by both analyst and patient, otherwise the patient is liable to fall again into the "black hole" of helplessness and despair. [1990, p. 213]

Will Tamara fly or fall? Only time will tell, when the "edge" of her analysis will no longer be under her feet but hopefully inside herself.

References

Logue, C. (1981). *Ode to the Dodo: Poems (1953–78)*. London: Jonathan Cape.
Tustin, F. (1972). *Autism and Childhood Psychosis*. London: Hogarth.
——— (1986). *Autistic Barriers in Neurotic Patients*. London: Karnac.
——— (1990). *The Protective Shell in Children and Adults*. London: Karnac.

17

The Absent Self

Francis M. J. Dale

Psychogenic autistic states are not to be associated with narcissism, because the autistic child has no sense of being a self, false or otherwise.

Frances Tustin

One of the most technically difficult as well as emotionally disturbing factors in work with autistic children is their damaged, distorted, or even absent "sense of self." In psychoanalytic therapy, this absent sense of self confronts the therapist with severe, and sometimes insurmountable, technical problems and therapeutic impasses. This is due to the subsequent absence of the most crucial element in the analytic relationship: the transference. With the autistic child, there either does not appear to be an awareness of other people—or "otherness"—or the child is incapable of forming the kind of relationship in which the transference can become the medium for symptomatic and therapeutic change.

In the following chapter, I would like to illustrate and discuss the process of a three year, twice-weekly therapy with a 3-and-a-half-year-old boy called "Jason," with particular reference to the development of a "self" and the modifications of analytical technique in the absence of the transference. However, before doing so it will be necessary to establish what we will be meaning when talking about "self."

Most commonly, when we talk about "self" we are referring to those uniquely individual characteristics by which we and others come to know and recognize ourselves. The *experience* of self is, however, more than an "image" or set of characteristics by way of which we know ourselves; it has something to do with the *feeling of being a "self,"* of having an "I"-ness, an *essence*, which is *more* than the sense of being different and unique from others. Part—and I would suspect, an essential part—of having a sense of self probably has to do with having a mind that can "think about differences," that can *know* about inside and outside, "I" and "thou." This of course poses another question: Where does self-consciousness, "mind," the capacity to "know," come from? In order to answer *this* question, we have to go back to a time in developmental history *before* the experience or the notion of being a self—an individual separate from others—was possible.

In her book *Autistic States in Children* (1981), Tustin defines autism as, "a body centered, sensation dominated state which constitutes the core of the self" (p. 3). She goes on to say that even when objects in the outside world *are* observed or interacted with, these are experienced as "being part of the body" (p. 3) and not separate from it. Mahler also stresses the importance of the infant's early sensory experience and sees it as forming the "crystallisation point of the feeling of self around which our sense of identity will become established" (Mahler 1968, p. 11).

Tustin believed that this sensation and bodily based state of self *preceded* the establishment of true object relations and that, in the period immediately after birth, the infant related to the world in terms of "his own body and its in-built dispositions" (Tustin 1981, p. 5), which "established his body as a basis for personal identity" (p. 5). However, early on, the infant's "body" is defined and experienced in terms of the mother/baby unit: what Mahler refers to as an "undifferentiated at-oneness" and Tustin a "flowing-over-at-oneness." The first *self* then, is both a combined or merged self, and a self that is defined by, and experienced as, *coterminous with the body*.

The part of the mother's body which is of most significance to the newborn baby, and in relation to which it has the most contact, is the breast. Any prolonged loss of contact with the breast can therefore have a detrimental impact on the development or the maintenance of a sense of self.

The primary cause of frustration in babies is *loss of contact with the breast*. Early on, this is not experienced by the baby as merely "loss of the breast" but more as the psychic equivalent to the loss of the *mother-baby-unit*. For the first few months of life, the mother—or more accurately the *mother as breast*—is not clearly differentiated from the self. All good experiences derive from an ongoing identification with the *self as breast*. Any disruption of this identity, or union with the "breast as self," can lead to the baby experiencing the breast—at this stage, emotionally and psychically equivalent to the mother as a *whole person*—as "not self."

In order to begin the long process of individuation—which involves an increasing capacity to deal with external reality or "not self" experiences—at some point, the baby *needs* to be able to differentiate between the illusion of the breast and self as one, and the self as being in relationship with the mother or breast *as a separate and autonomous person*. However, if this happens too early—before the baby's ego can cope with the knowledge of the mother's separateness—then the baby will feel overwhelmed by catastrophic, disintegrative states which cannot be thought about, processed, or experienced (Dale, 1996a). Autism is an attempt to manage these primitive, elemental states of catastrophic disintegration that result from premature "not self" experiences.

Jason

I first saw Jason—the little boy I am going to be talking about—from behind a one-way screen when he was being assessed by a child psychotherapist. Also present in the interview room were his mother, grandmother, and an educational psychologist. My first impression of Jason was of a boy who had no "connection" to his body, no sense of his or other peoples' physical/spatial boundaries. He moved around the room as though it were empty. If someone spoke to him or tried to get his attention, he would ignore them and behave as though they weren't there. There was a dreamlike quality about him which seemed to place him in another dimension where no contact with "reality" was possible (Dale 1996b).

He had been referred to a child guidance clinic because, at the age of 3 and a half, he was doubly incontinent, had never spoken or shown any sign of understanding language or any other kind of communication, and seemed to be "glued" to his grandmother—with whom he was living while his mother was working in America—to the extent that she could never go anywhere without him or leave a door in her house shut (as soon as he *lost sight of her*, he would become extremely agitated and distressed). The initial medical diagnosis was that he was either deaf, dumb, suffered from a congenital speech problem, or had congenital brain damage. The second diagnosis was autism— with which I concurred—and I agreed to take him on for intensive psychoanalytic treatment.

In the very first session, I had the impression that this child was not "there" in the room with me. He was present in body, but emotionally and mentally he was absent. It soon became clear that, in order to make contact with him, to "engage" him, I had to radically change the way in which I would normally interrelate with a child in therapy (Dale 1996c). I realized that there was no way in which I could understand or make contact with him, either by engaging with him through his play, or by means of verbal interpretation in the way in which it was possible with other children. Firstly, he did not "play." It was like watching a robot which was randomly programmed and which failed to respond to external impingements or perceptions in any meaningful way. I might as well have not been there—and he did not seem to be "there" either. Secondly, and perhaps following on from the foregoing, he was either deaf, or language, speech, "sounds" had no meaning or significance for him.

Being with someone you are supposed to be helping who fails to respond to you, who looks "through you" and who seems to be completely unaware of your existence, is a profoundly disturbing and unsettling experience. It can make you feel confused, frustrated, "empty," powerless, incapable of thinking, disoriented, and fragmented. Being with this psychotic little boy rendered me incapable of thinking. It was as if there was no "mind" there to think with, perhaps because there was no "object" (person) out there to be thought about. What I could do, though, was to observe. In stopping thinking about and trying to "understand" him (that is, trying to understand him from the point of view of my "world view"—Weltanschaung—and not his), a subtle but very significant change occurred in the way I began to relate to him (Dale 1996b).

I realized that the only way I could know him and communicate with him was to reach out to him with my attentiveness and to surrender (temporarily) my sense of having a separate identity. At times I had the unnerving experience of losing all sense of bodily awareness apart from my eyes just watching him (Dale, 1996c).

It became apparent that the process of "thinking" itself—in its logical deductive mode—was placing a barrier between us and any possibility of my understanding him. In the second session, I became completely absorbed in watching him, in following his every movement but without any attempt to understand or think about what was happening. This intense "watching" eventually brought about an altered sense of perception or reality—disembodiment—in which all I was aware of were my eyes, floating in space, watching him. There was no "body" attached to them, no separate self, no observing ego (Dale 1996b).

Following this session, I had to drive nearly fifteen miles across London to another appointment. That journey is lost to me forever. A part of me never made it. The first recollection I have following that second session is of coming back into my body and for several minutes not knowing who I was, where I was, how I got where I was, what I was supposed to be doing, or what this "thing" (that is, the car I was sitting in) was.

Fortunately, I was able to regain my composure and recover the use of my mind—which I had temporarily given up in order to connect with my patient—to think about what had happened. My understanding of what happened is as follows. In order to understand Jason I had to "give up" my separate identity and, psychically, "become him." In the process of identifying with someone as disturbed as Jason, one risks taking on board, in an undiluted, unprocessed way, the mental characteristics or emotional experiences of the person one is trying to understand or empathize with. It is important, therefore, when working with disturbed and, in particular, psychotic children, that we understand the nature of the primitive processes that may get activated in both therapist and child in the therapeutic interaction and those aspects of theory and clinical practice which are most helpful in understanding and managing the sometimes extremely stressful emotional and mental states evoked in the therapist (Dale 1996b).

It became apparent early on that Jason was in a confused or entangled relationship with his objects. Frequently, he was trying to "burrow" inside me or be covered up by me very much in the manner that Tustin describes in her book *Autistic States in Children* (1981) when she writes that: "They are preoccupied with burrowing inside other bodies and with seeming to put parts of themselves into other bodies" (Tustin 1981). I would like to illustrate this with some material from the third session.

Early on in that session, Jason had picked up a glass of water and put it to his lips, but instead of drinking it, the water dribbled out of his mouth down his front and onto the floor. I made a comment about him being a "leaky" baby who could not take in the food without it all spilling out. He rummaged inside a toy box and took out a rubber funnel with the spout end detached so that it looked very much like a breast with a hole where the nipple should be. Holding this close to his chest he began to rhythmically chant "Mum, mum, mum," followed by "Baba, baba, baba." He then picked up the glass, holding it out to me as if he wanted me to fill it with water. I did this and gave it to him. Holding the glass with one hand, he held his other hand up to my face and, this time, drank it on his own without spilling any. I sat down in a chair and Jason came up to me, pushed my legs aside so that he could come close to me, and climbed onto my lap. I said that he was like a baby who wanted to get right inside mummy. He then leaned very close and put his cheek next to mine. I said he wanted to be my baby. He then lay back across my lap gazing up at the ceiling. In the countertransference, I had the experience of holding a very small baby in my arms but one that was merged with and a part of me rather than having its own boundaries and individuality.

Following this, Jason climbed from me onto a window ledge where he sat looking out, pulling the lace curtains over his shoulders. It seemed to me that he had become an "inside baby looking out" and that he now had a sense of an internal space which was differentiated from an outside "not-self" space. I commented along these lines to him and, shortly afterwards, he seemed to accidentally brush against the glass, causing it to fall and break on the floor. While I was picking up the pieces of broken glass, Jason came up to me and slapped me on the face. I said that he was telling me off for being a "broken" mummy breast that could not hold him together and which felt to him to be in pieces and therefore no good to him.

The early sessions vividly portrayed Jason's dilemma as well as containing within them the main themes that were to be of central significance in the work that followed. In the above session, the loss of his mother appeared to be equated to a breast without a nipple. The funnel without a spout was experienced by him as a breast with a "hole," with no facilitating nipple to either help him gain access or to "hold him together" and help feel contained. The glass he could not at first drink out of represented the nippleless, leaky breast. In holding onto me with his hand, he provided himself with an "outside," a boundary or skin through which he could gain access to a breast which could feed and contain him. However, becoming aware of an outside also implied separateness and the trauma and loss associated with separateness or "not-self" experiences. Although it probably needed to be said, it did not help him when I commented about him being an inside baby who was aware of an outside, "not-self" space. For him, it was like a "slap in the face," a direct threat to his omnipotent phantasy that he was both merged with, and in control of, his object.

It also became clear that Jason was responding intelligently to what was being said to him and therefore understood words and what they connoted but that his understanding was both *limited* and *idiosyncratic*. He appeared to relate to objects—including myself—in terms of their shape and "feel" rather than in terms of their function or purpose. It was as if it were the *sensation* of objects that mattered and gave them meaning rather than their functional significance.

For the first four or five months of therapy, Jason did not appear to relate to me as someone who was truly physically or emotionally separate from him. In omnipotent phantasy, he treated me as an *extension* or *appendage* of himself which he only momentarily became aware of when he was frustrated or when he could not control me. If he wanted something, he would pull me over to it and then manipulate my arm or hand to turn the tap, or pick something up, or open the door to the room. I felt that he treated me very much like a puppet. I "belonged" to him, was a part of him, and therefore had no mind or will of my own. The only difference was that, in this case, puppet and puppet master were in the "same" body and shared the same boundary.

Much of what he did and how he related to me seemed to be *pre-symbolic* and concrete with little or no distinction between the subject or person and the thing or object with which it was equated. For example, for many months I had to struggle to stop him from eating the sand from the sand tray. He would typically do this at the beginning of a session or after a break in therapy. He would bury his hand under the surface and then watch as the sand trickled from between his clenched fingers as he held them close to his face (very much as the water had dribbled out of his mouth when he tried to drink from the glass). The smooth textured, flowing sand appeared to represent the *sensation* of a "boundary-less flowing into mummy experience," and the gritty *feel* of it, the unpleasant, oral *sensation* of the absent breast. Much later, when he had begun to feel more "held" by me and by the consistency and reliability of the therapeutic relationship, the "sand"—the "flowing away, shapeless mother"— was contained by the sand tray into which he would climb and curl into a fetal position.

Prior to this, however, I had to struggle with his insistence—even compulsion—to eat the sand. He devised cunning little strategies to prevent me from stopping him from eating it: He would push and pull me down to the floor, lead me over to the sink at the far side of the therapy room, or try to push me through the door and then run over to the sand tray to grab a handful and eat it. He would often "play" with the sand in what seemed like a teasing, provocative way—picking it up in his fist, holding it close to his face and giving me a knowing, artful look as if he were trying to lead me on: "Are you going to try to stop me? Am I about to eat it? What are you going to do?"

He also related to the funnel as a *sensory equivalent* of the breast which he could omnipotently get inside of and use as an extension of his mouth. He would put his face inside the funnel and put his tongue through from the inside so that the tip was poking through. Alternately, he would hold the funnel with one hand, stick his finger through with the other, and then suck or lick the tip of his finger as it poked through, treating his finger as if it were the nipple.

Although initially the sand, and other objects which he attempted to eat—like plasticine, soap, and even me—seemed to have equal significance for him (it was the shape and "feel" that mattered), gradually I gained the impression that his confusion with boundaries, between inside and outside and between "me" and "not-me," was diminishing. The beginning of a change in his conceptualization of boundaries and the capacity to perceive me as "other" or "not-self" emerged after about two months of therapy. The following are extracts from sessions seven to nine. Prior to the seventh session, he had experienced his first break in therapy, missing two sessions because of my taking a week's leave.

Seventh Session

Jason came into the room and immediately began pushing his hands into the sand and then tried to put handfuls into his mouth. I prevented him. He then started to pull me around the room, pulling me down onto the floor quite insistently. He then went out of the door, went along the corridor to another therapy room, and then down along the passageway to the toilet—pushing me away—clearly reluctant to go back to the therapy room. I said that he seemed to be wanting to explore all of mummy today (in other material, he related to the therapy room as "being inside mummy"). He did not want to go into the room ("mummy") he had been shut out of over the holidays. He then pulled me from the room, into the corridor, pushing me down to the floor, before going back into the room, where he again started running his fingers through the sand before attempting to eat it.

I again made a comment about him experiencing the sand as a kind of "flowing into mummy" which he could also make flow into him so that he could merge again with his "sand mummy" and have her inside (this seemed to me to be an indication of the lack of boundary he had between inside and outside, as if he experienced his body or self as amorphous with no shape or distinction between himself and "external" objects). He then came to me and sat on my lap and started to nuzzle up to me, laughing. He put his lips and face very close to mine, then he began to lick my cheek, my shirt, feeling my face and head with his hands. Then he pulled me up, leading me around the room, laughing—pushing me away from him—before coming back to me and doing the same again.

At the end of the above session, Jason was very reluctant to leave the room, holding on to the door jamb, trying to bite me, and struggling and kicking so much that I had to carry him bodily out of the clinic. At the time, I thought the break in therapy had severely dented his omnipotent phantasy that he was merged with and in control of me. Being inside the therapy room was experienced by him as literally *"being inside the mother."* Forcibly removing him from the room was the equivalent of *tearing him apart,* of stripping him of a *piece of his identity.*

Eighth Session

Jason continually tried to eat the sand today, constantly pushing me away when I tried to stop him. He also spent much of the session pulling and pushing at me to make me lie down on the floor in order to keep me away from the sand tray. He rummaged in the toy box several times, picking up the funnel and poking his finger through the hole. I said that he was wanting to fill the hole in the empty breast and to feed and fill himself. He came to me, pulled me to squat down on the floor, and then kissed me on the cheeks and on my mouth. He then went to the sink, picked up the soap, and put it in his mouth. I commented that he seemed to want to eat me, to take me inside like the soap. He laughed, went to the sand tray, and tried to eat the sand, and I again commented about him "wanting to have mummy inside, a kind of 'flowing' mummy he could take right inside." It is perhaps worth pointing out that he went from licking and "eating" me—with quite gentle bites on my cheek—to eating the soap and sand and making clear the link between the sand, soap, and myself as symbolic equivalents.

In the above session, there seems to be a confusion between "eating" me (licking and biting my cheeks) and eating the soap and sand, which *can* be taken inside in a concrete way. It is as if the "hunger" aroused by his wanting to "take me inside" and merge with me *cannot be symbolized*; it has to be *concrete.*

Ninth Session

He went straight to the sand tray, where he picked some sand up in his hand and stood there watching me. He brought his hand close to his mouth with sand in it, but instead of eating it, he let the sand trickle through his fingers into the tray. This was the first time he did not eat the sand when he did this. He then came very close to me and looked up at me very much as if he was saying "Hello." This was followed by Jason seeming to repeatedly test out my reaction to him by pretending to eat the sand. I had the impression that he *wanted* me to provide a firm, consistent boundary which he could come up against. He appeared to find my "No's" comforting and reassuring and, in some way, the equivalent of a nurturing, containing feed. At one point, he dipped the soap in the sand and put it into his mouth and then came back to me, touching my cheek with his lips then holding his head against mine. He then touched my lips with his, looking into my eyes closely all the time. Following this, he pulled me after him around the room. The feeling I had at the time was of my being very much attached to him as some sort of append- age. As he did this, he was humming "Mum, mum, mum."

Eventually, his capacity to "abstain" from eating the sand broke down and I had to lift the tray and put it onto the top of a cupboard out of his reach. When I did this, he looked up at me very intensely. Then he pulled me down to a crouching position and looked very closely into my eyes. He then kissed me on the mouth and cheeks by bouncing his lips off my face. I said that he was very much like a baby wanting to eat me up to get right inside me. I felt that this was both an acknowledgment of a link between the sand and me—in which there was both similarity and difference—and an acknowledgment of the boundary which I had provided between "me" and "not-me"—the "not- me" being the sand. I also thought that he experienced my putting the sand away as my confronting his wish to omnipotently substitute me as an object, which he could *not* take inside and which *does* have boundaries, with the "flowing sand mummy," which he could get inside and be enveloped by. In other words, I think he had come to the "real" object, the real mummy—me in the transference—as opposed to the sand or the not-real mummy.

I have quoted extensively from the above sessions because I think they show the beginning stages of Jason being able to replace a symbolic equation with the object as symbol. In the following months, although he seemed to want to be close—even "inside" of me at times—he became increasingly ambivalent, frequently refusing to come into the room unless his grand- mother came too. The room seemed to be associated with both positive experiences—being "inside" and a part of mummy—but, at the same time, because he was more aware of me as a separate person, he was also more in touch with loss and the pain of separation. At these times, the *therapy room itself* became identified with the empty breast—a black hole, a bottomless void—and the horrible, unbearable feelings associated with the loss of his mother. This became clear in a session where he just could not bear to stay in the room: moaning, crying, trying to get out of the door, and appearing completely inconsolable. I remember feeling at a loss, not really understanding why he was in such despair and not knowing what to do to help him in his distress. Just as I was thinking this, he came up to me and put his hand on my leg and it felt very much as if he was trying to reassure me by saying, "You're alright but I just can't be in the room today."

Eventually, I had to take him back to the waiting room, where he calmed down but still seemed disturbed and anchor-less, wandering around the clinic as if searching for something or someone. At one point, his grandmother asked, "What's happening with him today?" At that point Jason came up to me and touched my cheek with his cheek and then pressed his lips against my cheek before climbing up onto my lap, putting his arms around me and holding himself close to me. He then began bouncing his lips off my cheeks and face. His grandmother then clarified what was happening by saying, "He wants you but doesn't want to be in the room with you." I remember feeling incredibly sad and moved by this and, as before, sensed that *he* was reassuring me: "It's alright Mr. Dale, I know how hard it must be to understand me, to know how I feel."

I became aware—particularly through my supervision with Frances Tustin—that I had got into talking about "insides," about three-dimensionality, too soon, certainly before Jason was ready for it. While he was still living mainly in a two-dimensional world where he was more in contact with *surfaces* and the *shape* and *feel* of things, it would have been more appropriate to talk about his needing to be "covered up," stuck or merged with me rather than wanting to get inside me. Interpretations which implied he was *not* a part of me, or that he was not in control of me—as an appendage or extension—filled him with panic and despair. They also frustrated him because he could not bear the idea of things having to "come through space to him." He needed immediate gratification—no delay—very much like a small baby at the breast.

As he began to become more three-dimensional—more aware of boundaries and less merged with his objects—he reacted with increasing frustration to anything that blocked his access to being inside and in control of me, be it his grandmother or anything else which he had used previously to sensually and physically envelop him. He experienced his grandmother's and my "No's" as hard objects, which were equated with a hard, shutting-out breast. In one session, he tore a button off of his grandmother's dress as though he were attempting to "tear his way inside" her breasts. In another, he climbed onto her lap and started pushing and knocking at her breasts with his head as if he were trying to knock or butt his way inside her. When his grandmother eventually said "no" and pushed him away from her, he picked up a sharp-edged paperweight and crashed it down on the top of a cupboard so hard that he dented the surface. Not only was he showing his frustration and anger at the *shutting out hardness of her*, but he was also showing his realization that he could no longer control her or be merged with her through omnipotent phantasy.

On the other hand, as he became less two-dimensional—less "stuck to" or merged with his objects—he *needed* my firmness and that of his grandmother in order to locate himself in space "outside of his object" so that he could be *in relationship* to it. He also needed to connect to a hardness that "held him" rather than rejected him; this helped him discover an "internal space" where an interactive rather than a merged contact could be made and which would not leave him confronted with an internal vacuum, black hole, or nothingness. The loss of his mother seemed to be experienced by Jason as both a physical hurt or wound to his mouth as well as the loss of a protective skin or membrane *inside of which* he could feel "held together," integrated (at a sensory level) and at-one with his object.

The primitive level at which Jason seemed to function suggests that there is a phase of development which *precedes* true object relating which, if it is not properly negotiated and worked through, prevents *object relating proper* from developing. The evidence for this comes from various sources, in particular from the way Jason used hard and soft objects, the significance of various shapes and textures, and the function of the skin or surrounding membrane as a psychic "container." Hard objects seemed to be used in various ways by Jason and were experienced differently according to their function. Frequently, they were employed to ward off the painfully exposed rawness that resulted from the realization of loss. Loss was not experienced by him as losing some*one*, but more as having some*thing*, a *part of him*, his psychic "membrane" torn away. I would like to illustrate this with some material from the forty-eighth session shortly after Jason's mother—who had been visiting this country—returned to America.

Immediately following his grandmother leaving the therapy room, Jason picked up his plastic spade and began mouthing it, saying the word "mommy" repeatedly. He held out his arms for me to lift him up, but when I did, he began to scratch my face. When I looked at him, he became very upset, began to cry, and scratched at my face and neck so aggressively that I had to put him down. Here, I felt that the loss of his grandmother was experienced as him losing a part of himself, like a protective membrane or skin. This sudden rawness reminded him of the unbearable sensations and feelings associated with the loss of his mother, which are experienced at a very primitive level as the loss of the nipple/mouth contact. This is the "black hole," the "nothing" space left by the absent breast which he tries to "plug" or fill with the hard sensation of the spade in his mouth. The hardness is the equivalent sensation to the hardness of the nipple, which acts as a "bridge" or connecting link between the mouth/skin/breast shape.

What he wanted from me was the *sensation shape* which would *feel* like being enveloped and held by the breast/mouth connection. When he scratched my face, he was showing his unbearable frustration at finding the "wrong" face. My "shape" was right but my face was not. He became very upset, wandering aimlessly around the room with a forlorn expression on his face. Clearly, when he felt the loss of his mother so acutely, he could no longer hallucinate me into the right shape or appearance. Only his mother or grandmother would do.

When I put him down, he scooped up some sand and, putting it into a plastic jelly mold, pressed it into his chin. He again became very distressed, walking in circles around the room with tears streaming down his face. He then climbed onto the windowsill, where he sat looking out of the window repetitively saying "baby, baby." I felt that he was painfully in touch with the loss of his mother and, in looking out of the window, was saying something like, "She isn't here, where has she gone?"

Other material in this session suggested that his autistic objects were no longer working to protect him from the psychic pain of loss, and neither could he "wipe away" the loss by scratching out my "not mumminess" and merging with me or becoming enveloped by me. Several times he wanted to be picked up, only to begin tearing and scratching at my face and neck and the front of my shirt as though he wanted to rip and tear his way inside. When I interpreted to him that he couldn't bear being outside of or apart from me, he became very depressed, crying, running around in a distracted manner, and repeating over and over again "baby, baby."

At one point, I used a towel to wipe his eyes and runny nose, which seemed to calm and comfort him. He then took hold of my hand to guide the towel gently over his lips and cheeks. Whereas hard objects seemed to block out the absent object or plug the gap left by it, the towel seemed to act more as a transitional object which provided him with the sensation of the soft maternal breast which he could then merge into or become a part of.

Jason clearly felt comforted by the towel in a way in which he wasn't comforted by the hard objects which he normally used to hold himself together. He threw the jelly mold and some wooden bricks—which he used to tap his lips with—across the room. This made me think that he was rejecting them because they were not working any more. The specific function of the hard object which had failed him was their ability to provide a barrier or wall which protected him from being overwhelmed with the sadness and loss of the soft, enveloping, maternal experience. They were like hard pieces of carapace which protected him from becoming a collapsing jelly with no internal structure, nothing to hold him together.

This leads us to another function of hard objects. Rather than blocking, plugging, or shutting out emptiness, loss, falling apartness, they act to *facilitate* and mediate contact with the *sensation* object. The nipple is one such object. Its firmness acts as both a bridge and a *regulator*, connecting mouth to breast. However, as long as Jason denied or was unaware of the separate existence of the object, this kind of hardness—rather than being facilitating—was felt to be a frustrating impediment to the "flowing over at-oneness," the enveloping maternal softness of the breast.

As mentioned earlier, Jason needed both my hardness—when he experienced my resisting his attempts to control me—*and* my softness. Although he would sometimes fight against my firmness—sometimes for the whole of a session—he invariably showed a kind of recognition, relief, and sometimes even gratitude when I refused to give in to him and held my ground.

I think that somewhere he "knew" or sensed that without my "hardness" in opposing his omnipotent desire to be in control of and merged with me, that no differentiation, no recognition of self and "other" could begin. While he was in a merged or fused relationship with me, and especially his grandmother, he could not be sad, experience loss, or mourn his mother. As long as he was merged—*the same as*—his object, he could not become aware of loss or develop those psychic/cognitive structures to allow him to become aware of separation/loss, to be able to *think about it* or to do something to ameliorate the loss.

This suggests that "mindfulness"—the capacity to think, to be able to differentiate between self and other—can only develop when the autistic object begins to be given up. The loss of the object "as a part of the self" (the confusional autistic defense), left Jason exposed and vulnerable in a way he had never been before. In the process of therapy, he became *attached* to the maternal object rather than being "the same as" his object. Consequently, he began to experience loss as an unbearable tearing or ripping away of a *part of himself*—like a vital organ or function—at the same time as he had lost his omnipotent defenses against it. On the other hand, he was finding his objects as *real* sources of comfort which he could seek out and *relate to*. This can be

temporary, fractional

seen in the following extracts from around the end of his second year in therapy.

Extracts From Second Year of Therapy

Jason began the session by behaving in a teasing, provocative manner: pretending to eat the sand by putting it close to his lips and watching my reaction, tapping his spade against his lips, and smiling in a forced way as though he were saying: "I've got the flowing sand mummy and my spade breast, I don't need you." However, this challenging mood changed and he began moving towards me then away, each time coming closer until he lay across my lap. I immediately felt drowsy and lethargic and I experienced myself as a mother holding a very small baby. He then began very gently squeezing the tip of my index finger while making contented baby noises before putting my index finger between his lips and the inside of his mouth to rest against his teeth. It felt as though he was using my index finger as a nipple, which he was using to heal the hurt of the mother who had gone away.

He then began playing with my eyelids, opening and closing them, pressing his fingers hard against my eyes. I told him that he was not wanting to see me looking at him because then he would experience me as being outside of him and separate from him. Throughout this session it seemed that Jason was exploring with me whether or not it was safe to allow himself to become a baby—*relating* to a "mother"—and give up his autistic defenses. There were long silences in which there was a very close bond between us. The word which comes closer to describing it is "communion." There was no need to talk or interpret as it seemed that talking would sever the link being built between us.

In the following session, he again lay very close to me, repeatedly pressing on my eyeballs with his fingers, squeezing my fingers, and attempting to pull open my shirt. Holding the towel to his face, he came and lay on my lap and, taking hold of my hand, brought it up to his mouth. He placed my index finger inside his mouth to rest on his gums. With my other hand, he cupped his cheek. My eyes seemed to be associated with some breast gestalt of eyes/nipple/face where the eyes, like the nipple, made him feel held together and attached to his object. I felt that he was feeling that I "hold" him inside with my eyes just as the nipple holds him to the breast. Poking my eyes seemed to be about wanting to press his way inside or be enveloped by that part of me that "sees" him and connects him to me. He wanted to be merged with that part of me that holds him in my mind and makes him feel part of me.

At this point in his therapy, Jason was properly in the infantile transference. Feeling more "held together," he could now more safely have an inside without the fear of becoming "detached" from his object. Having an "inside" also meant he could have memories, thoughts, and imagination because now there was an 'inside space' to store them. He now had the beginning of a "psychic" skin which could contain experiences, thoughts, and thinking—and not just physically through autistic shapes and hard surfaces.

Discussion

I would now like to return to a consideration of the technical, theoretical, and therapeutic issues with which work with children such as Jason present us. The technical difficulty which poses the most serious obstacle to undertaking analytic psychotherapy is the absence of the transference relationship. In the early sessions with Jason, I did not exist as a separate person. In fact, initially, I felt as though I did not exist at all. Added to this factor, was the impression Jason gave of "not being there" in the room or of *residing in his body*.

The first technical issue therefore was to find a way of making an *impression*, creating an *impact*, of getting him to notice that there was someone else there in the room with him. Normally, of course, one would interpret, talk to, or interact with a child through their play. However, to begin with, none of these avenues of communication was possible. The only solution—which came more from desperation than established technique—was to *let go* and give up to the experience of being in a mindless, egoless state of "not knowing." Perhaps the closest description of this state in a nonpathological relationship is Bion's (1962) concept of maternal reverie, which describes the mental and emotional attitude in which the mother of a new born baby is maximally receptive to her baby's communications.

Perhaps newborn babies communicate in a similar way to the autistic child who is confused or entangled with his object. In discussing the way in which Jason related to his objects, Tustin suggested that the word "communion" was more appropriate than the word communicate. For a child or baby who, in unconscious phantasy, is merged with his object, there is no "communication" as such. One can only communicate with someone who is perceived as separate. One can, though, be "in communion" in a fluid, flowing way with the breast or skin of the mother *as though it were part of the self* which is what is implied by the terms "flowing-over-at-oneness" and "undifferentiated-at-oneness." Both suggest that the most primitive form of "communication" is

through communion. Once contact through communion has been established, then other forms of *communication* become possible.

However, as Rosenfeld (1988) has pointed out, when working with psychotic patients the way in which language is used and interpretations formulated needs to be specially adapted and modified in order to interact with and
catch hold of the patient's uniquely subjective experience. The following
comments, taken from some work of mine with a boy with psychotic features,
expands on this further.

In the psychotic, inner and outer space, self and not-self, are in a constant
flux so that the boundaries which normally limit the degree to which we can
get contaminated by other people's distress lose their effectiveness. Psychotics
have a unique facility for getting under our skin. Unfortunately, we all too
often use the one tool which can get through to the psychotic patient as an
instrument of defense. I am of course referring to language and its method of
employment in the interpretative technique. I feel that as therapists we often
fall into the trap of protecting ourselves with our talking and use of conceptual
frameworks from the full emotional content of what our patients are experiencing.

With the psychotic experience, which is so much more invasive and overwhelming (i.e., when *compared with working with a neurotic patient*), the
holding or containing provided by the therapist's "verbal understanding" just
isn't enough. The therapist has, first and foremost, to have the capacity—in
the countertransference—to take on board feelings which the patient would
experience as unbearable and uncontainable and to be able to "get this across"
to him.

Thinking can therefore come to act as a barrier which both protects and
prevents the therapist from being confronted with the naked reality of very
primitive feelings which haven't been filtered or transmuted by words. It is
one thing to verbalize the psychotic experience—we enter into quite another
dimension of reality when we have that experience for ourselves. In a sense,
one has to become *mindless* in order to become *mindful*. However, as Farber
(1966) has pointed out, the risk to the therapist of entering into the psychotic
experience is that of losing himself and not being able to find his way back.

This raises the question of what you "hold on with" when you "let go." It
isn't simply the verbal interpretative mode of thinking or our conceptual
framework because these have to be given up—or at least partially surren-
dered—in order to get there. I must admit that I don't know the answer.
However, my own experience suggests that when we do "let go," we don't
become completely mindless: There remains an area where we are still

thinking, but it is closer to an experiential or holistic thinking rather than logical deductive thinking (Dale 1984).

If it is correct that, *in the first instance*, thinking—in the logical deductive mode—is a barrier to understanding the experience of the psychotic, and perhaps particularly the autistic child, then this suggests that a fundamental shift in the therapist's attitude must be from adopting an active, problem-solving style of thinking to a more receptive, almost passive attitude where "being with the patient" and making oneself emotionally available is the preferred stance.

In concluding, I would like to look at the concept of self or "I"–ness as it develops in the autistic child. It would seem axiomatic that a sense of self cannot develop until there is a sense of ownership of one's body and an awareness of the boundaries between "me" and "not me." Until an awareness of one's body boundaries has become established, awareness of the "other," of "not self" experiences, is not possible. The question we need to address ourselves to is the "how" and the "why" of individuation—of the processes underlying and facilitating the development of a self.

In part, this will be determined by physiological and maturational considerations. At birth, not all of the peripheral nerves are myelinated, and the frontal cortex—the part of the brain associated with self-conscious awareness, forward planning, and abstract thought—is also not yet fully functioning. But the experience and the development of self is also dependent on the early establishment of a satisfactory attachment between mother and baby. It is the nature of this attachment and the failure of it at certain crucial points in development that I believe predisposes some vulnerable children to fail to move on from the normal autistic phase to develop an "I" which can relate to an "other."

Some comments made by a patient of Tustin's in her paper "The Development of 'I-ness'" (1994) provide the basis of an answer concerning those specific aspects of the mother/baby relationship that are crucial in fostering a sense of "I-ness." She reported her patient's early experience as "fluid-like," as "falling out of control . . . into boundless space, into nothingness" (p. 217), which felt to her as though she were "losing herself." One of her greatest anxieties was of not being remembered or held in her therapist's mind. Tustin writes, "Forgetting was the feeling of everything being spilled out of her and out of me. She experienced this as losing her sense of existence—of feeling 'gone'" (p. 218). As she felt more "held" and understood by her therapist, she became able to use a transitional object—a teddy bear—to help her feel "held together and attached to something" (p. 220). Implicit in this attachment is the development of an "awareness of solid objects as separate from the body" (p. 220), and this must be an essential prerequisite to moving from "'felt-self' to 'transitional' states" (p. 221).

It is here that Bion's notion of the function of the mother as a *transformer* of unknowable, unexperienceable, chaotic experiences—"alpha function"—is crucial in understanding how a sense of self develops. If the baby, like the patient outlined above, fails to find a "maternal skin" or "membrane" sufficient to protect it from the trauma of not-self experiences, then a *sensation self*, sufficient to meet the world with, will fail to develop. When a sensation self has not been adequately defined by physical, emotional, and mental contact with the mother, the sense of having a boundary which can contain an inside will result in the baby or patient experiencing themselves very much like a jelly or fluid which has no shape, form, or concrete substance—nothing around which a self can cohere.

As Jason began to relate to me as someone who could help hold him together with interpretations or "outer" functioning (that is, interactions with me which confronted him with an external or shared reality), he was then able to begin to relate to external objects less exclusively in terms of omnipotent hallucinatory wishes. At this juncture, the sensation qualities of objects and their psychic significance changed. The shape and texture of objects moved from being predominantly soft, flowing, fluidlike and without boundaries— such as the silky sand or his grandmother's breasts—to objects which have, inherent in their shape or texture, the idea or possibility of having an internal space—such as the jelly molds, the funnel, the saucer with the hole in the middle, and perhaps, latterly, my eyes—which could "see" him and hold an image of him inside.

The importance of the sand was that it provided Jason with the sensation that he had a skin, that he wasn't just a fluid "falling and falling out of control into a bottomless abyss, into boundless space" as described by Tustin's patient (1986, p. 217). Perhaps the confusional autistic child shares a dilemma similar to the "Invisible Man": Unless he is "stuck onto" something solid, something visible, he cannot be certain that he exists; and he cannot differentiate himself from his background, from other objects. The bandages which give him shape and texture are the "skin" that provides him with an inside, which is differentiated from an outside. Without the bandages or the containing skin of the mother or therapist, there is no "framework" around which a self, an identity, can cohere. This can only happen when a boundary to the self—initially a "body-self"—is established and confirmed in therapy in such a way that the feeling that something can be "taken in" and *held onto* is stronger than the experience and annihilatory anxiety that everything is always leaking and spilling away or falling apart.

Thus *before the transference can develop*, the therapist has to become a "container"—both physically and mentally—in order to provide the child with the experience of having an outside skin which "holds him together." For Jason, particularly in the early days and months of therapy, the "holding" had to be a *concrete* experience, *not* a phantasy; and it was probably more in the nature of an hallucination. He and I were a *merged identity* and it was only in minute incremental steps that he could gradually tolerate the fact that I was separate from him and not under his omnipotent control. Once he could *relate* to me rather than *be* me, it became possible for him to allow me to act as a "transitional" object, that is, an "object which the subject treats as being half-way between himself and another person" (Rycroft 1972). According to Winnicott (1980), the transitional object is the first "not-me" possession but, "the point of it is not its symbolic value so much as its actuality. Its *not being the breast* . . . is as important as the fact that it stands for the breast or mother" (p. 6) (my italics). For the infant, the important point about the transitional object is its "actuality." I suppose one might call it a *concrete symbol* in that, although it represents and stands for some quality or characteristic of an object or relationship, it has to be *more* than a mental representation; it *has* to be touched, seen and *interacted with*. To quote Winnicott again, "The transitional object is *not an internal object* (which is a mental concept). It is a *possession*. Yet it is not (for the infant) an external object either" (my italics) (Winnicott 1980, p. 11).

Working with these very primitive processes in the autistic child pushes us to the outer edge of our *own* sense of "I-ness" and leaves us with very little to hang on to in terms of shared realities, cognitive frameworks, and reality testing. However, it would seem that letting go these certainties, these mental safety nets—albeit temporarily—is a *prerequisite* for making contact with the autistic child. This is, after all, no less than a mother does for her baby. There can be no concept of individual self for the baby. In fact, there can be no concept at all. For a concept to be possible, there has to be conceptualization, and conceptualization requires self-consciousness and the capacity to think. Babies do not "think." They "sensate"; they feel; they "are" their experience. As with the confusional or entangled child, the experience of self for the baby has form and shape but little sense of a personal boundary that differentiates between self and "not-self." In the interplay with the mother, experiences, feelings, and sensations achieve an integration in a *mental sphere* or space which initially resides wholly within the mind of the mother. It is the capacity of the therapist to be capable of moving with relative ease between being mind*ful* and mind*less*—while being available in a very sensual and concrete way for the confusional child—that makes it possible for a more genuinely interactive process to begin to emerge. This is certainly how Tustin seemed to work. When I presented material from Jason's sessions, she seemed to listen as much with her body as with her mind. Frequently she would say, "Yes. That *feels* right," or she would disagree, as though she were tasting food and something was missing from the ingredients. First and foremost, she knew that to understand the autistic child, you have to get "inside his skin" and, in the process, allow him to get inside your own.

References

Bion, W. R. (1962). *Learning from Experience*. London: Heinemann.

Dale, F. M. J. (1984). The re-unification of Sundip: the bringing together of split-off parts of the personality in a boy with psychotic features. *Journal of Child Psychotherapy* 10(2):221–234.

———— (1996a). Troubles of aggressiveness. In *Troubles of Children and Adolescents*. London: Jessica Kingsley Publishers.

———— (1996b). Stresses in child psychotherapists. In *Stress in Psychotherapists*. London: Routledge and Kegan Paul.

———— (1996c). Troubles of Withdrawal. In *Troubles of Children and Adolescents*. London: Jessica Kingsley Publishers.

Farber, L. H. (1966). *The Ways of the Will*. New York: Basic Books.

Mahler, M. (1968). *On Human Symbiosis and the Vicissitudes of Individuation*. New York: International Universities Press.

Rycroft, C. (1972). *A Critical Dictionary of Psychoanalysis*. London: Penguin Books.

Rosenfeld, H. (1988). *Impasse and Interpretation*. London and New York: New Library of Psychoanalysis.

Tustin, F. (1981). *Autistic States in Children*. London: Routledge and Kegan Paul.

———— (1986). The Development of "I-ness." In *Autistic Barriers in Neurotic Patients*, pp. 215–236. London: Karnac Books.

Winnicott, D. W. (1980). *Playing and Reality*. London & New York: Penguin Books.

18

Expressions of Annihilation Anxiety and the Birth of the Subject[1]

Bianca Lechevalier

As patients emerge from autism, they show very clearly that they feel on the brink of "falling" or of being "dropped". . . . Quite literally and physically, they feel "let down" . . . on the edge of a chasm which opens before them.

Frances Tustin, "Falling"

"Why do I come to you?" 6-year-old Martine asked me as she lay on the floor sobbing. She had been in psychotherapy since she was 3-months old. Interrupting my attempts at an inadequate explanation, she added, "I will tell you why. I fall, I fall, I fall, I die, I die, I'm afraid to die." She continued to sob in front of her distraught mother. For my part, I shared the mother's feeling, and yet I also felt grateful on two accounts: to Martine for her capacity to tell me, with her own true words, her existential drama, and to Frances Tustin, who had helped me to approach the unthinkable anguishes of autistic children. I reminded myself that Tustin—with her experience and intuition of the most profound annihilation anxieties—knew how to express and to illustrate those anxieties in the very terms of those autistic children who emerge as subjects in the world, and with the emotional authenticity carried by the poetry of words.

---

1. Translated into English, from the original French, by Theodore Mitrani, Ph.D.

In this paper, I would like to examine the moment at which—becoming aware of his mortality—the subject enters an individualized bodily existence outside the omnipotent maternal fusion. According to Tustin (1990), the experience of the loss of the ecstasy of the "symbolon" provokes enraged despair, and the non-sense of the "diabolon" constitutes a shared experience with the analyst. The analyst's work in this very painful experience and the resultant "metabolon" have an essential role, which nevertheless allows for room for the mystery of the emerging process of the development of symbolic thought within the pain of de-fusion, loss, and mortality. Psychoanalytic understanding of autistic enclaves in adults—which at times become subject to overt somatization linked to the erotization of split-off and quasi-amputated body parts that are inaccessible to thinking—confronts us with the same problem.

The possibility of putting annihilation anxieties into words seems to me either to proceed or to accompany the awareness of mortality in a subject in agony at not being able to become. It is only then that such a subject can say, "I could die, I exist and I can become" and then integrate itself over time. This is particularly true when there are transgenerational pseudoidentifications with the dead, who are treated as if still alive. I wonder if, in certain cases of descendants of holocaust survivors, we could consider the existence of autistic enclaves which allow for the illusion of survival outside time and space of those unburied dead.

Martine, a Story of Grief

Martine was referred to me following a TV broadcast after which she was diagnosed as autistic by her mother at 3 and-a-half months of age. The fourth child of a business family, she was born one month premature following a planned and desired pregnancy. Prior to that pregnancy, a spontaneous abortion of another pregnancy in the eighth month due to placenta previa had triggered mother's depression. In the third month of Martine's gestation, the paternal grandmother died due to a violent pulmonary aneurysm.

During the first psychotherapy sessions with mother and infant, Mrs. J told me about a nightmare she had shortly after the death of her mother-in-law and which was accompanied by a pain in her left side. "I had a feeling that my mother-in-law was coming to look for me, and I was afraid she'd go away and die."

Martine's birth was uneventful. Her development up to her second month was apparently normal. She took to the breast, purring while sucking, and looked at mother, but she was very slow. The progressive weaning was experienced by mother as a very painful loss of a fusional bliss. Mother needed to brusquely return to her work as a businesswoman. Subsequently, she would leave Martine in the care of an employee. While telling me about this period, mother became aware that Martine's troubles emerged after the first time she was given the bottle, perhaps responding to a depressive episode about which she had not thought before.

At that time, Martine lost her "gaze," which became empty. She would actively turn both her head and eyes away when mother wanted to take her in her arms. There was some concern about torticollis as well as strabismus of an organic origin. Martine sucked on her bottle with fingers and arms stiffened, and she did not return her mother's gaze, which triggered despair in the latter. She no longer purred and she ceased looking about, keeping an empty gaze fixed on her own stereotypical finger movements. In the evening she would go through a crisis of anguish, bellowing and howling inconsolably at the slightest noise.

When I met Martine at the age of 4 months, she actively turned her head and gaze away and threw herself vigorously backwards. She was unable to anchor her gaze and her facial expression was pale and sad, her eyes ashen and empty. However, while I talked to her mother, it seemed to me that Martine turned her head a little bit, apparently listening. I wondered if some contact could be established between her and me by voice. I was concerned about the organization of autism in this baby. I suggested a conjoined twice-weekly psychotherapy of mother and baby. Martine's father was very cooperative.

During the second session, Martine seemed to be quite attentive to my voice. In the third session—having already approached mother's depression, her guilt feelings, and her prohibited desire to take care of her daughter by herself—we discussed the possibility of part-time work. Mother's voice changed in its nature and tonality, and Martine turned her head towards her in a listening attitude. She seemed to direct her gaze at her mother, and I remarked that she made sucking movements with her lips and tongue. We took note that Martine had moved from mono-sensuousness to poly-sensuousness, and toward a possible reinvestment of her buccal erotism in this poly-sensuousness, at the very same time as she rediscovered a relational exchange with her mother. However, the baby's depression persisted throughout many months, along with periods of regression, sleep difficulties, and separation anxieties of great magnitude.

When Martine was 10-months old, her parents expressed concern over this setback. She had lost whatever she had acquired and would isolate herself for long periods, lying down on the carpet and looking at small threads. No one seemed able to turn her away from her autistic retreat or withdrawal. During such moments of isolation, Martine would engage in the same stereotypical finger movements as she had in earlier months. We found that this setback corresponded with father's depression connected with his suffering from sciatica and the need for surgery. Afterward, when I was exploring the room, carrying Martine in my arms, we stopped in front of the mirror, and Martine recognized herself and smiled as her mother joined us from the side.

A month later, during an analytic session with an adult patient who was fearfully approaching childbirth, I was confronted with themes related to unburied Hindu sacred cows that appeared in one of this woman's dreams, evoking annihilation anguish and "vampire identification."[2] This patient's anxieties seem to be connected with a vampire identification with her grandmother, who died after the war subsequent to Nazi persecution. I fell asleep during that session and woke up abruptly, surprised by a dream in which I saw myself as a baby with a smiling face. I wondered about the process that led me to this narcissistic image.

I then recalled, in my associations, Martine and her jubilant mood when I was holding her in front of the mirror with her mother, whom she recognized, standing by us. I also recalled a snapshot of myself in the arms of my grandmother looking in a mirror. It seemed to be a double representation of a joyous baby and a supporting grandmother monopolized by a narcissistic identification as a defense against annihilation anxieties. I wondered how this grandmotherly countertransference would unfold in the process of recognition and differentiation and what would be the fate of the paternal transference.

At the age of 18 months, Martine began to walk. However, she frequently fell down. She walked in a precipitated way, as if space and objects did not exist. She staggered as if drunk or seriously dizzy. I was reminded of the whirlwind states described by Houzel (1995). She stumbled and, while yelling, she caved in to an interminable fall in which she could hold onto nothing and was not able to get up without mother's help. The latter, terrified, launched an accusatory look at me for having subjected Martine to this adventure in space and to the risk of a mortal fall. It would be only towards the

---

2. A term used by Wilgowicz (1991) in a paper she presented on the descendants of the holocaust survivors.

age of five years that Martine would acquire a stable walk. Throughout these sessions, she would climb up on a table or a piece of furniture and then jump off onto the sofa, facing the gap of separation with the help of my arms.

Both parents became concerned for a long time about Martine's falls. They initiated a line of medical tests in order not to overlook the possibility of a malignant tumor, as this became a leitmotiv. At the same time, her father had pericardial ailments and severe coronary infarct was diagnosed. "They have discovered it in time," the parents said. I would remind them of their feelings of guilt over not having proceeded with the necessary tests for their mother, who died brutally. Wasn't *she* always present in their fears and concerns for Martine? Father said: "It is because of her, Martine, that I became sick. I was very afraid for her sake. She demanded too much from me." Subsequently, he managed, for the very first time, to express his pain with regard to the loss of his own mother and his mental state improved.

After Martine acquired the capacity to walk, our greatest concern focused on the arrest and the progress of her expressive language. At this age, Martine pronounced a few words, while her capacity for comprehension was very well-developed. Anxiety seemed to hinder the emission of sound, which for her could be felt as a concrete loss of a bit of her body as well as an emotional loss, as the sound could fall into an endless void. This indeed seemed to be what she produced in her water games with an endless flow, and subsequently I interpreted this to her. At the same time, her drawings underwent a change. The whirlwind shapes were replaced by rings, either closed circles or snails within a gigantic helio-coidal shell. Martine agreed with my interpretations regarding the snail who protects the baby at risk of falling apart during the turbulence of change. Sketches of bodily presentations began to appear at the same time. When she drew a horse that seemed to carry her around the ring, I pointed out to her that the word "horse" is part of my name.[3]

It was during this period that Martine, now age 5, could be progressively educated in a preschool setting. On my part, I tried to maintain the confidence that I had had at the beginning of treatment. I had thought, during the first month, that having taken Martine into treatment so early would prevent the establishment of the organization of autistic defenses. This did not turn out to be the case. Despite very clear progress, we were still seriously concerned about the possibility of enclosure in a capsule of silence which would mobilize

---

3. Translator's note: the name "Lechevalier" contains the word "cheval," the French word for horse.

parental anxiety about death. In moments of progress, it appeared as if Martine could put into use the words that I would make available for her. At such times she would give expression to her pain and terror at separating from her feces. My interpretations were followed by singing sounds, which she enunciated with the same gesticulations which accompanied her bowel movements. She would repeat these sounds at home with her mother and would begin to sing. Acute bouts of fever accompanied these sessions.

Shortly after this, a very sweet, obedient Martine—the darling of her parents, given her fusional submission—was transformed into a little devil. Martine would scream both during session and at home at the slightest frustration. Separations at holiday times and at the ending of each session became dramatic events, given the emotional charge she expressed and the destructive aggression that required my using physical force in order to contain and calm her down. The appearance of foul language put an end to her physical fighting. Gesticulated games, in which a large lion roared and devoured me, allowed for a certain distance. It was during this period that Martine would demonstrate—with her body or with her dolls—anxieties of falling forever and disappearing in the dark, provoked by the slightest experience of frustration with me and the separation at the end of the sessions that was felt as a loss of fusion.

One day, Martine put into words her pain of existing separately. She sat down on my armchair and said, "I am Mrs. Lechevalier. Everything here belongs to me. The food, the babies, the house." She then started to sob inconsolably, dramatically expressing her pain as she let herself fall off the armchair, and she commented, "I am *not* Mrs. Lechevalier, I would like to be she." The word "I" appeared in her language. Several weeks later, just before the summer holiday break, Martine arrived to her session sobbing. She let herself fall down and then threw down her dolls, saying, "At your place too there are cemeteries, death is very sad." Her mother told me, "Close to our home there is a workshop for tombstones. We pass by in front of that shop." Was this Martine's way of approaching the tomb of her grandmother? I thought about Martine's history branded by grief and about my personal cemetery within my internal world which Martine was able to perceive. In the process of her becoming individuated as a subject within otherness, she was also becoming aware of death, and especially of the pain of mourning.

From that moment on, Martine's progress became surprisingly vigorous. It had to do both with her increasing capacity for expressive language and symbol formation and her accession to the sense of temporality. Shortly after, she staged—with the dolls from her drawer—her oedipal desire and her death-wish against her mother. At the age of 6 and one half years, Martine was enrolled in the first year of elementary school. On her return from summer holidays, she did not want to come to my office anymore. Her mother asked her to let me know the reason for her refusal. Martine said that she would like me to tell her (Martine) why she had been coming to see me. I tried to tell her about her history. Martine lay on the floor and began to yell and sob. She said, "You have not understood, I will explain that to you." Then she climbed up onto a small piece of furniture, just as she used to do in years past, and let herself fall down, imitating a chute. She commented, "I come to see you because I fall, I fall, I fall, I fall, I die, I die, death is sad. I do not want to die, I am afraid."

Martine continued to cry for a long time. Her mother became very upset by her pain. She remained silent. I thought about the precipitation anxieties described by Houzel (1995). Mother told her daughter that when Martine was in her tummy, she was very afraid that Martine would die. She said that she was in great pain because Martine's grandmother had just died and that she was very sad. I talked then about the baby-Martine, who felt herself falling forever when she would look into the sad eyes of her mother. Was she pulled into the depressive void of these eyes? Pulled into a black hole by mother's dead internal object? At that moment Martine went to the sink and drank some water and offered us a drink too.

Beginning with the following session, Martine declared that from then on she could come to her session by herself—leaving her mother in the waiting room and rejoining her by herself in the hallway—without the need for me to accompany her. In our first session alone together, she drew a house with a long pathway leading up to it. On one side she drew a mother with a baby in her tummy. A car on the pathway brought mother back home from the hospital.

The following Monday, Martine drew a little girl with budding breasts and a belly button alongside a house. Above her, Martine wrote her first name. Then she drew a tree with green foliage. A month later, in the sixth year of treatment, Martine's parents were able to take their first trip away. They chose Egypt. On their return, Martine announced that she was going to tell me the story of the Pharaohs. She described to me an omnipotent king and then drew the pyramid that her parents had visited. "He [the king] believed that he would live forever in his tomb. He needed a lot of food inside. This was a very long time ago. Now the Pharaoh is no more." Martine proceeded to draw herself beside the pyramid, running and playing with a rope without falling. One of her feet was on the ground, the other was elevated. She drew herself with abundant hair in profile, and one could notice a very large ear. A statue was positioned on a pedestal, separating Martine from the pyramid. Next to the pyramid she drew a castle and a large obelisque. In the sky there flew the parents' airplane.

During the following months, Martine requested that we keep telling her story in the form of "once upon a time." Soon after, she drew a house in which there was room for several generations: grandparents, parents, herself, and one of her two brothers with his fiancée. A month later, we were to mimic a visit to the cemetery. I had to be silent and Martine pronounced a prayer over the tomb of her dead grandmother, which she positioned in front of the mirror in my office. "If we pray very strongly," she said, "her smile will come into the mirror." Martine prayed and then said, "That's it, we have won . . . she smiled." Martine, the living-dead pharaoh, the tomb-out-of-time of her grandmother, became individuated as a small, mortal girl. She then became able to perpetuate, in her own smile, her acknowledgment of the souvenir of her grandmother. Reflected in my own countertransference experience in front of the mirror was a supportive grandmother—my own—and also my gratitude for the confidence established in me by my thoughts of Frances Tustin—thoughts that operate as a living memory, replacing the petrified memorial of autism.

Considerations of Adult Patients

There are fertile mutative moments when the renunciation of the autistic protective shell—which encompasses split-off pockets inaccessible to symbolic thinking—evoke emotional overflows in the course of change. We need to sort out the different components which constitute these crises. The first component is a reactualization, in the transference, of annihilation anxieties dating from the very beginning of life; these are sensed in a bodily manner, along with the rekindling of the memory of the sensual zones in which the anxiety was experienced, in a pre-perceptive mode without their relational recognition by the object. This can evoke a persecutory state and an escalation of acts of provocation as exemplified by the case of Sylvaine in her interaction with her boss at the office.

Sylvaine would keep yelling, "She wants to do away with me" for several consecutive sessions (her yellings reminded me of those of Martine.) "I want to kill somebody," she added, filling me with her gaze. She continued to report a dream, the interpretation of which calmed her down. In her dream, Sylvaine comes out of a bunker dating to the period of the German occupation. She is on the sand of one of the beaches where the Allies landed. Somebody suggests to her to build up a wall on the sand. This seems to her to be a mockery. The sand can crumble, fall away, disperse, and invade the openings of the bunker. She discovers—underneath some layers of sand—the skeleton of a man who wants to enclose her and drag her towards death. Her associations regard her father's brothers, one of whom had hung himself, the other committing suicide by a bullet to the head shortly after she was born.

In another dream, with an atmosphere of disquieting alienation, she perceives her mouth through the sensation of being filled by something odd and grainy, like sand. She cannot swallow. While telling me the dream, Sylvaine picks at the tiny protruding points of the sand-colored material covering the couch. She pulls apart the threads and seems to be fascinated, hooked by her finger and by her gaze to the yellow points, just like autistic children respond to reflections of light. I intervened by comparing her mouth to that bunker from which she emerged. She is invaded by sand, just like the emotions that crumble and fall down, dispersed into small grains on my couch. She is as if flayed alive with no skin to pull her together during this change which perhaps resembles the "landing of the Allies."

It seemed that she perceived me as her boss in the office who wanted to "get under her skin" and invade her mouth with gritty sand instead of with fluid flowing milk. Will she be able to pull herself together on my couch as she renounces her armor of aggressivity? Could she find in me both an envelope and sufficient support that might be internalized as a supportive bone-structure in order to facilitate her becoming a living subject, differentiated from the dead skeletons of her uncles? I wonder about the memory traces of Sylvaine's bodily perceptions of a small baby with bereaved parents— perhaps at the moment of weaning—traces which may find access to a symbolizable representation, thanks to the dreamwork and to its elaboration in the transference.

The hard sand in her mouth could be compared to John's "nasty prick" and to the sand in David's mouth and skin, as discussed by Tustin (1972), while the 'bunker' evokes images of the autistic armor, the second skin referred to by Bick (1968). In its absence, the subject—who is emerging with as yet no protection of a personal containing skin—hooks herself adhesively to mine, as to the threads of my couch cover. She suspects that her emotions, perceived as grains of sand, would splinter.

The second component is the re-erotization of frozen as-if-amputated bodily zones, inaccessible to symbolic thinking, which could—in certain cases of increased separation anxieties, due to interruptions in the analysis—provoke somatic reactions. The decrease of the split which facilitates this re-erotization may be a source of overflowing instinctual excitation. The latter increases due to the separation, which triggers the failure of the analyst's containing function. It seems to me that the risk of this is particularly serious towards the end of the treatment.

Aline, a musician, treated during her adolescence for severe mental anorexia, was afflicted by episodes of vertigo and angina, which prevented her from singing as a soloist in the "Passion According to St. John." Aline had numerous consultations with regard to repetitive failures of her love life and attempts at suicide. Her verbal expression had always been poor. She was named after her father's first wife, who died in childbirth. Aline's mother had lost all her teeth during her pregnancy. She became severely depressed during the first months of Aline's life and could provide only mechanical care for her baby. In treatment, as Aline reached the perception of her otherness and became successful in her love life, a cancerous tumor developed in her upper maxillary. At the time of writing this paper, her cancer has been cured.

Without lingering on the history of this very long analysis, I would like to present certain dreams with accompanied the access to her autistic enclave. These dreams, emerging on the eve of holiday separations, seem to me to illustrate some of Tustin's thoughts. In one dream, there is a tiny marble that splinters, and which Aline compares to a snail's shell (a shell which protects her against primary depression). In another, she has exzema. She does not believe that it can be healed with alcohol. Instead, cotton over her skin is required. We thought about her bare skin after the loss of the snail's shell—sensitive skin on which I inflict the excitation of the alcohol of separation, rather than the soft envelope of cotton. Subsequently, Aline commented on the bare skin as the testimony of the pain of existing alive on her own, separated in the otherness with bare personal thoughts.

I encountered the third component during analytic work with descendants of holocaust survivors. I will emphasize the particularity of their thought disorder. In reference to the theories of Frances Tustin, I wondered about the existence of autistic enclaves in some of those patients. Tustin quotes David Rosenfeld (1986) and Yolanda Gampel (1988), suggesting the encapsulation of trauma in the survivors of the holocaust horrors. Descendants of those survivors show a mode of functioning rich in associations and fantasies and accompanied by brilliant intellectual success co-existing side by side with moments of active struggle against the search for meaning. It seems to me that at those moments, there emerges a concrete gripping-on to a trace, which links with the history of the traumatized parents. Pseudoidentifications, acted and repeated in their destructiveness, have been variously described as "transposition" (Kestemberg 1982), "concretization" (Kogan 1993), "Vampire identification" (Wilgowicz 1991), and "radioactive identification" (Gampel 1993). I hypothesize a mode of adhesiveness dating back to the very beginning of life, upon contact with one or both depressed parents. Carried by nonverbal messages, a trace of horrifying significance for the parents, yet deprived of meaning for the child, can constitute an adhesive link in order to struggle against the perception of nameless dread and annihilation anxiety. This stifled clinging inhibits the subject's ability to become alive to his own life and mortality.

In my paper "Noah's Children" (Lechevalier 1993), I presented a number of clinical vignettes. The patient I called "Ham" lived through delusional moments in which he would wear a band around his head so that his thoughts would not be emptied in the specificity of his own identity. Dark sunglasses and incessant eye movements protected him from any emotional encounter. Ham's adolescence was marked by a severe anorexia. Later he reached a high level of scientific success. His father, a prisoner of the Nazis during the Second World War, had been subjected to the experimentation of ingestion of crushed glass and chlorhydric acid. During the treatment, Ham would talk about his struggle to prevent the perception, in an emotional encounter, of "the hole that sucks in and annihilates, like the black hole in physics." The awareness of his emotional link with his father and the relinquishing of his delusional system coincided with the eruption of Crohn's disease, which was diagnosed and for which treatment was established. For a very long time, Ham thought that the surgeon had left some inabsorbable compress inside him, which then became the source of terrifying pains in his stomach. In addition, according to Ham, the surgeon believed him to be a cold rational man of science as in fact he had been in earlier times. I linked this compress with Ham's new capacity to contain and understand his emotions, his suffering—that of his father—which he was accusing me, as the surgeon, for having introduced into him through the analysis.[4] Would his rational thinking go to the encounter and to the "absorption" of these new capacities? The subject, agonizing to become, wished for my acknowledgment within his mode of thinking in his quest for what he then called "something of a most profound mystery."

---

4. This is a case of pseudoidentification, concretization, thus his suffering is equated with his father's.

Genuine identifications in the transference allow analysands, such as Ham, to relinquish their attachment to the historical concreteness of the horror in order to invest in metaphoric mobility. In such cases, as in cases of autistic children, we facilitate the waking of their interest in the family history and the myths carried with it by the proceeding generations. The hopeful meaning, such as the newly found smile of the grandmother by Martine, allows the survival of a psychic reality inscribed in time. The autistic core allowed the illusion of the unburied dead surviving outside of time, thus triggering through this gripping-onto generational confusion, the impossibility of using the mythical stories of the original group in the service of conferring meaning on the present from within past significance, of weaving a story of their own personal history, and of having a vision of the future in using the active force of myths. The diffusion—by the renunciation of the autistic link with the depressed parent—allows the subject access to the awareness of his/her mortality as well as to the pain of existing alone while mourning the dead and remembering their history.

Conclusion

The analyst's recognition of annihilation anxieties from within his/her own countertransference experience is a moment of reciprocity and of differentiation. Both intra- and inter-psychic mobility—within an encounter which confers meaning to an emotion perceived in the body—allow for the emergence of the subject in his/her oneness and heterogeneity. Levinas (1991) asks,

> Isn't the vivacity of life an excessiveness, a rupture of the container by the uncontainable. A rupture of a form which ceases to be its own content formerly offered in the guise of an experience. The waking of the awareness with no awareness of the waking; a waking which remains a prime mover towards the other, and of which the reduction to intersubjectivity secretly hits the very subjectivity of the subject. [p. 101]

Waking up into awareness brings on a painful perception of "otherness" as well as of erotism, with its emotional, moving, and symbolizing representations. It is also the awareness of the pain of grief for oneself and for others— just like the red grains of the pomegranate which one of my analysands spoke of.

References

Bick, E. (1968). The experience of the skin in early object relations. *International Journal of Psycho-Analysis*, 49:484–486.

Gampel, Y. (1993). Penser la mémoire impensable de l'extermination. In *L'ange exterminateur*, ed., J. Gillibert, et P. Wilgowicz, pp. 3–4. Brussels: Edition de l'Université et Cerisy.

——— (1988). Facing war, murder torture and death in childhood. *The Psychoanalytic Review* 75:499–510.

Houzel, D. (1985). Le Monde Toubillonnaire de l'autisme. In *Lieux de l'Enfance 3*. Toulouse: Privat; et in D'Anzier (eds.) 1987.

——— (1995). Precipitation anxiety. *Journal of Child Psychotherapy*, 21(1):65–78.

Kestemberg, J. (1982). In *Generations of the Holocaust*, ed. M. S. Bergmann, and M. E. Sucovy. New York: Basic Books.

Kogan, I. (1993). Curative factors in the psychoanalysis of holocaust survivors' offspring before entering the Gulf War. *International Journal of Psycho-Analysis* 74(4):803–814.

Lechevalier, B. (1993). Les enfants de Noé: De la culpabilité à la beauté d'un sens retrouvé. In *L'ange Exterminateur*, ed. J. Gilligert and P. Wilgowicz, pp. 3–4. Brussels: Editions de l'Université et Cerisy.

Levinas, E. (1991). Entre nous. In *Essais sur le penser à l'autre* pp. 98–107. Paris: Grasset.

Rosenfeld, D. (1986). Identification and it vicissitudes in relation to the Nazi phenomenon. *International Journal of Psycho-Analysis* 67:53–64.

Tustin, F. (1972). *Autism and Childhood Psychosis*. London: Hogarth, New York: Jason Aronson.

——— (1986). *Autistic Barriers in Neurotic Patients*. London: Karnac Books.

——— (1990). *The Protective Shell in Children and Adults*. London: Karnac Books.

Wilgowicz, P. (1991). *Le Vampirisme de la Dame Blanche au Golem*. Lyon: Cesura.

19

Thinking:
a Dialectic Process between
Emotions and Sensations[1]

Didier Houzel

We shall help the child to turn to human beings . . . who will enable him to process his sensory experience in relationships with other people, by the development of expressive activities, and by percepts and concepts which enable him to live in the ordinary world.

Francis Tustin

Where do thoughts come from? This question has been largely debated among a number of philosophers since the seventeenth century. Two philosophical theses oppose each other, point by point: Nativism and Empiricism. Each theory contains arguments that support the opposition of the other. Thus, philosophical thought progresses, or rather moves in a sinusoidal way from one pole to the other, without ever being able to reach a definite solution. However, it would be a mistake on our part to disregard its import, since to begin with we need philosophical thought in order to articulate the questions that await us and the methods that might allow us to advance our knowledge.

Bion (n.d.) reminds us that philosophy is the ladder that we have climbed, the ladder that he recommends we do not reject. On the one hand, there is the theory of Nativism, in which Descartes, Leibniz, and Kant postulate that ideas precede experience and have the power to organize. On the other hand,

---

1. Translated into English, from the original French, by Theodore Mitrani, Ph.D.

is the theory of Empiricism, in which Hobbes, Locke, Berkeley, and Hume postulate the derivation of ideas from experience. However, the majority of empiricist philosophers do not limit experience to the perception of the external world through the senses. They make room for the experience of an internal world, which Locke calls *reflection*.

In contrast with Locke, Condillac excludes, *a priori*, any form of internal world in order to posit—as the sole origin of ideas—the data derived from the senses. This "sensualist philosophy" is illustrated by the metaphor of the statue upon which this philosopher confers one single sense, the sense of smell. It is from this single sensorial capacity that Condillac deduces all the faculties that characterize the human psyche: attention, which corresponds to the state of the statue having but one single sense, for example, the smell of the rose; memory, when one sensation persists while another fades; judgment, when the similarities and differences between sensations are compared, and so forth. It is the wonder of philosophical speculation that can make us derive all our mental faculties from the smell of a rose.

Of course, there has been no lack of argument raised against Condillac's "Sensualism." Let us consider one of these arguments. The suggested metaphor of the statue supposes a reflection upon the relationship established between the "being" with the faculty of sensuality and the "object" as a source of the sensations. The scheme presented by Condillac necessarily includes either a third observer capable of such reflection or a reflective capacity of the statue itself that cannot derive from sensations alone.

Frances Tustin's thinking dedicates a large place to sensuality. She defines autism "as a sensation-dominated state in which perception is elementary, restricted or grossly abnormal" (Tustin 1972, p. 107). She clearly describes the sensuality of the autistic child as a pathological sensuality that she qualifies as perverse. It is this perverse sensuality that dominates the use of *autistic objects*: "They have no phantasy associated with them. Psychogenic autism is a sensation-dominated state, and autistic objects are sensation-dominated objects" (Tustin 1986, p. 104). It is sensuality that the child employs in order to produce *autistic shapes*, those idiosyncratic impressions the child produces on its mucous membranes and its skin with its own bodily substances and with "autistic objects." It is sensuality that constitutes the child's *autistic shell*, in which it encloses itself as a shelter from the external world and that allows it to deny the terrifying presence of the other, which might drag it into destructive vertigo.

It is thus a matter of an abnormal use of sensuality. However, the question at hand is what kind of abnormal use? Does this constitute a fixation at a developmental stage that an autistic person cannot transcend, or is it a regression to such a state? Is it a pathological impasse that does not correspond to any normal developmental stage? Having followed, for a period of time, Mahler's hypothesis of a "normal autistic" stage, Tustin subsequently ended up choosing another hypothesis: that there is no "normal" autistic stage and, therefore, no regression to such a state. Autism is *always* a pathological state and autistic pathways—especially those of *perverse auto-sensuality*—are to be understood as defense mechanisms created in the face of unbearable, archaic anguish, and not part of a "stage" of normal psychic development.

Tustin remained preoccupied with this subject for the rest of her life and dedicated her last paper, "The Perpetuation of an Error" (1994), to it. She makes recourse to the concepts of *adhesive identification* (Meltzer et al. 1975) and *adhesive identity* (Bick 1986) in describing the autistic child's relationship to the world—which Tustin calls *adhesive-at-oneness*. She wrote, "In 'adhesive at-oneness,' the child feels *the same* as someone, stuck to them as an inanimate object" (Tustin 1994, p. 16). The mechanism of adhesive-at-oneness is quite different than that of "flowing-over-at-oneness," the latter being an experience of primitive oneness with the mother that heals the rupture caused by the "caesura of birth" (Tustin 1986) and allows for the awareness of separation from and identification with the object without catastrophic experience.

Although adhesive-at-oneness may be necessary for survival, it impedes access to a sense of otherness, that is, direct cognition of the separate existence of the other, which Tustin called "awareness of bodily separateness" (1990, p. 179) and which I refer to as "the separability of the object"[2] (Houzel 1995). Adhesive-at-oneness also impedes the formation of mechanisms of identification and subsequently the development of the internal world: ". . . that which is normally a fluid oscillation of normal states of 'at-oneness'—which foster empathy—alternating with an awareness of separateness has become frozen into an abnormal, perpetually rigid state of 'adhesive-at-oneness,' which impedes empathy" (Tustin 1994, p. 16).

It seems that the "error" Tustin denounced, with regard to a normal autistic stage, is the very error made by Condillac in his metaphor of the statue.

---

2. The term "separability" ("separabilite" in the original French) is borrowed from theoretical physics. In that field, two particles which were linked at one moment retain their differences with regard to some of their parameters (especially their spin) even when spatially separated.

The "being" dominated by sensuousness, yet deprived of any intrapsychic communication either with others or with him/herself (or rather, with his own internal objects), cannot develop a thought. This amounts to saying that there is no genetic continuity between sensations and ideas. We are often tempted to derive the latter from the former, to suppose that at first the baby would live within a world of pure sensations before it could transform these sensations into emotions and later link emotions to the presentations so that, ultimately, it would accede to thoughts, thanks to the linking of representations with words. It seems to me that, at times, this interpretation is given to the model proposed by Tustin regarding the development of thinking. Such an interpretation leads certain psychotherapists to veer off from their technique with autistic children, to decrease interpretative work in the transference in favor of offering sensual experiences to the child. However, I do not think that this linear outline corresponds to Tustin's theory, and I am sure— having worked with her—that she would not recommend our deviating from analytic technique in the aforementioned way.

Well then, where do thoughts come from? I will focus my reflections on a particular aspect of their genesis, namely the relationship between sensations and emotions. In fact, it seems to me that in accordance with the way that one conceives of these relationships, two different if not opposing technical and theoretical orientations are derived. I suggest that in one of these models, these relationships are genetic, while in the other they are dialectic. Thus, I propose a dialectic model of relationship between sensations and emotions.

While I was in supervision with Tustin, I was struck by the impression that she gave me of thinking with her whole body. I remember how she used to listen very attentively to my tentative English. After a while, she moved her hand softly, then her arms, then her whole body. It was only after this that she began to talk. This pattern suggested to me that her thinking did not derive only from her head but, instead, from her body as a whole. In my personal jargon, I call this "thinking with one's body." It seems to me that she had a way of receiving the messages that I conveyed to her, not only as information, but also as a dynamic exchange, and that her thinking was the outcome of dynamic impressions which she received with her whole body before she would give them a mental/verbal representation. It was this observation that lead me to inquire into the origin of our thoughts, a subject that Tustin—like her analyst, W. R. Bion—had always been preoccupied with.

Do our thoughts come from our bodily sensations or from our emotions (etymologically "that which puts us in motion")? I finally reached the hypothesis that while the emotions are at the very foundation of the process of thought formation, they have, however, to be presented with the help of the sensations. In this model, emotions are the psychic links that allow us to confer meaning upon our relational experiences, as demonstrated by Bion (1992). However, the sensations are the necessary material for the construction of the representations of such experiences. I suppose that when I would see Tustin moving her body before talking, she was becoming aware of bodily sensations that allowed her to bestow form to the emotions that emerged in her while she listened to the clinical material. I believe that this is the same process that occurs between a baby and mother in the very beginnings of object relationship and mental life.

Freud (1900) suggests a similar model in the "Interpretation of Dreams" when he describes what he calls "considerations of representability":

A thing that is pictorial is, from the point of view of a dream, a thing that is *capable of being represented*: it can be introduced into a situation in which abstract expressions offer the same kind of difficulties to representation in dreams as a political leading article in a newspaper would offer to an illustrator. [Freud 1900, p. 339–340]

In the relationship established between the self and the object, there is a representable part that may assume a shape while another part is not representable. For example, Bion pointed out that an emotion has no smell. The shapable part of our relational experience is that which is the most stable and perhaps the basis of the importance of visual perceptions in our representations, since it is these which we can best identify with and stabilize. If we represent an object relation as a dynamic system, the sensation could be considered as an invariant part of the system. In normal development, the sensation would allow us to recall the ensemble of the experience of which it is a part, much as the taste of a "madeleine"[3] allowed Marcel Proust to recall a whole chunk of his existence.

It is this aspect of sensation that leads us, says Tustin, to percepts and then to the concepts that we can share with others. The perverse sensuality of the autistic child—the autistic shapes it envelopes itself with—do not serve this function. On the contrary, these isolate the child from the external world,

---

3. Translator's note: A "madeleine" is a common shell-shaped French butter cookie, usually dusted with powdered sugar. The author here alludes to a well-known episode in Proust's classic *In Search of Time Lost*.

sealing it off from any communication, disallowing development toward any percept or of any sharable concept. These autistic sensations are not associated with dynamic experiences of object relationship, thus they do not have the powers of evocation and representation of normal sensations. Yet, I suggest they do contain a germ of meaning, albeit one which is extremely condensed. The psychotherapist needs to invest in an effort to slowly decondense and inscribe meaning within the dynamics of the transference relationship. This is the task in the psychoanalytic psychotherapy of autistic children. I would like to illustrate this point with a clinical vignette.

Clinical Material

Aline[4] is the eldest of two children. Her brother is 7 years old. Mother's normal pregnancy was carried to term, but the birth was difficult and there was concern that a cerebral lesion might be the cause of Aline's abnormal tonus. She began to walk rather late, at the age of 20 months. She was referred for child-psychiatric consultation regarding an autistic syndrome suggested by a lack of interest in her environment, absence of symbolic play, active avoidance of eye contact, and stereotypical behaviors. She would visually fix herself onto any artificial light. She started analytic psychotherapy three times a week at the age of 22 months. I will present her psychotherapist's notes regarding the seventh session.

Aline could not yet talk. The relationship with her psychotherapist was clearly established through ritualized pathways, through increasingly vivid looks, facial expressions, and, notably, smiles. One can see, in this material, the importance of Aline's sensorial behaviors and the psychotherapist's efforts to interpret them within the transference situation.

The Seventh Session

Aline entered very quickly into the playroom. She opened her toy box by herself, picked up a pencil, and tapped the small table while launching a look

---

4. I thank Mrs. Hennequin for allowing me to quote this material from a psychotherapy that she conducted with Aline. In the text I will refer to the psychotherapist with the expression Mrs. H. with regard to the articulation of interpretations and will further refer to her as "I" or "me" in the rest of the text.

in my direction. I, too, took a pencil and started tapping the table at the same pace as Aline while I say to her: "Hello, Aline! Mrs. H is back." She smiled. Then she took a second pencil and hit the carpet rhythmically while continuing to scrutinize me, as if to ascertain that I do the same. The hits became more and more distinguished and, in the rhythm, so much more regular. I too hit rhythmically. There emerged an intense moment of communication between Aline and me through both gaze and smile. I said: "Here we are! We really meet again!"

Aline let go of the pencils and clutched one drapery cord in one hand and then the other in her other hand. She joined the cords, then separated them and then rejoined them anew. I said, "Mrs. H. and Aline meet again, and then they separate; they meet again and then they separate. . . ."

Aline handed me one of the drapery cords and kept the other in her own hand. Then she sent it to me. I said, "Aline comes to see Mrs. H," and I sent the drapery cord back to her. Aline caught it and launched it behind herself. I said, "Aline goes away. We are away. We cannot see each other any more. . . ." This play continued in the same way for some time. Then Aline put her ear to the knob at the end of one of the drape cords as if to listen. She held onto it and sniffed it as if to sense its smell. She tried to move it behind her head, but the cord got entangled in her hairpins and I had to help her out. (I did not interpret this sequence, but we may hypothesize that Aline was exploring the different sensuous qualities linked to hearing and smelling of this drapery cord—a representation of a transferential object—and the gesture of placing it behind her head was a first representation of the process of internalization: placing the object in her thoughts.)

Later, she touched the hot water pipe of the radiator and looked at me intensely. I said, "It's hot!" Aline continued to touch another hot water pipe at the other end of the room. Alluding to her gesture of placing the drapery cord behind her head, I asked, "Is it also that when Aline is far away from Mrs. H. she remains with her, as a good memory in the head?"

Aline gathered all the pencils and placed them in a small jar. I said, "Now that Aline and Mrs. H. have found each other, it is like a mommy-jar to gather everything within it." Aline then returned to her toy box. She took out the bottle, which was empty. She tried to remove the nipple cover, but as she did not manage to do so, she extended it to me so that I could do it in her place. She sucked the nipple and bit it while she raised the bottle very high and directed her gaze toward the area of the unlit ceiling.

I asked her, alluding to mother's postpartum depression, "Are you feeling yourself a baby-Aline, all alone in taking her bottle without the eyes of a mommy H?" Slowly, she directed her gaze toward me, but she had some difficulty maintaining it for very long. She stopped sucking and replaced the nipple cover back on the bottle. I commented, "It is like a session that ends."

She moved toward the large desk, on which there was a lamp and a telephone—adult things. She pointed with her finger at the top of the desk as if she wanted me to give her something. She returned to her toy box and took up the bottle filled with the water that is provided for her use during the session. With a gesture, she asked me to open it for her and she proceeded to drink greedily. I said, "Oh, you are so thirsty for all the things of Mrs. H!"

She took a pencil and placed it inside the bottle. She seemed to want to retrieve it and, for that purpose, she quickly emptied the bottle. I helped her out so she would not get soaked, and I emptied part of the water into small glasses. She picked those up and drank their contents. Then she came back to the bottle, drank its contents, caught the pencil with her teeth, and, for a moment, held it in that way. She then put everything down and extended the bottle to me, apparently so I could refill it with water. Yet there wasn't any left (there's no plumbing for water installed in the room). I said, "There is no more water. It is like when we separate and there is no more session."

She took hold of two little jars, hit the table, and smiled with an air of satisfaction. She did not seem to wait for me to start hitting with her as in the beginning of the session. Then, she placed the smaller jar within the larger one. I said, "Coming to see me is like coming into a jar-Mrs. H in order to feel well held." She continued this game of "putting-in" for a moment. Then she extended one of the jars to me, as if asking for me to hold it. At the moment when I reached out to take hold of it, she pulled it back and laughed. She devised a peek-a-boo game, making the jar appear sometimes from one side and sometimes from the other. Then she tried to place the pencils inside the jars, but they would not stay in because they were too long.

I said, "Could we contain everything within the session if it were big enough?" (I did not refer to these pencils at the time as paternal objects, but it is possible that they had this significance, not unlike the pencil that she had inserted into the water bottle). Aline went back to playing with the knob of the drapery cord. She knocked it against the wall as if in order to find out whether or not it was solid (undoubtedly yet another effort of a paternal quality). I asked, "Is it solid enough at Mrs. H's?" She moved toward the door and climbed on a chair in order to reach the door latch, which she shook vigorously. I asked, "Is it well closed at Mrs. H's in order to contain everything?" (Again, a paternal quality: tightness). "Or are there holes through which everything can flow out." (I'm thinking about her saliva that dripped down frequently through her parted lips.)

She did not come down off the chair by herself but extended her arms toward me. I was surprised and moved by this vote of confidence expressed for the very first time. I took her and placed her on the floor (maybe she would have liked to end up in my arms), and I said to her, "You want very much that I help you out today."

Comments

The detailed story of this session illustrates the very concrete mode of communication of the autistic child. One could observe its motor and sensorial behaviors as sequences of gestures and sensations with no significance. The therapist postulates that there is a latent meaning in each and every sequence of the session and that her task is to extract this latent meaning in order to attempt to communicate it to the child. The paradox of the autistic child's communication is that its behaviors are not the manifestation of an emotional deficit but of the kind of emotional hyper-condensation that renders the task of decodifying both difficult and uncertain at the same time. The best guide for the psychotherapist is to let himself go with the unfolding of the session; to entrust himself to the flux of the transference and countertransference that would break him; and to allow himself to become "moved," in the most profound sense of the term. Only then will the therapist arrive at the point where a representation may germinate in his soul, out of which he might propose an interpretation to the child. This is what Tustin points out in the very beginning of her first book: "As I experienced it, I seemed to flow along with John, surfacing when I felt I had understood enough to venture an interpretation" (1972, p. 16).

An interpretation is but a hypothesis about the internal state of the child as it is expressed in the dynamics of the transference and countertransference. Its primary function is to demonstrate to the child that his communications have been received intrapsychically by the therapist, that the latter is reaching out to the child, and that, together, they will be able to give "form" to their exchanges. These are the "forms" that a child will be able to hold within himself and use to populate his internal world with.

It seems necessary to distinguish between the *relationship* and the *communication* in order to understand what takes place in the analytic treatment of an autistic child. One can be in a *relationship* with someone without being in *communication* with that person. Undoubtedly, this is what takes place with babies whose mothers suffer postpartum depression. The presence of the depressed mother is not experienced as an absence but as an attractive void, a destructive vertigo, a call with no return. It seems as if the child has felt itself sucked into and vampirized by this void to the point of annihilation. It is precisely in his struggle against these very primitive annihilation anxieties that the child establishes such autistic mechanisms.

I have named these primitive anxieties *precipitation anxieties* (Houzel 1989, 1995), since they are oftentimes expressed in behaviors of falling, experiences of vertigo, and in stories of destructive precipitations and also because they correspond to an irrepressible and annihilating anxiety provoked by the presence of an uncommunicative object. The image of the *black hole* of astrophysics comes to mind as an expression of this phenomena: a mass so condensed that anything that falls within its field of gravitation is swallowed up with no return.

The *communication* is a "return" that gives form and stability to the infant's relationship with the object. It is necessary that the object not limit itself to endlessly absorbing the messages addressed to it but that it be able to produce something mental. That is to say, the object must give these messages "form" and to return this form to the infant/sender, who might then feel itself contained and understood. Thus, instead of feeling itself pulled into a bottomless abyss, the infant/sender may feel itself invited to walk in unknown territory, without risk of destruction. During the treatment, interpretations serve the function of *communication*.

The autistic defenses have the tendency to bridge the traumatic gap that opens between the self and the object. Everything transpires as if the abyss were leveled. The autistic delusion of the negation of otherness, as described by Tustin, has precisely this role. All autistic maneuvers share the same function. They are survival maneuvers. No psychoanalytic treatment would be possible if these maneuvers were perfectly successful. Experience has shown that there often remains—especially while the child is still very young—a permeability to communication, an expectation of an object capable of receiving and decoding the messages addressed to it. However, these are hyper-condensed messages that one has to very patiently decondense.

This work is comparable to what Freud (1900) indicated regarding the condensed images of dreams. As we know, Bion (1992) was inspired by Freud's descriptions of "the dream work" and transposed this to the matter of the communication established between the baby and its mother. He called the "mother's capacity" to receive the hyper-condensed communications of her baby and to distill them to extract all the significance from them *the capacity for reverie*. It is this capacity for reverie that must operate in the psyche of the therapist for the benefit of the autistic child. The therapist must not fear letting himself be taken on dangerous paths, where he may be wandering for a long time until he can find his way. The rigor of the technique advocated by Tustin proves itself to be indispensable under these circumstances. It is the compass that guides the traveler in unknown and deserted terrain.

In the beginning of this paper, I presented a question regarding the origin of our thoughts. I would now like to reformulate matter in a different way, because I believe that any origin is mythical. It is only our need to explain that causes us to fix, here or there, the origin of a phenomenon. The exploration of autism prompts us to relinquish this desire for explanation. Wasn't it this that Bion (1970) recommended when he suggested to the analyst to eschew memory and desire?

In a certain way, the meaning the analyst can give to the material of a given session already exists, to begin with, in a condensed state waiting to hatch out as the opportunity may present itself: namely, the opportunity for *relationship* and *communication* with the object to be established. Things occur as if in a closed system. Autism makes room for a dynamic system at the heart of which stable forms can become organized. This leads me to make some remarks with regard to this notion of stability.

The specialists describe three forms of stability: "Hamiltonian" stability, simple stability, and structural stability. *Hamiltonian stability* refers to movement with neither friction nor acceleration. It is the type of stability postulated by Newton with regard to the movement of bodies in a void. *Simple stability* is discussed by Freud (1920) in "Beyond the Pleasure Principle" when he describes the return of the psychic apparatus to a minimum level of energy. *Structural stability* can exist in an open dynamic system, one in which there is an exchange of energy with the outside and in which a form can remain identical to itself even when the parameters of the system change, provided that it remains delimited within certain boundaries. A system with structural stability can have a self organization, namely, the forms within the organization are born and stabilized due to dynamics internal to the system. It seems that Freud is onto this concept of structural stability in "Beyond the Pleasure Principle," especially when he quotes Fechner, who touched upon this notion. Yet Freud stopped at the notion of simple stability—that could only take the system back to a weaker degree of organization.

The task of psychoanalytic treatment with the autistic child—one that is indeed quite difficult to accomplish—may be conceived of as the opening-up of a closed system, functioning under the principles of simple stability, in order to transform it into an open system, functioning under the principle of structural stability and endowed with the capacity for self-organization. If the goal is attained, then the sensual and repetitive world of the autistic child becomes a world of relationships—of communication and representations.

In *Attention and Interpretation*, Bion (1970) examines in detail the rapport between sensual reality and psychic reality. In this text, he clarifies his point of view on this matter, about which—in earlier contributions—he has been ambiguous. In fact, prior to *Attention and Interpretation*, it was not always easy to know whether Bion was describing the genesis of thinking as beginning from the sensual elements he called "beta elements" or whether he regarded the origin of thinking to lie in what he called "preconceptions": that is, the innate organizing forms of object relations. We find here, more or less, the Sensualist and Nativist points of view, which I have mentioned earlier in this paper. Bion then introduces a new concept that he designates by "O" and which corresponds to what he calls, ". . . ultimate reality, absolute truth, the God head, the infinite, the thing-in-itself" (1970, p. 26). The goal of the analytic treatment is to *become* "O." That which the psychoanalyst is interested in, invests his efforts in, and gradually guides the patient toward is "becoming O," "being O." The sense data are but vehicles in service of either masking or initiating the process of "becoming O." Bion writes:

> He [the psychoanalyst] knows phenomena by virtue of his senses, but since his concern is with "O," events must be regarded as possessing either the defects of irrelevancies obstructing or the merits of pointers initiating it, the process of "becoming O". [Bion 1970, p. 27]

The sense data are necessary for memorizing the data of experience:

> Memory depends on the senses. It is limited by the limitations of the senses in their subordination to the pleasure-pain principle. . . . [Bion 1970, p. 30]

More generally, about "knowledge"—which is, for Bion, an outcome of the (Knowledge) K-link—he says:

> I have postulated that a K-link can operate only on a background of the senses, it is capable of yielding only knowledge "about" something, and

must be differentiated from the O-link essential to transformations in O. [1970, p. 36]

Our fascination with the autistic child is most probably due to our attraction to the "ultimate reality" with which it confronts us. The paradox is that in order to bring the autistic child into our human world, it is necessary to transform the thing-in-itself into phenomena to be deployed within the transference and countertransference dynamics and to translate these dynamics into representations of which the material is a result of our own sensorial impressions. At the same time, it is necessary for us to continuously transcend the sense data in order to help the child to emerge from his enclosure within the state of adhesive-at-oneness, a stuck-to sensuality; we must help him to "become O," to become that which he is. We can see, in the session with Aline, that patient work has to be carried on by the psychotherapist, guided only by the rigor of technique of transference analysis and the elaboration of countertransference, with no preconceived agenda, with no lecture notes, with no adaptive aim— as Bion tells us, "without memory and desire."

Conclusion

The question presented in the beginning of this chapter remains unanswered. Having explored its content and having reached the point of reformulating it, I wonder if, rather than inquiring into the origin of our thoughts, it might be more fitting to raise the question of how our sense impressions might become the idiom for our emotions? Without sensorial experiences, we will be like the "Monads of Leibniz," with no door or window. We would be without material for the construction of our representations and for sharing of these with our fellow humans. We would have nothing with which to give form to and stabilize the fluctuations of the emotions which move us. On the other hand, no sensation, as violent as it might be, would be able to awake our emotional life if we were not already inscribed in the network of relationships and communications that establish our humanity. Not even the most fragrant of roses could bestow life upon Condillac's statue.

References

Bick, E. (1986). Further considerations on the function of the skin in early object relations. *British Journal of Psychotherapy* 2(4):292–301.

Bion, W. R. (1970). *Attention and Interpretation*. London: Tavistock.

——— (1992). *Cogitations*. London: Karnac Books.

Freud, S. (1900). Interpretation of Dreams. *Standard Edition* 4:1–626.

——— (1920). Beyond the pleasure principle. *Standard Edition* 18:3–64.

— Houzel, D. (1989). Precipitation anxiety and the dawn of aesthetic feeling. *Journal of Child Psychotherapy* 13(2):103–114.

——— (1995). Precipitation anxiety. *Journal of Child Psychotherapy* 21(1):65–78

Meltzer, D., Bremner, J., Hoxter, S., Weddell, D., and Wittenberg, I. (1975). *Explorations in Autism*. Perthshire, Scotland: Clunie Press.

Tustin, F. (1972). *Autism and Childhood Psychosis*. London: Hogarth.

——— (1981). *Autistic States in Children*. London: Routledge and Kegan Paul. Revised Edition (1992). London: Routledge.

——— (1986). *Autistic Barriers in Neurotic Patients*. London: Karnac Books.

——— (1990). *The Protective Shell In Children and Adults*. London: Karnac Books.

——— (1994). The Perpetuation of an Error. *Journal of Child Psychotherapy* 20:3–23.

20

Encounter
with Frances Tustin[1]

Geneviève Haag

David, who came to me aged ten years, was a striking example of a child with a binary split in his "body self" . . . a child whose first disturbance had split him into two halves with encapsulation reactions which had held him together.

Frances Tustin (1992, p. 59)

My encounter with Frances Tustin is one of the most significant events in my professional life. It has been a pleasure and a privilege of great enrichment that I share with a number of colleagues around the world. Presently, many psychoanalysts who work with autistic and psychotic children owe a debt to Tustin for the greatest part of their understanding of these states and for the precise technical indications inferred from them. Her work has allowed us not only to provide healing relief to a certain number of children who are encapsulated in this pathology, but it has also helped us to better understand and treat the archaic difficulties that operate in many other structures of greater complexity, such as adolescent "mental anorexia," borderline states, manic depressive states, and certain neuroses.

It seems natural that Tustin's research incorporates not only the work of other researchers on autism—such as that of Donald Meltzer, which is

1. Translated into English from the original French by Theodore Mitrani, Ph.D. An earlier version of a portion of this chapter was published in the *Monographies de la Revue Française de Psychanalyse*, Paris P.U.F.: 1994.

complementary to her own—but also the work of a number of psychoanalysts who (either mainly or exclusively) work with adult patients and who have focused their work on the narcissistic field of the psyche and its intricate links with the emergence of the object world.

After a brief personal reminiscence of Frances Tustin, I will try to present the essence of the import of her work, which was entirely dedicated to the understanding of autistic functioning. Tustin also addressed other infantile and childhood psychoses in counterdistinction to autism. The clarifications principally advanced by Melanie Klein are especially deepened by her understanding that autistic symptoms are frequently found in the so-called "symbiotic psychoses" (Mahler 1958) or confusional psychoses. Tustin, in her work with children and adolescents with various pathological structures, became ever more aware of what she called "autistic pockets" or "cores" in a variety of patients. This aspect of her work was further developed in her last books (Tustin 1986, 1990).

It seems impossible to present in detail the ensemble of Tustin's work except in attempting to paraphrase her writings in a scholarly way, which would be of little use. It is indispensable to allow oneself into her books. Therefore, I have chosen to focus on her discoveries through the connections that I perceive with other works in an attempt to locate them in the present day metapsychological efforts while, at the same time, presenting my own extensions, developed through my encounters with her work. Subsequently, there emerge certain questions that became the subject of my personal dialogue with Tustin. I will also briefly consider another important part of her work, consisting of the technical considerations and the analysis of therapeutic processes. Following this part of the chapter, I will present clinical material to illustrate certain observations and metapsychological extensions on this line of thinking that summarize my contribution to the understanding of identifications operative in the body-ego.

Frances Tustin: the Person

It was thanks to James Gammill[2] that Anik Manufras du Chatellier, Leni Iselin, and I became acquainted with Tustin's first book—*Autism and Child-*

---

2. A member of the British Psychoanalytic Society, trained by Melanie Klein, Gammill came to France in 1966, where he worked as a child analyst at the Claparede Institute, Neuilly, where he was our first supervisor. Through his association with the

hood Psychoses—shortly after its publication in 1972 and met her in person during the pre-congress of 1975 at the Tavistock Clinic. Tustin affectionately welcomed us and our clinical material. Besides our small French group, there was also Annie Bergman, Paolina Kernberg, Vicki Subirana, and other Italian and English colleagues.

This very first "supervision" marveled us, and it did not remain a single occurrence. After that time, we followed her to a number of small cottages where she lived in the London suburbs. The garden, the flowers, and sometimes a small swimming pool were her preferred environment. I came to know the treatment room that she mentions in the case of "Peter" (Tustin 1981)—very simple, a small stable remodeled by her husband—in the village in Buckinghamshire. The sobriety, the intimacy, and the rigor of the setting struck us (the drawers of one chest were closed by different keys, each for a different child, and there was a blanket on the small couch, her chair, and two tables).

I wish to emphasize the contrast between this simplicity and rigor, the acquisition of which she would often talk about with such humor (as she liked to say—with regard to her analysis with Bion—she "truly learned from experience"), and the overflowing of sensitivity and sensual capacity, a positive sensuality that emanated from her person as well as the musicality of her voice, the vividness of her vocabulary, the expressiveness of her gesture/body language, and the veritable chime of her laughter. (Once she stopped us to admire a rose bush growing by the gable of her house, and she pointed out how it kept changing colors throughout the budding and flowering stages.) It is not by chance that these capacities—along with her great emotional vibrancy and her profound capacity for containment, in a true poetic emergence—allowed her to discover, to comprehend, and to treat autistic children. In turn, those children whom she treated brought about the deepening of her passionate research into the area of infantile autism. The contribution of her work to the development of psychoanalysis was recognized in 1984 by the British Psychoanalytic Society, which named her an honorary affiliate member.

Kleinian group at the British Psychoanalytic Society and his acquaintance with Tustin, whom he highly appreciated, he helped us to establish a bridge with England for which we are thankful to him.

The Work of Frances Tustin

In 1966, Tustin published her first article on autism—"A Significant Element in the Development of Autism"—followed by "Psychotherapy with Autistic Children" (1967) and "Autistic Processes" (1969). Her first book, *Autism and Childhood Psychosis* (1972) presented an ensemble of her important initial discoveries, principle investigations, and efforts at theory building, which she would continue to deepen throughout her life. In fact, in every successive book—*Autistic States in Children* (1981), *Autistic Barriers in Neurotic Patients* (1986), and *The Protective Shell in Children and Adults* (1990)—Tustin created increasingly insightful variations on themes specific to the autistic syndrome and other infantile psychoses of both symbiotic and confusional types.

Tustin deepened her comprehension of autistic psychopathology, the nature of the anguish of the primary or psychotic depression, the nature of the autistic defense, and its various symptomatic aspects: the shell, autistic objects, autistic shapes, the impact of the body–ego, of developmental arrest, etiological concerns (the respective roles of innate predisposition and environmental factors), the dynamics of drives, technical implications, and the unfolding of the therapeutic process. Beginning with *Autistic Barriers in Neurotic Patients*, we can observe an ever increasing enlargement of Tustin's consideration of the autistic aspects of a number of other pathologies. In this work, she emphasizes the limiting impact of the autistic defense on emotional development, while in *The Protective Shell in Children and Adults*, she further develops her ideas on the protective aspects of this defense. This leads to an even closer consideration of the conditions and the vicissitudes of the concept of autism in reference to normal development. In contrast to her earlier works, she discards the term "normal primary autism" with regard to primitive states of unintegration.

The First Discoveries

Trained in the Kleinian tradition, Tustin quickly became aware that autistic children *do not fall* within the frame of reference of the understanding brought by Melanie Klein with regard to those psychotic children dominated by pathological projective identification. Tustin's patient "John" and others had shown her that the essential matter for them was to avoid, at any cost, the awareness of bodily separateness. The emergence of this awareness provoked a feeling of loss of a part of the body—especially, the mouth—along with "the button" of the breast. This confirmed Winnicott's intuition concerning the experience of "psychotic depression" (Winnicott 1958), and Tustin (1981/ 1992, p. 91) quoted him when he said:

> The loss might be of certain aspect of the mouth which disappear from the infant's point of view along with the mother and the breast when there is a separation at a date earlier than that at which the infant had reached a stage of emotional development which could provide the equipment for dealing with loss. [p. 222]

Clearly, this is not a matter of *actual* separation but of an acceleration of the *awareness of separation*, as Tustin has often underlined. The other elements of this "psychotic depression" or "primary depression" are the bodily sensations of falling forever and spilling out into annihilation. Henceforth, autistic maneuvers are understood as functioning to plug this gap in the body–ego, affording the child a state of permanent excitation, in order to feel itself. Tustin would eventually call this state "autosensuality" and would carefully differentiate it from "normal infantile autoerotism" (e.g., sucking). She described a variety of stereotypical autistic maneuvers, emphasizing "the role of autistic objects": hard objects held in the palm of the hand, or bodily contents kept in bodily orifices other than the mouth. She described one child's (David) elaboration of this feeling of being protected by an armor that covers over the emptiness and is only an *appearance* of tri-dimensionality.

At this stage, her work crossed paths with the work of Esther Bick (1968)—one of her instructors—concerning the "psychic skin" and the phenomenon of the "second skin" as well as the works of Winnicott (1960) regarding the "false self" and those of Deutch (1942) on the "as-if" personality. However, at this time, there are only brief remarks on these works, which were to be further elaborated upon at a later stage of Tustin's work. The remainder of her first book is dedicated to a tentative classification of autism and its differentiation from other psychoses. She defines four categories: *primary normal autism* as the state of unintegration, with absent or minimal awareness of separation providing the grounds for the progressive organization of transitional experiences; *primary pathological autism*, an abnormal prolongation of the aforementioned state (due to serious deficiencies of the environment or of the constitution of the child); *secondary encapsulated autism*, corresponding to Kanner's syndrome; and *secondary regressive autism*, corresponding to the symbiotic psychosis described by Mahler (once called "secondary autism" in the United States, in contrast to Kanner's Syndrome, which was called, "primary autism").

New Discoveries, Further Elaborations, and Revisions of Hypotheses

In her third book, Tustin wrote: "With each book, I feel I have become more closely in touch with the nature of psychogenic autism" (Tustin 1986, p. 12), and in the introduction to her last book, she says of the work: "Each new paper that one writes adds a few grains of further understanding" (1990, p. 11). She recognized the repetition and emphasized its usefulness for bettering the reader's understanding.

I will now consider in greater detail Tustin's second book, in which she contends with what would remain the main body of her *oeuvre* by introducing a more specific scheme for the development of *autistic objects*. I will then refer to the "grains of further understanding" in the context of a discussion of the mechanism of pathological autism, where I will also refer to Tustin's other books.

Tustin's second book, *Autistic States in Children* (1981/1992) covers material presented in those lectures she gave over five years, on an annual basis, at the Institute of Child Neuropsychiatry at the University of Rome. In the first chapters, she attempts to deepen our understanding of the relationship between "autosensuality," a term that she borrows from James Anthony; "primary normal autism," a term also used by Mahler; and "primary narcissism." She refers to Freud (1914) when he states:

We are bound to suppose that a unity comparable to the ego cannot exist in the individual from the start, the ego has to be developed. *The autoerotic instincts, however, are there from the very first, so there must be something added to auto-eroticism—a new psychical action in order to bring about narcissism.* [Tustin 1981, p. 4 (Italics Tustin's)].

By linking ultra-sensuality to the autoerotic drive addressed by Freud, Tustin adopts a rather Winnicottian intermediary position between the orthodox Freudian tenets of an "objectless" stage and the Kleinian tenets of an object relationship that operates from the beginning of life. Tustin advances the hypothesis of a period when objects are perceived in a bodily mode as *sensation objects*: a period in which the mother herself is perceived by the baby as a sensation-object and a part of his body. Tustin then makes an apparently essential observation from the point of view of debates with the whole trend of direct infant observation of an ethological nature—it seems to her essential to differentiate between the reaction to others, which are based on innate patterns, the smile, for example, and conscious awareness of the other as a distinct individual, as not-me. However, she also adds that this stage is not constant. In fact, we are to expect fluctuations between the stage of undifferentiation and the emergence of an awareness of separateness.

Tustin goes on to describe a very progressive process of differentiation between this "autosensual image" (mother)—a useful image, which helps the infant to experience the mother as continuous, as one who was originally not at all differentiated—and a "modified autosensual image" differentiated out of a real "not-me" mother who is recognized, owing to the frustration of having to wait.

Tustin concludes this important metapsychological passage by stating that during this process of adaptation, these activities and the transitional phenomena protect the baby from a too-brutal encounter with the "not-me" mother (Winnicott 1958). However, the psychotic infant is one who does not manage to establish sufficient transitional activities, and so falls back onto the use of autistic and confusional objects (Tustin 1981/1992). Tustin states, in Winnicottian terminology, that the way in which the infant gains awareness of the "not-me" is essential to the constitution of his individual identity. With this, Tustin brings a new specification to her classification, which does not abolish the preceding one. This regards the nature and the importance of the maneuvers used in the service of avoiding the awareness of the "stranger not-me." She specifies, for example, that encapsulated children seem to ensconce themselves in protective containers (e.g., underneath furniture and rugs). However, in fact, they only manage to cover themselves up in a bi-dimensional way with those objects of the external world that they perceive as an integral part of their own body. They do this thanks to the *prevalence of their tactile sensitivity* and the tactile aspects of others' sensual modalities.

At this point, Tustin introduces the notion of *sensation shapes,* a theme that she would fully develop only in her third book. She states that the encapsulated infant's world is of the order of concrete surfaces, physical and tangible. She suggests that

It is only as treatment helps him to bear the fact of his bodily separateness from the outside world that he shows that he feels he is separated from it by a barrier and indicates that he feels enclosed in a shell. [1981/1992, p. 53]

In proportion to the density of this phenomenon, Tustin distinguishes between *encapsulated children*, who are totally enveloped, and those whose original shell has been damaged, rendering them somewhat more differentiated, leading to greater suffering and obliging them to make recourse to a more complex mechanism of defense. This mechanism is the "encapsulation of segments" (Tustin 1981/1992, p. 54), of "not-me," that employs a very primitive obsessional splitting, which Tustin connects with post-autistic obsessionality, not unlike that described by Meltzer (Meltzer, et al. 1975).

Subsequently, Tustin discusses "primary pathological autism," or the "shell child" or "primary shell," as well as the "secondary shell" for those in segments. Again, she very carefully differentiates these encapsulated states from the confusional states in which there is a much greater differentiation between the "me" and "not-me." The latter are filled with highly persecutory projections and function mainly in a state of tri-dimensionality. She links these latter states with the schizophrenic mechanisms and illustrates the clinical picture with a marvelous image:

The confusional child is a Don Quixote who, clad in an ill-fitting suit of armour made from miscellaneous bits and pieces insecurely fastened together, tilts at windmills under the delusion that they are giants. The encapsulated child's armour is much more intact, for he has a stronger drive to integration and organisation. He is scarcely aware of the outside world and its 'windmills.'" [1981/1992, p. 65]

In a later part of this, her second book, we find a much more developed and richly illustrated version of her description of "autistic objects"—always well differentiated from the confusional and the transitional objects—followed by several chapters dedicated to various aspects of the therapeutic situation. In this section, she especially addresses the problems of body image, the vicissitudes of symbol formation, the notion of trauma, of "psychological birth and psychological catastrophe" (1981/1992, p. 96), a consideration of the thought processes, and the deep links between the evolution of intellectual capacities and emotional development, with a particular configuration of the role of aesthetic feeling.

The Development of an Understanding of Autistic Objects

The differentiation between autistic, confusional, and transitional objects appears to be of great importance, both from the point of view of the clinical work as well as Tustin's efforts toward theory building with regard to the acquisition of boundaries of the self and its pathologies. First she establishes a kind of timetable between the normal and pathological processes, making recourse to her notion of "normal sensation objects" that constitute the core of the ego. These she calls "normal autistic objects" ("self-objects," according to the terminology used by Fordham [1966] and Kohut [1971]). For example, one of the earliest sensation-objects would be the nipple that the infant experiences as indistinct from his own tongue. Here she declares that the infant is in the "cluster of sensation," which *is* his relationship to the breast.

Tustin then discusses how the intersection between the normal and the pathological is established. She emphasizes once again the quality of premature rupture that is the painful feeling of bodily separateness, also expressed in terms of the premature rupture of normal illusions and hallucinatory capacities. Here, "Instead of creating a valid working stimulation of the breast which enables them to use it when it comes, they develop fake artifacts that *replace* the breast for which they do not wait" (1981/1992, p. 118).

Additionally, Tustin writes about how precocious learning is linked to the normal transitional way, beginning with normal sucking—established within the absence—that is lacking in those infants. She considers this to be at the root of the enormous passivity and the renunciation of any effort characteristic of these children. At this juncture she already uses the word *barrier* in connection to activities of adaptation. These "prevent the development of thoughts, memories and imagination which, in normal development, compensate in some measure for the inevitable lack of complete satisfaction which being a human being entails" (1981/1992, p. 119). It is here that the role of "the negative" is completely obstructed. Tustin observes that if the infant has recourse to these autistic maneuvers, he avoids the slightest perception of the "black hole," defending himself against death, nothingness, and a hallucinated annihilation. One could say that, for these infants, the negative is experienced as a bottomless pit, which may be expressed in terms of absolute despair.

Tustin then raises a question regarding the "hard" aspect of the autistic object. She thinks that this "hardness" is derived from the muscular rigidity (of the grip) which accompanies situations of extreme tension. At the edge of the pit, the psychotic child attaches himself to a hard object, which he will be able to grip onto in moments of danger, the "nameless dread" (Bion 1962). These children allow us to have a glimpse into the experience of this terror during temper tantrums, which are inevitably unleashed when their "shell" is damaged.

The therapeutic implications of such discoveries are of great import, since the therapist has to prevent himself from being manipulated as an autistic object (inanimate) and must also avoid brutally tearing away either the autistic objects or maneuvers. Instead, it is a matter of helping the child to progressively renounce the use of these in response to *straightforward interpretations of the primitive anguish that the child signals at a given moment.* The differentiation between the autistic object and transitional object is therefore fundamental. One must bear in mind that the autistic object is a "me-object" rather than a "not-me object," in Winnicottian terms.

It is between the hard autistic object specific to the shell of encapsulated children and the transitional object that Tustin locates a third kind of object: one that is soft and more difficult to distinguish from the transitional object; one that is more specific to confusional children. One of the principle distinctions between the transitional and the soft autistic object is that the latter is not a unique object. Its use is of an autosensual nature, similar to the "hard autistic object," yet it does not have the rigidity of surface-contact of the hard autistic object, and does not completely obliterate the awareness of the "not-me." In Tustin's exact terms, "soft confusional objects support the delusion of being enveloped in a veil, a fog, or a mist" (1981/1992, p. 133). She often talks about those psychotic children who use both types of objects.

Tustin's experience corresponds to my own: While the "shell type" autistic children use hard objects exclusively (an important diagnostic element), confusional children—and those autistic children in a confusional phase during the process of treatment—use both types of objects, oscillating between moments of intense "psychotic depression," which they attempt to fill in by reversing to states of bi-dimensionality, and moments of perception of a tri-dimensional space, along with some degree of awareness of separateness. I wish to emphasize here that, in these chapters in which Tustin discusses the aforementioned types of objects, only briefly does she address the subtle self-caressing as part of the register of soft sensations that are always surface sensations—an important autistic maneuver, not to be mistaken for the use of soft substances utilized in confusional behaviors.

I have discussed these chapters on autistic objects in detail, not only because of their great clinical usefulness and their demonstration of the links between

Tustin's and Winnicott's theories but also in order to provide a springboard into the following metapsychological discussion regarding the development of the ego and the establishment of the boundaries of the self.

Discussion of the Mechanisms of Pathological Autism: A Dialogue with Tustin

The principal elements of the following theoretical discussion are presented in Chapters 8 and 9 of Tustin's book *Autistic States in Children* (1981/1992).[3] In my discussion, I will make certain links between her contributions and those of other authors.

In the aforementioned two chapters, Tustin addresses questions that emerge quite naturally in light of her clinical descriptions and her initial attempts at psychopathological mapping. Thus I raise the first question: What brings about the sense of amputation in the experience of bodily separateness? Tustin takes up the problem of the sensation-ego, the loss within the sensation-ego, and the analysis of the initial forms of projection.

Loss in the Sensation-Ego

Discussing her patient "John," Tustin writes:

> He felt, for instance, that his mouth lost an exciting cluster of sensations for which, even afterwards, he was destined to grieve. A sensuous impression which he had taken for granted as being "there" was suddenly "not there." [1981/1992, p. 88]

It seems to me that this is an example of a form of "negative hallucination," as described in the work of Andre Green (1982). Tustin states that, for the autistic child, this sensation of lack becomes "catastrophic" (the abyss) and is immediately plugged up by the "positive hallucination" of a "stranger not-me": The carrier of the projection of the "too hard" is itself the carrier of the muscular contraction at the brink of annihilation. Such a hallucination may

---

3. Translator's note: In this section Haag refers to material found in chapters 6 and 7 in the 1981 edition or chapters 8 and 9 in the 1992 edition of *Autistic States in Children*.

also be the carrier of the projection of predatory forms of atavistic instinctual elements, poorly transformed in misdirected dynamics of drives. Although Tustin does not elaborate, she makes it clear that it is her understanding that both the negative and the positive hallucination—registering as sensations of hardness and discomfort—are also a part of the normal functioning necessary in facilitating the birth of awareness of the self and objects. Tustin suggests that "when the child becomes able to tolerate the fact that hard, uncomfortable 'not-me' experiences are a part of 'me-ness' and of the 'me,' the toughness and resilience necessary to tolerate the 'not-me' developed (1992, p. 87).

Tustin then presents her considerations regarding the precursor of projection: the *flowing-over at-oneness* associated with "adhesive identification" (Bick 1968) is earlier than projection and identification, which imply some degree of a sense of bodily separateness from the mother and infant. She credits Imre Hermann (1929), who had already mentioned this "overflowing" as a precursor mechanism to projection. I find that this notion is close to Green's (1971) thoughts on projection, especially his idea of "excorporation" in the constitution of the dynamics of the drives. If this "excorporation"—of that part of the body in which tension is felt (Green 1971)—is not received by an external object, the "projective field" fails to materialize.

Subsequently, I raise the following question: Isn't it at this junction that, instead of the establishment of a brief experience of "not there," which might stimulate a thought (at a pre-perceptive stage) about that which would return, there is the amputation or the "gone-forever" that the child needs to plug up immediately and continuously through the use of the hard "positive hallucination" discussed by Tustin? Through our understanding of this junction, we may be better able to comprehend the way in which the hallucination—sustained with the help of autistic objects—replaces the love-object, since in normal development the object and the ego are to be borne progressively within the dynamics of "normal projective identification" (Bion 1957, Rosenfeld 1965), which calls for an object that receives both the excesses of positive libidinal excitation as well as those of aggression. The return of the projected—with minor transformation—seems then to contribute to the constitution of a primary boundary.

I have reported in a number of papers, and also in my presentation to the Paris Psychoanalytic Society (Haag 1991b), on the expression given by children within the transference relationship to the feeling of the return of the overflow or the "excorporation," which creates the perception of an undulating shape, perhaps the first form of a containing boundary.

Certainly, Green's notion of "excorporation" could also be linked to the flow of primitive emotions in terms of bodily softness—as addressed by Tustin in later papers—which would take place in the "flower-over-at-onement," implying that in the beginning there is merely a surface experience. The term "projection" is more adequately used (as both Green and Tustin observe) in a state of tri-dimensionality, implying the acquisition of an initial boundary, a "psychic-skin" (Bick 1968) or "skin-ego" (Anzieu 1985), along with a minimum of space between the bodies, or rather the primary body images.[4]

The First Forms of Splits in the Sensation-Ego

Tustin considers the split "hard/soft" to be of great importance. We have come to learn through her observations that the autistic child expels the unbearable hard. Yet, at the same time, he reaffixes to himself the refabricated, mastered, and repossessed "lost bit," as if the remaining sensation of softness was linked to annihilation. Tustin suggests that the decrease of this split would indicate the sensation of elasticity. She also discusses the way she conceives of the primary normal integrations, thanks to the "marriage" of the primitive sensations of soft and hard, as they are respectively associated with the qualities of receptivity and penetration, in a kind of primary bisexuality, which (following Tustin) both Houzel (1987) and I (Haag 1983) have insisted upon in our discussions. While emphasizing the mystery of the process of the transformation of sensations into psychic experiences, Tustin indicates that the acquisition of this elasticity, which she links with adaptability, is the pivotal point of the capacity to establish the feeling of reality.

At this point, I would raise the following question: Is the sensation—the feeling of elasticity between the hard or solid and the soft or mushy—not given from the beginning by the qualifier "almost" and by the return of the "excorporated," and later the projected, thanks to the function of the external object and later the internal object? This would take place within the dynamics of the double interpenetration mouth/gaze, upon which both Meltzer (1982) and I have placed heavy emphasis. I also wish to note the importance placed on the function of "the gaze" by Pasche (1975) and Racamier (1989) as well as on what is regarded as the "differentiating return of the projection"

4. Autistic children show us through their own slow development the successive stages of body image formation (Haag 1990, 1991a, 1991b). The first feeling of bodily separateness seems to arise from the head to head situation.

and the adjustment of "almost," as discussed by Chasseguet-Smirgel (1988) regarding the importance of all differences for the acquisition of the feeling of reality.   —

Transformation of Bodily Sensation into Psychic Experiences and Thoughts

I am in agreement with Tustin that, for now, despite the ongoing efforts of a large number of workers, there remains considerable mystery about the matter of the transformation of bodily sensation into psychic experiences and thoughts. For me, this theme has been a matter of ongoing consideration (Haag 1991b). I think that it would be helpful to link it to the work of the phenomenologists such as Strauss (1935) and Maldiney (1973), who have worked through the relational and emotional qualities of sensations and their importance in the establishment of the feeling of individual "authenticity." Strauss (1935) states that the sensorial certainty of the external world cannot be derived from *individual* sensations. He suggests that one would lack this sensorial certainty if the individual sensations were other than those of differentiation and limitation of the original relationship of the feeling of the "I" and of the world (differentiated with regard to subject and object).

It seems to me that we are here very close to the notions of a sensation-ego and sensation-object as described by Tustin. The phenomenological study of the relation between "feeling and moving and feeling and perceiving" along with the "birth of the object," merit our attention. However, my main interest is the problem of the *emotional quality of the sensations,* which would then be in the realm of memorable psychic content—should they circulate freely—that may lie precisely in this to-and-fro rhythm of the experience of an undifferentiated surface.

Through these primitive processes of "excorporation" or "overflow," which are (as Green and Tustin have shown) also dynamic qualities, we approach the place of primal thinking, which anchors the sensorial impressions in their proper emotional cement. This "emotional cement" would yield the memorable and usable traces for our most profound communications as well as for the autistic creation.

The aftermath of the perception-awareness of one's knowledge of the "separated me" and of logical thought could have no truth, depth, or authenticity without the inseparable link with the sensation-self from which it emerges. Strauss (1935) advances a beautiful hypothesis in this regard: that the "perception as knowledge" remains unsatisfied, in as much as an essential moment for it is a "pre-logic" moment, since the "perception as knowledge" remains fully subjective and particular. The quality of objectivity that needs to be found within the perception yet cannot be found is nothing more than the sensorial certainty of the feeling. Later, in responding to doubts concerning the great subjectivity of feelings, Strauss says that if the feeling is subjective, it is at the same time in relationship with the "Other," with the world. However, this relationship is proper and individual. This is why this relationship is not knowledge (Strauss 1935).

While Tustin does not quote these authors, she does allude at a certain point to Jung (Tustin 1981/1992, p. 207). My own encounter with Maldiney has contributed much to my increased understanding of autism (Haag 1984). It may be that the deepening of the understanding of these pathologies and these areas of the psyche would require that Freudian psychoanalytic thinking decrease the split and catch up with a lost part in the direction of the Jungian and phenomenological (Binswangerian) disciplines.

Autistic Shapes

I would like now to return to Tustin's work in order to approach the mystery of "shapes." In 1985, Tustin presented her as-yet unpublished paper on "Autistic Shapes" to the GERPEN[5] in Paris. I would like to try to describe a particular relationship between the "shapes" of the sensation-ego, as defined by Tustin, and the formation of the "container" and thinking.

In Chapter 17 of *Autistic States in Children* (1981/1992), which she titles "Thinkings," Tustin relates an extraordinary dialogue with "Peter," during which this child provides her with the word "shapes" (p. 202) to describe the autosensual maneuvers that create a kind of "round-about" which keeps spinning, thus "skipping" over the opening into that stomach-like area of the mind where transformations take place. This opening that is "skipped" is, at best, a place filled with fantastic monsters.

Tustin then describes herself as obliged to concentrate on her own thoughts when the child turns his back to her. When she communicates to Peter the

---

5. *Research Group of Infant and Child Development*, a group founded and promoted by James Gammill, dedicated mainly to the organization of encounters with foreign analysts of Kleinian, post-Kleinian and Winnicottian approaches, in order to deepen infant and child development observations and the study of psychotic and borderline states.

outcome of her own "digestive process," which has taken place in what she would later call her "stomach-mind" (p. 208), the child relaxes and can think and exchange thoughts with her. In conclusion, Tustin asks:

> [Is Peter's material] talking about the transformation of sensations into percepts and concepts by the activities of a stomach-mind in which digestive processes have to occur?. . . . As the stomach provides connections between his "hard head" and his "soft-bottom," [the child] feels he has a container for his thoughts. [1981/1992, p. 208]

She seems to capitalize on the theory of support in which the digestive process of need-satisfaction is confused with the transformation process of the sensations-emotions, first expelled, "excorporated," and then returned in a tolerable manner when "sensations-shapes in his bottom can become thoughts in his head" (1981/1992, p. 208). Thus, we may infer that in the absence of a "stomach-mind" provided by the external object, "shapes" remain on the surface in a state of confusion between the internal and external or, more precisely, with the annihilation of the internal that is subjugated to the repetition compulsion.

One may ask: what constituents of thinking would derive from the soft-sensation-shapes in connection with the hard-sensation-tongue? Tustin suggests that

> This exciting object in the middle of the stomach is probably the extrapolation from the earlier infantile experience of soft mouth encircling the hard exciting cluster of sensations aroused by the nipple-tongue. [1981, p. 206]

Thus, we may assume there is an encircling aspect of containment operating in the "shapes." This must be the aspect of "contour" of the shapes. One clinical finding is clear: The autistic infant often engages a hard object in their mouth (e.g., sucking their own tongue) or hand, while lips and part of the skin is actually lost until such time as the exchange of "gaze" with the other becomes sufficiently established. Thus, they demonstrate that it is a matter of soft and firm tactile sensations.

In chapters 7, 8, and 9 of her third book, Tustin (1986) further develops her discovery and understanding of "shapes." She states that these shapes carry the roots of the tactile sensation of sound, smell, taste, and sight, which

". . . seemed to be 'felt' rather than heard, smelled, tasted or seen" (1986, p. 120). In this context, she hypothesizes about the infant's normal inbuilt disposition to form shapes: "vague formations of sensation" (1986, p. 121) carried out by shape-producing body substances. She says that,

In normal development, this shape-making propensity will soon become associated with the actual shapes of actual objects, which result in the formation of percepts and concepts. [1986, p. 121]

I wonder if we might make a connection between these "vague formations of sensation," which render form to the container, and the aforementioned perception of an undulating and then encircling form, which seems to emerge from the reflex invagination, the return of the instinctual tension. Tustin suggests that these "shapes" are probably "innate forms" (1986, p. 85–86), undoubtedly inherent in the vital elements. For example, the mass of clinical material suggests an instinctual movement and attraction to an object sensed as twirling or whirling. Houzel (1987) also provides numerous clinical examples of and theorizes about this phenomenon. The problem is the rhythmical establishment of the reversal of this drive or attraction, which installs itself in the sensation of encirclement. The autistic child, who does not encounter this "background of return," must repeatedly master the turbulence by either creating it himself or by creating a different rhythmic structure, which provides a sensation of containment beyond the feeling of encirclement (Haag 1986, 1991a).

Tustin also notes that those autistic infants who make use of the sense of sight are fascinated by the sight of rounded shapes. In part, I have likewise encountered those ravishing moments in front of a full moon or the setting sun (Haag 1989) and balloons and hoops of all kinds. These contemplations, like those productions of labyrinthine or kinesthetic forms of tactile round "shapes," seem to be connected with a desperate search for a sense of continuity, of existence in sameness and in circular time, which imparts a positive value of survival to the repetition compulsion.

We might see a connection between these "shapes"—that seem to belong to the realm of projection and resemble the tactile quality of the contour of containment, which uses moving images—and the "formal signifiers" as defined by Anzieu (1987) with regard to certain dream images or the phenomena of depersonalization in adult patients that refer to the movement of objects or of shapes in space. According to Anzieu (1987), the "formal signifiers" are psychic representatives, not only of certain drives but also of a diversity of forms, of organization, of the self, and of the ego' representations of space and bodily states, chiefly representations of psychic containers. I have shown that the first prefigurative sketches of children—and probably the decorative motifs in many cultures—pick up these shapes as representations of containment: rhythmic traces, double spirals, circles, or intersecting axes (Haag 1990). Progressively, they become part of the backdrop for the emerging scenes and figures of the internal and external theaters as well as of the very framework of our lives.

Autistic Obstacles in the Way of Symbol Formation

This theme was the specific focus of a conference arranged by the GERPEN in Paris in May 1988 in which Tustin's paper "To Be or Not To Be: A Study of Autism" was presented.[6] In that paper, after a short review of her principle discoveries (e.g., the formation of the autistic shell as a defense against specific bodily terrors), Tustin develops original formulations with regard to symbol formation. She evokes the "symbolon," the primitive whole object, that is broken into two pieces in order to be used after separation for the purpose of reciprocal recognition, and the illusion of continuity on the level of the erogenous zone, in which the partial object is then a complementary part included in the body. Normally, this experience is maintained within autoerotism. Tustin emphasizes the constitutive importance of the "ecstasy" of this first experience, which apparently cannot be tolerated in cases of autism.

In contrast, in states of frustration, rage produces the *diabolon*. Tustin writes:

> The Greek word *diabollo* literally means "to throw through". . . . It is a "diabolic" situation for these children when they feel that their projections of extreme states, such as rapture and tantrums, are "thrown through" a "nothingness" instead of being caught by a reflective human being, who may not understand them immediately, but who listens and thinks and so gradually becomes able to understand sufficiently to help them. [1990, p. 56]

---

6. Although Mrs. Tustin could not attend this conference, her paper was translated into French and read by Daphne Nacht and was later published in French in the GERPEN Bulletin.

one has to have an ex obj —

For Tustin, these two normal states—the symbolon and the diabolon—are not subject to reflective thinking. It is their reception, mentalization, and reflection by the external object that produces the "metabolon" (1990, p. 57), which assumes the task of recognizing and accepting the passionate states of ecstatic excitation and diabolic disappointment. We have no doubt that the projective mechanisms of autistic children are obstructed if there is no experience of a receptive object. The autistic withdrawal into two-dimensionality is produced automatically, perhaps to the extent that "if the infant's projections are not caught, its sense of existence evaporates into nothingness" (Tustin 1990, p. 55).

However, in normal development, as in the therapeutic process,

> It is the metabolizing of the sensation-dominated impulse-driven passions of the "symbolon" and the "diabolon," that leads to symbol formation. This fuels the development of an active fantasy life, which dispenses with the need for autistic sensation objects and autistic sensation shapes. These have been palliatives and suppressants that have arisen to blunt the sharpness of intense states of "being," and the dread of "not being." Obstruction of states of exaltation and tragedy, and the lack of expression of such states through the containment of creative activities, has meant that life has lost its savour . . . the appetite for life becomes well-nigh extinguished. Everything is flat and uninteresting. Autistic patients seem half-dead. They are trapped in the limbo of "to be" or "not to be." [1990, p. 58–59]

The Steps of Recovery: the Return to Psychic Life

Tustin refers to the therapeutic process in the last chapters of her final book (1990). She teaches us not to lose our temper in the face of the volcanic eruptions of raw states of excitement and ecstasy or of rage, which inevitably produce temper tantrums from the moment these children begin to feel a better chance for receptivity in the budding awareness of an external world of objects, even of part objects. The need to bear a psychotic phase in which projective identification, initially rather exaggerated, oscillates between schizophrenic dangers and manic phases is made clear in all these chapters on technique.[7]

The post-autistic's obsessional symptoms less vociferous than the manic

---

7. The importance and the technical difficulty encountered with these manic

✳ fantasy is "better than" autistic objects, shapes! Why
✳ and creativity is just containment!

ones are not always cause for a better prognosis, as there may be powerful explosions. (There is a risk of moving from an "encapsulated autism" into a "segmented autism," according to the classification presented at the beginning of this chapter.) Tustin always insists on the firmness of containing the intensity of the capacity of observation[8] and the therapist's empathy as vehicles for the translation of preverbal language and for the reception of intense projections. Here, she recommends a more active and propositional attitude. The therapist needs to intervene in a limiting way in times of overflow, provided of course, that within the analytic setting this intervention is accompanied with—or swiftly followed by—an appropriate interpretation.

Tustin brings up an essential point with regard to the phenomenon of primitive rivalry encountered beyond the oedipal triangulation, and indeed beyond the phenomenon of rivalry in terms of the part-object relations as described by Klein (i.e., baby and penis within Mother's tummy): it is a matter of the breast (Tustin 1972) filled with a rival "mouthful of sucklings" (Tustin 1990, p. 192).

Recent Revisions and Dialogue

When Tustin prepared the revised edition of *Autistic States in Children* (1981/1992), she especially modified two chapters, which she mailed to me along with a letter (Tustin 1991) in order to communicate the essentials of her thinking to her colleagues in France and to announce the forthcoming publication of her "Revised Understanding of Psychogenic Autism" in the *International Journal of Psycho-Analysis*. Tustin's revisions can best be summarized by quoting from her letter to me (November 11, 1991). Here she confirms that she no longer uses the term "primary normal autism," mainly because the term "autism" has become too associated with pathology but also because

> I do not believe that the autistic syndromes develop from a regression to a normal autistic stage in very early life. It seems to me that they emerge rather from a precocious aberration in the human relationship when the

stages, which I have often encountered in my work, seem to me insufficiently emphasized in Tustin's writings and triggered some of my direct questions to her.

8. Tustin insists on the need for training in infant observation according to Esther Bick's technique.

course of normal psychological development was blocked and deviated towards a pathological line. This becomes apparent only later when a child is recognized as autistic. That is, at the age of one or two. The deviation is produced at a stage of sucking. . . . This obstructed psychological development is aggravated over time. [Personal communication 1991]

In chapter three of the revised version of *Autistic States in Children* (1981/ 1992), she discusses the vicious cycle as she conceives of it presently. The central point remains the dramatic awareness of a bodily separateness, even though she insists on the fact that *the shattered fusion is not a normal fusion.* In terms of identifications, she takes up a formulation previously presented in her fourth book (1990). She points out that *adhesive equation* impedes that very early oscillation between moments of normal fusion and moments of partial awareness of separateness, which allows for the unfolding of development. She defines *adhesive equation* as "a delusory state in which the child feels *stuck to and 'at one' with the mother in a pathological unchanging way* (the normal states of flowing-over-at-oneness do not have this rigid, unchanging quality)" (1992, p. 31). Tustin believes that the concept of adhesive identity, advanced by Bick, regards a less compact phenomenon and can more readily be observed in schizophrenic children who have some degree of awareness of separateness. She explains that adhesive identity is deployed in the service of decreasing this awareness. She believes that these pathological adhesive processes obstruct the development of primary identification. With regard to the definition of primary identification, she relies on Freud (1921, a, b) and Fairbairn (1941) through Grotstein, (1980) and proposes the metaphor of "rootedness."

At this point, I would like to introduce a personal note regarding discussions of normal and pathological adhesiveness. I believe that the adhesiveness described by Bick is also a normal phenomenon and is a part of the background of primary identification. What I have come to formulate converges with what Tustin describes as *the rhythm* that needs to be established in these processes. The problem of differentiating between normal and pathological adhesiveness seems essentially to reside in the problem of the "temporary," of the "momentary," as if this "stuck to" state needed to bounce back rapidly towards a self as a carrier of a minimum feeling of separation (Haag 1991b).

In that same chapter, Tustin (1992) establishes greater junctions with Bick and Anzieu with regard to the "feeling of having a skin," without forsaking her previous references to Bion and Winnicott. She also refers to the recourse made to autism as a possible defense in the face of schizophrenic confusions.

In fact, in the clinical situation we can often recognize frequent mixed states in which one can feel the "to and fro" between these two defensive systems.

In my last scientific exchange with Tustin, I presented to her the principle elements of this discussion and their rapport with the ideas of other authors referred to in this paper. I also presented to her some reflections, in part with regard to the importance of the notion of rhythmicity as it is grounded in certain clinical experiences, which add to her own formulations of the "rhythm of safety" (Tustin 1985, p. 268), and in part with regard to the manic-depressive phase that these children go through during their healing.

With regard to the loss of the sensation-ego (e.g., the loss of the part of the mouth), in terms of a permanent negative hallucination—due to the absence of reception, transformation, and reflection on the part of the external object—she confirmed that, in fact, this negative hallucination is the "black hole" of the psychotic depression. She also agreed with the *rapprochement* made between her own formulations regarding flowing-over-at-oneness and Green's formulations regarding excorporation.

With regard to the "rhythm of safety," I proposed to her the formulation— derived from my clinical experience with several autistic infants—that the restoration of the feeling of "flowing-over-at-oneness" may be experienced in the very primitive tactile reestablishment of eye contact, in which the child might find the bottom/floor in the "head-eye." When this "bottom" is lost, the child falls behind the eyes and subsequently needs to make recourse to autistic maneuvers. It seems to me that, to begin with, the restoration of the bottom/ floor provides a perceptive awareness of the rhythmical containing shapes, such as undulations or folds, which relate to the flow and ebb discussed by Tustin. At the same time, a sensation of a folding over or invagination in the link seems to establish an awareness of bodily joints. The loss of the bottom/ floor and of the joints might take place in the transference relationship, either following a physical absence of the therapist—which equals the loss of the regular rhythm of sessions—or within a given session when there is a mental absence of the therapist.

Concerning the bottom/floor, Tustin pointed out to me that Ogden (1989) calls this the "sensory floor," while Grotstein (1980) calls it a "psychic floor." In Tustin's letter, she continues:

> I found your relating the feeling of having a "bottom floor"-"sensory floor"-"psychic floor" to the restoration of eye contact very apposite. Also, I found your relating awareness of "undulations" or "folds" to an aware-

ness of "sensation shapes" arising from the rythmical ebb and flow very interesting and apposite.

A British psychoanalyst wrote to tell me of a conversation he had with a man, who had been blind from birth who said that his dreams were composed of "shapes and movement." Undulations are both shapes and movements. [1991]

I pointed out to Tustin that these phenomena, as they connect with her point of view, have allowed me to formulate a sense of rhythmic exchanges in the two-dimensional "common substance." Freud (1921a) refers to the term of common substance in a footnote at the end of his chapter on identification. The brutal rupture of this rhythm (due to the real or mental absence of the external object, or to the child's incapacity to bear it) would suggest an additional formulation with regard to the origin of bodily "amputation," which links with Tustin's formulation of the "rhythm of safety." She agreed with the aforementioned formulations.

With regard to the manic-depressive phase of a rather serious or prolonged nature that I have found in almost all the processes of recovery in autistic children, I suggested that, clinically, there arrives a moment in which the body–ego seems to be nearly repaired when a manic state erupts. The depressive feelings of a melancholic nature are very rare and yet at times are nevertheless demonstrated in the expression of a very weak feeling of one's self, in which the patient feels himself to be very small and under constant threat of being smashed. In contrast, these depressed feelings may be violently projected into the therapist, who feels himself to be impotent, devalued, and so forth. My hypothesis is that, in these states, a feeling of bodily separateness of a whole body and a whole self (while the whole object is becoming perceived) is emerging along with a greater capacity for mentalization.

Thus I agree with Meltzer (Meltzer et al. 1975) when he describes these manic states as phantasies of repenetration into internal "compartments," now structured in the body of the object for the purpose of either sexual or anal co-excitation and, in the latter case, along with phantasies often of a very perverse nature. It seems then that there emerges a new dread of being rejected from the head (mind) of the object, and that this new capacity for imagining bodily compartments is used in the manic defense. Tustin specified that, for her, this is the obsessional component of the manic defense.

In my experience, the firm denunciation of these maneuvers and the invitation to rejoin the therapist in his/her head (mind) is often the most effective technique in such a situation. Tustin confirmed that it was a matter of the head-mind in the service of mentally digesting that which has been projected.

A Contribution to the Understanding of Identifications Operative in the Body–Ego: Clinical Case Discussions

As it may be seen in the above, the intertwining of my psychoanalytic practice with infantile psychosis (especially autism), with my experience in infant observation according to Bick's method, and with the analysis of the archaic core of neurotic and borderline adults has stimulated my interest in the nature of primitive bodily identifications. I will here attend particularly to the aspects of the skin, skeleton, joints, muscle tone, and motility that seem to be of particular importance within the archaic core.

I call the identifications discussed in this section of my paper *intracorporeal identifications* (Haag 1994). This term reflects my evergrowing impression that identificatory links—established both before and within the realm of part-object relations—are indispensable components of the image of a "relational body." I use the latter term in resonance with the old term of "relational motility" and as distinct from "visceral motility," which depends on the autonomous nervous system. I will focus this portion of my discussion especially upon the function of gaze/attention in the integration of the tactile, auditory, labyrinthine, and olfactory "envelopes," as well as upon their contribution to the formation of the "skin–ego" and the incorporation of relational links within the large axial body joints and the joints of the limbs. Finally, I will discuss the nature of the identifications in play and I will link them with contemporary metapsychological considerations regarding the formation of the self, the nature of the drives, the emotions, and the anxieties involved in these processes.

The Back, the Background, the Gaze and the Skin: the Pivot between Two- and Three-Dimensionality

I have had experience working with quite a number of children under the age of two who have suffered from etiologically varied developmental arrests, manifested especially in psychomotor symptoms—such as stiffening—and lack of interest in the exploration of space and objects. During their psychoanalytic sessions these children "explained" to me, in a preverbal language, their need to find concomitantly—and within a close relationship of attention—both the tactile experience of the "contact of the back" and the interpenetration of reciprocal gazes allied with softness. This experience of concomitance seems to give them the sensation-feeling that something is entering into the back of the head, where it imprints certain qualities and contributes to the creation of a "back-space" in which interrelations are unfolding.

This "back-space," an experience of a background with a floor, is instrumental in helping these children to overcome the panic and fear of exploring the depths of external space. Also, the interpenetration of the reciprocal gaze facilitates an uprightness, and the achievement of a sense of verticality that may be quickly used in both the development of the psychic vertebral axis and in the pathway "nipple-penis."

Clinical Material

I will proceed by reporting a very detailed case example of a 20-month old child whose behavior is similar to behaviors seen in seriously autistic children at the point when they regain eye contact in the transference. It is common at such times for the child to get very close to the therapist's eyes, as if entering them, thus creating a "Cyclops effect." Following this, the child will quickly stick himself to the back of the therapist's head.

I will also present material from the treatment of a 4-year old boy— emerging from a "Kanner-type" state of autism—who showed me, through her gestures, a recapitulation of this issue at a time when his verbal language began to bud. This material will be followed with some vignettes from my analytic work with adults and finally a number of theoretical considerations.

1. Observations of a "First": Bruno at 20 Months of Age

I will present here Bruno's rather elaborate demonstration of the "construction" and "destruction" of his "back," which took place following a concomitant experience of a renewed back-contact and interpenetrating gaze which allowed him to begin moving in external space. Prior to this episode, Bruno might have attempted to stick and unstick flat objects. This time he picked up two interlocking blocks and tried to join them together. Then he separated them. He turned his back to me then turned once again toward me, threw away behind himself some objects that were in front of him, and picked up a small cube. He then looked straight into my eyes, placing the cube between his eyes for a moment. Then he raised the cube gently to the center of his forehead and moved it up along the cranial midline, all the way to the back. Following this, he placed the cube tenderly against his neck and let it slip down his back.

He paused shortly, turned around, and acted in a sort of angry way, dispersing the toys behind himself, throwing them away in all directions with large sweeping movements accompanied with onomatopoeic utterances of discontent. He repeated this sequence twice. The second time, with the toys dispersed yet again all over the place, he turned toward me and symmetrically, with his two hands, energetically pulled the hair from the middle of the back of his head forward, assuming an air of emptiness. I had the impression that he had become a facade.

He seemed to be demonstrating that something initially good, which passed from the gaze to the contact with the back, had subsequently become bad and blown up—perhaps due to an intrusive experience of penetration—or an internal conflict or due to an attack from this first background object. Subsequently, Bruno needed to swiftly bring forward, as on a flat surface, whatever remained attached—in this case his hair—and to place himself at the surface in a perfectly symmetrical relationship to it. Along with the withdrawal of his "story," he gave me the impression that the inside, connected with the back-space, had disappeared. There was only one wall left as the back and the front had become confused. Was he recalling the time when I first saw him, at the age of 1 year at the institution, where he was lying stiffly on his back with his arms symmetrically clamped over his clothes? At that time, he had no hand-mouth contact. While he kept some degree of eye contact laterally, he avoided any frontal gaze. This would happen, for example, when one would bend over towards him on the changing table. In this tactile, adhesive, clamped and sticking state he could not accept a frontal gaze, which required foveal fixation and a distancing that created in front of him an abyss or an antero-posterior gap. Lying on his stomach was intolerable to him. I took this to be connected with his then vital need to maintain the sensation of back-contact.

2. Paul: A 4-Year-Old Autistic Child on His Way
Toward Considerable Improvement

Paul has been treated analytically for Kanner-type autism since the age of 20 months, at which time his symptoms were typical of the syndrome. Following intensive interpretative work focused on the penetrating, aggressive/predatory, devouring and distancing aspects of the gaze, eye-contact was established very gradually between 2 years and 3-and-a-half years of age. Expression of verbal language followed at the age of 3-and-a-half, when he began to articulate his first sentences. Then, for a few sessions, he showed interest in two small, almost similar, oval-shaped containers.

This similarity seemed to make him rejoice. He placed the containers by each other and made believe he was putting something inside one, then the other, saying: "Paul pours milk." Then he turned around and closely watched the central heating radiator. This radiator had two protruding pipes at each end: one large and almost flat and the other long, L-shaped, and pointed with a bolt with a rounded concavity at its tip. He picked up the container formerly used to fill up the two oval dishes, approached the large flat pipe, pretended to fill it up and said: "Pshitt." He proceeded to do the same with the pointed L-shaped pipe. Leaning firmly with his back against the wall, he slowly brought his right eye up to this pointed pipe as he kept looking me straight in the eye. He seemed to be "thinking," and he picked up a small stuffed goose made of very soft material, with a soft felt beak, which in the past had helped him out considerably to re-find the amputated contour of his mouth.

He returned to the radiator's "pipe-beak" and placed the soft beak of the goose over the hard metallic "beak" of the radiator as he brought his eye up to this doubly penetrating object. Then he positioned himself in front of the pipe and made the soft beak penetrate the concavity of the bolt at the tip of the hard beak. I could then interpret, in the transference, that baby-Paul needed not only to drink good milk but also to have the good soft eyes of a mother entering into his eyes and to have a soft eye-beak with which to enter mother's eye.

With this, Paul left the radiator corner and—holding the goose firmly in his hand—walked along the walls striking the goose intensely in an "imprinting" manner. He slowed down in front of a sharp pencil mark he had made a very long time before as a representation of penetration. Thereafter, at times, he would regain his gaze—he would often be gazing at it with the same jubilation which accompanied his progressively steadying gaze.

He proceeded with the symbolic game of feeding a small puppet, which he then placed in a tiny cradle with a teddy bear by its side. He proceeded to lie flat on his back on the couch, looking at me happily. Suddenly he got up and—standing upright on the couch—said "Daddy," as he pointed to the edge at the corner of the wall against which the couch was placed. He said, "The corner," and placed himself standing, making a few jerky movements, his spine against the edge. He became slightly excited and there followed an oedipal scene and a castration fantasy (having the tip of his finger cut).

3. Adult Cases

Experience has shown me that the aforementioned sequence—either in part or whole, and more or less extended in time—is to be found in almost all cases of autism and in cases of psychosis with a strong autistic component. In cases of adults in analysis, these observations relate to at least two kinds of phenomena: (a) *Certain phenomena of depersonalization,* which appear during the work with neurotics and borderline patients with an autistic core: a sensation of vertigo with, for example, the back stuck against the wall; danger of an antero-posterior gap opening up should the "gaze" and the backrest combine; loss of the sensation of the backsupport (Grotstein 1980); the sensation of a hole in the back, and so forth; (b) *Dream images.* Grotstein mentions dreams in which the patient drives a car from the back seat. I have also encountered this kind of "gap-opening" dream between the need to drive forward and the need to stay stuck behind at the same time. In other dreams, the patient is usually behind someone, usually a man who provides a sense of security. Some children try to position themselves "inside our backs." This seems to take place at an advanced period prior to which, in a more autistic state, we can approach or can be approached only from the back. At such times, patients seem to be trying to stick their backs against ours.

4. Theoretical Considerations

The observation regarding the back-rest naturally relates to the definition of what Grotstein (1981) first called the "background object of primary identification" and that presently Grotstein (1990) prefers to call the "background presence"—apparently a self-object in Kohut's (1971) sense—which denotes a state of partial fusion (e.g., symbiotic Siamese twins). He relates this concept to Sandler's (1973) "background of safety," to Winnicott's (1951/1975) "environmental mother," and to Bion's (1967) innate "preconceptions." Grotstein proceeds to liken it to the "dream screen" and, in his "dual track theory" (1979) refers to it as a "guardian of the nascent feeling of object constancy," prior to the establishment of object-representations, at which time it is transformed into a divine concept associated with the superego and with the ego ideal.

Adhesive identification, as described by Bick (1968, 1986) is relevant to the nature of the identifications discussed in this paper. She considers this a defensive mode of being "stuck onto" in two-dimensionality, skin to skin, or by any other sensorial modality that assumes the tactile aspect of a suction tentacle, (Symington 1995) as well as in imitation, such as echolalia. This defense is meant to protect against the dead-end, where one can either fall endlessly or liquefy (postnatal anxieties). But Bick also discusses a normal developmental process, quoting Greenacre's (1970) notion of the ontogenetic defenses of the organism, which appear early on and are later transformed into the mental defense mechanisms of the mature ego.

Bick also refers to Gaddini's (1969) discussion of the role of primitive imitation in the formation of identificatory processes. Bick states that she is attempting to outline the processes of the most primitive holding-together of the infant's body–ego, as this is formed conjointly by the mother-and-the-infant-in-the-family. Thus, she emphasizes also the environment's group character as an external containing object, which is of great interest with regard to what I call the *normal adhesive component of group envelopes*. In her teaching, Bick (1982) advances the hypothesis of an "adhesive position" similar to the notion of the paranoid-schizoid and depressive positions.[9]

I believe that we need to differentiate between normal and pathological "adhesive identity" since this defense operates also in pathological autistic states. The latter are states in which it is primarily used as a defense against any feeling of bodily separateness functioning as pure auto-sensuality against any object-related emotional link. At the same time, it seems to me that there is a primitive kind of emotionality operating in this two-dimensional fusion. I would relate it to Meltzer's (1988) considerations of the "aesthetic object" as well as to emotional modalities of prenatal life. Might the feeling of ecstasy be two-dimensional—a kind of "stuck onto," or "fused-with" feeling—where the sense of a separate identity is more or less abolished?

Maldiney (1982)[10] suggests that we are here letting ourselves go more or less fully into "autistic" contemplation, and he states that there is no art without autism. Milner (1955) also addresses this problem, stating that

> The basic identifications which make it possible to find new objects, *to find the familiar* [my italics] in the unfamiliar require an ability to tolerate a temporary loss of sense of self, a temporary giving up of a discriminating ego. [p. 97]

---

9. Personal communication in my supervision with Bick and published in a booklet of Bick's supervision notes of infant observation edited by H. Haag (1984).

10. Personal communication.

On the same page she also suggests that it may require the state of mind described by Berenson (1950) as "the aesthetic moment." It seems that the aforementioned problem of differentiation is located essentially in the problem of the "temporary." It is as if this "sticking-to" needs to dart back towards the self, somewhat like the clapping of hands. In contrast, in pathological adhesiveness, the "stuck-to" has to remain rigidly glued to an inanimate, emotionally nonvibrating object. Is the dread of being sucked in—as into a whirlpool or quicksand—a corollary of this "stuck-onto," like the suction tentacle which Bick describes, defending against anxieties of liquefaction and of falling forever?

In the pathological case, there is no experience of a supple external object which "glues itself on" thanks to its "capacity for reverie" (Bion 1962) or "primary maternal preoccupation" (Winnicott 1965). In the rhythmic and especially labyrinthine and auditory experiences—in prenatal memory traces as well as in the holding postnatal oral experience—cradling and feeding give one the feeling that the "glued onto" of the initial emotionality returns in the movement to and fro, first experienced with bodily substances (Tustin). Later and gradually, a tiny spatial leap, leaning on a budding confidence in the return of the response—adjusted and transforming at the same time and sufficiently similar but with the small difference—may be manifested especially in eye contact.

Grotstein (1981) insists on an important quality of the background object: the phantasy of a newfound container whose elasticity is tested by psychic contention (as related to stress). In his "dual track theory," he proposes that the baby functions with both a feeling of separation and with a beneficial adhesive identification at the same time. I subscribe to this point of view.

Let us reconsider what the aforementioned children have shown us about the role of the gaze/attention in the passage of the "glued onto" from the back into its internalization in the sense of an envelope, a "backdrop of thoughts" (Anzieu 1985), or dream screen, and so forth. In these observations, I strongly feel that we are at the pivotal point between two- and three-dimensionality. I propose the following formulations: The problem is that of the moment and of the way in which the surface-ego invaginates in order to give a sense of a circular envelope to the image of the embryonic body. Perceptual depth is established between the background presence—probably of an adhesive and two-dimensional nature—and the lateral presence. Muscle erotism and a kinesthesis of erectility in the functioning of erogenous zones (the tongue-nipple encounter; a certain erectility of the eye) participate in the establishment of a sense of depth on a reflex backdrop, connected to the "Moro reflex" of gripping.

Psychically, a small gap in mother's response becomes the founding transformation of asymmetrical psychic relations. This small gap both inhibits and facilitates the elastic play of visual-tonicomotor asymmetries and of binocularization preprogrammed in neurophysiological development (Bion 1967).

The mystery is that the adhesive moment of identification is, at the time, both "thought-less" and an instance of the most intimate contact, which is also the instance of discovery, of invention, and enlightenment. Even in pathological autistic states, this quality is not absent. Indeed, Meltzer and colleagues (1975) point out the autistic child's extreme sensitivity to the emotional states of others. Yet these same children are totally defenseless outside the shell of hypersensuality in which they find refuge. I suggest that there seems to be a split in the primitive emotionality, as rooted in the sensation, and which calls for further study, especially with regard to the archaic roots of affect.

We have refined our concepts in order to differentiate normal projective identification (Bion 1962) using a receptive container (Meltzer 1982) from pathological projective identification, also called intrusive identification, as discovered by Klein (1946) in psychotic states. By the same token, I believe we need to distinguish between pathological adhesive identity and normal adhesive identity. The normal version would be the "stuck onto" that imprints, that assimilates itself to, including the component of similarity in both affective and cognitive phenomena as well as in normal group rituals. It seems that presently, this adhesive identity is usually called "massive projective identification."

What would be the difference between the adhesive and the projective forms of identification? Indeed, the projective contains the adhesive within a three-dimensional experience, within an existing sense of a primary enveloping and encasing skin (Green 1974) and accounts for a phantasy clearly communicated both by children as well as by some thoughts and dreams of adults: getting "stuck to" or "clinging onto," with a tiny spatial leap, inside someone's head, while the other sticks "something" inside his own head almost as in a mirror image. Additionally, it may be a matter of the absorbent imprinting nature which may flow from the kinesthetics of oral experience imprinted in its tactile origin (Anzieu 1985, Freud 1923) upon the backdrop of thoughts and the screen of dreams.

Autistic children show that only the revival of the gaze/attention allows them to make this spatial leap within a common skin, which envelopes two vesicles on their way towards differentiation. Anzieu's (1985) excellent contributions are highly relevant and important with regard to the qualities of this skin-function.

Freud's observation about oral erotism was later elaborated by Winnicott (1965). In my own clinical experience, I can confirm how clearly we may detect two essential components in the sucking situation: (1) *A skin-background* as provided by the peripheral caressing of the hand. When placed for a nap on their stomach, some babies will place one hand on their neck in order to retain the tactile component. (2) *The dual interpenetration of both nipple/mouth and eye to eye*. Abundant clinical material from my work with autistic children shows that the thumb is directed into the mouth only following the reestablishment of the gaze. In contrast, sucking—as a complex integrated and integrating memory of the breast—is rarely a part of the autistic child's auto-erotism or auto-sensuality (Tustin 1990) due to the more archaic nature of these maneuvers. Meltzer's (Meltzer et al. 1975) work on the "dismantling of the perceptual apparatus" is relevant for further consideration here.

I agree with Botella's (1977, 1984) analysis of the role of normal erotism in the duplication of links: namely, the possibly nonviolent appropriation of body and psychic zones involved in the movement of fusion as a pivot between the adhesive and the three-dimensional symbiotic. Surely the first experiences of sucking contribute to the emergence of "the head" in the body image.

Besides the issue of splitting, as I have elsewhere discussed (Haag 1988), there remains the issue of the common skin for two, or of a given aspect of either the body or the psyche in common for two, also addressed by McDougall (1989). We may say that, prior to the establishment of the primary skin, the bodily anxieties are those of falling endlessly and liquefying, according to Tustin (1975, 1985) and Rosenfeld (1984). According to these authors and to my own experiences, these anxieties seem more primitive than the splintering anxieties, the latter being an aspect of oral sadism in the dynamics of projective identification of a three-dimensional body image.

Tustin points out that between the two sets of anxieties there appears the phantasy of a sphincter-less tube-ego, which no doubt underlies all vampire anxieties linked to circulatory tubes on a most primitive level. My experience also confirms this observation. Rosenfeld (1984) observed that the appearance of solidification of contents in the digestive process suggests that the "container" has improved. Nevertheless, the fantasy of a sphincter-less tube-ego within an erect body remains an important element at the core of anorexic adolescents (Kestemberg and Dëcobert 1972, Tustin 1986).

Mother and Baby in the Two Halves of the Body:
the Lateral Object of Primary Identification

1. Clinical Examples

I discovered the vertical axial joint in pathology long before I discovered its significance for growth. The pathological phenomenon, especially evident with autistic children, is a vertical split of the body image. This was described by Tustin (1981) as a binary split of the body–ego in children whose encapsulation was intended to hold the two body parts together.

I have provided a large number of examples to that effect from my own practice (Haag 1985): The little girl Arielle compared the two halves of the body to two parts of a small house connected by a hinge, and also to two identical boxes alternatingly glued together and unglued. She indicated that she had to lie down and keep herself rather stiff in order to keep the two halves together. Another girl, Celine, would keep her hands and her feet "glued" on either side of the center line of a decorative tile, itself placed at the center of a hallway, while watching with riveted eyes the extremities of her limbs, glued onto the sides of that median mark.

A third little patient, Allina, had a particular need to take hold of somebody's hand in order to "do things." One day, she drew a picture herself with her teacher as a double body covered on the one side and with two confused arms on the other. I have an ever-growing conviction that this common maneuver of autistic children—to have someone do things for them—is related to a phantasy of one half of their body confused with half a body of another person. Some autistic children walk around as hemiplegic, not using half of their body, while manifesting no spastic symptoms.

In analysis with adults, there may occur bodily transformations such as a difference in size between one half-body and the other in which the larger half carries the smaller; sensations of loss in one half of the body; or medically uneventful hemi-convulsions. The operative impact of this issue may also be observed in the hand activity of the analysand lying supine on the couch. Relevant examples from dreams abound: Shortly before a break, a patient dreamt that he jumped from one rock to the other with somebody behind him. Suddenly, he noticed that the person behind him had disappeared. He then saw, on his left, a country road. At a distance, he saw a ruined mill with a damaged mechanical wheel in the water. One aspect of this dream suggests that the loss of the analyst from behind (the background) is linked—by the loneliness of the left part of the self—with a damaged object. The right side would seem to be lost on its trail in the background. This loss may be condensed with and aggravated by the envious attacks of the combined internal object mill-mother and mechanical wheel-father.

Bearing such clinical realities and experiences in mind, I was struck during numerous observations of infants between 4 months old and 8 months old to realize—in contrast with the aforementioned dissociations—the importance of the junction between the right and left sides, of self carriage and self-holding between the two hands and the two feet. The junction is clearly reflected in the quality of feeding, care, and attention provided to the baby. I also often observe how the abrupt distancing of a person, particularly attentive to the baby, provokes the movement of an as-if magnetized departure of the right arm of the baby, which seems to connect itself with the body of the distancing adult. For example, in one case of a five-month-old baby, the left hand kept pulling at the right "departed" arm, as if to catch it. An 8-month-old baby had its left hand clutched onto the middle finger of his right hand, as if the latter had departed in the direction of mother.

In a contrasting example of a 3-and-a-half-month-old baby left a little too long on the rug, one could see that after a while the right hand needed to invest an effort in order to join the mouth and, in failing to do so, fell back in its place. Equally failed was the right hand's efforts to join the left hand and to hold it. This inadequacy persisted and exacerbated during half an hour in a state of great dis-ease, despite the baby's desperate efforts. The moment Mother returned, the baby manifested excellent junction of self carriage of the right hand with the left.

2. Theoretical Considerations

Subsequent to my encounter with Grotstein's work on the "background presence," I coined the term "lateral object of primary identification" in my effort to theorize about my description of "the mother-and-baby-in-the-two-halves-of-the-body" (Haag 1985). The identification of the two sides of the body with the two parents is better known, albeit on a symbolic level, and seems to be detected in observation of the second year of life. The former identification discussed here seems to function on the same level with part-objects and with certain functions of objects, especially that of "holding." At the same time, there seems to already be a certain degree of bisexuality of some primary parental qualities.

For example, in the case of the mother and baby in the two halves of the body, the paternal quality seems to be indicated in the link, the pivot, the hinge, and the median axis. This conceptualization is in keeping with that of the aforementioned background presence. I suggest that the background presence extends in part into the vertebral axis (father) and in part into the lateral presence of primary identification (mother). Wouldn't that configuration evoke the image of our guardian angel? These phenomena are undoubtedly an important link in the autoerotic work of disengagement of the two glued half-bodies. The work is as indispensable for the owning of one's body as is thumb-sucking, which, beginning at an earlier level, participates at length in the disengagement of the feeling of a combined envelope/skeleton which sustains the initial mentalized reveries.

The detailed analysis of hand articulation shows rather exciting details of the balance between envelopes and penetration, emotional nuances of possession, and so forth. It seems certain that these phenomena contribute to the release of the appropriation process of the upper limbs and of the trunk. It truly seems that the body image is progressively acquired from top to bottom.

The Appropriation of the Lower Limbs around the Line of Horizontal Splitting: Limb and Head Joins with the Trunk

1. The Incorporation of the Lower Limbs

At the age of about 5 months, babies begin to grasp their lower limbs, to pull at them, and to experience their attachment within body-parts dynamics, in which the body unity is centered around the horizontal axis of the pelvis. At times, these attempts at self-carriage seem to show an intertwining of the more advanced movement along the vertical line and those budding along the horizontal axis.

Another indication of the later-date integration of the lower limbs is their ready use, in times of conflict, for the expression of expulsion of painful feelings and the localization of bad objects. For example, a 4- to 5-month-old baby, during an adjusting process in his crib, is given the bottle for the first time by an infant specialist in the mother's presence. He "expresses" having adopted the bottle in his upper part thanks to an excellent initial adaptation. Yet, in his lower part, the lower limbs—rather than articulating in their usual way—show a movement of expulsion of a partially "bad" experience.[11]

---

11. Videotape of the Psychology and Applied Pedagogy Center (CAAP) 4, Rue de Varenness 94370 Sucy en Brie, France.

Likewise, a 7-month-old baby demonstrates that his whole body resonates with the feeding experience, his right side leading rhythmically in correspondence with the arrival of the spoon while the left side received and swallowed the food. He showed only through his legs that, as his mother said, he did not like fish: the left leg kept attacking the right leg (Haag 1985).

It took me a long time to realize and to understand the relatively belated appearance of the need to bend in the evolution of the autistic child: to fold over in half, either when standing or when lying down, as if in quest of verification of the existence of his very own hinge. By the same token, we can presently better understand the extended periods of manic states that emerge in the treatment of formerly autistic or psychotic children. During these periods, the central phantasy is that of repossessing the other in a mutual incarceration of a tyrannical and torturing nature—usually set in a dark underground location—which evokes a common bottom that may or may not be accompanied by anal masturbation (Meltzer 1976). This seems to be the last stronghold between body and phantasies within the abnormalities of anal erotism on the threshold of gaining sphincter control, which marks the "end" of the body. This state evolves along with the elaboration of depressive feelings subsequent to the awareness of the total body separateness.

Thus it seems that the appropriation of the lower limbs is a concomitant of the development of erogenous anal and sexual zones. It is at this nodal point that we may perceive a more mentalized ego with the hypochondriacal junction as part of the manic/melancholic, psychosomatic and visceral difficulties on the one hand, and on the other, the problem of hysteria along with the horizontal split of the body image known since Freud.

2. The Small and Large Joints of the Limbs

These joints are also primitively invested as limbs, especially the hand and finger joints. In the upper erotic illusion, the hand is the first representation of the breast. The contemplation of the hand joints seems to be a part of this auto-erotism.[12] The wrist joint is an object of special contemplation and becomes a target of attack at times of unhappiness. The shoulder and the

---

12. My thanks go especially to Jocelyne Delegay Siskou for having called my attention to the small articulations. That became very useful in understanding certain psychotic children's self-mutilation inflicted on the small joints.

knee[13] are especially linked to the roundness of the breast, while the elbow is linked to a phallic-aggressive element. In all cases of a serious pathology, the joint as a junction represents the link between a part of the member/self and an objectified part, usually the distal part of the limbs.

3. The Junction of the Head on the Trunk and the Neck Joint

Briefly, the patent signs of a serious problem seem to me to occur late in development and in the therapeutic process. In normal development, babies in observation between 10 months and 12 months show indications of a new awareness of "thinking" as located in the head. This localization is manifested by their placing their little picture books over their heads. My present understanding is that, prior to this stage, the head in the body image is welded to the trunk, both in the background object and in the median access. It is to be noted that when the child of about 2 years of age goes into space by walking, primitive body anxieties are concomitantly revived along with the unfolding process of individuation. At this time, many children manifest tiny maneuvers of getting into one's back: putting the head in between the shoulders, making use of threads, cloth, and links in order to place them around their head, neck, or shoulders.

Are such phenomena linked with the fact that more mentalized anxieties, which by now respect the unity of the body as a whole on its way toward gaining sphincter control (limits), are especially felt on the level of the neck? If so, this would be the pivot between psychotic and neurotic bodily anxieties.

Conclusion: Practical Considerations

How can we help our patients to change? The refinements discussed in this paper put us more at ease with regard to bodily manifestations and their corresponding levels of identification. In my opinion, what helps the patient to change is to be considered on a number of registers. On the one hand our improved communication to the patient of our knowledge of the nature of primitive anxieties of which he/she suffers succeeds best at the right moment

---

13. Special thanks to Dr. James Gammill for his beautiful observations regarding shoulder and knee.

to create a bridge of understanding, which reestablishes an active link with the solid elements of the primary relationship.

On the other hand, primitive anxieties are initially often conveyed in adhesive and projective ways. As discussed by Sidney Klein (1980), this requires us to find our bearings against the background that is our own analysis, within our professional group, and in our own research. Thus, we may be less frightened of allowing ourselves to become the back-father or mother or right-arm-mother or the skin envelope in the countertransference, since any virtually objectifying maneuver is bound to revive the most archaic anxieties with their corresponding defenses. The work within the transitional space (Winnicott 1951) is often a necessary stage which allows the patient to develop a constitutive autoerotism as an essential element of the "owning-up" in the process of bodily separation.

I hope to have been able to share with the reader the great richness and the vitality of my exchanges with Frances Tustin. Her discoveries with regard to autism are at the very core of our attempts at broadening and developing the Metapsychology in order to be able to account more precisely for recently written-about clinical phenomena, not only in the autistic child but in a variety of pathologies.

References

Anzieu, D. (1985). *Le Moi-Peau*. Paris: Dunod.

——— (1987). Les signifiants formels et le moi-peau. In *Les Enveloppes Psychiques*, pp. 1–22. Paris: Dunod.

Bick, E. (1968). The experience of the skin in early object-relations. *International Journal of Psycho-Analysis* 49:484–486.

——— (1982). Personal communication.

——— (1986). Further considerations on the function of the skin in early object relations. *British Journal of Psychotherapy* 2(4):292–301.

Bion, W. R. (1957). The differentiation of the psychotic from the non-psychotic part of the personality. *International Journal of Psycho-Analysis* 38:3–4.

——— (1962). Learning from experience. In *Seven Servants*. New York: Jason Aronson.

——— (1967). *Second Thoughts*. London: Heinemann.

Botella, C., Botella, S., and Haag, G. (1977). En deca du sucotement. *Revue Francaise Psychanalyse*, 5–6:985–992.

Botella, C., and Botella, S. (1984). L'homosexualite inconsciente et le travail du double en seance. *Revue Francaise* 3:687–709.

Chassequet-Smirgel, J. (1988). *Les Deux Arbres du Jardin*. Paris: Edition des Femmes.

Deutsch, H. (1942). Some forms of emotional disturbance and their relationship to schizophrenia. *Psychoanalytic Quarterly* 40:301–321.

Fairbairn, W. R. D. (1941). A revised psychopathology of the psychosis and psychoneurosis. In *Psychoanalytic Studies of the Person*. London, Tavistock (1952) pp. 28–58.

Fordham, M. (1966). Notes on the psychotherapy of infantile autism. *British Journal of Medical Psychology* vol. 39.

Freud, S. (1914). On narcissism. *Standard Edition* 14:67–102.

Freud, S. (1921a). Group psychology and the analysis of the ego. *Standard Edition* 18. London: Hogarth.

——— (1921b). The ego and the id. *Standard Edition* 19. London: Hogarth.

——— (1923). The ego and the id. *Standard Edition* 19:3–63.

Gaddini, E. (1969). On Imitation. *International Journal of Psycho-Analysis* 50(4):475–484.

Green, A. (1971). La projection: de l'identification projective au projet. In *La Folie Privee*. Paris: Gallimard, 1990.

Green, A. (1974). L'analyste, la symbolisation, et l'absence dans le cadre analytique. *Rev. Franc. Psychanal.* 5–6:1191–1230.

——— (1982). La double limite. In *La Folie Privee*, pp. 292–316. Paris: Gallimard, 1990.

Greenacre, P. (1970). Fetish objects. *International Journal of Psycho-Analysis* vol. 51, pp. 447–456.

Grotstein J. (1979). The dual track theorem. Unpublished manuscript.

——— (1980). A proposed revision of the psychoanalytic concept of primitive mental states: part I. *Contemporary Psychoanalysis* 16:479–546.

——— (1981). Primal splitting, the background object of primary identification and other self-objects. In *Splitting and Projective Identification*. New York: Jason Aronson.

——— (1990). Nothingness, meaningless, chaos and the "black hole." In *Contemporary Psychoanalysis* 26(3):257–290.

Haag, G. (1983). Racines Précocissimes De la Détérmination Sexuelle ou Biséxualité dans la Relation Orale. *Les Textes du Centre Alfred Binet*, pp. 69–72. Juin 1983.

——— (1985). La mère et le bébé dans le deux moitiés du corps. *Neuropsychiatrie de l'enfance*, 36, (1):1–8.

——— (1986). Hypothèse sur la structure rythmique du premier contenant. *Gruppo* 2:45–53.

——— (1988). Réfléxions sur la structure rythmique du premier contenant. *Gruppo*, 2:45–55.

——— (1989). Représentation de la groupalité originaire dans les problématiques adhésives en thérapie familiale psychanalytique. *Gruppo* 5:85–94.

——— (1990). Le dessin prefiguratif de l'enfant, quel niveau de representation? *Journal de lapsychanalyse de l'enfant* 8:91–29.

——— (1991a). De la sensorialite aux ebauches de la pensee chez les enfants autistes. *Revue Internationale de Psychopathologie* 3:51–63. Paris: PUF.

——— (1991b). Du sensible au symbole et à la pensée à partir de la clinique psychanalytique des états autistiques: précisions et interrogations. Paper presented at the Conference of the la Societé Psychanalytique de Paris, France, June.

——— (1993). Fear of fusion and projective identification. *Psychoanalytic Inquiry* 13(1):63–85.

——— (1994). Contribución ala compresión de las identificacion en juego en el yo corporeal. Revista cie Psicoanalisi's Argentina 5.l., No. 1 pp. 85–102.

Haag, M. (1984). A propos des premières applications françaises de l'observation requlière et prolonger d'un nourrisson dans sa famille selon la méthode d'Esther Bick: des surprises profitables. Vol. 1, Paris: HAAG.

Hermann, I. (1929). Das Ich und das Denken, Imago, 15.

Houzel, D. (1987). Le concept d'enveloppe psychique. In *Les Enveloppes Psychiques*, pp. 23–54. Paris: Dunod.

Kestenberg, E. and J., Decobert, S. (1972). *La Fain et le Corps*. Paris: PUF.

Klein, M. (1946). Notes on some schizoid mechanisms. In *Envy and Gratitude and Other Works*, pp. 1–24. New York: Dell.

Klein, S. (1980). Autistic phenomena in neurotic patients. *International Journal of Psycho-Analysis* 61(3):395–401.

Kohut, H. (1971). *Analysis of the Self*. New York: International Universities Press.

Mahler, M. (1958). Autism and psychosis: two extreme disturbances of identity. *International Journal of Psycho-Analysis* 39(1):77–83.

Maldiney, H. (1973). *Regard, Parole, Espace*. Lausanne: L'age d'homme.

——— (1982). Personal Communication.

McDougall, J. (1989). *Theatres of the Body*. London: Free Association Books.

Meltzer, D., Brenner, J., Hoxter, S., Weddell, D., and Wittenberg, I. (1975). *Exploration in Autism*. Perthshire, Scotland: Clunie Press.

————— (1976). The relation of anal masturbation to projective identification. *International Journal of Psycho-Analysis*, 47(1):56–67.

————— (1982). The conceptual distinction between projective identification (Klein) and container-contained (Bion). *Journal of Child Psychotherapy* 8:185–200.

————— (1988). Exposé bref au GERPEN à propos d l'identification projective. *Bulletin du GERPEN* 13:61.

Milner, M. (1955). The role of illusion in symbol formation. In *New Directions in Psychoanalysis*, ed. M. Klein. London: Tavistock.

Ogden, T. H. (1989). *The Primitive Edge of Experience*. Northvale N.J.: Jason Aronson.

Pasche, F. (1975). Realite psychique et realite materielle. *Nouvelle Revue de Psychanalyse*.

Racamier, P. C. (1989). *Antoedipe et Ses Destins*. Paris: Apsygee Editions.

Rosenfeld, D. (1984). Hypochondriasis, somatic delusions, and body scheme in psychoanalytic practice. *International Journal of Psycho-Analysis* 65:377–388.

Rosenfeld, H. (1965). *Psychotic States*. London: Hogarth Press; trad. francaise, Diatkine, G., Gibeault, A. et Miller, J., Vincent, M. *Etats. Psychotiques*. Paris: Puf, 1976.

Sandler, J. (1973). The background of safety. *International Journal of Psycho-Analysis* 41:352–356.

Strauss E. (1935). *Von Sinn der Sinne*. Berlin: Springer Verlag. Trad. Francaise, Thines, G. et Legrand J.P.: *Du Sens des Sens*. Grenoble: Millon Jerome, 1989.

Symington, J. (1995). La ventouse tentacule. In *Les Liens d'Emérveillement Toulouse*, Erés pp. 45–49. English version: The suction tentacle. In *Primitive Mental States* vol. I (Eds. K. Koustoulas & S. Alhanati) Northvale, N.J. Jason Aronson (in press).

Tustin, F. (1966). A significant element in the development of Autism. *Journal of Child Psychology and Psychiatry*. vol. 7.

————— (1967). Psychotherapy with autistic children. *Bulletin Assn. Psychotherapy*, Vol. 2 No. 3.

————— (1969). Psychotherapy with autistic children. *Bulletin Assn. Psychotherapy*, Vol. 2 No. 3.

————— (1972). *Autism and Childhood Psychosis*. London: Hogarth.

————— (1981). *Autistic States in Children*. London: Routledge and Kegan Paul. Revised Edition (1992). London: Routledge and Kegan Paul.

———— (1985). The rhythm of safety. In *Autistic Barriers in Neurotic Patients*. London: Karnac pp. 268–284.

———— (1986). *Autistic Barriers in Neurotic Patients*. London: Karnac Books.

———— (1990). *The Protective Shell In Children and Adults*. London: Karnac Books.

———— (1991). Excerpt from letter Nov. 11, 1991. Unpublished.

Winnicott, D. W. (1951). Transitional objects and transitional phenomena. In *Through Paediatrics to Psychoanalysis*. London: Hogarth, 1975.

Winnicott, D. W. (1958). Transitional objects and transitional phenomena. In *Collected Papers: Through Pediatrics to Psycho-analysis*, pp. 209–242. New York: Basic Books.

———— (1960). Ego distortion in terms of true and false self. In *The Maturational Process and the Facilitating Environment*, pp. 140–152. New York: International Universities Press.

———— (1965). *The Maturational Process and the Facilitating Environment*. New York: International Universities Press.

Index

Second reading 4-12-08